A CHRISTIAN
PHILOSOPHICAL
JOURNEY

A Christian Philosophical Journey

Kenneth Schenck

TRIANGLE PUBLISHING

A Christian Philosophical Journey
Kenneth Schenck

Direct correspondence and permission requests to one of the following:

E-mail: info@trianglepublishing.com

Web: www.trianglepublishing.com

Mail: Triangle Publishing
Indiana Wesleyan University
1900 West 50th Street
Marion, Indiana 46953
USA

Unless otherwise noted Scripture quotations are from *New Revised Standard Version Bible* (NRSV), copyright © 1989 by the Division of Christian Education of the National Council of Churches of Christ in the United States of America, and are used by permission. All rights reserved.

Scripture quotations marked (NIV) are taken from The Holy Bible, *New International Version®*, *NIV®* Copyright © 1973, 1978, 1984, 2011 by Biblica, Inc.™ Used by permission. All rights reserved worldwide.

Scripture quotations marked (NLT) are taken from the *Holy Bible*, New Living Translation, copyright © 1996, 2004, 2007 by Tyndale House Foundation. Used by permission of Tyndale House Publishers, Inc., Carol Stream, Illinois 60188. All rights reserved.

Scripture quotations marked (KJV) are taken from the *King James Version* of the Bible.

ISBN: 978-1-931283-51-9 (pbk)
ISBN: 978-1-931283-64-9 (ebk)

Printed in the United States of America.

ACADEMIC AND PEER REVIEW

Authors typically invest thousands of hours in the process of providing a textbook for you—drawing upon their own expertise, collaborating with others in their discipline, researching, and writing. They have collected and organized the important topics of the subject matter in a form they believe is most beneficial for your learning. In addition to the significant investment the authors make, publishers solicit the assistance of other experts and professors in their quest to provide excellent learning resources.

Excellence is enhanced through peer reviews. These reviews are a very important part of the process of publishing any textbook as experts in the field critically examine the author's work. Reviewers read the text carefully and usually provide the publisher with dozens of pages of critical comments. These comments range from strengths such as affirmation about content and writing style to suggestions about deficiencies—chapter organization, information regarding current research, documentation, form and style matters, as well as debate pertaining to the author's viewpoints. The author is provided with the review comments and are given opportunity to respond—and in many cases does additional researching, rewriting, and discussing issues and questions that are raised.

This textbook is no exception to the peer review process. Professionals in the field of philosophical studies, have invested hundreds of hours reviewing this text. The Publisher is especially thankful to the reviewers who have given their expertise, time, and wisdom in reading and commenting on *A Christian Philosophical Journey*. Their contribution adds significantly to the content and quality of what you are about to study.

With gratitude,
Nathan Birky
Publisher
Triangle Publishing

DEDICATION

I dedicate this book to my father, M. Lee Schenck, who passed away when it was in its final stages of editing. My father was not only a reasonable man, but a model of virtue and "the good life." Serving God was his *summum bonum,* and his life showed anyone who knew him what it meant to love your neighbor.

CONTENTS

ACKNOWLEDGMENTS

Many hands have made this book far better than it would have been if I had written it in a vacuum. The first bits of the book were written for the entry-level philosophy classes I taught for years in the undergraduate program at Indiana Wesleyan University (IWU). Indeed, I got my teaching job at IWU by God's providence because they needed someone to fill their philosophy classes for a year, and Bud Bence thought I might turn out to be a "thoroughbred" who could teach competently in more than just New Testament. One year stretched into two, and I honed my knowledge of philosophy by teaching ethics and contemporary philosophy.

I blogged a good deal of this book, which gave me the benefit of immediate feedback from Internet passersby, often specialists in various areas of philosophy. "Lay philosophers" helped me know what was alarming or unclear. My colleagues at IWU, especially Chris Bounds, were often at hand to clarify points where I misunderstood orthodoxy or the perspective of some particular philosophy. Philosophy teachers from IWU's College of Adult and Professional Studies unit read chapters with a view to adult students. Individuals including Paul Garverick, R. B. Kuhn, Scott Burson, Brian Fry, Steve Horst, Bob Whitesel, James Harless, Dave Ward, Keith Drury, and Russ Gunsalus read portions of the manuscript.

Nathan Birky and Laura Matney at Triangle Publishing, as well as Jerry Pattengale and others who oversee Triangle, were incredibly patient in waiting for this multiyear venture. Thank you for trusting in me. Evelyn Bence did painstaking editing work to improve the style and normalize the text. A book written over half a decade is bound to have numerous inconsistencies of format and approach. Her incredible eye for detail brought significant improvement for which students should be very grateful. Several reviews also gave good insights to help focus the book in terms of audience and consistency.

I thank the Fulbright Commission and the Ludwig-Maximilians Universität of Munich, Germany, which unknowingly created a space for me to finish the textbook. Although I took the Fulbright to write on other subjects (and did), the first two months of my Fulbright sabbatical were dedicated to finishing this book. There is something incredibly fitting about writing on philosophy in Germany, which birthed the likes of Immanuel Kant and G. W. F. Hegel, not to mention Friedrich Nietzsche and a host of lesser-known but significant thinkers.

I thank my family as always for enduring my writing projects. I often hijack my wife Angela's attention for her feedback on my style or tone. My children are often forced to hear about things most young people only endure in a classroom. If my father had not died suddenly last week, I would have dedicated the book to my children, in hope that they might one day grow to be philosopher kings and queens. Perhaps it is fitting that I finally thank my father and mother for raising me to be a thinker. My father was not only a reasonable man, but also a paragon of virtue and a life well lived. And it was with my mother that I first honed my skills at debate (smile). Thank you, Mom and Dad, for a wonderful heritage.

Good Friday, April 6, 2012

UNIT 1

PROLEGOMENA
(things you say before saying something)

CHAPTER 1

WHAT IS PHILOSOPHY?

What to Get from This Chapter

- You are a philosopher. Strive to be a good one.
- Philosophy stands at the heart of all other areas of study.
- The ideas of reality, truth, and value work in life. God has made it so.
- A life without questions is the life of a slave.

Questions to Consider

- What is a philosophy?
- What are the kinds of questions a philosopher asks?
- Why would I want to think philosophically?

Key Words

- Philosophy
- Second-order questions
- Socratic method

© istockphoto.com

1.1
WHY PHILOSOPHY?

Everyone is a philosopher. Not everyone is a good philosopher, but everyone is a philosopher. For example, do you think it is wrong for me to shoot you? Then you take a position on an issue of ethics. Do you think that the chair you sit on is real? Then you believe something about reality. Are you able to follow my reasoning? Then you have views on what is logical and/or true. These are all subjects of philosophy.

We make philosophical decisions every day and have countless philosophical positions on life. Should I go the speed limit? Was that person telling me the truth? Who am I? Is this really what I should be doing with my life? What do you think about abortion, evolution, war, or poverty?

Philosophy stands behind all other fields of study. It is the subject that asks what every other subject is about! More important, it asks what truth itself is, what it means to exist, and what is truly valuable. For Christians, of course, true philosophy, true "love of wisdom," eventually leads us to questions of God and faith.[1] Interestingly, this conclusion itself is our answer to a philosophical question. We cannot have any thoughts about anything without what we call "reasoning."[2]

> **Philosophy** asks questions about the nature of reality, truth, and value as well as about the nature of all other subjects.

Postmodernism rejects the idea that our reason can have anything like a neutral or objective view of the world or of truth.

First-order question: asks about something.

Second-order question: asks about asking about something (i.e., about a first-order question).

Philosophy of religion: asks questions about the nature of religion and God.

Philosophy of science: asks questions about the nature of science and scientific inquiry.

Psychology (in the philosophical sense): asks questions about the nature of the human mind and/or soul.

Philosophy of art: asks questions about the nature of art.

Philosophy of history: asks questions about the nature of history.

To be sure, a number of philosophical voices deny that these questions have answers or even make sense as questions. These are some of the voices of **postmodernism**. In philosophy postmodernism is a movement that strongly rejects the idea that our reason can have anything like a neutral or objective view of the world or of what is true.

Postmodernism can refer to many things, so we should not fall into the fallacy of thinking we can dismiss something simply by putting that label on it. If we believe in truth, it may just be that there are some true aspects to postmodernism. Indeed, if we define postmodernism in this way—a rejection of human reason's ability to be completely neutral or objective about truth—then it should be clear that there are both Christian and non-Christian versions of postmodernism.

Having said that, the most pessimistic postmodern voices would question whether any truth (as opposed to individual opinion) exists—or even if our words truly mean anything at all. Other postmodern voices suggest that we cannot know anything about what the world outside ourselves is really like or whether a God exists. We will want to consider these voices, not simply to dismiss them but to see if we can learn anything from them.

Ultimately our lives would fall apart if we ever took some of these theories and tried to apply them to the real world. For example, what would happen if I treated my supervisor's words as if they could mean anything I wanted them to mean? Even the most radical postmodern individuals act as if their words are trying to say something. And they step out of the way of moving traffic—as if the car heading in their direction were a real force. In short, truth and reality "work." And as Christians, we believe that there is a God behind everything that makes them work!

1.2
THE QUESTIONS OF PHILOSOPHY

Philosophy is the subject that looks at every other subject and asks what it is doing. We have a name for that sort of question: it is a **second-order question**, a metaquestion. A **first-order question** asks about something, for example, did you take out the trash? Second-order questions ask about first-order questions: What is "trash"? Should someone take out the trash? Who should take out the trash—husbands, male children? Is trash real? The table below gives several second-order or "meta" subjects in philosophy.

The philosophy of religion asks second-order questions such as, does God exist? or if God is good, why doesn't God stop evil? The philosophy of science asks questions such as what makes one scientific theory better than another? and are scientific theories really about the way the world is? The philosophy of art, the philosophy of history, and other "philosophy of" areas ask similar questions about their own disciplines.

However, we can boil down the topics of philosophy even further. Philosophy ultimately asks three basic kinds of metaquestions about everything else: questions about reality, questions about truth, and questions about value. These three types of questions relate to the three fundamental branches of philosophy: metaphysics, epistemology, and axiology.

Metaphysics is the branch of philosophy that asks questions about the nature of existence and reality. Is the world outside myself real? What is its nature? Where did it come from?

Epistemology is the branch of philosophy that asks questions about the nature of truth and sound reasoning. What is good thinking? How do I know that I know what I think I know?

Axiology is the branch of philosophy that asks questions of value. What is the meaning of life? How should we live? What makes something beautiful?

By the end of this book, you should recognize in the questions above a number of sub-branches of philosophy such as cosmology, logic, ethics, and aesthetics. In fact, it might be useful to reduce everything we have said thus far into a set of basic philosophical questions. Your answers to these questions constitute a major part of your view of the world.[3]

> **Metaphysics:** the branch of philosophy that asks questions about existence and reality.
>
> **Epistemology:** the branch of philosophy that asks questions about truth.
>
> **Axiology:** the branch of philosophy that asks questions about value.

© istockphoto.com

1 DOES GOD EXIST, AND, IF SO, WHAT IS GOD'S NATURE? From a Christian standpoint, this is the most important question of all, the answer of which plays into our answers to all the other questions. Questions about God relate to branches of philosophy including metaphysics and the philosophy of religion.

© istockphoto.com

2 WHAT IS THE NATURE OF THE OTHER THINGS THAT EXIST? Are we ideas in the mind of God? Is matter something different from spirit or mind? Is there even such a thing as spirit? These questions relate to metaphysics and its sub-disciplines.

© istockphoto.com

3 WHAT CONSTITUTES GOOD THINKING? What aspects of truth can we simply assume are true and which ones do we need to argue for? What is a good argument? These questions relate to the study of logic.

4 HOW DO I KNOW WHAT IS TRUE? Can I trust my senses? Can I trust my mind? Does God reveal truth that can bypass my human reasoning? How do I know that I really know what I think I know? These questions are matters of epistemology. The chapters that follow begin with epistemology because, from where we sit in the world as thinkers, we cannot get to any of the other questions until we have at least tentatively answered it.

5 WHAT IS A HUMAN BEING? Am I simply a biological machine? A being created in the image of God? These are questions of psychology in the philosophical sense as well as questions of axiology in terms of human value.

6 HOW SHOULD I LIVE IN THE WORLD? Are there rules that everyone must follow? Do other individuals count when making decisions? What is a fulfilled life? These questions relate to ethics, a branch of axiology.

7 HOW DO HUMANS BEST LIVE TOGETHER IN THE WORLD? Should we have no ruler but simply follow God's law? Should we have a king? Should materials be owned privately or shared in common? These are the topics of social and political philosophy, including economic theory.

8 WHAT MAKES SOMETHING BEAUTIFUL? What is truly art and what is not? What constitutes good art? Is beauty truly in the eye of the beholder? These are the questions of aesthetics, a branch of axiology.

9 WHERE IS HISTORY HEADED? Is history simply a cycle of similar events repeating themselves? Is history headed toward a particular set of climactic events? Is the future alterable, or are we simply playing out an inevitable scenario? These are matters of the philosophy of history.

If you know what you think about these questions, you know your conscious perspective on the world. In reality, we behave far more in terms of our unconscious rather than our conscious minds. But clarifying our surface beliefs is a good first step toward knowing ourselves.

1.3
LIBERATION: THE GOAL OF PHILOSOPHY

© shutterstock.com

Most people in the history of the world have recognized how little freedom they have. Perhaps most of those who have lived on this planet have subscribed to a certain **fatalism**, a sense that the world is driven by forces beyond our control. We are born into a set of circumstances we did not choose, and most humans in history have not had the option of moving very far from the constraints of that beginning. In many respects, the Western world has afforded unprecedented possibilities for change and mobility that few others in history have known. In such a culture, it is easy to believe that you are freer than you actually are.

Yet much of this freedom is also an illusion. How many in the Western world truly understand *why* they believe or do the things they do? How many people have truly chosen the beliefs they have with a significant awareness of the other options? You do not freely believe what you believe unless you are free to choose some other belief. And how are you free to choose another belief if you do not know any other option?

I can become president of the United States even if my parents cleaned toilets for a living. It is all too easy to see these sorts of possibilities for change. But what about the person who is born into a family that hates people of a different color or the man who was raised to view women as inferior to men? It is all too easy for such people to go through their whole lives as a slave to a view they did not choose for themselves, that they inherited from their native environs. This person is no freer in this area than a slave chained to the galley of a ship, because he or she has never considered

Fatalism: the sense that the world is driven by forces beyond your control.

Illustration of Plato's allegory of the cave

Philosophy is about giving you the freedom to choose your views more freely.

"Know yourself" was the sign at the entrance to the ancient Greek temple of Delphi.

any other possible way of looking at the world. Such people have been pushed along by the beliefs of their parents or environment without ever examining them.

In his book *The Republic,* the philosopher **Plato** tells a story related to such slavery.[4] In his **allegory of the cave**, some men are chained in a cave their whole lives. All they know are the shadows on a wall, shadows cast by figures moving behind them that they cannot see. One day one of them is freed and comes to realize that all he has seen his whole life are shadows of the true reality that has been behind him all along. Plato then has us imagine that this individual returns to the cave. Would not his companions think that he was speaking nonsense if he were to tell them of the outside world? Would they perhaps even kill him if they could get their hands on him?[5]

Plato suggests that there is a similar difference between those who have seen the light of the truth and the bulk of humanity that never leaves its darkened cave. Of course we will want to look later at exactly what Plato considered to be the light. But the allegory, this symbolic story, is a fair analogy for becoming truly human by examining the beliefs you have inherited and either making them your own or adopting better ones.

Philosophy in this respect is about freedom, about true freedom of the mind and heart. The purpose of examining your philosophy is not so much to change your views as it is to allow you to choose them more freely. To be sure, we can never totally free ourselves from the internal and external forces at work on our thinking. Factors are at work in our subconscious minds that we will never fully know consciously.

But we can become freer than we were when we started our philosophical journeys. Some ancient Greek sayings are very appropriate to this task ahead of us. The first was an inscription that stood at the entrance to the temple at Delphi. The sign read "know yourself." This slogan is a great way to capture a good deal of the philosophical venture, the part that has to do with philosophy freeing us.[6]

Another quotation comes from one of the best-known philosophers of all time, **Socrates**. When he was on trial in Athens for "corrupting the youth" with his ideas and allegedly teaching them not to believe in the gods, he made the bold claim that "the unexamined life is not worth living."[7]

The Death of Socrates, 1787 (oil on canvas), David, Jacques Louis (1748–1825) / Metropolitan Museum of Art, New York, USA / The Bridgeman Art Library

Socrates chose to die rather than to stop his philosophical quest. Of course most of us do not feel that strongly about examining our lives. Yet asking questions is one of the most important paths to truth and freedom, to a more authentic human existence. Indeed self-reflection is one of the key characteristics that distinguishes us from other animals. In a sense a person who has never examined his or her life or beliefs is not yet fully human. Plato gives Socrates's argument:

> Someone might say, "Surely if you leave the city, Socrates, you can spend the rest of your life in peace, minding your own business."
>
> It is really hard to make some of you understand my answer to this. If I tell you it would be disobedience to the god to do as you say, and therefore that I cannot mind my own business, you will not believe that I am serious. But if on the other hand I tell you that the best thing you can do is to discuss virtue daily, along with the other subjects about which you hear me examining myself and others, if I tell you that the unexamined life is not worth living, you are even less likely to believe me.
>
> Yet what I say is true, even if it is not easy to convince you.

Plato, *Apology* 37–38

> The wisest person is the one who realizes he is not truly wise.
>
> **Socrates, in Plato, *Apology* 23b**[8]
>
> Socrates testified at his trial that "the unexamined life is not worth living" and chose to die rather than to stop asking questions.

To be sure, not all questions are helpful. And some ask questions from a cynical or unbelieving heart. But asking questions in itself—even about matters of faith—is not contrary to faith. Indeed, some people are afraid to ask questions of their beliefs *because* they lack faith; they are afraid the answers will prove their beliefs to be false.[9] But other people ask questions *in* faith, unafraid of the answers or the complications, because they have faith that what they believe is in fact the truth.

As we finish we should mention something else, the subject of the next chapter. For Christians, truth—including the truth about ourselves—is not simply a matter of something we can reason out. As Jesus says in the Gospel of John, "If you continue in my word, you are truly my disciples, and you will know the truth, and the truth will make you free" (8:31–32). Christians claim that we cannot fully know truth by discovery, by questioning. For us, the starting point for truth of the most important kind is to follow Christ. For Christians, the most important witness to Christ is Scripture. Christians see the first half of the Bible, the Old Testament, as a foreshadowing and anticipation of Jesus's coming. Then the

Visitors stand outside the entrance to the Garden Tomb in Jerusalem, Israel. It is a first-century rolling-stone tomb and one possible site where Jesus's body was laid.

BIOGRAPHY

SOCRATES

All we know about Socrates (ca. 470–399 BC) comes from things that his followers (and detractors) wrote about him, especially Plato. In that sense he is like Jesus, whom we know about only through the writings of others.

By all accounts, Socrates seems to have spent his time asking questions of important people and then publicly shaming them by unraveling their answers. His method of investigation is called the **Socratic method**. The Socratic method asks questions of someone else and then in turn asks more questions of their responses. The goal is by each round of questions to eliminate some answers and pursue more fully those answers that seem to hold the most promise.

Ultimately Socrates seems to have thought that only the gods were truly wise (if in fact he believed in them). Plato's *Apology* gives an account of the trial that sentenced Socrates to death. In it Socrates tells how a friend of his had visited the **oracle of Delphi**, a priestess who purportedly spoke for Apollo, the god of prophecy. When asked if Socrates was the wisest person alive, the priestess agreed that he was.

Socrates, supposedly shocked, embarks on a campaign to see if in fact he was wiser than the "smartest" of his day. He embraces the role of a "gadfly"

that flies around irritating the leaders of Athens. In the end he concludes that he is the wisest, because he at least realizes that he is not wise. He concludes that the one who recognizes one's own lack of wisdom is the truly wise person.

When reading Plato's stories about Socrates, it is not always easy to know where we are truly hearing about the ideas of Socrates and where we are hearing Plato's. But most would attribute to Socrates himself the conviction that to know the good is to do the good. The idea here is that if your insight/thinking is straight, then you will live and behave correctly.[10]

Reality probably does not bear this idea out. In actuality, our behavior comes far more from things going on in our brains below the surface than from ideas of our conscious minds. But we can still embrace this philosophy. Ideally our thinking and actions would be in sync with each other. It is definitely a goal that we can embrace and for which we should aim.

At the end of his trial for "corrupting the youth" and not believing in the gods of the state, Socrates is found guilty and eventually sentenced to death by drinking hemlock. He could have escaped, and Plato's book called the *Crito* presents the attempt of some to get him to agree. But he does not, and Plato's *Phaedo* describes his death as he increasingly feels less and less of his body.

Photo Credit: Herm of Socrates (469–399 BC), Greek philosopher, Roman copy after a Greek original from second half of the 4th century BC, marble
De Agostini Picture Library / G. Dagli Orti / The Bridgeman Art Library

second half of the Bible, the New Testament, is God unpacking the significance of Christ's coming, his death, and his resurrection in the earliest church. We will talk more about Scripture as God's revelation in chapter 4.

For us as Christians, ultimate truth and ultimate value are thus more about a person—Jesus Christ—than about a set of ideas. The most important truths, we believe, are revealed rather than discovered by reason. The most important truths are far deeper than the mere rational, and they usually involve faith. By faith we believe that there is a world outside ourselves and that God has made it possible for us to know true things about it. The next chapter discusses specifically how we as *Christians* might ask questions about reality, truth, and value.

1.4
CONCLUSION

At the heart of what you think about everything is philosophy, whether you call it that or not. If you have a position on right and wrong, that is ethics. If you have thoughts about how politics should work, that is social and political philosophy. If you have a position about what art is, or how science works, or how we tell history, those are all philosophical positions. They are second-order questions that step back and ask questions about questions. We cannot even avoid philosophy when it comes to religion, for as soon as we ask what religion is or should be, we have asked a philosophical question. Philosophy is the study of the study of everything else.

We are all philosophers, but some of us are better philosophers than others. Some of us are more aware of why we think the way we do than others. The more reflective we are in our thinking, the freer we are in our positions. Otherwise we are simply a slave to the forces on us from our culture, personalities, and traditions. And the more options we know, the more likely we are to pick good ones.

KEY TERMS

- philosophy
- postmodernism
- first-order questions
- second-order questions
- philosophy of metaphysics
- philosophy of epistemology
- philosophy of axiology
- fatalism
- allegory of the cave
- Socratic method
- oracle of Delphi

KEY PHILOSOPHERS

- Socrates
- Plato

PHILOSOPHICAL QUOTATIONS

- "Know yourself." (Delphic oracle)
- "The unexamined life is not worth living." (Socrates)
- "The wisest person is the one who realizes he is not truly wise." (Socrates)
- To know the good is to do the good. (Socrates)

KEY QUESTIONS

1. What does it mean to be a philosopher and what is the benefit of thinking about philosophical questions? How has postmodernism challenged the legitimacy of doing philosophy? Anticipate and explain how a Christian might object to doing philosophy.

2. In what way does philosophy stand at the core of all the other subjects you might study in college?

3. What are the three fundamental branches of philosophy? Name and identify some of the overall questions that philosophy asks.

4. In what way might asking questions lead to personal freedom? Are all questions permissible? Is there ever a time when you should not ask a question?

5. What do you think about the two Greek mottoes: "know yourself" and "the unexamined life is not worth living"? To what extent do they reflect important or legitimate pursuits? How would you suggest Christian faith steers such pursuits?

6. What is the Socratic method? Do you ever use it when you are trying to find the truth? Should you?

NOTES

1. The word *philosophy* derives from two other Greek words, *philos* (love) and *sophia* (wisdom). The parts of a word do not necessarily tell you what a word means, but in this case "love of wisdom" is not a bad picture of what philosophy is, especially for a Christian.

2. It is of course possible that God might put thoughts in our heads or that God might direct our reasoning.

3. The questions that follow were inspired by James W. Sire, *The Universe Next Door: A Basic Worldview Catalog*, 4th ed. (Downers Grove, IL: InterVarsity, 2004). Many would call these "worldview" questions: questions that get at the lenses through which we view the world.

4. Plato, *Republic*, 514a–520a.

5. This last statement is probably an allusion to the death of Socrates. See later in this chapter. In Plato's *Republic*, it is Socrates who tells the allegory of the cave. But Plato's later writings probably do not record things that Socrates actually said. By then Socrates had become merely the voice of Plato, a character in stories Plato wrote to portray his own philosophy.

6. The other part is about the world outside us and how we should live in it.

7. Earlier in the trial, Socrates says, "Men of Athens, I honor and love you; but I will obey God rather than you" (*Apology* 29). Acts 4:19 possibly alludes to Socrates's statement; the disciples say to the ruling council in Jerusalem, "Whether it is right before God to obey you rather than God, you decide" (my translation).

8. I have tried to paraphrase excerpts from philosophers in this book to make their thinking more accessible. For Plato, I have generally started with *Plato: The Collected Dialogues*, ed. E. Hamilton and H. Cairns (Princeton, NJ: Princeton University, 1961).

9. Certainly we will not be able to determine the answers to some questions, and many of us are not equipped to ask certain questions. There is no shame in a faith that acknowledges the limits of reason.

10. This is a paraphrase of Socrates's sense that "virtue is knowledge" (e.g., *Meno* 87c). Although everyone agrees that Socrates held this position, it is hard to find a quotation that states it crisply and in the form of a final conclusion. *Gorgias* 460b comes close: "When you truly learn something, your life adjusts accordingly" (my paraphrase). See also Socrates's sense that all wrongdoing is based on ignorance in *Apology* 37a and *Gorgias* 509e.

What to Get from This Chapter

- All Christians are philosophers, because they take positions on basic philosophical questions.
- Some Christians have objected to the relevance of secular philosophy because of its non-Christian presuppositions.
- Some Christians have objected to any philosophical approach that overemphasizes reasoning or evidence as the path to truth.
- Some Christians claim that Christians should assume rather than argue for basic Christian beliefs.

Questions to Consider

- What are some objections to philosophy?
- What are your presuppositions?
- How objective can a person be?
- What are some Christian answers to the basic questions of philosophy?
- How do faith and evidence relate to each other?

Key Words

- Presuppositions
- Objectivity
- Faith
- Evidence

© Kevin L. Welch

2.1
CHRISTIAN OBJECTIONS TO PHILOSOPHY

Philosophy classes are sometimes stereotyped as unfriendly to Christian faith. Even some early Christians considered philosophy an opponent to faith, especially in the years before Christianity became the dominant religion of the Roman Empire.[1] The best known is **Tertullian** (ca. 160–235), who famously asked the rhetorical question, "What does Athens have to do with Jerusalem, the Academy with the Church?"

By the "Academy," Tertullian referred to **Plato's Academy** in Athens, the philosophical school founded by Plato in 385 BC and then closed by the Christian emperor Justinian in AD 529. Some have considered the closing of Plato's Academy by Christian powers as the beginning of the "Dark Ages." With a thinly disguised anti-Catholic bias, these and other historians have termed the subsequent years the "Middle Ages," spanning the "death" of culture (equated with Greco-Roman culture) and its rebirth or "renaissance"

> **Plato's Academy:** The philosophical school founded by Plato in 385 BC. The Roman emperor Justinian I closed it in AD 529, a date that some call the beginning of the "Dark Ages."

in the 1400s and 1500s (see chap. 14). Although most of us continue to refer to the "Middle Ages," we should be leery of how this term effectively dismisses a thousand years of Christian history.

Here is the passage in which Tertullian poses his famous question:

> Where do those "fables and endless genealogies," "unprofitable questions," and "words which spread like a cancer" come from? When the apostle [Paul] wants to restrain us, he expressly names philosophy as what we should guard against. Writing to the Colossians, he says, "See that no one deceives you through philosophy and empty deception, after human tradition, contrary to the wisdom of the Holy Spirit."
>
> Paul had been at Athens, and in his dialog had become acquainted with the human wisdom that pretends to know the truth while in reality corrupting it . . . What indeed has Athens to do with Jerusalem? What agreement is there between the Academy and the Church? . . . By contrast, our instruction comes from "the porch of Solomon." . . . Away with all attempts to produce a Christianity mixed with Stoic, Platonic, and dialectic composition! . . . We do not want any other belief in addition to our faith.

Tertullian, *Prescription against Heretics* 7[2]

School of Athens, from the Stanza della Segnatura, 1510–11 (fresco), Raphael (Raffaello Sanzio of Urbino) (1483–1520) / Vatican Museums and Galleries, Vatican City / Giraudon / The Bridgeman Art Library

Of course Colossians 2:8 does not refer to philosophy in our sense. Rather, Colossians addressed a form of Judaism that was overly concerned with angels and physical discipline. Indeed the kinds of passages Tertullian had in mind—1 Timothy 1:4; 2 Timothy 2:23; and Titus 3:9—all refer to Christian teaching about the Jewish law. These biblical texts do not refer to philosophy in the way that we—or Tertullian—refer to it.

Even Tertullian himself was not truly opposing philosophy, but *non-Christian* philosophies. Indeed, as we will see in the next section, Christians have regularly taken positions on the basic questions of philosophy. Tertullian ironically was thus a philosopher as well: someone whose thinking operated on the basis of certain Christian **presuppositions** or presumptions about God, himself, and the world. We are all philosophers because we all take positions on the basic philosophical questions—either intentionally or by happenstance.

Presuppositions: beliefs that one *assumes* before reasoning rather than for which one argues on the basis of evidence or reasoning.

The greatest Christian opponent to philosophy as it normally operates was the Danish philosopher **Søren Kierkegaard** (1813–1855).[3] In his writings Kierkegaard was particularly keen to dismiss a faith based on reason, denying that we could figure out the answers to the most important questions of life with our rational minds. For example, in his book *Concluding Unscientific Postscript*, Kierkegaard attacked the claim that "the rational is real and the real is rational."

He countered with his belief that "subjectivity is truth," by which he meant that truth is not something that you can prove or for which you can argue. It is something personal that is not based on arguments but on what one might call **blind faith**. Truth involves what one might call a **leap of faith** in the absence of clear reasons to take that leap.[4] **Objectivity,** in contrast to **subjectivity,** is the idea that a person can think without bias, that we can come to correct conclusions by human reasoning alone and thereby arrive at something like a "God's-eye view" on truth.

> Faith cannot exist without risk . . . If I can understand God objectively, I do not have faith. But precisely because I cannot do this, I must have faith. If I wish to preserve my faith, I must constantly work to maintain objective uncertainty, so I remain out in the deep, over seventy thousand fathoms of water, still keeping my faith.

Søren Kierkegaard, *Concluding Unscientific Postscript* 2.2[5]

Despite Kierkegaard's opposition to an overly rational faith, he remains one of the most significant Christian philosophers. He opposes a reason-based philosophy, but he is a philosopher nonetheless. Of course many Christian thinkers disagree with Tertullian and Kierkegaard. At the same time that Tertullian was blasting any relationship between Christianity and Athens, the Christian theologian Origen (ca. 185–254) was integrating Platonism with his beliefs. And thinkers such as C. S. Lewis have seriously opposed the notion that faith is blind.[6]

Indeed, one Christian branch of philosophy is called **apologetics**, which studies how to defend Christian faith, usually with rational argument. (It is not about being sorry for your faith.) You might remember from chapter 1 that Plato's *Apology* was about Socrates's defense at his trial. So apologetics, often connected to 1 Peter 3:15, is being prepared to give an answer when you are on trial for your faith.[7] We will discuss the relationship between faith and reason more carefully in the final section of this chapter. Suffice it to say, Christians have different views on the appropriate emphasis given to each of the foundations of belief. When you are done reading this book, you are the one who has to decide which approach you will follow.

Leap of faith, blind faith: phrases commonly used to refer to the idea that faith is not based on evidence or reasoning but is rather a "leap" without sure footing, made without seeing where we are leaping.

Objectivity: the idea that we can form conclusions without bias and thus attain somewhat of a "God's eye" perspective on truth.

Apologetics: the study of how to defend your faith, usually on the basis of rational argument.

1 Peter 3:15: "Always be ready to make your defense to anyone who demands from you an accounting for the hope that is in you."

2.2
CHRISTIAN POSITIONS ON THE ISSUES

In the first chapter, we boiled down the basic issues of philosophy to nine basic questions. Even those who have argued that philosophy is not Christian have addressed these questions in one way or another because they are **worldview** questions, questions that get at a person's fundamental perspectives on reality. For some of these questions, the Christian answers are clear-cut. Christians have answered other questions in varying ways. In those cases we might be able to identify a range of possible answers rather than a distinctly Christian position on that issue.

Before we run through these basic philosophical questions with Christian eyes, it is important to clarify what we mean by the word *Christian*. Here we make clear distinctions between "historic" Christianity and what we might call "cultural" Christianity or social groups that identify themselves as Christians. A person might be a Christian in terms of social identity and yet hold to none of the beliefs or practices of historic Christianity.

For example, the twentieth century saw a great deal of conflict between Irish Catholics and Protestants, and much of this conflict took place with at least a veneer of Christian rhetoric attached. However, neither the Roman Catholic Church nor the Anglican Church sanctioned partisan violence, and the actions of opposing groups often stood definitively outside the boundaries of historic Christianity. When we speak of Christian answers to these philosophical questions, we mean answers that are in the flow of *historic* Christianity. While many Christian groups disagree on many things, Christians share in common a good number of core beliefs and practices and have done so since the earliest days of Christianity.

Further, almost all Christian groups have worked out these beliefs in dialogue with the Bible, the Christian Scriptures. Even the Roman Catholic Church, despite what Protestants sometimes think, holds that its beliefs and practices are the inspired working out of biblical teaching in the church. Thus the Bible also plays a significant role in identifying a belief or practice as Christian.

1. Does God exist, and, if so, what is God's nature?

This issue gives us a good example of a "historic" Christian belief. Many people in the world are "Christian" by social group—some even go to church. Yet many of these do not believe that God exists, or they have serious questions about

> **Worldview:** the lenses through which a person understands reality. Such perspectives are often more a function of what goes on "deep down" in one's head than of our conscious ideas and reasoning processes.

© istockphoto.com

BIOGRAPHY

SØREN KIERKEGAARD

Søren Kierkegaard (usually pronounced in English as KYIRK-i-gard) was a Danish philosopher who lived from 1813 to 1855. He had a melancholic personality, captured well in his extreme decision not to marry the love of his life. Instead, he took a leap of faith and surrendered her to God, as Abraham did Isaac. He perhaps thought that God would reward him by returning her to him somehow. Instead he soon found her engaged and then married to someone else.

We can see much of Kierkegaard's thought as a response to two aspects of his environment: complacent Danish Christianity and the optimism of Georg W. F. Hegel's philosophy. He encountered Hegel's widely popular philosophy while at university and took an immediate dislike to what he saw as its irrelevant optimism. In the days that followed he formulated his "three stages of life."

The first is the "aesthetic stage." The person at this stage either lives for pleasure (as Kierkegaard himself did a great deal while at university) or like Hegel pursues abstract philosophical ideas with little relevance to life and living. Kierkegaard wrote in his journal at university, "What I really lack is to be clear in my mind *what I am to do*, not what I am to know."

The "ethical stage" is when a person stops living for the moment and begins to recognize the role of duty and personal responsibility. This person lives recognizing his or her past and with a view to the future, not simply for the moment. Unlike the trajectory of Hegel, the ethical stage brought a person to make meaningful choices rather than spending one's time in irrelevant philosophical speculation. As the title of perhaps his most important work displays, you come to make choices: *Either/Or*.

But Kierkegaard saw a "religious stage" as the true goal. One took a leap of faith beyond reason, just as Abraham did when he attempted to sacrifice Isaac. Reason and duty would have told him to stop. Kierkegaard here critiqued the ethic of another popular philosopher, Immanuel Kant. Kant's famous "categorical imperative" insisted that if something was your duty, it was *always* your duty without exception.

Based on his works *Fear and Trembling* and *Concluding Unscientific Postscript*, Kierkegaard earned the title the "father of existentialism." Existentialism is a philosophical approach that emphasizes the importance for each person to define who he or she is. In these works Kierkegaard argued that "truth is subjective" and that it was impossible to construct a philosophical system because truth was individual and personal.

Photo Credit: Portrait of Soren Kierkegaard (1813–55) 1922 (engraving), German School (20th century) / Private Collection / The Bridgeman Art Library

God's existence. A group in England known as the "Sea of Faith" movement styles themselves "non-realists" when it comes to language about God.[8] Proponents do not believe that God actually exists as a person but think the idea of God is real and accomplishes good things in the world.

Nevertheless, the historic belief of Christianity is clearly "that he [God] exists and that he rewards those who seek him" (Heb. 11:6). The "orthodox" Christian belief is that God is a Being who exists apart from the existence of any human being. Indeed, historic Christianity believes that while there is only one God, God has always existed as three distinct persons—Father, Son, and Holy Spirit.

Christians further believe that God created the world and have historically held that the world is distinct from him. God has "all power" and "all knowledge" in relation to the creation. They believe that God is good and loves what is created, but that God is also just. We will discuss some variations on these basic themes in the unit on the philosophy of religion, but these are some of the most commonly held Christian beliefs.

2. What is the nature of the other things that exist?

© istockphoto.com

If we find virtual unanimity by Christians on the existence of God, we have a variety of Christian positions on the second. At one extreme, we have individuals like George Berkeley (1685–1753) who believed that matter did not really exist and that we were thoughts in the mind of God. The early-church Christian School of Alexandria included Origen (ca. 200), whose Platonist leanings led him to see our spiritual side as more real than our physical bodies.

Some Christian thinkers today—while affirming basic Christian beliefs about the afterlife—have argued that we do not have "souls" apart from bodies.[9] In that sense, they would argue that there is no such thing as a nonphysical existence apart from material of some sort or another. We will discuss their ideas in our unit on the philosophy of the psyche.

However, most Christians today are dualists. Today's *dualists* believe that reality consists both of the material and the nonmaterial, the natural and the supernatural realms, if you would. When we get to the unit on the philosophy of science, you may be surprised to learn how recent this kind of dualistic thinking is.

3. What constitutes good thinking?

We have already seen in this chapter that a number of significant Christian thinkers such as Tertullian and Kierkegaard have questioned the possibility of "good thinking" on the basis of reason alone. While most Christians accept the basic rules of logic, it is essential for the Christian thinker to have a place for faith in his or her thinking as well. We will argue in the next section that faith need not be contrary to reason, but the need for faith does imply a lack of *evidence*. On all subjects, faith provides the missing piece between what we see and the full picture that only God sees (cf. Heb. 11:1).

© istockphoto.com

As we look at Christian history, we find some variety of thought about the proper formula for faith in relation to evidence. On the one hand, we have thinkers such as Thomas Aquinas (1225–1274) and C. S. Lewis (1898–1963) who have seen faith in highly rational and evidentiary terms. On the other end of the spectrum are people like Søren Kierkegaard who have seen faith more along the lines of "blind" faith.

4. How can I know what is true?

© Kevin L. Welch

Chapter 4 in this book is titled "What Is Truth?" In addition to the subject of good thinking, which we just mentioned, it will ask what the proper sources of truth are. Clearly reason and experience play a significant role in the way we arrive at what we think is true. Accordingly, a number of Christian *rationalists* such as René Descartes (1596–1650) have seen reason as the key to truth. Yet we could also mention Christian *empiricists* such as John Locke (1632–1704) who thought our experiences were the path to truth. Others such as Immanuel Kant have seen a combination of the two as being essential (1724–1804).

However, Christianity introduces other very important elements into this equation, sources of truth *revealed* by God. Evangelical Protestants see the Bible as the most important source for truth about the most important aspects of life. The Roman Catholic Church and the Orthodox traditions have further argued that the church is also essential in the interpretation of the Bible. Charismatic and Pentecostal traditions—including holiness traditions—have generally seen direct revelation from God (through the Holy Spirit) as a regular part of revelation as well.

5. What is a human being?

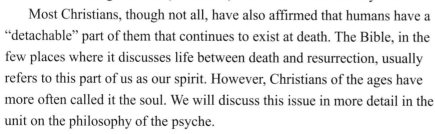
© shutterstock.com

Christians do not believe that humans are simply biological machines or simply the product of mindless evolution. Certainly we are biological machines, and some Christians do believe in a God-directed evolutionary process. But historic Christians believe that humans are much more than highly sophisticated animals. Christians believe that human beings are created in the image of God (Gen. 1:27) and are thus intrinsically valuable.

Most Christians, though not all, have also affirmed that humans have a "detachable" part of them that continues to exist at death. The Bible, in the few places where it discusses life between death and resurrection, usually refers to this part of us as our spirit. However, Christians of the ages have more often called it the soul. We will discuss this issue in more detail in the unit on the philosophy of the psyche.

6. How should I live in the world?

We can speak of a fundamental Christian *ethic* that boasts the teaching of Jesus, Matthew, Paul, James, and John in the New Testament. That ethic is love of God and love of our fellow human. The New Testament books treat these two commands as their foundational, rock-bottom ethic, and Christianity has followed its lead. To be sure, many Christians and Christian groups throughout history have endorsed hatred, but we can question to that extent whether they have been properly Christian.

However, as we will see in the chapter on ethics, we would be wrong to restrict questions of living to action. The ancient world, and Christianity as a part of it, emphasized proper character and virtue more than proper action. So we find some Christian groups that have emphasized proper action (sometimes becoming somewhat legalistic in the process). And we find others that have emphasized relationship with God (in one way or another) as the key to Christian existence in the world. Some groups—such as the Lutheran tradition—have actually deemphasized ethics because it tends to focus us on our own "works" more than on God's work.

7. How can humans best live together in the world?

We cannot speak of a common Christian belief on how society or an economic system should be organized. Some Christians argued for the "divine right" of kings in the 1600s. Yet many American Christians would say democracy is most Christian. We similarly find among Christian ranks both pacifists and those who believe in St. Augustine's just-war theory. Further, we find ardent Christian supporters of the capitalistic system and others who believe a socialist society would be most Christian in nature. We will discuss these ideas as well in our chapter on social and political philosophy.

8. What makes something beautiful?

Neither can we speak of any distinctly Christian position on the subject of aesthetics, except perhaps that whatever is truly beautiful will cohere with God. We might find some Christians who argue that art can be "true" only if it is representational and thus actually looks like something in the real world. But most Christians today would likely consider such a view impoverished. The main issue of Christian debate in aesthetics today is whether we can consider material of questionable content to be true art. We will discuss these issues in the chapter on the philosophy of art.

9. Where is history headed?

Historically, Christians have affirmed in what is called the Apostles' Creed that Christ "will come again to judge the living and the dead." Although some have questioned whether we should take Christ's second coming as a literal event yet to come, Christianity has traditionally believed that Jesus will return to Earth one day and will set the world straight. At that time the dead will rise, and evil will be banished forever.

And yet significant pockets of Christianity question whether Christ will come to interrupt human history in this way. For example, many Christians today on a popular level operate as if judgment is a matter of dying and then going to heaven or hell—which is not the historically Christian position on this issue. Further, among those who affirm the second coming, we find differing perspectives on the events that will lead up to it. Some see the world getting better and better in preparation for Christ's return. Others think the world will get worse and worse. We discuss these perspectives in greater detail in the chapter on the philosophy of history.

We can see from the preceding sketch that, while there are certain core beliefs on certain issues, we cannot really speak of a single Christian worldview that encompasses all the philosophical questions. On most of the questions of philosophy, we find a variety of Christian responses throughout the ages. The chapters that follow will explore these issues in greater detail and give you an opportunity to work through the questions yourself.

2.3
FAITH AND REASON

Thus far in the chapter, we have argued that while some Christians have opposed certain forms of philosophy, all Christians are philosophers because they have views on the questions of philosophy. As we end the chapter, we need to discuss an issue that gets at the heart of Christian opposition to philosophy where it has occurred. What role does revelation and faith play in what Christians believe?

A good place to begin talking about revelation and philosophy is to notice that all thinking is, well, thinking. As we will discuss at greater length in chapter 4, we simply cannot get away from a basic sort of reasoning. We cannot "understand" anything without basic patterns of thought. Tertullian used it; Kierkegaard used it. When we articulate faith, we use basic reasoning.

It is thus somewhat misleading to speak of faith versus *reason*. Unless you believe that every individual thought you have is directly revealed to you by God and that there is no logical connection between each of your thoughts, you use reason all the time. You think; you make connections from one thought to the next. Rather than faith versus reason, what we should contrast is faith versus *evidence*. We will explore this topic in more detail in chapter 4: "What Is Truth?"

For the moment, we would claim that Christian thinking differs from other thinking not so much in the thinking itself, the "rules" of good thinking that we will discuss in chapter 3; rather, Christian thinking differs from other thinking because of the *presuppositions* by which it operates. As we noted earlier, a presupposition is something you assume *before* you start reasoning rather than something you necessarily argue for. Presuppositions are somewhat like axioms in geometry. You do not try to prove that two points make a line. You assume it and use it to prove other things.

So Christians assume any number of beliefs and interpret the world through those assumptions. For example, when a Christian reads the gospel stories, he or she will read them with the belief that miracles can actually happen. Belief in the possibility of miracles is a presupposition, and we likely come to different conclusions about the Gospels depending on whether or not we start with this belief.

Some Christian philosophers have argued that certain Christian beliefs are almost exactly like axioms. I believe that God exists, even though I cannot prove it. It is a presupposition that I bring to the world when I am trying to understand what is going on. I assert belief in God *by faith* in the absence of absolute evidence.

Reformed epistemology goes one step further. You know from the previous chapter that epistemology is the branch of philosophy that asks about how we can know anything. Reformed epistemology argues that a number of beliefs about reality are **properly basic**, like axioms, such that we do not need to argue for them. It does not worry about trying to evaluate these beliefs in terms of faith versus evidence, as we did above. It holds that we could hardly function in the world without assuming certain basic beliefs.

So how could we function if we did not assume that the world exists outside ourselves and that the people we see have minds that are at least similar to ours? **Alvin Plantinga** has argued that belief in God is so intrinsic to reality that it is not only beyond reasonable doubt; our existence and our thinking all presuppose the existence of a God who makes existence and

Reformed epistemology: an approach to truth that considers certain beliefs, such as the existence of other minds, as **properly basic**—beliefs without which we could not even function in the world. Such beliefs are "warranted" without argument.

Alvin Plantinga: along with Nicolas Wolterstorff, one of the originators and main proponents of Reformed epistemology.

truth possible. He believes the world does not make sense unless we assume God's existence.[10]

It is no coincidence that Reformed epistemology is identified with a particular Christian tradition: the Reformed tradition. Reformed Christians, who trace their origins to John Calvin (1509–1564), believe that only specific individuals whom God has chosen to be saved will make it to heaven. You can see that it makes sense for such a person to believe that no proof or warrant is needed for belief in God. Those whom God has chosen will obviously see the truth of God's existence with or without logical proof.

Most Christian traditions probably would agree that logical proof is not the most important part of faith in God. You do not need to be able to prove God's existence beyond a reasonable doubt to justify belief that God exists. Perhaps it is also no coincidence that those who believe that *we* must decide whether to believe in God sometimes see a larger role for reason to play in convincing others.

Reformed epistemology is philosophy—in fact it is hard-core philosophy. It would not object to philosophy itself as a subject. However, it might object to an approach to philosophy that did not largely start by assuming the core beliefs of Christian faith. This is especially true of a postmodern Christian approach to truth very similar to Reformed epistemology called **radical orthodoxy**.[11] It would emphasize that philosophy is not Christian unless it assumes *all* the essential elements of Christian faith.

> **Radical orthodoxy:** a postmodern approach to truth claiming that, since we cannot be objectively certain about what is true, we should assume all the essential beliefs of Christianity without argument.

Reformed epistemology argues that we can assume certain beliefs without argument, yet it has a very rational flavor. Postmodernism claims that we cannot be certain that our reasoning is sound and leads us to truth. In this light, radical orthodoxy argues that, since you cannot prove what is true, we should assume *all* the essentials of Christian faith in our thinking. Whereas Reformed epistemology might argue that belief in God is properly basic, radical orthodoxy would assume without argument a full-blown belief in the Trinity, the virgin birth, and many other things that clearly are not properly basic to human thought.

Before we leave this chapter, we note that our minds are really much more than our conscious thoughts. If we are to believe the field of neuropsychology, we are aware of only the tip of the iceberg of what takes place in our brains. Considering this fact, we wonder: to what extent are we playing games when we act as if philosophical arguments and ideas are really the "heart" of our perspective on the world? What if, in fact, we behave the way we do because of things going on much "deeper" inside us than we realize? We hope to have a good deal of insight on these sorts of issues by the end of our philosophical journey.

2.4
CONCLUSION

Only God can be completely objective because only God knows all the facts and how they relate to each other. We can try our best to interpret the evidence we have without unfairly reading our own biases into it, but we will never be completely successful. Indeed, some Christians do not think we should even try. Some Christians believe we should quite intentionally assume a particular Christian interpretation no matter what the evidence seems to say. They would either say that faith is blind or argue that, since everyone starts with certain presuppositions, we may as well start with Christian ones.

It is true that all thinking involves presuppositions, but some assumptions would seem to be more basic and necessary than others. We could hardly make our way through this world without believing that the world around us is real in some way, but we can debate whether some Christian beliefs are this "properly basic." In the end, Christians have had a range of different beliefs over time on the basic questions of philosophy, some of which seem more obvious than others. Almost all of our beliefs are some mixture of faith and evidence. Many Christians believe that it is reasonable to believe in God and Christ, even if significant faith is involved.

KEY TERMS

- Plato's Academy
- presuppositions
- blind faith
- leap of faith
- objectivity
- apologetics
- worldview
- Reformed epistemology
- properly basic
- radical orthodoxy

KEY PHILOSOPHERS

- Tertullian
- Søren Kierkegaard
- Alvin Plantinga

PHILOSOPHICAL QUOTATIONS

- "What does Athens have to do with Jerusalem, the Academy with the Church?" (Tertullian)
- "If I can understand God objectively, I do not believe." (Kierkegaard)

KEY QUESTIONS

1. Do you agree more with Tertullian and Kierkegaard about philosophy or C. S. Lewis and other apologists? Why?

2. Before you go further into this book, what quick answers would you give to the basic philosophical questions? Do you think your ideas will change as you work through this book?

3. What do you think about the idea that some beliefs are "properly basic"? Would you include belief in God?

4. How does radical orthodoxy strike you? Should we largely bracket our essential Christian beliefs from critical examination and ignore questions about them that others have asked?

NOTES

1. Christianity became a legal religion in AD 313 by the Edict of Milan of the Roman emperor Constantine. We might say it became the dominant religion of the empire *politically* at that time (though certainly not in reality) and then *legally* in 392 when Theodosius forbade all other religions. Of course pagan worship continued long after throughout the empire.

2. All quotations from the ante-Nicene church fathers in this book are paraphrased on the basis of the translation by Philip Schaff, *The Ante-Nicene Fathers*, 10 vols. (Peabody, MA: Hendrickson, 1994).

3. The other philosopher was Georg W. F. Hegel in *Phenomenology of Spirit*.

4. Kierkegaard did not actually use either of these phrases. His phrase was actually a "leap *to* faith."

5. All paraphrases of Kierkegaard's *Concluding Unscientific Postscript* began with the translation by H. V. Hong and E. H. Hong (Princeton, NJ: Princeton University, 1992).

6. C. S. Lewis's book *Mere Christianity* is a classic rational defense of Christian faith.

7. It is important to recognize that 1 Peter is not strictly talking about a defense of Christian ideas based on rational argument. First Peter probably pictures a setting where Christians are on trial and required to testify in their trial defense, in other words, to "give their testimony."

8. See, e.g., Don Cupitt, *Sea of Faith* (London: SCM, 1994).

9. For an exploration of the issue, see *In Search of the Soul: Four Views of the Mind-Body Problem* (Downers Grove, IL: InterVarsity, 2005).

10. See especially Alvin Plantinga, *Warranted Christian Belief* (New York: Oxford University, 2000).

11. See especially James K. Smith, *Introducing Radical Orthodoxy: Mapping a Post-Secular Theology* (Grand Rapids: Baker, 2004). While many proponents of radical orthodoxy are Reformed in their theology, not all are. The postmodern element is sufficient in itself as a basis for this position.

UNIT 2

PHILOSOPHY OF KNOWLEDGE:
EPISTEMOLOGY

CHAPTER 3

CLEAR THINKING: LOGIC

© istockphoto.com

3.1
THINKING IN TWO DIRECTIONS

What to Get from This Chapter

- Logic is the branch of philosophy that explores good reasoning.
- Deductive thinking starts with certain assumptions and deduces other truths from them.
- Inductive thinking starts with a collection of evidence and induces possible truths from it.
- The syllogism stands at the heart of deductive and propositional thinking.
- Informal fallacies stand at the heart of most bad thinking in ordinary life.

Questions to Consider

- What does good thinking look like?
- What are some key fallacies people use in arguments?

Key Words

- Logic
- Proposition
- Premise
- Fallacy

In the first chapter, you learned that **logic** is the branch of philosophy that distinguishes good thinking from bad thinking. There are two basic sorts of good thinking: (1) where your conclusion *must* be true if your assumptions and reasoning are good, and (2) where your conclusion is *probably* true if your reasoning and evidence is good.

The first kind of reasoning—your conclusion *must* be true if your logic is good—is called **deductive reasoning**. Figure 3.1 pictures deductive reasoning as an upside down V. In general, deductive thinking starts with certain assumptions and then shows what must be true if those assumptions are true. Much of math, particularly geometry, is deductive in nature.

Figure 3.1

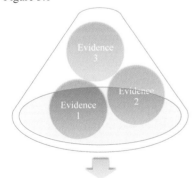

Deductive Reasoning

Logic: the branch of philosophy that explores the nature of good thinking.

Figure 3.2

Inductive Reasoning

Inductive reasoning, on the other hand, is more like the normal V in Figure 3.2. You gather evidence and then hypothesize *possible* or *probable* conclusions given the evidence you have. Most scientific thinking is inductive, where you form hypotheses to try to explain a set of data.

This chapter sets out some of the basic rules and mistakes people make when thinking and arguing both deductively and inductively. It is concerned not only with whether a **proposition** or "truth claim" is true or false; it is about valid and invalid ways to move from one thought to the next.

We should also make clear the difference between a proposition and the statements we often make in ordinary language. "I'll never forget how happy I was to get that dog" is not a proposition. For one thing, it is a hyperbole, an exaggerated comment. You may very well forget, especially if you grow senile in old age. Propositions are usually literal rather than metaphorical or figurative statements.[1]

People sometimes throw around the word *always* in an exaggerated way. Consider this statement: "People are always happy when they get dogs." Of course this statement is not true as a proposition, because many people do not like dogs, and sometimes even individuals who generally like dogs do not like the ones they get. To be true, a proposition must *always* be true.

For this reason, it is important to distinguish proverbs and most statements in the Bible from propositions. Take Proverbs 22:6: "Train children in the right way, and when old, they will not stray." This is not a proposition, because it is not something that is *always* true. It is a general principle that is *usually* true, but sometimes through no fault of their parents children choose to go down the wrong paths.

A great example of the "proverbial" nature of biblical statements appears in Proverbs 26:4–5, which says in succession, "Do not answer fools according to their folly," and then in the next verse, "Answer fools according to their folly." Since one of the rock-bottom principles of logic is the *law of noncontradiction*, both of these statements cannot be true as propositions. But because proverbs are not statements of absolute truth but of general truth, both of these statements are true as proverbs. An absolute truth is one to which there are no exceptions. By a "general" truth, I mean one that is generally true but with some exceptions.

It is important to recognize that the vast majority of biblical statements are not meant as propositions; they are not made as absolute statements of truth that do not have exceptions. Here we are talking about statements of truth rather than commands. And we are not talking about the many figurative and metaphorical statements in the Bible. Jesus in particular seemed to have used metaphor and hyperbole extensively in his teaching, as we see in his use of parables.

Deductive reasoning: reasoning to what *must* be true given certain assumptions.

Inductive reasoning: reasoning to what is *probably* true given certain data.

Proposition: a truth claim.

Take Jesus's intriguing statement to the Syro-Phoenician woman in Mark 7:27: "It is not fair to take the children's bread and throw it to the dogs." For starters, this is a metaphor. We might literally render it, "It is not right for me to cast a demon out of a non-Jew," with a supporting statement, "My exorcist ministry is for Jews." Neither of these statements is a proposition. If it were, it would be false—or Jesus did wrong when he then went on to cast the demon out of the woman's daughter.

In the end, the books of the Bible were written to address ancient Israelites, Romans, Corinthians, and so forth. The statements in these writings were made not only in these contexts, but in terms that people from these ancient cultures could understand. It is the exception, rather than the rule, to find propositional statements like "there is one God, the Father . . . and [there is] one Lord, Jesus Christ" (1 Cor. 8:6), and even it may have had nuances to its original readers that are different from the ones we hear.[2] The first meaning of biblical statements virtually always, if not always, is connected to their historical-cultural contexts. The work of applying them to other times and places, as well as determining whether they are exceptionless, is a sacred task we need to do together, "working out our salvation with fear and trembling" (Phil. 2:12). The Bible is central for us as Christians to meet and know God, so it is desirable for us to read it with as much understanding as possible.

3.2
THINKING DEDUCTIVELY

If you have ever had a class in geometry, you will no doubt remember having to prove things like "the measures of the angles of a triangle add up to 180 degrees." These kinds of statements are called theorems. To prove them, you drew on a number of "givens" that your geometry textbook did not try to prove. These were things you were supposed to *assume* were true, like "two points make a line" or "parallel lines never meet."

These are great examples of deductive reasoning. You start with certain assumptions or presuppositions and then make conclusions about what *must* be true as a result. Because of the way deductive thinking works, we have to make a distinction between whether your logic is **valid** and whether your final conclusion is **true**. To say that a deductive argument is valid is to say that the logic works. If your **premises**, your assumptions, are true, then your conclusion must also be true. At the same time, your argument can be valid

Figure 3.1

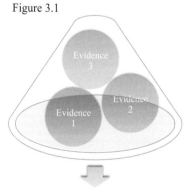

Deductive Reasoning

logically and yet your conclusion be false because one or more of your assumptions is false.

The ancient Greek philosopher Aristotle was the first person we know to lay down the rules of logic. He described the kind of thinking we were talking about in the previous paragraph as a **syllogism**, an argument that reaches a particular conclusion given certain assumptions. Take the following example:[3]

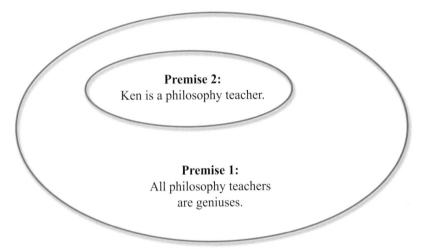

Premise 2:
Ken is a philosophy teacher.

Premise 1:
All philosophy teachers
are geniuses.

Conclusion: Ken is a genius.

This syllogism is called a categorical syllogism, because its premises make definite assertions about everything in a certain category.[4] The logic of the syllogism is *valid*, so that if the premises are true, then the conclusion *must* be true. However, it is not at all likely that all philosophy teachers are geniuses. So although the logic of the syllogism is valid, we cannot trust the conclusion because one of the premises is false.

An entire course in logic would extensively explore the various kinds of syllogisms and how they work. Good thinkers follow these sorts of principles whether they know them officially or not. In the above example, the logic of the syllogism works because the first premise talks about everything in a certain class, and the second premise talks about a subset of that class. Therefore, the conclusion about that subset *must* be true if the first premise is true.

The certainty of deductive logic gives us one tool for *disproving* certain ideas. If we can show that certain ideas inevitably lead to a false conclusion, we can show that one of those premises is certainly false. This kind of argument is called a ***reductio ad absurdam*** or reducing a line of thought to an absurdity. It is a kind of contrary-to-fact argument where you show that if certain premises are true, they would imply that some other conclusion was true as well. But since that other conclusion is not true, one of the premises leading to that conclusion must be false.

Syllogism: a pattern of reasoning in which the conclusion must follow if your assumptions are true.

Premise: the assumptions you make when making an argument.

Valid syllogism: a syllogism whose logic works correctly, whether the conclusion is true or not.

True syllogism: a syllogism for which both the logic is valid *and* the conclusion is true because your premises are true.

Take our syllogism above, which resulted in the conclusion that Ken is a genius. If you can show that, in fact, Ken is not a genius, then you know that one of your premises must be false. If you know that Ken does in fact teach philosophy courses, then the faulty premise must be that "all philosophy teachers are geniuses." This premise must be false because it leads to a false conclusion.

Deductive logic is like math: either you get it right or you get it wrong. If the logic is valid and the premises are true, the conclusion *must* be true. It makes no more sense to disagree than it would to argue about whether 1 + 1 = 2. If the logic is invalid, then we say that the conclusion is a **non sequitur**, a common Latin expression that means "it does not follow." Mistakes in deductive reasoning are usually mistakes in the way the argument is set up, **"formal"** fallacies.

> *Reductio ad absurdam*: a line of deductive thinking that results in a false conclusion, thereby implying that one or more of the premises in the argument is false.
>
> **Tautology**: two statements that say the same thing.
>
> **Formal fallacy**: a fallacy where the logical structure of the argument is invalid.
>
> **Non sequitur**: Latin for "it does not follow," when a person's conclusion does not follow from his or her argument.

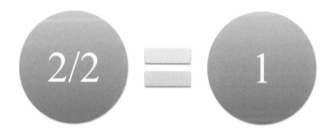

We should mention one more aspect of deductive logic, namely, the **tautology**. A tautology is when some claim is equal to itself. So the statement "he is single because he is not married" is a tautology, because you have simply said the same thing in two different ways. It can be helpful to recognize a tautology, because sometimes people think they are saying something that advances an argument when in fact they are simply saying the same thing in a different way.

3.3
THINKING INDUCTIVELY

As previously noted, inductive reasoning is a second form of good thinking. Here one gathers evidence and hypothesizes possible or probable conclusions based on that evidence. In life, we are constantly observing and drawing conclusions from what we see. I notice that you are walking around with a limp, so I ask you, "Did you hurt your leg?" We gather evidence hardly without thinking of it. Then we test our hypotheses against the data.

The scientific method, which we will explore in more detail in chapter 8, is a great example of solid, inductive reasoning. You identify a question and

Inductive Reasoning

gather relevant evidence in relation to that question. Then you form hypotheses that you test against the data until a hypothesis emerges that accounts so well for the data that it merits being considered a theory.

Much is made in some Christian circles of the difference between a theory and a fact. For example, you sometimes hear of arguments between scientific creationists and evolutionists over whether evolution is fact or theory. Both should be able to agree, however, that evolution is a scientific theory. Inductive reasoning is about *probabilities* given the evidence rather than about *certainties*. Facts are certainties. Theories are about probabilities. In science, if something has been tested enough to be called a theory, then it is the most probable reading of the evidence at this time, a reasonable thing to believe for the time being, even though it is not absolutely certain.

BIOGRAPHY

ARISTOTLE

Aristotle lived from 384 to 322 BC. We can think of him as the third great philosopher in succession in Athens after Socrates and Plato.

He was born in Macedonia, directly north of Greece. When Plato did not name him as successor at his Academy, Aristotle left Athens for a time. He eventually returned and founded his own school in Athens, the **Lyceum**. In the interim he had tutored Alexander the Great, who would later "conquer the world." Alexander took experts in science with him on his military conquests as a result of Aristotle's influence.

Aristotle was perhaps the most prolific writer of all ancient philosophers. His writings span all the fields of philosophy. The very word *metaphysics* comes from Aristotle's work—"after the physics" in the collection of his writings. Aristotle also founded the study of logic, and he suggested that any event had four basic "causes": (1) the material involved (material cause), (2) the truths that give "form" to what happens (formal cause), (3) the **efficient cause** or what directly caused something to happen, and (4) what results from the event (final cause), which we do not normally think of as a cause.

He disagreed with his teacher, Plato, on many subjects. For example, Plato believed that learning was remembering ideas our souls had known before they took on bodies. Today most of us will find Aristotle's perspective more attractive. He believed we recognize things because we have observed their essential characteristics before (empiricist).

In ethics, Aristotle is known for the golden mean—the idea of moderation in all things. He also taught that the ultimate good was happiness and that all other goods derive their value from the fact that they lead to happiness. He further thought of virtue as a habit, that we can become more virtuous by acting virtuously. We become courageous by acting courageously.

His social philosophy was based on the idea that "a human is a political animal" and thus that we could not be truly happy unless we live in a just society. His "household codes" give us essential background to some New Testament teaching on the home. Principally, we find that the idea that the husband is the head of the wife was a value of ancient Mediterranean culture in general rather than a distinctly Christian idea.

I notice that every tree in my yard has leaves. I form a hypothesis: all trees have leaves. I might walk around my neighborhood and test this hypothesis. Perhaps I come across a dead tree without leaves, so I have to modify it. All *living* trees have leaves. Continued observation will further modify my hypothesis in more than one way. All healthy trees have either leaves or needles at some point during the year. After extensive travel, testing, and modification of my hypothesis against the data of the world, I will at some point upgrade my hypothesis to a theory.

However, I cannot (at least not in philosophy class) consider it a fact that all healthy trees have, have had, and will have either leaves or needles at some point during the year. Neither I nor any human is capable of observing all trees. Who knows? Maybe one day a tree will arise that has something else.

> **Informal fallacies:** fallacies that involve false assumptions and problems with the content of an argument.

A theory is thus nothing to sneeze at. It is a hypothesis that has stood up against extensive testing. But it is not a fact. And inductive reasoning by its very nature tends to be open ended for possible modification on the basis of new evidence. Even when one has all the relevant evidence, inductive reasoning involves interpretation and thus can still be open ended.

In this section, however, we are primarily concerned with logical errors people make when they are reasoning inductively. Fallacies of inductive reasoning tend to be **informal fallacies** in contrast to formal fallacies, which are more a matter of deductive reasoning. Formal fallacies have to do with the way an argument is set up, the structure of an argument. Informal fallacies often have to do with false assumptions and the specific claims of an argument being wrong in some way.

We should point out that we are here talking about fallacies of invalid inductive *reasoning* not about whether a person's conclusion is true or false. Someone might come up to me and say, "I can tell you're a man because you have short hair." This person has committed a logical fallacy; the length of a person's hair is not logically linked to his or her gender. The conclusion was true: I am male. It is this person's *logic* that was in error, even though the conclusion was correct for other reasons. The remainder of the chapter summarizes the significant kinds of informal fallacies of logic that people make when using inductive reasoning.

Fallacy: Appeal to Force (*argumentum ad baculum*)

It should be obvious that forcing someone to hold a certain position does not make that position true. The law usually will reject a confession from a suspect that has been coerced. Force is the stuff of power and politics, but it is not the stuff of logic. You cannot change what is logically true by torture or pressure.

Fallacy: Appeal to Emotion (*argumentum ad populum*)

Debby Boone famously sang a song called "You Light Up My Life." One line says, "It can't be wrong, when it feels so right." Whatever merit this thought might have in other contexts, it has no merit in logic. Whether or not something is true logically has nothing to do with feelings or emotions.

Fallacy of Subjectivism

Closely related to the appeal to emotion is the *fallacy of subjectivism*.[5] Something is not true or false logically because of what I want to be true or false. For example, the question, does God exist objectively, apart from human thinking? has nothing to do with whether I like the idea of God or whether it works for me. It is not a matter of my motivation to believe or disbelieve.

The question of whether God exists objectively depends on, well, whether or not God exists objectively. To be sure, you can find conceptions of God out there that *do* both subscribe to the belief that God exists and hold that this belief is a matter of human subjectivity. But this is not the kind of existence we were asking about—whether a Being exists apart from human thinking and the actions to which that thinking leads. When you are talking about this kind of existence, then God exists or does not exist regardless of my feelings or desires.

Fallacy: Appeal to the Majority

If the fallacy of subjectivism is the idea that something is not logically true or false because of your *individual* desires, then it is similarly true that something is not logically true or false simply because a majority of individuals wants it to be true or false. In general, truth or falsity in logic is not a matter of vote. Whether or not an idea is true or false is a matter of, well, whether it is true or false.

Is it raining right now outside in the normal sense of what it means to rain? The answer to this question is not a matter of a vote. Either it is literally raining or it is not.[6]

Fallacy: Appeal to Improper Authority

In this and the next fallacy, we shift to slightly different logical ground, namely, when bringing other people into arguments makes sense and when it does not. In some circumstances it might make sense to put weight on a person's claims because of who that person is, that person's credibility. Take a victim of a crime who is mentally stable, knew his or her attacker, has no apparent ulterior motives, and observed the person who attacked. This person certainly seems a credible authority on the identity of the attacker. This credibility does not *prove* guilt absolutely, but it may argue for truth *beyond reasonable doubt.*

© istockphoto.com

In many cases, however, it is clear that we rely on the opinions of individuals who are not really appropriate authorities on an issue. "Everyone's entitled to their opinion." But as true as this idea is, it does not mean that everyone's opinion is equally valuable or likely to be true.[7] *Informed* opinion is, at least logically, more valuable than an individual's whims and fancies. In the realm of thinking, opinion is worthless unless it has reasonable arguments behind it.

The fallacy of improper authority is a real issue in matters of religion and politics. For example, a person who does not understand or know the science involved in climate change or evolution is not competent to evaluate the weight of the evidence with regard to the *science* surrounding those subjects. He or she could theoretically have received revelation from God on these issues, but he or she cannot be an authority on the science. Similarly, a person may know something true that God has revealed to him or her while reading the Bible, but such individuals cannot be authorities on the original meaning of the Bible unless they know the original languages, the historical background, the history of interpretation, and the process of reading in context (exegesis). It is a great privilege to live in a democracy, but not all opinions are created equal.

© istockphoto.com

Fallacy: Argument against the Person (*ad hominem*)

It is often effective in debate to attack your opponent rather than the actual *issue* you are debating—effective rhetorically but not logically. Politics is rife with this sort of sleight of hand. So-and-so is in a picture with this other so-and-so—thus I illogically transfer what you do not like about the one to the other. So-and-so cusses a lot or had an affair, therefore I illogically suggest so-and-so's ideas on some unrelated issue must be wrong. So-and-so is a liberal or a conservative or a communist or a fascist or unpatriotic—death by labeling the person. I dismiss this person's thinking on a particular issue, not by arguing against this person's position, but by suggesting he or she belongs to an untrustworthy group.[8]

But logically you cannot dismiss the truth of an idea by attacking the person who holds the idea. Whether or not an idea is true or false depends on, well, whether or not the idea is true or false. It does not depend on the person who has the idea. In the Bible, Satan knows that Jesus is the Son of God (e.g., Matt. 4:6), and demons themselves believe in the one God (James 2:19). These are untrustworthy sources who on these occasions believe true things.

© istockphoto.com

Genetic and Circumstantial Fallacies

Two related fallacies are the *genetic fallacy* and the *circumstantial fallacy.* The genetic fallacy is to say that something must be false because of the reasons someone came to the idea. Here are some examples of the fallacy. Sigmund Freud suggested that people believe in God because they want a father figure to take care of them. Karl Marx famously called religion the "opiate of the masses." But even if these scenarios proved to be true for many—let's say that some people believe in God because they want divine help or to make life bearable—that motivation would not *logically* disprove the existence of God. Whether or not God exists depends on, well, whether or not God exists.

The circumstantial fallacy argues against a person's position by pointing out the circumstances in which the person is making the claim. "Isn't it true that the district attorney has cut you a deal if you will testify?" It may be true, but that does not *logically* lead to the conclusion that the witness is lying to get a deal.

For this reason, circumstantial evidence is of varying value in a trial. From a practical standpoint, it can be very compelling. Let's say I find my son with cookie crumbs and chocolate smears around his mouth, a trail of crumbs leading back to a cookie drawer that is opened, with a box of cookies opened and standing upright in the drawer. I did not actually see my son take or eat the cookie. I am not an eyewitness to the "crime." Nevertheless, it is reasonable to infer that he in fact has just eaten a cookie from the drawer.

At the same time, this circumstantial evidence does not logically prove that he did. He could have been framed by one of his clever sisters, without him even realizing it. For that matter, space aliens or a mischievous angel might have set the whole thing up. This scenario gives us a good illustration of the difference between what is *logically* necessary and what is possible or even probable.

When the maturing person finally realizes that he will always remain a child, that he can never dispense with protection against strange powers, he lends to these forces the characteristics of his father; he himself creates the gods whom he fears, whom he seeks to win over and to whom indeed he entrusts his own protection. Thus the drive of longing for a father is identical to the need for protection against the consequences of human weakness.

Sigmund Freud,
The Future of an Illusion[9]

Fallacy: Appeal to Ignorance

Sometimes someone will argue that because you have not or cannot prove one thing to be true, the opposite must be true. "Prove it. You can't prove I did it." Of course the fact that I cannot prove that you did something says nothing definitive about whether you did it or not. Either you did it or you did not, and my ability to tell which does not affect anything.

Sometimes people use this fallacy in relation to God's existence. "You cannot prove God exists; therefore God must not exist." This argument commits the fallacy of ignorance. An individual may certainly think he or she has *no reason* to believe in God. But this fact does not in any way serve as a proof that God does not exist.

Fallacy: Hasty Generalization

One of the most frequently committed logical fallacies is that of hasty generalization. You draw an inference when you do not have enough information to do so, or perhaps you ignore important information that should be considered. This fallacious reasoning often accompanies the commission of other fallacies.

Fallacies of Composition and Division

The fallacy of composition is when you assume something is true of a whole group of things because it is true of some of the things within the group. We see this fallacy at work in what sociologists call in-group/out-group dynamics. People tend to pick positive individuals or traits from the groups to which they belong and then ascribe these particular characteristics to the whole group. "America is a Christian nation, whose people are honest and want to help the world." But obviously the United States has its share of sin and dishonesty.

Similarly we tend to pick negative traits or examples from other groups we do not like and paint the whole group with the same brush. "You have to watch out for such and such a group; they steal or lie or cheat all the time." "All Muslims are terrorists." "Catholics do not believe in the Bible." This is the stuff of prejudice—and often the fallacy of composition.

By contrast, the fallacy of division is when you take something that is true of the whole and then apply it to all of its parts. The fact that a team loses a ball game does not mean that every individual on the team played poorly or worse than those on the other team. The fact that an administration as a whole makes bad decisions does not mean that everyone in that administration agreed with those decisions or thought them the best course of action.

Fallacy: After This, Therefore Because of This (*post hoc, ergo propter hoc*)

One frequent expression of hasty generalization is the assumption that because something happened after something else, the first thing must have *caused* the second thing. For example, let's say I touch your earlobe, and then immediately someone across the room gets up and leaves the room. It might be tempting to think that the touch had something to do with the person walking out, but it is not at all a logical certainty. We especially have to be careful about this fallacy when looking at historical events and trying to ascribe praise or blame to some alleged cause. Just because something happens before something else—this does not prove that the first was the cause of the second.

Fallacy: Correlation (*non causa pro causa*)

A related fallacy is when you assume something that *correlates* or happens concurrently with something is the *cause* of that thing (*non causa pro causa*). Let's

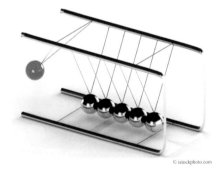

© istockphoto.com

say that one year both the crime rate increases in a particular city, and, at the same time, a large number of people move away. It is of course possible that the rise in crime is causing some people to leave town. But it is also logically possible that the rise in crime *correlates* with the people leaving town and that the two events are unrelated. One has to be very careful when doing research not to assume a cause-effect relationship without sufficient evidence. Things can happen at the same time without being related causally.

Fallacy of Diversion

The fallacy of diversion involves changing the subject in the middle of debate. Some of the fallacies we have already mentioned can serve such a diversion, for example, attacking the person instead of his or her position. One common form of diversion confuses the potential consequences of a course of action with the validity of the action itself. For example, it may very well be that prohibiting certain drugs could lead to people selling them illegally and a whole host of undesirable consequences. However, such consequences, abuses that others commit, would not necessarily mean that prohibiting those drugs was inappropriate. Whether or not some course of action is right or wrong is a question distinct from whether others might take advantage of or do bad things in light of the situation it creates.

Another form of diversion is a *straw man* argument. In this fallacy, you create a portrait of your opponent's position that looks a little like it but is actually not quite the same as what the opponent is claiming. Most of us would have a hard time beating up your average weight lifter or wrestler. But we could probably vanquish quite easily a version of one stuffed with straw. In the same way, it is easy to dismiss someone else's argument when he or she is not in the room and you are misrepresenting that person's position.

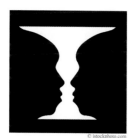

Fallacy of Equivocation

The fallacy of diversion involves a change of subject. The fallacy of equivocation changes in midargument the sense of the words you are using. Take the quip, can God make a rock so big that he cannot lift it? The person who poses this question usually wishes to argue that it does not make sense to say that God is all powerful.

But this person has mixed up two distinct concepts associated with the word *can*. One has to do with power or ability, and the other has to do with possibility. Christians do not normally suggest that it is possible for God to do everything (e.g., to fail), for "everything" includes things that contradict each other. Christians believe rather that God has all power or, as some Christian philosophers put it, that God can do anything that is logically possible.

The answer to the question, can God make a rock so big that he cannot lift it? is thus no, precisely because God is all powerful. God can (has the power to) lift any rock. But he cannot (it is not possible) for him *not* to be able to lift a rock. The question is worded in a way that plays into the fallacy of equivocation.

Fallacy: False Alternative

Another fallacy is to present an either/or option, when in fact other alternatives exist. Either you love me or you hate me. Either you favor the war or you do not. Life is seldom this simple. Here are two more examples: if you do not believe every word of the Bible is true, then you do not believe any of the Bible is true; if you believe in evolution, then you do not believe God created the world. These last two statements are examples of fallacious thinking even if we believe every word of the Bible is true and do not believe in evolution.

For example, there are Christians who believe that God created the world *through evolution*. They may be wrong, but they represent another possibility for which the either/or sentence above did not allow. And if for some strange reason someone believed that Lot's wife turned into mustard rather than salt (see Gen. 19:26), that would not imply that this person did not believe in the resurrection or that we should love our neighbors. This is the fallacy of false alternative.

One notable example of the fallacy of false alternative is the **slippery slope fallacy**. A slippery slope refers to the idea that if you start down a certain path or line of reasoning, you will not be able to stop before you reach an undesirable end. If we let students dance at our college, then next they will try to get permission to drink. So let's not allow dancing to stop the slippery slope there.

In real life, slippery slopes can actually have some substance to them. It is a good idea not to let your teenage son or daughter be alone in an empty house with his girlfriend or her boyfriend if you don't want certain things to happen. But logically, it is not an absolute certainty that one thing will lead to another. Other alternatives exist.

Fallacy: Begging the Question (Circular Reasoning)

Yet another fallacy is begging the question, which is when you assume your conclusion in your argument. You cannot use the fact that Ken said he never lies to prove that Ken never lies. What if I am a flagrant liar? You cannot assume something you want to prove in order to prove it.

Circular reasoning can be tricky because we aren't always aware of our own assumptions. "Christians are gullible because they believe that someone rose from the dead." But you're assuming that it is impossible for someone to rise from the dead. How do you know that for sure?

© Kevin L. Welch

Fallacy: Complex Question

A related fallacy is the complex question, such as in some cases when a lawyer leads a witness by asking, "When did your anger issues stop?" The attorney here is assuming that the person had anger issues. The question thus asks a follow-up question when no one has yet established the answer to the first question, namely, "Did you have an anger problem?"

3.4
CONCLUSION

In a world where so much seems uncertain, the rules of logic remain clear and indisputable. There are coherent and fallacious ways of thinking, arguments that are valid, and arguments that are invalid. We live in an age when opinion sometimes seems to count as much as expertise and every opinion is considered as valid as any other. In such a context, the rules of logic provide at least one irrefutable measure by which to evaluate certain claims and arguments. If we do not share "ground rules" like these for thinking in common, it will prove very difficult for us to communicate with each other or to decide between conflicting positions.

Deductive reasoning is when you draw a conclusion based on premises you assume. In such reasoning, if your premises are true and your logic is valid, the conclusion must follow without exception. Inductive reasoning starts with a body of evidence and creates hypotheses to explain the data. Along the way, we regularly see all sorts of bad reasoning. You might subtly change the subject or attack the person instead of the argument. You might mistake an exception for the rule or falsely stereotype everyone in a group. Sometimes we try to disguise feelings as arguments when they are none of the sort. We present false alternatives or create fear by invoking a slippery slope. The more we are able to think coherently and avoid fallacious thinking, the more empowered we will be to sort out truth from falsehood.

PHILOSOPHICAL QUOTATIONS

- "Religion is the opiate of the masses." (Marx)

KEY TERMS

- logic
- deductive reasoning
- inductive reasoning
- proposition
- valid and invalid logic
- true and false statements
- premise
- syllogism
- *reductio ad absurdam*
- formal fallacies
- *non sequitur*
- tautology
- Aristotle's Lyceum
- efficient cause
- informal fallacies
- fallacy: appeal to force
- fallacy: appeal to emotion
- fallacy: appeal to majority
- fallacy of subjectivism
- fallacy: improper authority
- fallacy: *ad hominem*
- genetic fallacy
- circumstantial fallacy
- fallacy: appeal to ignorance
- fallacy: hasty generalization
- fallacy of composition
- fallacy of division
- fallacy: *post hoc, ergo propter hoc*
- fallacy: *non causa pro causa*
- fallacy of diversion
- fallacy of equivocation
- fallacy: false alternative
- slippery slope fallacy
- fallacy: begging the question
- fallacy: complex question

KEY QUESTIONS

1. What is the difference between inductive and deductive reasoning?

2. What is the difference between a valid syllogism and a true one?

3. Evaluate the chapter's claim that biblical material is not propositional in nature for the most part. Argue either for or against this claim.

4. What were the key contributions of Aristotle to philosophy?

KEY QUESTIONS

5. Get a copy of an editorial page or locate a website where someone takes a position on an issue. Evaluate the arguments used. What logical fallacies can you find?

6. Identify the informal fallacy in each of the following statements:

- "I see the guy who shot her was white. That's the way white people are—very violent and dangerous."
- "I just know she's innocent. I can feel it."
- "Angels don't exist. I've never seen one."
- "That boy has cried wolf twice now, and there was no wolf. So there will be no wolf this time either."
- "Quantum physics is a bunch of bunk, because that's what my mom (who is no good at science) told me."
- "You believe that all religions are equally valid because if you believed otherwise we would fire you."
- "The president's foreign policy is obviously bad. After all, he cheated on his wife."
- "Either you believe in absolutes, or you don't believe in any right or wrong."
- "The economy started to tank after he became president; he must have caused it."
- "Premarital sex is wrong because it is wrong to do sexually immoral things."
- "If we let immigrants continue to speak their own languages, before long no one will speak English here anymore."
- "Paul couldn't have written 2 Timothy, because most scholars do not think he did."
- "I know you killed him, because I saw you leaving the building after the murder."
- "This rock is millions of years old because it has this fossil in it. This fossil is millions of years old because it was found in this rock."
- "I'm not out to get you, Frank. You think everyone's out to get you because you're a paranoid schizophrenic."
- "If a person has ever had a homosexual relationship, we should keep that person away from our children, because the vast majority of child molesters are repeat offenders."
- "He's a Muslim because he's a Palestinian, and Palestinians are mostly Muslim."
- "God is the greatest Being we can conceive. But he wouldn't be the greatest if he didn't exist in reality as well as thought. Therefore, God exists."
- "God would never want us to make an exception to the rule not to lie because God would never want us to do wrong."

NOTES

1. George Lakoff and Mark Johnson have made a good case that not only speech but even our concepts are ultimately metaphorical in nature. See *Metaphors We Live By* (Chicago: University of Chicago, 1980). Nevertheless, the distinction between literal and metaphorical stands when we think of the literal as the ordinary use of words and metaphors as an unusual use of words based on comparing them to other things that are unlike them.

2. Interestingly Paul does not exactly word this statement like a proposition, introducing it with the relativizing phrase "for us there is . . ."

3. Technically this second premise is a "some" premise. The four types of premises are (1) all x's are y's, (2) no x's are y's, (3) some x's are y's, and (4) some x's are not y's.

4. The two other kinds of syllogism are the disjunctive syllogism, where the premises say either this or that is true, and the hypothetical syllogism, which follows an "if-then" format.

5. In fact, we might consider the first three fallacies in our list subjectivist fallacies of a sort: the appeal to force, the appeal to emotion, and the appeal to the majority.

6. I want to stress the phrase *normal sense* for more than one reason. We are avoiding a host of postmodern concerns here and taking a pragmatic view of reality and knowing. Regardless of the ultimate ontological and epistemological status of what we are saying, this language works as well as any human language.

7. Most modern governments wisely incorporate a representational element into their systems. While on the one hand practicality forces representation—it is hardly feasible for millions of people to be involved in every vote—it is also logically desirable for those most informed and capable to make key decisions. The United States and most modern governments are thus technically republics rather than pure democracies.

8. This last example also smacks of the fallacies of division and composition. This person has a viewpoint in common with a certain group; therefore the person is a part of this group (fallacy of composition). This group is bad; therefore this individual within the group is bad (fallacy of division).

9. Paraphrased from Sigmund Freud, *The Future of an Illusion*, trans. J. Strachey (1928; New York: W. W. Norton, 1975), 32.

© Kevin L. Welch

CHAPTER 4

WHAT IS TRUTH?

What to Get from This Chapter

- The three tests for truth are the correspondence, coherence, and pragmatic tests.
- The Bible, the Spirit, and the church can play roles as sources of truth.
- Kant's epistemology synthesized the strengths of both the rationalist and empiricist approaches to truth.

Questions to Consider

- What are the three tests for truth?
- What role does the Bible play in truth?
- What roles do reason and experience play in truth?
- What was Kant's synthesis of rationalism and empiricism?

Key Words

- Truth
- Hermeneutics
- Rationalism
- Empiricism

4.1 THREE TESTS FOR TRUTH

How do you know that you know what you think you know? We have been discussing some key ingredients in the answer to this question in the previous two chapters. In chapter 2 we looked at the relationship between faith and evidence, as well as the role that presuppositions play in what we think, the *assumptions* that underlie our reasoning. In chapter 3 we discussed the *process* of thinking. In particular, we laid out the difference between good thinking and bad thinking or valid and invalid reasoning.

In this chapter we consider different *sources* of knowledge and the key ways to *assess* whether such claims are true. Where do we go to find truth and what criteria should we use to decide whether something is true or false? To some degree or another we all measure truth by three basic "yardsticks."

First, we decide whether a claim is true by comparing the claim with what we can observe around us. We see if it *corresponds* to our experiences of the world. This is the **correspondence test for truth**.

Second, we see whether a claim makes sense in itself. Do all the parts of the claim fit together with the others? Does the idea contradict itself at some

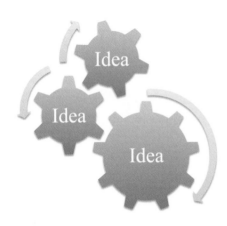

Correspondence test: an approach to truth that asks whether a claim corresponds to the evidence.

Coherence test: an approach to truth that asks whether a claim is coherent both with itself and with your prior assumptions.

Pragmatic test: an approach to truth that asks whether a claim "works" on some level, whether it is a useful or beneficial idea.

Empiricism: an approach to knowledge that views experience as the principal path to truth.

Rationalism: an approach to knowledge that views reason as the principal path to truth.

point? And does the claim fit with what we already assume to be true, with our starting points? We might call this measuring stick the **coherence test for truth**.

Finally, we regularly measure an idea by whether it "works" for us in some way. Despite all our truth talk, the **pragmatic test for truth** is perhaps the strongest force behind what people end up affirming in practice. This test for truth can function on more than one level. It can function on a subjective level, where certain ideas "work" for me whether or not they work for anyone. Other ideas seem to work fairly well for most human beings, even though we may not be able to prove them absolutely.

We all inevitably use all three of these tests for truth as we go about life. We test the evidence; we fit ideas together; we see if they work for us. But various philosophers throughout history have often emphasized one of these approaches while downplaying the others. For example, **empiricists** tend to emphasize that truth is a matter of our experience, of what we perceive with our senses. "Seeing is believing," an empiricist might say. Empiricists emphasize the correspondence approach to truth.

By contrast, **rationalists** emphasize the importance of presuppositions and coherence when determining what is true. "Don't let your eyes deceive you," they might say. Plato believed that learning was remembering truths that your soul already knew before you were born. You did not learn new information as you looked on the world; you were born with all that truth already in your mind. Few would follow him straightforwardly today, but he illustrates an extreme version of how a rationalist might emphasize thinking over experience when determining what is true.

Finally, postmodernism has recently given significant power to the pragmatist position by drawing attention to the uncertainty of our knowledge: We cannot set ourselves apart from the world as God can, to see the world exactly as it is. We have no choice but to look at the world from where we are, stuck in our bodies in a specific time and place. All our thinking proceeds from assumptions that we can neither prove nor disprove. Our knowing thus involves faith on a fundamental level. And the decisions we make between competing truth-claims are based largely on our sense of which conceptions of reality work better than others.

We will give a fuller discussion of postmodernism in chapter 15. In this chapter we will rehearse the historical debate between those who have seen either reason or our sense experiences as the best path to truth. But before we start that discussion, we need to explore what role the Bible—as well as the Holy Spirit and the church—might play in a *Christian's* quest for truth. How might the Bible serve as a measuring rod of truth for a Christian believer?

4.2
THE BIBLE AND TRUTH

You may know a children's chorus that says, "Jesus loves me; this I know. For the Bible tells me so." Historically Christians have believed in several sources of truth that hold an authority higher than that of mere human reasoning or experience. The Bible immediately comes to mind, especially for Protestant churches. Yet we might also mention Pentecostals, charismatics, and holiness groups for whom experiences of the Holy Spirit have often played, in practice, an equally strong role in hearing God's voice.[1] Roman Catholics and Eastern Orthodox churches would further point out the role of the church throughout the centuries in understanding the Bible and God's ongoing will in the world.

In general, Christians acknowledge a legitimate role for all three of these distinct sources of truth: (1) Scripture, (2) the church throughout the ages, and (3) the Holy Spirit.[2] They may have different formulas for the relative importance of each of these sources, but they acknowledge all three as part of the truth equation. For example, Catholic and Orthodox traditions strongly affirm the authority of Scripture, even though we often hear that they do not. They differ, however, in their sense that the church (as they understand it) is the only reliable guide to which *interpretation* of the Bible is correct. Similarly, while Pentecostal traditions put a premium on direct revelation from the Holy Spirit, they usually receive these revelations when interacting with the words of Scripture. Finally, even a "Scripture only" tradition like the Reformed church sees a role for the Holy Spirit and the church in helping believers know how to apply the Bible appropriately to contemporary life.

As we saw in the second chapter, it is the nature of philosophy to ask "metaquestions"—questions that follow up on the kinds of claims we have just mentioned. For example, one crucial metaquestion in this discussion is, what is the meaning of words in general and the words of the Bible in particular? You do not have to drive far in any city in America to discover dozens of different churches identified by signs naming different denominations. No doubt the Bible plays a role in almost all of them, yet they have differing interpretations and often quite different beliefs.

This fact has long played a role in the Roman Catholic and Orthodox critique of Protestantism. From the time of Martin Luther, Roman Catholics predicted that giving each individual the authority to interpret the Bible would result in almost as many interpretations as people reading it.[3] And indeed the Protestant Reformation has resulted in a massive fragmentation of Christianity into thousands of individual groups, all of which think they have the right interpretation.

Further, some Protestant groups would critique Pentecostals and other more "Spirit-oriented" interpreters of the Bible because their "spiritual" use of the Bible seems inevitably to lead to an almost endless number of interpretations for one passage. Ten people can think the same words in the Bible can mean ten different things based on what they think the Spirit is saying to them.

"It means this to me."

"Really? It means this to me."

It is beyond the scope of this book to delve very deeply into the philosophy of language, also known as **hermeneutics**. Hermeneutics is that branch of philosophy that asks how meaning and communication take place, what it means to say some text means something. One of the most convenient ways to think of communication is in terms of a text, its author, and its reader.[4] Of course a text need not be written. A smoke signal is a sort of text, as are the motions of sign language. As such, the "reader" could actually be someone listening to you talk or a blind person who feels a Braille text.

Hermeneutics asks second-order questions about the relationships between authors, readers, texts, and meaning. It asks questions not only about how these relationships work, but about how they *should* work. Interestingly, the question of language has been one of the dominating issues in philosophy these past hundred years, even among Christian philosophers of language.

Up until the early 1900s, a theory of language prevailed that we might call the "picture" theory of language; a word corresponds to something I picture when I hear it. Take the following comment on words by St. **Augustine** in the early 400s:

> No one uses words except as signs of something else. So we can understand what I call signs: those things we use to point to something else. Accordingly, every sign stands for a thing, for what is not a thing is nothing at all.

Augustine, *On Christian Doctrine* 1.2[5]

Here Augustine reflects the simplistic view that a word is a "sign" to cue in your mind the remembrance of some "thing." I see the word *cat* which cues in my mind the thing: a cat. The appeal of this view of language is that it seems to work on a very basic level. It evokes images of how many people suppose a child learns words.

Applying this view of language to the Bible, one might suppose that each of its words points to one meaning. Understanding the Bible—indeed, understanding any word—would then become a matter of knowing the right meaning behind each word, behind each "sign" in turn. We might think that

Hermeneutics: the branch of philosophy that asks how meaning takes place and is communicated; the philosophy of language.

the meaning of the Bible is thus generally obvious. We get a good translation, one that has identified the correct words in our language that correspond to the right meanings, and we are set to hear the voice of God.

However, this view of language is imprecise at best and misleading at worst. More than anyone else, the twentieth-century philosopher **Ludwig Wittgenstein** (1889–1951) pioneered what seems to be a more accurate understanding of language. He pointed out that the meaning of words is primarily a matter of how they are *used*, not of some fixed thing to which they point.

Wittgenstein recognized that we cannot know the meaning of a word like *fire* unless we know what **language game** a person is playing with the word, what a person is "doing" with the word. These games connect to particular **forms of life**, the distinct contexts in which various words are used.

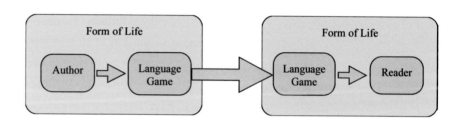

For example, if we are talking about the word *fire* in the context of a firing squad, then the rules of the game tell certain people to shoot someone. The meaning of the word *fire* in this context does not correspond to some "thing." It is a command to do something. If someone runs into a room and yells "fire!" in an alarming voice, it is a different language game. The rules of this game tell us that we should hurry out of the room quickly to safety. In each case, if we do not know the "game" an author is playing in his or her form of life, then we cannot know the intended meaning.[7]

Following this general train of thought, Wittgenstein suggested, "If a lion could talk, we could not understand him."[8] The reason is that we do not know the language games of the forms of life in a lion's world. We might be able to give approximate definitions in English for every word the lion said and still have no clue what he was actually saying.

A good example of this dynamic is when the Nazis demanded that General Anthony McAuliffe surrender at the Battle of the Bulge. He sent them back the answer, "Nuts!" The Germans knew what a nut was, but they could not make sense of McAuliffe's response because they did not know this particular *use* of the word in one American language game.

The implication of this discussion for understanding the Bible is immense. First, we recognize that most Bible readers approach the text with what we might call a **premodern** hermeneutic (see also chap. 15). A premodern hermeneutic, as it relates to texts, is one that reads texts from the standpoint of the reader's own language games and forms of life without realizing that the meaning of these texts was originally a function of someone

> Think of the tools in a tool-box: there is a hammer, pliers, a saw, a screw-driver, a rule, a glue-pot, glue, nails and screws. The functions of words are as diverse as the functions of these objects.
>
> **Ludwig Wittgenstein,**
> ***Philosophical Investigations* 11[6]**

Language game: a particular way that a word or set of words is used in a particular form of life.

Form of life: Wittgenstein's way of referring to a specific context in which words are used.

else's language games and forms of life.[9] The text in question is not read in context, on the *text's* terms, but on the terms of the person doing the reading.

Premodern hermeneutic:
unreflective interpretation in which a reader is largely unaware of the difference between how the words strike him or her and their original meanings.

Modernist hermeneutic:
interpretation that attempts to read words in their original contexts, often with over-confidence in the result.

Postmodern hermeneutic:
interpretation that in one way or another recognizes the limitations of our ability to know the intended meaning of texts with absolute certainty.

A **modernist** hermeneutic, by contrast, attempts to read the biblical texts on their own terms, in terms of their original audiences. These were not originally one book from God *to me*, but scores of books written in three different languages over perhaps a millennium *to people who have been dead for two or three thousand years*. On the assumption that God meant their first audiences to understand them—a reasonable assumption—they must have been written in the language games of these ancient contexts, which often differed from ours today.

Are there human "forms of life" and accompanying "language games" that are common to all humanity? Almost certainly. If so, such meanings could be understood by all people in all times and places without much explanation. But many assume more common ground than is probably the case. Even basic human categories such as love play themselves out in quite different ways in different cultures and settings. They are approximately the same but with some differences in the specifics.

Some of the most exciting developments recently in biblical studies have to do with the social world of the Bible.[10] These studies suggest a host of basic ways in which our modern Western culture differs from the cultures in which the books of the Bible originated, categories such as individual identity, family, money, and worldview. Even as simple a word as *I* apparently had significantly different connotations in the biblical worlds than it does in the United States today.[11]

This section is titled "The Bible and Truth" because the Bible is the primary source of truth for evangelical Christians. But it is clear from this discussion that the topic is far more complex than most Christians imagine. Those who simply read the Bible and do what it seems to say to them may only be doing what they *think* the Bible says, given who they are, rather than what it was *really* saying. They may be reading the text to mean something quite different from what it really meant to Isaiah or Paul.

Evangelical scholars have spent a good deal of energy unfolding a method by which we might with integrity connect the worlds of the Bible with our world.[12] For example, in 1 Thessalonians 5:26 Paul encourages the ancient Christians at Thessalonica to "Greet all the brothers with a holy kiss" (NIV). But few Christian men today would go up and greet someone in their church with a kiss. The meaning of this act in ancient Thessalonica was quite different from the meaning it would have in a Western church today.

At the same time, we can do things that accomplish the same basic purpose—to show brotherly love to one another and to affirm that fellow Christians are family. Instead of a kiss, we might greet someone with a hearty handshake. In this instance, doing exactly what they did two thousand years ago does not accomplish the same thing as it did back then. The significance for us is simply not the same. The person who blindly applies the words of the Bible directly to today will sometimes stray from its true purposes.

More recent days have seen attempts to move beyond a purely modernist approach to the Bible to one that returns to the possibility of hearing a more direct voice in the Bible's words. Because these attempts come after the era of the modernist approach, we might call them *post*modernist. They are often much like the premodern paradigm in that they may not primarily be concerned with the original meaning of the biblical texts. They will probably be more concerned with what these texts might mean for us today. The difference is that the postmodernist more knowingly chooses this focus, while the premodernist is largely unaware of the distinction to any depth.

Some postmodernist approaches to the biblical text do not leave it with any real voice at all. Purely **reader-response** approaches ignore any original meaning the words might have had and replace it with the way the words strike some particular interest group. These approaches often give the reader complete control over the Bible's meaning. We will also discuss briefly the deconstructionist approach to language in chapter 15. It denies that words have any stable meaning at all—even to a particular reader or reader group.

Other developments in recent years are more positive. The **two horizons** hermeneutic draws largely on the work of **Hans-Georg Gadamer** (1900–2002), who pictured the process of understanding as a "fusing" of the "horizon" of the reader with the "horizon" of the text.[13] In this scheme, Gadamer was largely unconcerned with the historical author behind a text.[14] A person might take into account historical features of a text, but the goal is not to get behind the text to its history but to fuse your world with the text's world as we have it.[15]

Gadamer's approach to texts stands on the edge of the transition from modernism to postmodernism. On the one hand, he pictures understanding as a genuine engagement with the text as something other than yourself. On the other hand, he did not believe we could come to the text objectively. We have no choice but to come to texts with all the traditions of understanding we bring with us.

In that sense Gadamer's account of understanding finds it inevitable that a Christian will come to the biblical text with Christian understanding in tow. Some who have pursued Gadamer's approach find this element in his equation very attractive. Is it in fact a good thing for Christians to come to the biblical text with certain Christian understandings in place? If Scripture itself can be ambiguous, is it helpful that Christians come to it with many beliefs and practices in common, things that presumably God has helped the church throughout the ages unfold?[16]

> **Reader-response hermeneutic:** an approach to texts that focuses on the way a particular reader or group of readers understands it.
>
> **Fusing the two horizons:** in Gadamer's hermeneutic, the idea that readers inevitably bring their world to a text, including any traditional interpretations of that text that have impacted them; readers then engage in a hermeneutical circle in which the "horizon" of their world fuses with the "horizon" of the text.

For example, the belief that Jesus is fully God is a common Christian belief. We Christians believe that Scripture points in this direction. However, this truth is not as frequent in the New Testament texts as we might imagine it to be. It is as much the fact that we Christians read the biblical text through the eyes of Christian history that leads us to see it clearly in the text.[17] In far more ways than we usually realize, our Christian glasses influence the way we read the Bible.

Different Christian traditions will no doubt continue to combine these elements of the equation differently. But when we ask in what way the Bible is a source of truth, our discussion shows us three basic ways. First, the Holy Spirit speaks to us collectively and individually through the biblical texts. Some think that the Spirit chooses to speak mostly the same way over time through the same Scripture, without breathing new meanings.[18] But we can all surely agree that if we could be certain that the Spirit was speaking, that message would indeed be a valid source of truth.

Most Christians also agree that the original meanings of the Bible witness to the ongoing speaking of God throughout the history of biblical times. Each book in some way represents God speaking to its particular audience. Further, when we read these books in context, it is not difficult to see a flow and progress of understanding even among the individual books of the Bible themselves. For example, the New Testament books seem to have a fuller understanding than the Old Testament books. But we can see truth in each book, many Christians would say an inerrant or infallible one, as it related to God's purposes for each original audience.

Finally, we recognize in the church throughout the ages a potentially rich, perhaps even essential, set of lenses through which to appropriate the Bible. If the books of the Bible themselves have played into the hands of numerous competing versions of God's story, perhaps the version that Christians hold most in common is the version that sets the story straight. We suspect that Protestant Christians will increasingly value this piece of the puzzle throughout the rest of this century.

Before we leave this discussion, I want to underline some of its philosophical implications for the Bible as a source of truth. Far more thinking is involved in interpreting and applying the Bible than most people realize. Even the most able scholars have areas of unreflective thinking where they are unaware of their assumptions. Unless the Holy Spirit is directing our thoughts in such moments, we will likely mistake our own voice for God's.

We use a good deal of reason particularly when we are trying to fit the various parts of the Bible together. We can believe that none of the parts of the Bible conflict with the others and still acknowledge that there are a lot of statements that at least *seem* to conflict with others. Paul says, "a person is justified by faith apart from works prescribed by the law" (Rom. 3:28). James says, "a person is justified by works and not by faith alone" (2:24). Neither Paul nor James tells us how to fit these seemingly conflicting statements together! That is to say, *the Bible* does not explicitly tell us how faith and works go together. To a significant degree, we have to reason out the answer, often relying heavily on the Christian tradition from which we come.

In the previous section, we discussed how *to apply* to today the verse, "Greet all the brothers with a holy kiss." It is important to point out that *the Bible* did not give us the answer to this question. First Thessalonians was a letter *to ancient Thessalonians*; God did not tell Paul to include a footnote on how to apply the truths of the letter to a different cultural context. *We* are forced to find the points of continuity and discontinuity between "that time" and "this time."

The long and short of all these observations is this. We Christians rely on the Bible as God's Word to us. The Bible is God's instrument for forming us—our hearts, our wills, our minds. But we cannot bypass the role that reasoning plays in interpreting the Bible. We certainly pray for the Spirit to direct our reasoning, but without reason we cannot come to any conclusion on what "the Bible" as a whole says or about how to apply such a conclusion to today.

Nor can we eliminate the role our past and current experiences play in our readings of Scripture. Our experiences shape the questions we ask and what aspects of the biblical text stand out to us. Our experiences create a sort of common sense that leads us to see some verses as clear and others as unclear. Our denominational backgrounds and the broader culture to which we belong serve as filters as well. We should try to be as objective as we can in relation to the forces at work on us, but Gadamer is surely correct when he tells us we inevitably bring hermeneutical "baggage" with us to any text.

The Bible is a unique source of truth for the Christian, but our interpretations of it do not bypass our reason and experience. Even when I have a direct revelation from the Holy Spirit, I inevitably interpret it with my human reasoning. I not only have a finite perspective on the universe, but I have that perspective stuck "within" my head. The person who thinks that he or she simply reads the Bible and does what it says—God said it, I believe it, that settles it—can be a dangerous person, for this person is vastly unaware of the forces at work on one's personal understanding. This person is wired to mistake his or her own thoughts for the thoughts of God.

© istockphoto.com

4.3
REASON VERSUS EXPERIENCE

© istockphoto.com

Philosophy students often find the two-thousand-year debate over whether reason or experience is a more important path to truth exasperating, and not without cause. The conclusion reached by **Immanuel Kant** (1724–1804)—that *both* are intrinsic to knowing—can seem anticlimactic and obvious. But if we cut through the tiring repetition and get to the heart of the matter, we see a crucial question of epistemology that we are still wrestling with today.

Perhaps we can see the underlying issue better if we start with Kant's solution. Is reason or experience the dominant path to truth? Kant "broke the tie" by saying that both were involved—that the *content* of my knowledge is largely a matter of my senses and experiences. Thus the empiricist is partially right. But the *organization* of that content is something I don't get from experience. It is something my mind does to the content I get from my senses. Thus the rationalist is partially right.

Kant put it this way:

> There can be no doubt that all our knowledge begins with experience. For how should our faculty of knowledge be awakened into action if objects did not affect our senses . . . In order of time, therefore, we have no knowledge prior to our experience, and with experience, our knowledge begins.

> —∞—

> But thinking, which is limited to objects of experience, nevertheless is not derived entirely from experience, but . . . there are without question elements of thinking that exist in the mind *a priori* [prior to experience].

> —∞—

> The uniting together of all impressions [from our senses] requires us to synthesize them into a unity in our consciousness.

> **Immanuel Kant, *Critique of Pure Reason*** [19]

Kant is basically saying that we must have something in our minds that makes sense of our experiences, that connects them together so they become meaningful. For example, I can experience a horse and I can experience a horn, but I cannot experience a unicorn. Experience may account for my idea of a horse and horn, but it cannot completely account for my idea of a unicorn.

Of course Kant was not interested in unicorns. He was concerned with things like how we can understand one event to cause another or how we can say an event is right or wrong. These are issues that philosopher **David Hume** (1711–1776) had raised just prior to Kant. Hume was the empiricist to end all empiricists. Kant once summarized Hume's impact on him by saying that "he interrupted my dogmatic slumber."[20] Kant's most important ideas were to a large extent his attempt to grapple with problems raised by Hume.

For example, Hume recognized that empiricism alone cannot account for the idea of cause and effect. I can experience one event happening after another. But these are simply a succession of experiences, one right after the other. The idea of one event *causing* another is not something I experience with my senses. Accordingly, Hume questioned whether the idea of cause and effect really made sense at all, although he no doubt got out of the way of passing carriages just the same.

> Suppose someone . . . suddenly came into this world. Certainly he would immediately observe a continuous succession of objects, and one event following another. But he would not be able to discover anything further. He would not . . . be able to reach the idea of cause and effect . . .
>
> All inferences from experience, therefore, are effects of custom, not of reasoning.

David Hume, *Enquiry concerning Human Understanding* 5.1[21]

Kant, however, did not want to conclude in Hume's pessimistic and skeptical direction. Instead, he suggested that my *mind* rightly organizes the two experiences into a pattern of cause and effect. The idea of cause and effect is a valid way my mind puts two successive experiences together, even though this "glue" does not come from the experiences themselves.

Think of it this way. Most computers come with word processing software. But until you begin to put letters and words into a document, it remains blank. In a similar way, Kant implied that our minds come with certain "software" that stands ready to process the input of our senses. In philosophy we say this kind of software is **a priori**, because it is there "from before" the time we experience anything. But it is our experience that inputs specific content into the "documents" of our knowledge. Before experience, our knowledge is a blank page, even if there are elements of cognition or knowing that are already in place.

Take another issue Hume raised—something called the fact-value problem. Hume suggested that there is nothing in experience that can get us from a fact to a moral value we put on that fact. We can experience someone

> Thinking without content is empty, intuitions without a conceptual framework is blind.
>
> **Immanuel Kant, *Critique of Pure Reason***[22]

BIOGRAPHY

IMMANUEL KANT

In Immanuel Kant's entire lifetime (1724–1804), he never ventured more than a hundred miles from his hometown of Königsberg, Prussia (today Kaliningrad, Russia). Although his early writing was popular among his contemporaries, he wrote his most enduring works in later life. *The Critique of Pure Reason*, which he wrote in his late fifties, would become one of the most important books in the history of philosophy.

In the preface to his book *A Prolegomena to Any Future Metaphysics* (a summary of the ideas in the *Critique*), Kant wrote that the empiricist David Hume had woken him from his "dogmatic slumber." Hume had shown him that empiricism could account for only the content of our thoughts, not for the shape those thoughts took in our mind. To explain the organization of our thought, the synthesis of information in our minds, Kant suggested that our minds operate within certain a priori categories such as space and time or cause and effect.

Kant believed that these categories, the frameworks by which we understand the things that we sense, are "transcendental." Although some scholars interpret Kant differently, Kant seemed to believe that the categories by which we understand the world are universally true. On the one hand, these categories come from our minds, not from the world itself. In that sense, we cannot know the world as it is in itself; we can only know the world as it appears to us, as it is organized by our minds. We cannot understand the world without using transcendental categories like time and space, cause and effect, and believing that the things we perceive have substance.

On the other hand, Kant was inclined to think these categories were, in reality, universally true, even though our minds impose them on the data of our senses. Some who have followed Kant have accepted that our minds construct reality while they reject the claim that those constructions are universally true.

Kant argued that several other beliefs follow naturally from these transcendental categories, namely, our belief in God, the existence of the soul, and human freedom. We cannot be consistent with the way our reason makes sense of the world without also affirming these beliefs.

But the way Kant affirmed them flowed straight from his philosophy. For Kant, for example, freedom meant that you act in accordance with universal reason. It did not mean that you could do whatever you want to do. And the moral law for him was a function of conclusions that flowed directly from our built-in categories of reason.

Kant used the phrase *categorical imperative* to describe his understanding of ethics. Kant's thinking seems to be that if something is an imperative, a "must do," then it is "categorically" a must do. Kant believed that if something was right or wrong, then it was *always* right or wrong without exception.

killing an innocent person (a fact). But the moral judgment, the *value* we place on that act—that it was wrong, immoral, or evil—does not come from our experience of it. Moral judgments, Hume pointed out, are not something that come from our experiences. He accordingly considered such value judgments meaningless, although he refrained from murder just the same.

Once again, Kant suggests that God has created our minds with certain "moral software" that glues together events with values. Our minds have built-in or "innate" categories by which to process these sorts of things and glue them together. Our minds thus rightly glue together causes to effects and facts to their values. Kant also included the ideas of space and time as categories built into our minds to process experiences. We will discuss Kant's thoughts on metaphysics in chapter 7, "What Is Reality?"

Kant did not end the discussion back in the 1800s. Indeed, in many respects he only got it going full speed. We will look at the impact of his thought on the philosophy of the past two hundred years in chapter 15 on postmodernism. For now, he gives us a good perspective from which to summarize the debate between rationalists and empiricists from Plato to Hume.

Rationalists, with their emphasis on reason as the best path to truth, have tended to see truth as something that is a priori, already available to our minds in some way apart from our experiences. They tend to think that we have **innate** knowledge that we are born with. On the other hand, empiricists have tended to see our knowledge as almost totally derived from our experiences.

Today Western culture by and large leans toward the empiricist side of things. It is harder for us to relate to **Plato**'s philosophy (rationalist) than it is for us to relate to Aristotle's (empiricist). For example, Plato believed that "all learning is only remembering."[23] Our souls preexisted our bodies in heaven, where they already were acquainted with universal truth. Learning in our bodies is thus about the process of remembering consciously the things our souls already know a priori.

Most of us will find Plato's notion of how learning takes place

> **a priori:** "from beforehand"; in epistemology, the idea that certain knowledge or categories exist in our minds prior to experience.
>
> **Innate:** "born with"; in epistemology, the idea that we are born with certain knowledge or categories a priori.

School of Athens, from the Stanza della Segnatura, 1510–11 (fresco), Raphael (Raffaello Sanzio of Urbino) (1483–1520) / Vatican Museums and Galleries, Vatican City / Giraudon / The Bridgeman Art Library

BIOGRAPHY

FAMOUS RATIONALISTS

Plato (ca. 427–347 BC):
Plato suggested that the world around us that we experience with our senses is far less real than the world we can access with our minds (see chap. 7, "What Is Reality?"). The world of our senses is a world of shadows cast by the truest world, the world of ideas. The things we experience with our senses are like copies or images of the ideal patterns that we can only contemplate with our minds. Our minds know these ideas because our souls had access to them before they became imprisoned in our bodies. Learning is thus remembering this innate knowledge rather than a matter of gaining new knowledge.

Photo Credit: Plato (429–347 BC), ca. 1475 (oil on panel), French School (17th century)
Bibliotheque de la Faculte de Medecine, Paris, France / Archives Charmet
The Bridgeman Art Library

Gottfried W. Leibniz (1646–1716):
The depth of Leibniz's rationalism did not come through clearly until his unpublished writings became better known in the 1800s. Leibniz's two principles of reason were already known: his "law of contradiction" and "principle of sufficient reason." Truths of reasoning are truths we can know apart from experience. The law of contradiction says that two contradictory claims cannot both be true, and we know this must be the case even before we have any relevant experiences. Truths of reasoning are thus *necessary* truths.

On the other hand, principles of sufficient reason relate to truths of fact. These truths are *contingent* rather than necessary truths; they did not have to be true but turn out to be. As human beings, we come to know these sorts of truths through our experiences. Leibniz's unpublished writings have shed considerable light on what he was thinking here. For Leibniz, all the things that happen to us in life are dictated by reasons we will never fully know. Of all the possible things that could be, some cannot coexist because of the law of contradiction. Those things that do exist are the greatest number of possible things that could coexist.

In the end, Leibniz followed Spinoza in believing that all truths are already determined and known by God. Experience thus does not contribute to truth, even if we as humans seem to come to know truth by this path. In theory, all truth could be known through reason alone.

Photo Credit: Portrait of Gottfried Wilhelm Leibniz (1646–1716) (oil on canvas), German School (18th century) /
Niedersachsisches Landesmuseum, Hanover, Germany / Flammarion / The Bridgeman Art Library

René Descartes (1596–1650):
Descartes is known as the founder of modern philosophy primarily for the way he drew attention to the question of certainty in what we know. He notoriously set out to doubt everything he could doubt and to accept as true only those things that he could conceive *clearly and distinctly*. The perceptions of his senses were the easiest for him to doubt, securing him his place among the rationalists. Descartes suggested that I could be dreaming what I think I am experiencing. Descartes then found it possible to doubt his own thoughts, for an evil demon could be manipulating them. What I cannot doubt, he famously suggested, is that I am thinking. "I think; therefore, I am."

Believing that he had established a point of certainty, he proceeded to argue that God existed, because any conception of God "clearly and distinctly" includes the idea that God is a *necessary* Being. Descartes thus thought God must exist. And if God exists, God is not an evil demon who would try to deceive us by making us perceive the world outside our minds vastly differently than it is. Thus I can trust my mind as it thinks about the world outside it.

Photo Credit: Portrait of Rene Descartes (1596–1650) ca. 1649 (oil on canvas), Hals, Frans (1582/83–1666) (after) /
Louvre, Paris, France / Giraudon / The Bridgeman Art Library

Baruch Spinoza (1632–1677):
Spinoza took from Descartes the idea that truth is a matter of what we can conceive of clearly and distinctly. But whereas Descartes saw knowing as a matter of our souls understanding a material world outside our minds, Spinoza believed that everything was one basic thing, God. The truths we associate with our thought and the truths we associate with the world are both truths about "God" that we can discover through reason. Experience is not necessary to learn any truth. All such truth is predetermined, and understanding involves coming to accept it. In this Spinoza partially resembles the Greek Stoics, although he did not oppose emotions to the extent they did. One's emotions involve truths that one must accept.

Photo Credit: Benedict Spinoza (1632–77) (oil on canvas), Dutch School (17th century)
Herzog August Bibliothek, Wolfenbuttel, Germany / The Bridgeman Art Library

strange. We much more readily identify with Aristotle's idea that we derive all the ideas in our minds from our experiences of the world. In other words, our knowledge comes **a posteriori**, "from after" we experience things. St. Thomas Aquinas, whose ideas drew heavily from Aristotle, summed up this position best when he said, "There is nothing in the mind that was not first in the senses."[24]

If Hume took a purely empiricist approach to its logical conclusion, it was John Locke (1632–1704) who had first set down the ground rules, earning him the title "founder of modern empiricism." First of all, Locke supposed, we begin with a **tabula rasa**, a "blank slate."

> *All ideas come from sensations or reflections.* Let us suppose the mind to be, as we say, a blank slate, empty of all characters, without any ideas. How does it come to fill up? . . . Where do the materials of reason and knowledge come from? To this I answer, in one word, *experience*. From it all knowledge originates.

John Locke, *Essay concerning Human Understanding* 2.1.2[25]

We have sensations of the world that create simple ideas in our minds. We see the color blue and the parts of a flower. Our minds put these simple ideas together to form complex ideas, such as our idea of the whole flower in all its aspects. Examples of such complex ideas included "beauty, gratitude, a man, an army, the universe."[26] Although these are complex ideas made up of simple ones, the mind considers them as one entire thing.

Hume called Locke's sensations "impressions" and was more imaginative in his examples:

> When we think of a gold mountain, we only join two consistent ideas, *gold* and *mountain*, with which we were formerly acquainted. We can conceptualize a virtuous horse because, from our own feeling, we can conceive of virtue. And we can connect this idea to the figure and shape of a horse, which is an animal familiar to us. In short, all the materials of thinking are derived either from our outward or inward sentiment. The mixture and composition of these things belongs alone to the mind and will.

David Hume, *Enquiry concerning Human Understanding* 1.2

But as Hume would later point out, Locke lacked any basis in his theory to account for the "glue" that stuck some of our most important ideas together. So in Hume's empiricism, relationships like that between cause and effect did not clearly go together. We make these sorts of connections without

a posteriori: "from afterward"; in epistemology, the idea that knowledge comes only after experience.

a clear basis in experience. If we go with a pure empiricism, Hume would seem to be right. We need some suggestion such as Kant's to come to our rescue if we are to consider some of these connections true rather than just coincidences or, as he put it, "habits." Any theory of knowledge that does not involve both the mind and experience would seem to be inadequate.

So what does this historic debate have to say about reason and experience as sources of truth, especially for a Christian? It says that experience does not automatically equal truth. Kant rightly pointed out the fact that my mind processes the evidence I get from my senses. I apparently do not know the world as raw experience but as *processed* experience. My mind organizes my experiences according to its rules.

This raises the question of how accurate the "rules" of my mind are.[27] Kant brings his faith in God into play here—surely God has given us good software. But if our minds are "fallen," affected by sin—not to mention limited in what they can grasp and see—the accuracy of the way my mind processes experience is called into question.[28] We came across this issue in the previous section when we pointed out that we do not have the Bible as "raw truth," but we inevitably interpret and process its truth with our minds.

4.4
CONCLUSION

What are the best sources of truth, especially for the Christian? To varying degrees, people of all times and places have regularly used at least three tests for truth, whether they have ever heard of them or not. Does a hypothesis seem to correspond to the evidence I have? Do my ideas fit together with each other, or are they contradictory? Does an idea help me function in my day-to-day living, or does it more likely bring difficulty or pain?

If God's Spirit reveals something to you, it is absolutely reliable and definitive. The problem is that some mistake their own thinking for that of the Holy Spirit. It is thus very important for Christians to help each other "test the spirits" to see if they are really from God (cf. 1 John 4:1).

Scripture is not only a collection of God's words to people at different times and places in the past. God uses it today as a whole to form us and inform us of his will for today. In it we see the story of God walking with his people and reaching out to the world, culminating in Jesus Christ coming to earth, taking on our humanity, dying to reconcile us to God, and rising victoriously over death. Our reason and experiences are still a part of our appropriation of the Bible, but they do not prevent God from changing us

BIOGRAPHY

FAMOUS EMPIRICISTS

Aristotle (384–322 BC):
Plato thought that ideas exist on their own, in heaven. Our souls know them before they enter our bodies, and thus truth is something our minds know innately. However, for Aristotle, we come to knowledge only by experiencing things with our senses. Universal truth is something we abstract from our experiences, not something built into our minds even before birth. Before experience, our minds are like a blank tablet with only the potential to have things written on them.

Photo Credit: Marble head of Aristotle (384–322 BC) / Kunsthistorisches Museum, Vienna, Austria / The Bridgeman Art Library

John Locke (1632–1704):
We might call Locke the "founder of modern empiricism" for the way he steered philosophy, at least in Britain, away from the rationalism of continental Europe (Descartes, Spinoza, Leibniz) and toward empiricism. Like Aristotle, Locke considered our minds to be a "blank slate" (tabula rasa) prior to experiences from our senses. We have *sensations* of the world and *reflections* on the workings of our own minds that result in simple ideas (each part of a flower; the color blue). Our minds then rightly connect simple ideas into more complex ideas (a blue flower).

At the same time, Locke continued to believe that the things we experience have "substance" behind them. The substance behind our sensations is matter, and the substance behind our reflections is mind. Thus like Descartes he believed that the world consisted of two basic substances, mind and matter, in a mind-body dualism.

Photo Credit: Portrait of John Locke, ca. 1704 (oil on canvas), Kneller, Sir Godfrey (1646–1723) (studio of) / Private Collection / Photo © Philip Mould Ltd, London / The Bridgeman Art Library

George Berkeley (1685–1753):
Along with Locke, Berkeley affirmed that experience was the source of all our knowledge and denied that we have any innate knowledge. But he disagreed with the dualism of Locke and Descartes, that

mind and matter are two different substances. Locke had distinguished between two different bases for our experiences of the material world. Primary qualities are aspects of the world that exist independently of our experiencing them (e.g., shape) while secondary qualities exist only as a result of our experiencing them (e.g., color).

Berkeley denied this distinction, saying that all the qualities of the world exist because someone is experiencing them, in particular, because God is perceiving them. Berkeley thus denied that any material substance underlies the world of our perception at all. Rather, "to be is to be perceived" (*esse est percipi*). He was an idealist who believed that, apart from God, the only kinds of things that actually exist are ideas.

Photo Credit: George Berkeley, engraved by Bocquet, illustration from 'A catalogue of Royal and Noble Authors, Volume III', published in 1806 (litho), English School (19th century) / Private Collection / Ken Welsh / The Bridgeman Art Library

David Hume (1711–1776):
Hume developed and refined Locke's empiricism to its ultimate, logical conclusion. He called Locke's sensations "impressions" and believed that these correspond to ideas we have in our minds. Hume also followed Locke in seeing complex ideas as conglomerates of simple ideas. But Hume strongly argued that no idea we have makes sense unless it corresponds and originates with sense impressions.

Accordingly, Hume questioned Locke's and Descartes's claims that matter and mind are substances that underlie our experiences. Berkeley had denied that matter underlies our experiences, but he had accepted that idea underlies them. Hume denied both, finding the notion of underlying substance—which cannot be experienced—meaningless. Hume also questioned notions like cause and effect, the existence of God and the soul, as well as the connection between events and moral significance. In his view, none of these connections or entities could be experienced and thus are meaningless notions.

Photo Credit: David Hume (1711–76) 1766 (oil on canvas), Ramsay, Allan (1713-84) / Scottish National Portrait Gallery, Edinburgh, Scotland / The Bridgeman Art Library through Scripture. Indeed, God has already used the past two thousand years of Christian history to shape the way we read the Bible.

Reason and experience are both involved in the way we process knowledge of any kind. Experience gives us most of the content of our thinking. But our minds organize our experiences according to ways that are common to all normal human brains. Our brains come with "software" that knows how to process time and space, cause and effect, perhaps even right and wrong to some degree. We also grow up with some basic ways of thinking about the world, paradigms and worldviews that we inherit from our parents and cultural environment. More than any of us can realize, these also affect the way we understand the world around us.

KEY TERMS

- correspondence test
- coherence test
- pragmatic test
- empiricism
- rationalism
- hermeneutics
- language games
- forms of life
- premodern hermeneutic
- modernist hermeneutic
- postmodern hermeneutic
- reader-response hermeneutic
- two horizons hermeneutic
- a priori
- a posteriori
- innate
- tabula rasa

KEY PHILOSOPHERS

- Plato
- Aristotle
- Augustine
- René Descartes
- Baruch Spinoza
- Gottfried Leibniz
- John Locke
- George Berkeley
- David Hume
- Immanuel Kant
- Ludwig Wittgenstein
- Hans-Georg Gadamer

PHILOSOPHICAL QUOTATIONS

- "If a lion could speak, we would not understand him." (Wittgenstein)
- "There is nothing in the mind that was not first in the senses." (Aquinas)
- "I think; therefore, I am." (Descartes)
- "To be is to be perceived." (Berkeley)
- "Thinking without content is empty, intuitions without a conceptual framework is blind." (Kant)

KEY QUESTIONS

1. What are the three "tests" for truth? Which do you find the most persuasive? Why?

2. What do you think the proper relationship is between the Bible, the Spirit, and the church as sources of truth for a Christian? Why?

3. Do you agree with the claim that a great deal of what we call "the Bible" basically amounts to traditions we have inherited about how to interpret and connect together diverse biblical statements and apply them to today? Why or why not?

4. Do you agree that reasoning is always involved in our appropriation of the Bible? That our experiences significantly affect the way we read it?

5. Articulate your personal opinions: In arriving at truth, what are the respective roles of reason and experience? To what extent do our minds organize our experiences beyond the experiences themselves? For example, how might personality or life story impact our interpretation of our experiences?

NOTES

1. Certainly these groups have such spiritual experiences primarily in encounter with the biblical text. However, their engagement with the text in such instances has sometimes been somewhat superficial. The determinative element in the equation is more the ever-changing voice of the Spirit through the text, not some fixed meaning of the text itself.

2. By the "church throughout the ages," we are not speaking of one church in particular (e.g., the Roman Catholic Church), but to all true Christians throughout the centuries, no matter the visible church to which they have belonged. By "true Christian," we mean someone who has the Spirit of God within (cf. Rom. 8:9). But we will leave it up to God to decide who such people are.

3. The Catholic Renaissance scholar Erasmus put it this way to Luther: "You say, 'What does an assembly of the church have to do with understanding Scripture when not one of them may genuinely have the Holy Spirit?' I reply, 'What, then, does some independent group of a few have to do with it, in which it is even more likely that none of them have the Spirit?' . . . Now every Tom, Dick, and Harry wants you to believe him when he says he has the Spirit of the gospel." Paraphrased from *Erasmus and Luther: Free Will and Salvation,* ed. E. Gordon Rupp and Philip S. Watson (Louisville, KY: Westminster John Knox, 1978), 42.

4. George Lakoff and Mark Johnson have pointed out that this scheme is based on "conduit" and "container" metaphors for communication. They suggest we might reasonably use other metaphorical grids as well to discuss language. See *Metaphors We Live By* (Chicago: University of Chicago, 1980), 10–13.

5. All quotations from Augustine in this book are paraphrased on the basis of the translation by Philip Schaff, *The Nicene and Post-Nicene Fathers*, Series 1, 14 vols. (Peabody, MA: Hendrickson, 1994).

6. Ludwig Wittgenstein, *Philosophical Investigations*, trans. G. E. M. Anscombe (Englewood Cliffs, NJ: Prentice Hall, 1958), 6.

7. Subsequent philosophers of language have further developed Wittgenstein's functional approach to language. Key here is the speech-act theory of J. L. Austin, *How to Do Things with Words* (Cambridge, MA: Harvard University, 1962); and John R. Searle, *Speech Acts: An Essay in the Philosophy of Language* (Cambridge: Cambridge University, 1970).

8. Wittgenstein, *Philosophical Investigations,* 223.

9. Although he did not use the precise language we are using here, the most important work on precritical interpretation of the Bible is Hans Frei, *The Eclipse of Biblical Narrative* (New Haven, CT: Yale University, 1980).

10. One of the pioneers of this field of study is Bruce J. Malina. See, e.g., *The New Testament World: Insights from Cultural Anthropology*, 3rd ed. (Louisville, KY: Westminster John Knox, 2001).

11. In particular, the ancient Mediterranean world was largely a "collectivist" culture in which a person's individual identity was embedded within the groups to which one belonged. Biblical individuals thus defined themselves primarily on "external" factors such as gender, family, and race. Identity was thus fixed from birth rather than a matter of choice or psychological development.

12. Typical books that explore such methods include Grant R. Osborne, *The Hermeneutical Spiral: A Comprehensive Introduction to Biblical Interpretation*, rev. ed. (Downers Grove, IL: InterVarsity, 2006); and Gordon D. Fee and Douglas Stuart, *How to Read the Bible for All Its Worth*, 3rd ed. (Grand Rapids: Zondervan, 2003).

13. Gadamer's main work in this regard was *Truth and Method* (1960).

14. Another author who similarly did not consider the world "behind" the text accessible to the modern reader is Paul Ricoeur. See especially *Interpretation Theory: Discourse and the Surplus of Meaning* (Fort Worth: Texas Christian University, 1976).

NOTES

15. The primary purveyor of the work of these individuals for biblical hermeneutics is Anthony C. Thiselton, *The Two Horizons: New Testament Hermeneutics and Philosophical Description* (Grand Rapids: Eerdmans, 1980).

16. Although Gadamer is no doubt correct that we inevitably bring considerable "baggage" to biblical interpretation, the goal of reading in context seems legitimate. We may not be able to be completely objective, but we can strive for objectivity. In that sense I personally think it is wrong to choose *only* a contextual focus or *only* a reading located in a community of readers. These both seem legitimate readings of the biblical text and both seem to hold out distinct benefits.

17. Take a statement like John 10:30, "I and the Father are one" (NIV). We as Christian readers are prone to hear in this verse an affirmation of Christ's divinity like the Father. In context, however, Jesus is speaking primarily of the agreement between him and his Father on this topic.

18. In addition to Grant Osborne, *Hermeneutical Spiral* (see n. 12 above), a notable example of this position is Kevin J. Vanhoozer, *Is There a Meaning in This Text?* (Grand Rapids: Zondervan, 1998).

19. All paraphrases of Kant's *Critique of Pure Reason* in this book are based on the translation by J. M. D. Meiklejohn (New York: Prometheus, 1990). These three paraphrases are taken from pp. 1, 95, and 79 respectively.

20. A paraphrase of Kant, from his Preface to the *Prolegomena to Any Future Metaphysics*, par. 260.

21. David Hume, *Enquiry concerning Human Understanding.* Paraphrase of Hume's own original 1748 English wording.

22. Kant, *Critique*, 45.

23. Plato, *Meno* 81.

24. Thomas Aquinas, *De veritate* 2.3.19.

25. John Locke, *Essay concerning Human Understanding.* Paraphrase of Locke's own 1690 English wording.

26. Locke, *Essay concerning Human Understanding* 12.1.

27. In chapter 9 we will mention the impact of brain science on this discussion. A key reference here is George Lakoff and Mark Johnson, *Philosophy in the Flesh: The Embodied Mind and Its Challenge to Western Thought* (New York: Basic Books, 1999).

28. For further exploration of this idea, see James K. A. Smith, *The Fall of Interpretation: Philosophical Foundations for a Creational Hermeneutic* (Downers Grove, IL: InterVarsity, 2000).

UNIT 3

PHILOSOPHY OF RELIGION

© istockphoto.com

What to Get from This Chapter

- Christians disagree over how important or convincing rational arguments for God's existence are.
- Cosmological arguments argue that the existence of the world requires the existence of a Creator.
- Miracles and religious experience have been key verifiers of Christian faith from the beginning.
- Teleological arguments claim that the complexity of the world requires the existence of an intelligent Designer.
- Moral arguments claim that an ingrained sense of right and wrong requires the existence of a Creator of morality.
- Ontological arguments claim that our very ability to conceptualize the Most Perfect Being entails the existence of that Being.

Questions to Consider

- Can we prove the existence of God?
- What are some reasons to believe in God?

Key Words

- Apologetics
- Cosmological argument
- Teleological argument
- Ontological argument
- Moral argument

5.1
DO WE NEED PROOF?

People always have reasons why they believe in the existence of God, even if they are not fully conscious of them. Various philosophers have offered their own suggestions—some positive, some negative. Augustine (354–430) thought we were made for God, and so our hearts would be restless until we found peace in him. Sigmund Freud (1856–1939) argued it was because people wanted a father figure powerful enough to keep them safe from the world. Ludwig Feuerbach (1804–1872) thought God was a projection of all the best virtues of humanity taken as a whole. Meanwhile, Friedrich Nietzsche (1844–1900) thought God was an idea the weak used to gain power over those stronger than them.

In chapter 3 we learned about the genetic fallacy. Even if some skeptics turn out to be right about the *reasons* some people believe in God, it would not disprove the existence of God. The genetic fallacy confuses *why* someone

> You made us for yourself, and our hearts are *restless* till they find rest in you.
>
> **Augustine, Confessions 1.1**[1]

The heavens are telling the glory of God; and the firmament proclaims his handiwork.

Psalm 19:1

Atheist: one who does not believe that God exists.

Agnostic: one who is uncertain whether God exists, especially one who does not believe it is possible to know for certain.

Apologetics: the study of how to defend your faith, usually on the basis of rational argument.

In the Trinity Term of 1929 I gave in, and admitted that God was God, and knelt and prayed: perhaps, that night, the most dejected and reluctant convert in all England.

C. S. Lewis, *Surprised by Joy*[6]

believes something with the veracity of *what* that person believes. This chapter discusses arguments about *whether* God exists not *why* people believe in God's existence.

For some people, deciding whether God exists seems to be a question of personal benefit: Why should I believe in God? What's in it for me? But if God exists as something other than an idea in our heads, if God is an actual Being who thinks and acts regardless of us, it doesn't really matter whether God's existence is to our advantage. If God exists, God exists, whether it is convenient for me or not.

Other people sincerely disbelieve (**atheists**) or doubt (**agnostics**) God's existence. They may not be more immoral than those who say they believe in God. Indeed, many atheists live very "Christianly." Some people disbelieve or doubt the existence of God because their heads simply cannot "see" it, not because they are trying to run away from God.

In the rest of this chapter, we look at some of the classic arguments for the existence of God. Not all Christian thinkers believe such arguments are necessary or even helpful. We have already encountered some of these issues in chapter 2, where we discussed "Faith and Reason." Is belief in God really a matter of blind faith rather than argument? Can we actually prove God's existence by reason, or will we find that rational argument comes up short? Does rehearsing the classical arguments contribute more to doubt than to faith?

Some voices would say so. The branch of Christian philosophy that traditionally defends Christian faith using rational arguments is called **apologetics**. Although the word *apology* has taken on the sense of telling someone you are sorry for something you have done, an apology in this context means a defense by way of argument. The writing known as Plato's *Apology*, for example, is a presentation of Socrates's trial, during which Socrates *defended* himself in argument before the men of Athens.

Some Christians in the past have put a high premium on the likelihood of reason leading you to believe in God.[2] C. S. Lewis (1898–1963), for example, aimed in several of his writings to show not only that Christian faith was reasonable, but that reason virtually compels a person to such faith.[3] Another popular Christian author of the late twentieth century, Josh McDowell, wrote *Evidence That Demands a Verdict*[4]—the title suggesting that an objective consideration of the facts not only allows for faith but in fact demands it as the clear conclusion. As we will see, Thomas Aquinas (ca. 1225–1274) argued in the medieval period that the existence of God could be rationally demonstrated by observing God's effect on the creation.[5]

We have also seen in chapter 2 that some Christian thinkers object to the idea that God's existence is provable through Christian reason. Indeed, some believe the attempt to prove God's existence through reason is dangerous or even antithetical to faith. Søren Kierkegaard (1813–1855) claimed that "If I can understand God objectively, I do not have faith."[7] Blaise Pascal (1623–1662) is known for saying that "the heart has reasons that reason can't know," implying that faith ultimately is not a matter of rational proof.[8] In more recent times, individuals including William Placher have playfully suggested that Christians should be "unapologetic" about their faith.[9] To them, to orient oneself around rational proofs of Christian faith is something like corrupting God's thinking by subordinating God's thinking to flawed human reasoning.

You will have to decide which approach you think is more correct. The approach we take in this book is that faith in God is not irrational, even though human reason probably cannot *prove* the existence of God. Christians have traditionally believed that we come to faith only because God initiates a relationship with us and enables us to respond to him. The starting point for our faith is thus not proof of God's existence, but that God has come to us, and we have responded accordingly. Even more important, the God we might be able to prove by rational argument is not yet the Christian God, for Christians have historically believed that Jesus Christ stands at the heart of who God is. From a Christian standpoint, any understanding of God that does not view his identity through the lens of Jesus Christ is thus at least an incomplete understanding of God.

> We can't understand anything about God's actions in the world unless we accept the principle that he wanted to blind some of us and enlighten others.
>
> —⁓—
>
> God wants to move our will rather than our intellect. Perfect clarity in understanding would help our intellect but handicap our will.
>
> —⁓—
>
> The heart has reasons that reason can't know.
>
> **Blaise Pascal,**
> ***Pensées,* 566, 581, 277**[10]

5.2
ARGUMENTS FROM CAUSE AND EFFECT

One of the oldest and best-known arguments for the existence of God is the **cosmological argument**, particularly the cause-effect version of it. It basically argues that

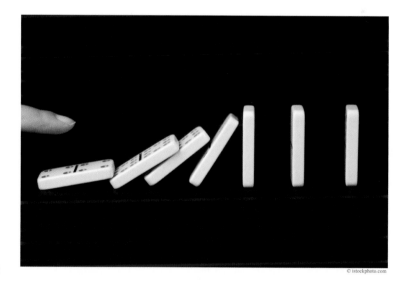

© istockphoto.com

"something cannot come from nothing," therefore something must have caused the world to exist. It must have had a Creator, a supreme cause. Most have also heard a common response: then where did God come from? We will address this objection below.

> **Cosmological argument:** the argument that God must exist in order to explain where the world came from.

Over the centuries, various thinkers have used various kinds of cause-effect arguments to try to prove God's existence. Some seem to work better than others. I propose the following version of the cosmological argument:[11]

1. The universe seems to have had a beginning. We apparently can trace a chain of causes and effects in the physical world back to a point "in time."

2. We currently have no scientific explanation for that beginning. We have no explanation for what "caused" or began the process of creation.

3. It is reasonable to suggest that something "beyond" this universe, some nonuniverse force, caused that beginning.

As many Christian thinkers have pointed out, whatever the cosmological argument leaves us with, it is not yet the *Christian* God. At most it suggests a very powerful Creator. Indeed, the form of the argument we have made above does not even imply a Creator that is *all* powerful! Nevertheless, the argument seems to make sense and implies that belief in a "Creator" is perfectly reasonable. The atheist at present has no alternative explanation for why the universe "suddenly" decided to begin.[12] He or she must instead have faith that science will one day discover such an explanation or that such an explanation exists even though we have no access to it.

We most associate the cosmological argument with **Thomas Aquinas**, who in his *Summa Theologica* advanced five proofs for God's existence. The first three are versions of the cosmological argument. We will consider the first two now and the third in the next section.

> It is clear and obvious to our senses that some things are in motion in the world. Now anything that moves is moved by something else . . . And if the something else that moves it is moving, it must be moved by something else. This situation cannot go back infinitely . . . So we must eventually arrive at a First Mover, unmoved by anything else. And everyone understands this Mover to be God . . .
>
> In the world of senses, we find a succession of efficient causes. We do not find any instance where something is the efficient cause of itself. Then it would have to exist before itself, which is impossible. Now it is impossible that such efficient causes could go back infinitely . . . Therefore, we must admit the existence of a First Efficient Cause, to which everyone gives the name, "God."

Thomas Aquinas, *Summa Theologica* I.q.2 a.3[13]

Here we see two arguments, one from motion and one from cause. Aquinas's argument from motion is basically a Christianized version of an argument made some 1,500 years earlier by Aristotle. In the world, we observe one thing moving another. Aristotle could not imagine that this process of one thing moving another could go back forever, so he suggested a "First Mover" that was not moved by the world but gave the world its first "push" to get started.

This form of the argument has not convinced many people in recent times. For example, Galileo Galilei (1564–1642) set out the law of inertia several hundred years after Aquinas. According to this rule, a body in motion tends to stay in motion, while a body at rest tends to stay at rest.[14] No doubt to Aristotle and Aquinas, it appeared that something had to keep pushing in order for an object to move; they were not really aware of friction. But

BIOGRAPHY

THOMAS AQUINAS

Thomas Aquinas, an Italian monk, lived from circa 1225 to 1274. He has been called both the "angelic doctor" and the "dumb ox." Aquinas stands as the greatest philosopher-theologian of the Middle Ages. Even today, the Thomistic school of philosophy continues, especially in Roman Catholic circles.

One of Aquinas's great contributions to philosophy was the preservation of Aristotle in the West. Up until the time of Aquinas, Platonic philosophy had exerted the greater influence through the thinking of individuals such as Augustine (354–430). However, Aquinas did not resurrect Aristotle on his own. We have rather to thank Islamic philosophers such as Avicenna (Ibn Sina, ca. 980–1037) and Averroës (Ibn Rushd, 1126–1198) for this feat, who themselves had an influence on Aquinas.

Aquinas basically divided the things we can know into truths that we can know through our reason and truths we can know through revelation. He did not

believe our minds were completely corrupted by sin. We could actually know many truths about the world simply by using good reason. At the same time, he did not believe that the truths we could know only from revelation—from the fact that God has revealed them to us—were irrational. Truths known only by revelation make sense, and we can illustrate them by analogy.

Accordingly, Aquinas offered five famous proofs for the existence of God in his *Summa Theologica*, most of which are forms of the cosmological argument. Here he shows himself indebted to Aristotle's idea of a "Prime Mover" and his understanding of causes and effects.

Aquinas is known for a number of other key ideas about God and Christianity that some continue to believe today. For example, he is most responsible for the Roman Catholic understanding of transubstantiation, the idea that the underlying substance of the bread and wine in Communion becomes the literal body and blood of Jesus. He promoted the idea of earlier thinkers such as Boethius that the essence of God is existence itself, and that God's being is "simple," without any parts.

theoretically the motion of the world could go back infinitely.[15] If an astronaut throws a ball into space, it will continue at the same speed forever unless it runs into some other force. David Hume (1711–1776) made a similar objection to Aquinas's arguments. How do we know that the motion cannot go back infinitely?

By contrast, the argument we advanced above is a form of the argument from cause, corresponding to Aquinas's second argument. When expressed as a proof, as Aquinas expressed it, it argues that for every effect there must be an "efficient" cause. An **efficient cause** is the thing that directly causes something else to happen. Aristotle, on which Aquinas based much of his philosophy, set out four basic causes, some of which we might not really consider to be causes today.[16] The idea of an *efficient* or immediate cause, however, continues to make sense to us. In modern times, William Lane Craig has especially advocated this argument by drawing from the *kalam* argument of certain Muslim philosophers.[17] If something has a beginning, it must be the effect of a cause.

Efficient cause: the most immediate and direct cause of an event.

It seems unwise to make this statement with such certainty, since we scarcely know how causation exactly works, especially with universes as a whole. However, assuming the universe had a beginning, it certainly seems rational to suggest that something caused it to begin. This explanation seems more reasonable than the suggestion that it did not have a precipitating cause.

We must also dismiss the simplistic response: then where did God come from? The form of the cosmological argument we are making applies to things we observe *within* this universe. *In this universe* effects generally have causes.[18] When we make this statement, we imply nothing about whether creators of universes such as this one must have causes. By the rules we have laid down, any Creator stands "beyond" or "outside" the creation in essence. To observe rules within the creation thus says nothing about the rules of the Creator.

© istockphoto.com

Although it is foolish to base one's belief in God on the current state of scientific thinking, it does no harm to mention that science currently favors a beginning for the universe. We mention just two reasons. The first has to do with the "mass" of the universe, the amount of stuff in it. Every bit of matter as we know it has a certain gravitational pull.[19] Theoretically if the universe had enough matter in it, the universe might one day stop expanding and collapse on itself. If that were the case, someone might suppose that the history of the universe is simply an endless cycle of expansion and collapse leading to another expansion (the so-called oscillating big bang theory).

But astrophysicists do not currently think that the universe has enough mass for that to happen. They believe the evidence currently points to a single beginning to the universe. Christians do not have to agree with all the particulars of current astrophysics to enjoy the secular conclusion that the universe had a beginning. At least for the moment, science has refuted David Hume, who thought it just as possible that the universe did not have a beginning.

A second argument has to do with the fact that the universe is constantly in the process of cooling down. Newton's second law of thermodynamics observes that the workings of the world inevitably turn various forms of energy into heat. The long and short of it is that things tend to disorder from order over time. There is no such thing as a machine that can go on forever without putting more energy into it. The work you do now eventually dissipates as friction and heat, never to be recovered.

Eventually, at least if things continue as they are, the universe will cool down to absolute zero. The energy in the universe will convert to heat and all the heat will spread out evenly throughout the universe until everything is cold, cold, cold. By the same token, the universe could not be infinitely old or else the heat would have already dissipated. This fact points to a beginning, and thus David Hume is foiled once again.

Of course we should never base our faith on the "God of the gaps," the God whom we bring into some gap in our understanding.[20] History since the scientific revolution has witnessed Christian after Christian staking their faith on some unexplained aspect of science. And history has witnessed those gaps getting filled in time and time again. So the cosmological argument does not prove the existence of God. But it does suggest that, at least with regard to the matter of causation, it makes more sense to believe in a Creator than it does not to.

Now that we have finished discussing cause-effect as an argument for the existence of God, it might be interesting to *assume* God's existence and ask what the notion of cause-effect might imply about God in relation to the creation. Let us assume by faith, for example, that God in some way created the world "out of nothing," **ex nihilo** in Latin. Jews and Christians increasingly believed that God created the world out of nothing from about AD 200, when a group known as Gnostics argued that matter was intrinsically evil and that it had existed eternally alongside God.[21] The Jewish and Christian response was to affirm that God had not only formed matter but had created it out of nothing.

If God created the universe out of nothing, then God must have enough power to create it. In other words, the idea that God created the world out of nothing would seem to imply that God is all powerful or **omnipotent** in

Creation ex nihilo: creation of the world "out of nothing."

Omnipotent: all powerful.

relation to the universe. The implication is that God has the power to do anything that is possible to do with the creation. Of course Christians have historically affirmed that God is all powerful without having to follow any line of reasoning such as this one. It is at least interesting to note that the idea of God being all powerful fits with the idea that God created the world out of nothing.

Hands of God and Adam, detail from The Creation of Adam, from the Sistine Chapel Ceiling, 1511, Buonarroti, Michelangelo (1475–1564) Vatican Museums and Galleries, Vatican City / The Bridgeman Art Library

5.3
MIRACLES AND EXPERIENCES OF GOD

Most people do not believe or disbelieve in God because of their assessment of the evidence. Indeed, it is not even clear that people believe or disbelieve in God because of their experiences. Two people can have nearly identical experiences and interpret them completely differently. The same experience that deepens one person's faith in God may lead to deeper doubt for the other.

Nevertheless we must reckon religious experience a far more potent "proof" of God's existence for most people than any rational argument one might offer. In a sense, such experiences are a type of cause-effect argument for God, by which a person reckons the existence and involvement of God in the world as the best explanation for an event that happens to him or her. **Miracles** seem to fall into a similar category of argument for God's existence. A miracle is something that does not seem explicable given the normal operation of cause and effect. It is something that seems beyond "natural" explanation, requiring a "supernatural" cause.

Miracle: an event that is not explicable on the basis of normal scientific, cause-effect reasoning.

David Hume, the famous skeptic, argued in his book *An Enquiry concerning Human Understanding* that no amount of eyewitness testimony could justify belief in a miracle.[22]

A further argument Hume made had to do with the consequences of relying on experiences of God and eyewitness testimony to miracles. Considering that most religions have claimed miracles and experiences of their gods, he said, we would have to conclude that all religions are true. But since these same religions contradict each other, we have no reason to consider the experiences or miracles of *any* of them to be legitimate.

A miracle is a violation of the laws of nature. Because firm and unalterable experience has established these laws, the proof against the possibility of a miracle is . . . as absolute as any argument from experience we could possibly imagine.

David Hume,
An Enquiry concerning Human Understanding 10.1[23]

Perhaps the best-known response to Hume on these sorts of issues has been that of **C. S. Lewis.** In his book *Miracles*, Lewis argued,

> Now of course we must agree with Hume that if there is absolutely "uniform experience" against miracles, if in other words they have never happened, why then they never have. Unfortunately we know the experience against them to be uniform only if we know that all the reports of them are false. And we know all the reports to be false only if we know already that miracles have never occurred. In fact, we are arguing in a circle.
>
> **C. S. Lewis, *Miracles*[24]**

In other words, even if the overwhelming majority of professed experiences of God and reports of miracles were false, it could not disprove the legitimacy of *all* such claims.[25]

It seems almost impossible to prove or disprove whether or how often genuine miracles or experiences of the "divine" might take place. Such experiences can be highly convincing to the individuals involved, but the legitimacy of one person's religious experience is rarely apparent to someone else. And it has become increasingly difficult in a quantum world to determine what the precise boundaries might be between what is "natural" and what is "supernatural," indeed, if even this distinction makes any sense at all. A person who recovers from cancer might very well do so because of a precise combination of material causes and effects brought on by chemotherapy, all of which could in theory be accounted for scientifically. On the other hand, God may very well "fiddle" regularly with quantum particles here and there.

Religious experiences will thus play varying roles in an individual's faith. Hume was at least right to point out that people of all religions claim to have experiences of the divine, and almost all religions would point to various miracles as proof of their legitimacy. Christian tradition would say that people have faith because God "invites" them, and they respond appropriately.[26] But this confidence seems to be something deeper than some specific religious experience. It would not seem as Christian to see (1) specific experiences *or* (2) reason as the ultimate basis for faith; rather, they are varying paths by which God as the true underlying cause can draw people of varying personalities to faith in him.

Clearly miracles and religious experiences play a very important role for Christians. The Gospels tell us that Jesus was someone who did "signs and wonders." Even the non-Christian Jewish historian Josephus records that Jesus did startling deeds.[27] The ancients categorized Jesus in part as a miracle

Christ walking on the Sea of Galilee (gouache on paper), English School (20th century) / Private Collection / © Look and Learn / The Bridgeman Art Library

worker. Regardless of how skeptical you are, the burden of proof is squarely on anyone who would deny that Jesus did things that observers categorized as miracles.

Similarly, the early-Christian Paul, in the face of opposition in the city of Corinth, reminded this church that he had performed miraculous deeds when he was with them (2 Cor. 12:12)—a very foolish thing to say if he thought they might disagree with him. And the author of Hebrews refers back to signs and wonders that accompanied those who brought the message of salvation (Heb. 2:4). We have to conclude at the very least that the followers of Jesus and indeed the early Christian leaders themselves did things that their audience considered miracles. Many believers throughout the past two thousand years—and many today—continue to give witness to events they cannot explain as normal occurrences.

Of course the most important miracle of all is the resurrection of Jesus from the dead. No reputable historian—not even an atheist—would suggest that Jesus was not a real person who lived and died in Palestine some two thousand years ago. Nor is there any serious debate over the question of whether he died by crucifixion at the hands of the Romans. True, about once every generation someone on the fringe tries to push the idea. But no rational consideration of the evidence gives a second thought to such a shoddy suggestion. The evidence is overwhelmingly conclusive against such idle speculation.

For example, most scholars recognize the high probability that the non-Christian Jewish historian Josephus and the Roman historian Tacitus both referred to Jesus as a historical individual who died during Pilate's administration.[28] Even more definitive is the evidence from the writings of the early-Christian Paul. It is universally agreed that the early-Christian Paul wrote the New Testament letters of Galatians and 1 Corinthians. In Galatians in particular Paul claims to have met with "James, *the Lord's brother*" in Jerusalem three years after he became convinced Jesus was the Messiah (Gal. 1:19). It is the virtually unanimous conclusion of biblical scholarship that this meeting took place *less than ten years after Jesus's crucifixion*. Regardless of whether you agree with what Paul thought about Jesus, it boggles the mind to imagine how one might reasonably argue that Jesus was not a real person.

At that same time, Paul claims to have met with Peter, the same person that all the New Testament Gospels depict as a key follower of Jesus while he walked the earth. In 1 Corinthians 15:5 Paul says Peter (also called Cephas) was the first person to whom Jesus appeared alive after his death, information it is reasonable to assume Peter shared with Paul back then, *less than ten years after the crucifixion.* Paul makes all these claims in the context of people who oppose him, people who disagree with him on various matters and would love to undermine his truthfulness and authority. In short, it would require a conspiracy theory of novelistic proportions to conclude that Jesus was not a real person. Indeed, it is hard to imagine how one could make a reasonable case that Peter did not make a real claim to have seen Jesus alive after he had died.

It seems beyond reasonable doubt that Peter—and many others whom Paul mentions as eyewitnesses in 1 Corinthians 15:3–8—were convinced they had seen Jesus alive after his crucifixion. Other individuals would claim to be the Jewish Messiah and would die at the hands of the Romans. No religions have survived in relation to them. No Jew would have expected the true Messiah to die, let alone at the hands of the Romans. It is hard to imagine anything but a vastly demoralized group of Jesus followers after the crucifixion. Certainly none of these facts prove the historicity of the resurrection, but they certainly argue that many of those who followed Jesus believed they had seen Jesus after he died.

It is also more than reasonable to conclude that Jesus's body was unaccounted for in the days after his death. For example, when Matthew tells of rumors about "what really happened" to Jesus, he tells us that those who disbelieved thought his followers had stolen his body (Matt. 28:11–15). In other words, their argument *against* Jesus's resurrection assumed that Jesus's body was not available. Matthew indicates that the rumor about the disciples' stealing Jesus's body was current at the time he was writing. We cannot prove how far back this rumor went in time, but it does show that even some who disbelieved accepted an empty tomb.

Although Paul is not explicit about Jesus's body, he seems to assume continuity between the physical body that dies and the spiritual body that rises (e.g., 1 Cor. 15:44). The "perishable" body puts on imperishability; the mortal puts on immortality (1 Cor. 15:53 NIV). Because Paul considers Jesus's resurrection and believers' future resurrection to be similarly categorized (e.g., Phil. 3:21), it is reasonable to think he believed Christ's resurrection body to be the transformed version of Jesus's earthly body and thus that Jesus's earthly body was no longer on earth. And he surely would not have thought such a thing if the location of Jesus's body was known.

We have no reason to doubt traditions that point to violent martyrdom for many of these early Christians. Peter and Paul in Rome, James in Jerusalem—according to tradition almost all of the primary followers of Jesus died for their beliefs. We do not have to prove all of these claims to show that key early believers were so convinced they had seen Jesus after his death that they were willing to die rather than change their stories.

If you believe in the possibility of resurrection, the evidence points strongly to Jesus as an example. Obviously if you do not allow for such a possibility, you will find some other way to account for an empty tomb and convinced eyewitnesses. But for those with faith, it is more than reasonable to believe God raised Jesus from the dead.

© istockphoto.com

5.4
ARGUMENTS FROM ORDER AND DESIGN

A second set of arguments for the existence of God has to do with the order of creation. If one finds a watch, **William Paley** (1743–1805) famously suggested, one automatically assumes there must have been a watchmaker. You do not think for one moment that the watch has just happened to come about by chance. So it is with the order of nature, Paley suggested. Something like a eyeball is complex enough to suggest it must have had a designer. The argument that an intelligent Designer must exist to explain the order and complexity of the world is called the argument from design or the **teleological argument**.

Much has happened since the 1700s when Paley made this argument from design, an argument that he was not the first to make by any means. Interestingly, David Hume had already made some fairly significant arguments against the argument even before Paley's more widely read book. For example, Hume questioned exactly how good an analogy the watchmaker example is. How do we know that design works on the level of universes the way it works with watches?

Then of course in the 1800s, Charles Darwin (1809–1882) argued that complexity was simply a matter of chance evolution, where more-complex forms of life tend to dominate over time because such organisms are better equipped to survive than less-developed ones. Because belief in evolution became so widespread in the twentieth century, most philosophers came to reject the teleological argument for the existence of God altogether.

The late twentieth century also saw the rise of **chaos theory**. Chaos theory suggests that, while it is unlikely that any *specific* instance of order would come about randomly, it is mathematically a virtual certainty that order of *some* kind will occur by chance over time. "You couldn't do that again if you tried," but by accident every once in a while "truth is stranger than fiction."

Suppose I find a watch on the ground, and I ask how the watch came to be there. I would never think . . . that for all I knew, the watch might have always been there . . . Rather, at some time, at some place or another, an artificer or artificers must have made the watch . . .

Every indication of design that existed in the watch exists in the works of nature. The difference in the case of nature is that it is even greater design, in a degree which goes beyond all calculation.

William Paley,
Natural Theology[29]

Teleological argument: an argument for the existence of God that suggests the existence of an intelligent Designer is necessary to explain the complexity and order in creation.

Chaos theory: the idea that pockets of random complexity tend to develop as a virtual mathematical certainty.

Advocates of the teleological argument have not stood still either. Intelligent design theory has argued that there is "irreducible complexity" in the world that cannot be explained strictly on the basis of chance or undirected evolution.[30] Similarly the English philosopher **Richard Swinburne** (b. 1934), while accepting evolution, has argued that even evolution proceeds according to certain laws. He argues that there are "laws of nature" that embody a design to the universe. Why do things consistently fall down instead of up? Why is it that "for every action there is an equal and opposition reaction"? He would say that the fact that the universe operates according to laws leads to the question of a Designer who created those laws and put them in play.

> The universe is characterized by vast, all-pervasive temporal order, the conformity of nature to formula, recorded in the scientific laws . . .
> The orderliness of nature is a matter of the vast uniformity in the powers and liabilities of bodies throughout endless time and space . . . Science cannot explain why all bodies do possess the same very general powers and liabilities.

Richard Swinburne, *The Existence of God*[31]

Although it is often discussed separately, we here discuss another argument for God's existence, namely, the **moral argument** for God's existence. It also is usually based on the idea that there is a certain design or structure to the world that requires the existence of a particular kind of Designer. The argument typically goes something like this:

1. At various times, humans exhibit a strong sense of right and wrong that goes beyond personal advantage or "natural" explanation.

2. Some "supernatural" cause must thus have placed this moral impulse inside us.

Immanuel Kant (1724–1804) was one of the first to make this kind of argument. Kant believed that a moral law was part of the rational fabric of the universe. It is something that is entailed by rationality itself, and we can determine the right course of action by following logic. Beyond this moral structure, Kant believed we also make a mental connection between acting morally and the greatest possible happiness. This connection, Kant said, has no basis in this world, because acting morally in this world often does not lead to happiness.[32] Therefore, he argued, a God must exist beyond this world both who has created this connection in our minds between morality and reward and who will also bring about such reward in the next life.

> Two things fill the mind with ever-increasing wonder and awe, the more often and the more intensely we reflect on them: the starry heavens above me and the moral law within me.
>
> **Immanuel Kant, *Critique of Practical Reason*[33]**

> We know that men [sic] find themselves under a moral law, which they did not make, and cannot quite forget even when they try, and which they know they ought to obey.
>
> **C. S. Lewis, *Mere Christianity*[34]**

Moral argument: the idea that the fundamental human sense of right and wrong cannot be explained without recourse to a moral Creator.

Many people do indeed believe that everyone has a basic sense of right and wrong built into them, a kind of universal conscience. Aside from serial killers and psychopaths, it seems reasonable to many people to think everyone deep down really knows what they should or should not do. However, if there is a common core of human conscience, it is probably limited to certain basics. We find significant variety among what various humans have found morally obvious depending on when and where they have lived. Most cultures have a sense that mothers should protect their children and that incest on this level is abominable. But common morality among humans is somewhat limited to these sorts of things.[35]

Sistine Chapel Ceiling: Creation of Adam, 1510 (fresco), Buonarroti, Michelangelo (1475–1564) / Vatican Museums and Galleries, Vatican City / The Bridgeman Art Library

C. S. Lewis's account of the argument may be a little more forceful than Kant's. For Lewis, the specifics of right and wrong are not as important as the fact that humans feel strongly about right and wrong in the first place, whatever the specifics. Some will find this argument persuasive, and others will not. An evolutionary biologist, for example, might attribute such drives to instincts deeply ingrained in our brains that contribute to our survival as a species.

But we do not think it is necessary to prove God's existence. The approach of this particular book only expects that God's existence will likely prove to be reasonable. Is it reasonable to suggest that the basic "laws" of nature and the complexity of the world come from a supreme Designer? Yes is surely the obvious answer. We have no reason to believe that the evidence at any one time will *demand* this verdict. Indeed, those who take this approach to evidence may end up creating more doubt for themselves than certainty.

So let us end our discussion of design in the creation by posing the issue the other way around. If we assume that God designed the universe ex nihilo, what can we likely infer about God's attributes? With regard to God as the cause of the universe, we concluded that God must be all powerful— omnipotent—with regard to the creation, since God made it out of nothing. We must conclude that God, as the Designer of the universe out of nothing, is all knowing or **omniscient** with regard to the design of the universe. This argument does not necessarily seem to entail that God must know everything that *actually* happens or will happen (although Christians have historically believed these things). But it implies that God knows the entire design of the universe and thus all its potentialities.

This line of argument says nothing about what God might do with such knowledge. But it does imply a few interesting things about what God knew about the creation when creating it. People sometimes try to apply the

Omniscient: all knowing.

particulars of *human* knowing to God that probably do not apply. For example, we as humans often distinguish knowing something in one's head and knowing it by experience. But if God created everything out of nothing, then God knows everything in as full a manner as anything can be known. God does not need to become human to know what it is like. Indeed, God does not have to sin or be evil to know what it is like. If God created the world out of nothing, then God created the possibility for all these things and knows them better than any human ever could. God thus can learn nothing by becoming human, nor does God learn anything on the cross, experientially or rationally. Such knowledge is implied from the notion of God as Designer of the world from nothing.

5.5
ARGUMENTS FROM EXISTENCE

We want to consider two final arguments for the existence of God that are sometimes made in relation to the idea of existence itself. The first is often associated with the cosmological argument and was Aquinas's third argument for the existence of God, sometimes called the **argument from necessity** or contingency. Aquinas's argument runs something like the following:

1. Some things have only a *possible* existence: it would be possible for them not to exist.

2. If everything was of this sort, then it would be possible for there to be a point when *nothing* existed.

3. But if there were a point when nothing existed, then nothing could come into existence.

4. Therefore there must be at least one *necessary* Being, which we call God.

This argument made much more sense in the time prior to the scientific age. If, as we are now taught in high school, matter can neither be created nor destroyed, it would seem that we could use this argument to consider matter to have a necessary existence, at least from our current point of view.[36] We can think of God as the only necessary Being to be sure, but it seems difficult to prove it given where we stand.

A final argument for the existence of God is the **ontological argument**, first put forward by Anselm (1033–1109). We might summarize it as follows:

1. We can imagine the greatest possible Being; the greatest possible Being can exist in our thoughts.

2. But a Being that exists in the world is greater than one that exists only in the mind.

3. Therefore, the greatest possible Being must exist in the world as well as in the mind.

Immanuel Kant, who believed in God, rejected Anselm's argument as incoherent. He argued basically that Anselm's argument mixed two different kinds of claims: one was about the world, and the other was about ideas. Mixing the two together was like mixing apples and oranges or playing two different games on two different fields. The premises do not connect to each other.

One thing that helps us understand Anselm—and Descartes, who later advanced a similar argument—is to realize that he tended toward the idealist end of the spectrum where reality is closely related to ideas. For Descartes, for example, if you could conceive of something clearly and distinctly, it was in all likelihood true.

In more recent times, **Alvin Plantinga** has advanced some new versions of the ontological argument.[37] One of his chief claims is that belief in God is "properly basic." Belief in God is so fundamental to life that we cannot imagine a universe without a God. Even those who think they do not believe in God must presuppose God's existence in all their thinking. The existence of God is thus a part of making our way through life, comparable to our believing that other people and objects actually exist or that other people have minds as we do.

> **Argument from necessity:** the argument that if all entities had only a possible existence then conceivably nothing might exist. Since something does, there must be at least one Necessary thing.
>
> **Ontological argument:** the argument that if we can conceive of the greatest possible Being, it must also therefore exist.

5.6
CONCLUSION

No argument would seem to prove beyond any doubt that God exists. Nevertheless, the arguments of this chapter tell us it is reasonable to believe in a Creator. Science has no explanation for *why* anything exists even if it has become very good at describing *how* things exist. And whether one accepts evolution or not, the laws and patterns of the universe exhibit an order that might easily be explained by way of an intelligent Designer. In the end Christians have traditionally believed that God more *makes* his existence known to us than that we find God through the evidence of the world. Faith in God is a warranted personal belief.

© Elizabeth Welch

In his *Pensées*, the philosopher Blaise Pascal once suggested that the decision to believe in God was like a wager everyone was forced to take in life, often called **Pascal's Wager**. He argued that if you bet in favor of God's existence, you stood to gain everything if you proved to be right. On the other hand, you stood to lose nothing if you proved to be wrong. He thus considered the choice for belief an infinitely better wager.

Pascal's Wager: a thought experiment proposed by Blaise Pascal in which a person has to wager in life whether to believe or not to believe in God. He proposed that belief in God was a much better bet than choosing not to believe in God.

This wager is not a proof or argument for God's existence. It is simply a reason why an unsure person might choose to live in faith rather than disbelief. Many Christians resonate with this idea. They find that their faith in God fills their lives with meaning and purpose. They are content to live their lives in faith even though they are not able to prove God's existence. Even so, we would argue that faith in God's existence is perfectly reasonable.

KEY TERMS

- atheist
- agnostic
- apologetics
- cosmological argument
- efficient cause
- ex nihilo creation
- omnipotent
- miracle
- teleological argument
- chaos theory
- moral argument
- omniscient
- argument from necessity
- ontological argument
- Pascal's Wager

KEY PHILOSOPHERS

- Anselm
- Thomas Aquinas
- Blaise Pascal
- David Hume
- William Paley
- Immanuel Kant
- C. S. Lewis
- Alvin Plantinga
- Richard Swinburne

PHILOSOPHICAL QUOTATIONS

- "You made us for yourself, and our hearts are restless till they find rest in you." (Augustine)
- "The heart has reasons that reason can't know." (Pascal)
- "Two things fill the mind with ever-increasing wonder . . . the starry heavens above me and the moral law within me." (Kant)

KEY QUESTIONS

1. What are the five different arguments for the existence of God presented in this chapter? Try to explain them as if to another person. Which do you find the most convincing? Which do you find the least convincing?

2. How important do you think it is to be able to argue for God's existence? Should we be able to prove it? Does it need to be reasonable? Would you expect it to be a matter of blind faith?

3. How important is religious experience to you? Do you believe that miracles can take place today? Give a brief explanation. How would you recognize a miracle; what constitutes a miracle? What do you think of the historical evidence for Jesus's resurrection from the dead?

4. Why do you think people believe in God's existence, or why should they believe in God's existence? What is the best reason?

NOTES

1. All quotations from Augustine in this book are paraphrased on the basis of the translation by Philip Schaff, *The Nicene and Post-Nicene Fathers*, Series 1, 14 vols. (Peabody, MA: Hendrickson, 1994).

2. Louis Pojman in fact quotes a Roman Catholic statement from Vatican I (1870): "If anyone says that the one and true God, our creator and Lord, cannot be known with certainty with the natural light of human reason by means of the things that have been made: let him be anathema." *Philosophy of Religion: An Anthology* (Belmont, CA: Wadsworth, 1987), 1.

3. The two best-known are *Miracles* and *Mere Christianity*.

4. Josh McDowell, *Evidence That Demands a Verdict* (San Bernardino, CA: Here's Life, 1979); and newer editions.

5. Some more recent apologetic works include the almost instant classic, Lee Strobel, ed., *The Case for Christ: A Journalist's Personal Investigation of the Evidence for Jesus* (Grand Rapids: Zondervan, 1998); R. C. Sproul, *Defending Your Faith: An Introduction to Apologetics* (Wheaton, IL: Crossway, 2003); William Lane Craig, *Reasonable Faith: Christian Faith and Apologetics*, 3rd ed. (Wheaton, IL: Crossway, 2008).

6. C. S. Lewis, *Surprised by Joy: The Shape of My Early Life* (New York: Harcourt Brace, 1955), 221.

7. Søren Kierkegaard, *Concluding Unscientific Postscript* 2.2. All paraphrases of Kierkegaard's *Concluding Unscientific Postscript* began with the translation by H. V. Hong and E. H. Hong (Princeton, NJ: Princeton University, 1992).

8. Blaise Pascal, *Pensées*, 277.

9. William Placher, *Unapologetic Theology* (Louisville, KY: Westminster John Knox, 1989), e.g., 12.

10. The paraphrases and numbering of Pascal quotes in this book are made from the 1897 French edition compiled by Léon Brunschvicg. Cf. Blaise Pascal, *Pensées* (Paris: Flammarion, 1976).

11. The word *time* in the argument is not exactly appropriate, given that time as we know it would not exist "before" the beginning. The beginning would have been both the beginning of space and time. *Before* is thus a highly metaphorical term, the literal meaning of which we do not know.

12. Again, the word *suddenly* is highly figurative here, because there would not have been any time, at least in this universe, prior to the beginning.

13. All paraphrases of Aquinas in this book start from *The Summa Theologica of Saint Thomas Aquinas*, Fathers of the English Dominican Province, trans., revised by D. J. Sullivan (Chicago: Encyclopedia Britannica, 1952).

14. This law would later become Newton's first law of motion.

15. However, we will argue in a moment that Newton's second law of thermodynamics implies a beginning to the universe for different reasons.

16. See p. 36 above. The other three were the (1) material cause (the stuff out of which the thing caused is made), (2) the formal cause (having to do with the nature of the thing caused), and (3) the final cause (strangely having to do with the consequences of what is caused).

17. William Lane Craig, *The Kalam Cosmological Argument* (New York: Barnes & Noble, 1979).

18. It is true that discoveries on the quantum level have significantly muddied the water here. Apparently some things can happen on that level without apparent causes. The universe as a whole of course at least seems to exist on a diametrically opposite scale.

19. Newton's law of universal gravitation.

NOTES

20. A phrase used by Kenneth Miller in reference to basing your faith on something that science has not yet explained. *Finding Darwin's God* (1999; repr., New York: Harper Perennial, 2007). Historically, many such gaps have eventually found themselves filled in by science!

21. It is highly debated by scholars of the Old Testament whether the Hebrew of Genesis 1:1–2 originally had creation ex nihilo in view. Apart from it, we do not find a possible reference to such creation until the first century BC in a Jewish writing (2 Maccabees 7:28). However, it is even debated whether 2 Maccabees has creation out of nothing in mind.

22. Hume's argument is somewhat peculiar given that he was known for arguing that because we can consider things true only on the basis of direct experience, we cannot prove that an effect is indeed caused by the event that came before it. So it is remarkably inconsistent for him to suggest that the absence of the experience of a miracle by one person up to a point in time might in any way count as evidence for what others have experienced or of what might be experienced in the future.

23. This is a paraphrase of Hume's own original 1748 English wording.

24. C. S. Lewis, *Miracles* (1947: repr., San Francisco: HarperSanFrancisco, 2001), 162.

25. A recent treatment of miracles in the New Testament is Craig Keener, *Miracles: The Credibility of the New Testament Accounts*, 2 vols. (Grand Rapids: Baker Academic, 2011).

26. Christian traditions of course disagree on the degree of human freedom involved in that response.

27. Josephus, *Antiquities* 18.63–64.

28. See Josephus, *Antiquities* 18.63–64; and Tacitus, *Annuals* 15.44.

29. Paraphrased from Paley's 1802 edition in English.

30. E.g., Michael J. Behe, William A. Dembski, and Stephen C. Meyer, *Science and Evidence for Design in the Universe* (San Francisco: Ignatius, 2000).

31. The quote is from Richard Swinburne, *The Existence of God* (Oxford: Oxford University, 1979) as quoted in Louis J. Pojman, ed., *Philosophy of Religion: An Anthology* (Belmont, CA: Wadsworth, 1987), 41, 42.

32. Indeed, in Plato's *Republic*, Plato has a character named Thrasymachus argue to Socrates that it is ideal to be able to get away with doing evil while everyone else thinks you are good.

33. Paraphrased from Kant's conclusion to the work as translated by T. K. Abbott in Kant's *Critique of Practical Reason and Other Works on the Theory of Ethics* (New York: Longmans, Green, 1883).

34. C. S. Lewis, *Mere Christianity* (1952; repr., San Francisco: HarperSanFrancisco, 2001), 23.

35. As with psychopaths, we can allow for the possibility that there are sick cultures that are unhealthy and dying. The Ik people of Uganda would seem an excellent candidate. See Colin Turnbull, *The Mountain People* (New York: Simon & Schuster, 1972), although his method has been questioned.

36. Whether this notion is true on the quantum level is another question. The quantum level is when we get down to a level smaller than the atom.

37. Alvin Plantinga, e.g., in *God, Freedom, and Evil* (New York: Harper & Row, 1979); also *Warranted Christian Belief* (Oxford: Oxford University, 2000).

38. Blaise Pascal, *Pensées, 233.*

CHAPTER 6

THE PROBLEM OF EVIL

What to Get from This Chapter

- The problem of evil is the question of how a good and all-powerful God could allow evil to continue to exist in the world.
- Some philosophers have altered their sense of either God's power or goodness to address the issue.
- Moral evil is evil that results from the choice of a being; "natural evil" refers to pain and suffering that is a consequence of nature.
- The soul-making theodicy suggests that pain and suffering can be good because they can help us grow and thrive as humans.
- The free-will theodicy suggests that a world in which beings can choose to do good or evil is a better world than one where we are forced to do good.

Questions to Consider

- What is the problem of evil?
- What is evil?
- What are the best answers to the question of evil?

Key Words

- Problem of evil
- Theodicy
- God's directive and permissive will

© Kevin L. Welch

6.1
DEFINING THE PROBLEM

Perhaps no one has put the problem of evil so succinctly as Archibald MacLeish in his play *J.B.,* about Job in the Bible. In the script, the character who represents Satan taunts, "If God is God, he is not good. If God is good, he is not God."[1] What the character is saying is that if "God is God," if God is all powerful and can do anything, God must not truly be good. Surely a good God, so the argument goes, would do away with evil, if powerful enough to do so. By the same token, if "God is good," then—so the argument goes—presumably God is not powerful enough to do away with evil. He must not be "God."

This conundrum is traditionally called **the problem of evil**. Throughout history, any group that believed its gods were powerful—*and* loved them—has struggled with this question in the face of defeat or suffering. It is no coincidence that MacLeish expressed this issue by way of the biblical book of Job. Job is a righteous person who does everything that God requires

> **Problem of evil:** the question of why evil exists if God is both good and powerful enough to stop it.

of him (e.g., 1:8). Indeed, it is exactly this point that Job's "friends" dispute. They believe that Job must have done something wrong to bring such suffering on himself (e.g., 4:7).

But when God shows up at the end of the story, he rebukes Job's friends for their insistence that Job is suffering as a punishment for his own sin (42:7). No sin on Job's part has brought on his sufferings. We, the audience of Job, know that Job was being tested by "the Satan" to see if Job would be loyal to God. But Job never learns it in the book. One point of Job is that the righteous can suffer even though they have done nothing to deserve it.

We should not be too quick to dismiss the argument of Job's comforters. Their logic is indeed found in other parts of the Old Testament. In Joshua 7, when Israel loses in battle against the city of Ai, the explanation is that defeat was caused by the sin of someone named Achan in their company. Once the offender is stoned and purged, Israel is victorious against the city.

This approach to suffering is a part of what is sometimes called deuteronomistic theology, since it is expressed so well by the book of Deuteronomy, especially chapter 28. If Israel would keep God's commandments, it would be blessed. But if Israel would not keep God's commandments, it would suffer. This theology of history permeates the books of Joshua, Judges, 1 and 2 Samuel, and 1 and 2 Kings, as well as other books of the Hebrew Bible. These books give us one side of the biblical equation.

Yet other parts of the Old Testament, such as Job, wrestle with this theology, especially on an individual level. Jeremiah 31:29 and Ezekiel 18:2 both record a saying in Israel from the time of Jerusalem's destruction in 586 BC: "The parents have eaten sour grapes, and the children's teeth are set on edge" (Jer. 31:29). The generation that went into captivity was punished, *not for their own sins*, but presumably for the sins of their parents:

> All this came upon us,
>> though we had not forgotten you;
>> we had not been false to your covenant.
> Our hearts had not turned back;
>> our feet had not strayed from your path.
> But you crushed us and made us a haunt for jackals;
>> you covered us over with deep darkness!"

Psalm 44:17–19 NIV

Both Jeremiah and Ezekiel argue that God will no longer punish descendants for their parents' sin. Rather, the person who actually does the sin is the one who will die (e.g., Ezek. 18:4).

Greek philosophers also wrestled with this issue. Allegedly, the philosopher **Epicurus** (341–270 BC) put the question this way: "Do the gods want to prevent evil, but are not able? Then they are impotent. Are they able, but not willing? Then they are malevolent. Are they both able and willing? Then why is there evil?"[2] But Christians probably wrestle with this issue more than most other religions because Christianity has such a heightened sense of God's love for the creation. Perhaps the first verse that any Christian child learns is John 3:16: "For God so loved the world that he gave his only Son, so that everyone who believes in him may not perish but may have eternal life."

Christians also have a heightened sense of God's power and of God already having begun the process of taking care of evil. We believe he has started this process by sending Jesus to die for the sins of the world. So why does evil still linger on so powerfully? Why do genocides continue to take place with no sign of abatement? This is the problem of evil, the topic of this chapter.

6.2
GOD'S POWER AND GOODNESS

© istockphoto.com

Various thinkers have addressed the problem of evil by adjusting their view of God's power or God's goodness. For example, Jewish thinkers such as Harold Kushner and Walter Kaufmann preferred to think of God as willing but unable to prevent the Holocaust. For them, God is good but not powerful enough to eliminate such evils from the world. Similarly, **process theology** sees God evolving and developing along with the world. Thinkers who hold this philosophy think that God might very well get to the point someday where he can put a final end to suffering and pain. But God is not quite there yet. Process theologians usually see the world as part of God's body.[3] They might say that God is developing just as the world is evolving.

Most people who believe in God, however, are not as likely to question God's power. The notion of God as powerful seems to be one of the most fundamental understandings of what a god is. More often than not, explanations for the problem of evil address the question of God's goodness rather than God's omnipotence.

In the preface to his book *On the Genealogy of Morals*, Friedrich Nietzsche (1844–1900) boasted that even at age thirteen he was already preoccupied with the problem of where evil came from. "My solution to the

> **Process theology:** an approach to reality that sees God evolving and developing along with the world, which is usually thought to be a part of God (panentheism).

Calvinism: a Christian system of thought that emphasizes God's sovereign control and direction of the world.

God's directive will: when God directly causes something to happen in the world.

God's permissive will: when God allows something to happen in the world but does not directly cause it.

No seemingly random ability, action, or movement exists in creatures that is not governed by God's secret plan, with the result that nothing happens, except what God knowingly and willingly decrees.

John Calvin,
***The Institutes of the Christian Religion* 1.16.3**[6]

John Calvin, French theologian and religious reformer, (1509–1564), Miniature / De Agostini Picture Library G. Dagli Orti / The Bridgeman Art Library

problem at the time was to give God the honor of being the father of evil."[4] Nietzsche of course did not believe in the existence of God. He is known especially for the statement "God is dead; we have killed him."[5] As distasteful as we might find Nietzsche's flamboyant disregard for Christianity, we must take seriously at least one aspect of his thought on the origins of evil.

If God created the world out of nothing, then he must at least be *indirectly* responsible for the existence of evil. God made the world in such a way that evil was possible. He may not be the *direct* cause of evil. He may not be the *direct* cause of everything that happens in the universe. But God created a universe where such things can and do happen. If God is entirely good, it raises the question of why he would do so.

Christians believe that God is sovereign, king, over the creation. God does not have to fight against evil, as in some dualistic systems with two supreme beings, one good and one evil. Christianity is not like Zoroastrianism, where the good being Ahura Mazdā struggles eternally with the evil being Ahriman. Yet God does not prevent evil from happening, despite the fact that he is capable of doing so. If God is entirely good, why doesn't he prevent it or stop it for good?

Despite the fact that Christians believe God created the possibility of evil, we find different Christian approaches to *how* evil came about in the world. On the one end of the spectrum are certain extreme forms of **Calvinism** that believe God directly orchestrates all the evil of the universe. Calvinism is a branch of Christianity that took its departure from John Calvin in the 1500s. We will discuss Calvinism more extensively in chapter 10. In its most extreme form, "hyper-Calvinism" believes God caused Satan to rebel against him, while also making the first human, Adam, to sin. In his great "mercy," however, God now causes relatively few people to be saved—all of whom God caused to be sinful in the first place.

To be fair, **John Calvin** himself did not teach that God had orchestrated the "fall" of Satan or the original sin of the first human, Adam. Rather, Calvin believed that it was possible that Adam might not have sinned against God as he did. But *after* Adam sinned, all humans subsequently have been born into the world "totally depraved," unable to do any good at all in their own power.[7] People will unavoidably do evil unless God directly causes them to do good.

However, in the most extreme form of Calvinism, God has determined on a microlevel everything that happens, has happened, and will happen in the universe, as in Islam. Accordingly, no real claim is given that God loves anyone but those toward whom he shows favor. At the same time, "good" might be defined as whatever God does. Anything God does is good because that is the definition of good.[8] If God causes one of his favored ones to die of painful cancer, then that is good because God has done it.

This approach to God's "goodness" seems to make little sense of the idea of *good* or *love*. The normal understanding of *love* involves genuine desire for the benefit of the beloved. But in these forms of Calvinism, God makes people do things that anger him and then shows his "justice" by punishing and destroying them. Others God makes do things that anger him, and then he shows his great "love" and "goodness" by not punishing them. But since someone must be punished, he punishes his Son, Christ, instead.

Whatever this god is, it seems dubious that it is the God of Jesus or the bulk of the New Testament.[9] We would, in contrast, make a distinction on some level between God's **directive will** and God's **permissive will**. God's directive will relates to things that God directly causes. God's permissive will, on the other hand, relates to things that God does not stop, things that God allows to take place.

The hyper-Calvinist perspective makes *everything* a function of God's directive will. In our opinion, it seems difficult to consider such a god good in any meaningful sense of the word. Most forms of Christianity, however, including mainstream Calvinism, allow at least some place for God's permissive will.[10] Most would not make God directly responsible for all the evil that has ever taken place in a directive sense (cf. James 1:13–14). Rather, they would try to explain why God has allowed evil to take place despite his goodness.

6.3
WHAT IS EVIL?

© istockphoto.com

If we are going to ask why God allows evil to exist and occur, we need to define exactly what it is in the first place. At this point, someone might suggest a very "theological" definition, maybe that evil is anything that does not conform to the will of God or glorify God. This person might then suggest that it is not really evil when bad events happen to people, because every one of us is a sinner who has done wrong and deserves judgment. Indeed, someone might even argue that God's love shows itself in the fact that God does not simply obliterate the whole world.

Perhaps that is the right answer. But it does not fit very well with the way we normally talk about love or about what is good. We certainly experience things like cancer, catastrophes, and senseless violence as bad events that often at least seem out of character with the normal definitions of love and what we would expect a loving God to do or allow.

On a most basic human level, we categorize things as "good" or "bad" by whether they bring us pleasure or pain, benefit, or harm. Such pleasures and pains can quickly come into conflict with one another. The pleasure someone gets from a night of drinking might issue in a painful headache the next morning. By the same token, the pain of pulling out a splinter might avoid the greater pain of a later infection.

In this "street-level" discussion, evil is not a thing, like a piece of coal. It is a description of something that happens. People sometimes talk about evil as if it were a thing, as if there were such a thing as "pure evil." Christians from time to time have even talked about our having an "evil nature," a thing inside of us that might be removed or need to be suppressed. But evil would not seem to be a matter of something you could look at or remove from a person surgically. In that sense, God did not create *a thing* we call "evil." He created the possibility of people committing evil *actions*, but God probably did not create evil *things*.

Other Christians have considered evil to be the absence of a thing, the absence of good. **Augustine** (354–430) said that there was no *efficient* cause of evil but only a *deficient* cause. Some *thing* does not cause evil but rather the absence of some thing brings about evil, namely, the absence of good.

> You should not try to find an efficient cause for a wrong choice. It is not a matter of something present but of something missing . . . We understand darkness and silence . . . These are not things we perceive present but things that are not there to perceive . . . We never see darkness except when we stop seeing . . . silence can only be perceived by not hearing.
>
> **Augustine, *The City of God* 12.7**[11]

> The depravity and evil intent of both humanity and the Devil, as well as the sins that arise from them, have not originated in nature, but from the corruption of nature.
>
> **John Calvin,**
> ***The Institutes of the Christian Religion* 1.14.3**

Thus we have Augustine's observation from his *Confessions,* cited in the previous chapter: "You made us for yourself, and our hearts are restless till they find rest in you." For Augustine, the absence of God's presence results in evil. If something was entirely evil, it would completely cease to exist altogether. So to Augustine, even Satan must still have at least a little good in him, or he would cease to exist!

Augustine may have a helpful thought here, if we take his words to mean that people do evil because they are lacking something. However, if we take his language straightforwardly, he seems to treat good as a thing, which seems to commit the same basic error as those who treat evil as a thing.

It seems more accurate and helpful to think of *good* and *evil* not as nouns but as *adjectives*, as descriptions of intentions and motives rather than as things themselves. Paul says of eating foods, "I am convinced, being fully persuaded in the Lord Jesus, that nothing is unclean in itself. But if anyone regards something as unclean, then for that person it is unclean" (Rom. 14:14, NIV). We might infer from Paul's discussion of when to eat and when not to eat certain things that immoral action is primarily a function of *context*.

For example, to have sex is not sinful in itself, as an act. However, it becomes a sinful action in various contexts, such as if you have sex with someone who is not your spouse. The Bible does not even treat killing as an evil action *in itself*. The Bible never prohibits killing in battle or as an act of capital punishment. It is rather the context of such killing that makes it evil.[12]

Some Christians have wondered how it is that Adam, the first human in the biblical story, could have been tempted when he was a perfect human. Certainly the text of Genesis does not raise this question, but it nonetheless provides a good way to help us work out our thinking on these issues. If we approach evil as a matter of context, we can still account for Adam's temptation even though he has no evil drive inside him. His drive, uncorrupted by sin, is to excel and to learn. What was wrong was not the drive, but the context in which Adam expressed that drive, namely, toward something he was forbidden to eat.[13]

We might even suggest that if a particular action is wrong in every circumstance, it is so only because no context exists in which the action could be considered right. Thus the action itself would still not be intrinsically wrong, but the action would be wrong *in every context* in which it might be done. When we approach the question of evil from this perspective, God does not directly create any evil in the world. The world God created was thoroughly good and might in theory have remained thoroughly good. Yet at the same time God created the possibility that morally neutral actions might take place in the wrong contexts, thus making them evil because of the decisions of humans and other created beings.

So it is certainly true that pleasure and pain seem to be "good" and "bad" on a street level. Yet it is not clear that in themselves they map directly to good and evil. Pleasure is not always truly good, and we should distinguish between **moral evil** as a matter of intention and pain as a consequence of nature. **Natural "evil,"** which I would not even call evil, refers to adverse events or situations that create pain and misfortune, but that do not happen because of some person or being's intention.

For example, a person trips and breaks her leg. That person experiences pain and inconvenience, but one might argue that no person or being has caused it. Of course it is possible that some angel or demon, that Satan might

Evil is an act of will whose objective is inappropriate given its context.

© istockphoto.com

Natural "evil": bad events that occur apart from human or "supernatural" intention, perhaps better called natural pain or suffering.

Moral evil: bad events that occur because of human or "supernatural" intention.

Is what is right loved by the gods because it is right, or is it right because the gods love it?

Plato, *Euthyphro* **10a**

We might put Plato's question this way: "Is good, good because God says so? Or does God say it's good because it's good?" In other words, is "the good" something that is absolute beyond the gods, to where we might judge the gods themselves by its standard? If Zeus kills an innocent person, is he guilty of murder in the same way an ordinary Greek would be considered a murderer? Or is such a killing "good" simply because Zeus himself has done it?

Philosophers have raised the same question in relation to the Christian God. In Genesis 22 God commands Abraham to sacrifice his son Isaac. God does not go through with it, but the question arises: if God commands you to kill your son, has God commanded you to do something immoral? Should you disobey him to do what is right?

The view that considers good to be anything God says is good is called the divine command theory. So if God commands the Israelites to kill all the women, children, and animals of Jericho, then that command must, by definition, be good. On the other hand, most Christian thinkers throughout history have believed that God's nature is good, such that God in effect could never make a truly evil command. Such a command would be contrary to his nature, and thus no possible world exists where God truly commands evil. You can never be disobeying God when you refrain from evil, and you will never be obeying the true will of God if you do evil.

directly cause people to break their legs. If so, then we would not categorize such an event as natural "evil" but as *moral* evil, where moral evil refers to the consequences of some *being's* bad intentions. But if no person, human or supernatural, caused her to break her leg, then we might better call it "suffering" rather than evil.

6.4
THE SOUL-MAKING THEODICY

A **theodicy** is an explanation of God's justice in the light of the existence of evil. Two primary theodicies have emerged over the course of Christian history: the **soul-making theodicy** and the **free-will theodicy**. The earlier of these two shows up in the writings of **Irenaeus** in the late

© istockphoto.com

Theodicy: an explanation of God's justice in the light of the existence of evil.

100s and has been advanced in various ways in recent times by individuals including John Hick and C. S. Lewis.[14] The basic idea is that suffering and pain help us grow up, make us better people. They improve our souls and are thus soul making.

Because Irenaeus was apparently the first Christian to suggest in any detail something like this approach to the problem of evil, the soul-making explanation is sometimes called the Irenaean theodicy. Irenaeus argued in this way:

> Someone might say, "Then why didn't God make humanity perfect from the beginning?" Tell this person that . . . everything is possible for God. But created things must be inferior to him who created them, from the very fact of their later origin. It is not possible for things created recently to become uncreated.
>
> But since they are not uncreated, they obviously fall short of the perfect . . . So it was possible for God himself to have made humanity perfect from the beginning, but humanity could not receive this perfection, since humanity was still infant . . .
>
> —⚬—
>
> If humanity had no knowledge of the opposite, how could it have instruction in what is good? . . . Just as the tongue understands sweet and bitter by tasting them, the eye can tell between black and white because of seeing and the ear recognizes distinctions in sounds by hearing. The mind is the same. Its experience of both good and evil gives it the knowledge of what is good, and it becomes more tenacious to preserve the good by obeying God.

Irenaeus, *Against Heresies* 4.38.1, 4.29.1[15]

We might compare this approach to exercise or weight training. Anyone who has been on bed rest, even for several days, knows how quickly muscles atrophy. Inactivity makes us weaker. Conversely, exercise builds muscle by "tearing down" the weaker muscle then replacing it with stronger muscle fibers. The soul-making theodicy thus pictures a world that functions like a jungle gym. As we face obstacles, we get better, stronger. What we call evil may actually be good for us, like liver or spinach. "You intended to harm me, but God intended it for good" (Gen. 50:20 NIV). C. S. Lewis also, at least in the period before the painful death of his wife by cancer, spoke of suffering as something God uses to make us grow.[16]

What are we to make of this theodicy? On the one hand, it is true that not all pain is ultimately bad. Sometimes pain can lead to greater happiness, like an unpleasant shot that helps you get over a serious illness. Of course recognizing pain's potential payoff is usually of little comfort when we are in

[Pain] is His megaphone to rouse a deaf world.

C. S. Lewis,
The Problem of Pain[17]

We are like blocks of stone out of which the sculptor carves the forms of men [sic]. The blows of his chisel, which hurt us so much, are what make us perfect.

Shadowlands[18]

Man [sic] is in the process of becoming the perfected being whom God is seeking to create. However, this is not taking place . . . by a natural and inevitable evolution, but through a hazardous adventure in individual freedom . . . If, then, God's aim in making the world is the "bringing of many sons to glory" [Heb. 2:10], that aim will naturally determine the kind of world that He has created.

John Hick,
Evil and the God of Love[20]

the middle of the suffering. Nevertheless, we can find some truth even in Friedrich Nietzsche's famous saying that "what does not kill me makes me stronger."[19]

From a philosophical standpoint, it is not clear that death in itself is evil or even that suffering is. They are usually undesirable to us, to be sure. But it is not clear that they are evil. As unreassuring as it is, it is quite possible that the problem of evil sometimes looms larger to us than it should, because we do not have a good sense of the overall picture or of what is ultimately of greatest importance. We think our individual lives to be more significant than they really are in the vast scheme of things. We exaggerate the significance of our pains and pleasures.

And we should probably point out that our insignificance becomes infinitely greater if there is no God. If there is no God, then—while we may become infinitely significant to ourselves—we turn out simply to be biological machines meaninglessly concerned with our own fortunes and circumstances. If undirected, atheistic evolution is the ultimate explanation of what a person is, then there is no goodness—or evil—to the world at all. The fittest survive, the weak get eaten, and neither outcome really matters one way or another beyond the feelings of the few, insignificant animals involved.

Certainly it is the fallacy of subjectivism to think that something is true just because it is convenient for me. Yet the existence of God would seem to be the only hope for suffering having any real meaning at all beyond ourselves and those who care for us. Ironically, while the continuance of suffering raises the strongest objections to the idea of a God of love, it is only the notion of God's love for the world that makes suffering significant at all beyond the chemical reactions in the brains of a half dozen *Homo sapiens*.

© istockphoto.com

When we think of the soul-making theodicy, we are especially thinking about the potential of *natural* "evil" to lead to positive outcomes, although the same concept could apply just as well to the effects of moral evil. We should remind ourselves again that there are different perspectives on whether God directs such natural evil or allows it. From one Christian point of view, God directly causes hurricanes, tsunamis, and tornados, car accidents, and fires. From another, God allows these things to happen as the natural outworking of the laws of cause and effect that God placed into the universe. Sometimes a frame of metal going one direction collides with a frame of metal going another, and the people in these cars get hurt. From this approach, the question is why God did not *stop* the cars, not why God *caused* them to collide.

But why would God design a world that works this way in the first place? Even if God does not orchestrate hurricanes to kill people, why did

God create a world that creates hurricanes by the laws of cause and effect? Could not an all-powerful God have made a world where growth could take place without the inordinate amount of suffering that has taken place in this world over the course of history?

For these reasons, many Christian philosophers would suggest that the soul-making theodicy is inadequate in itself as an explanation for why a loving God created a world that grows in this particular way. This observation leads us to the more dominant theodicy, the so-called free-will theodicy of Augustine. We should not presume, however, that we will ever find a full explanation that leaves us with no questions at all. Even biblical figures such as Habakkuk, Job, and various psalmists had questions about the ways of God. At the end of this chapter, we will inevitably conclude that we must ultimately decide whether we have faith in God's goodness and power. This side of eternity, we will not likely find an entirely satisfying answer to the question of why God allows so much suffering.

6.5
THE FREE-WILL ARGUMENT

The most popular explanation for the existence of evil is the free-will theodicy. The basic thrust of this explanation is that a world in which humans have relatively free choice is better than a world in which they do not. But if people have free choice to do good or evil, then some will make bad choices, and evil will result.

The one who is usually credited for this argument is Augustine, although Augustine's version of it was a little more nuanced than our explanation. For Augustine, it was the first human, Adam, who had the free choice to do good or evil. Because he chose to disobey, the entire world became "fallen." Although Adam was free to choose, we are not free to choose good today.[21]

The strength of Augustine's understanding of **the Fall**—Adam's choice for evil and the subsequent evil that has followed—is that it explains both the existence of moral and natural evil. On the one hand, the choices of Satan and Adam to sin were free-will choices.[22] God did not make them sin, and they had the freedom *not* to sin if they had so chosen. God is thus not directly responsible for the origins of evil. Satan and Adam are.

On the other hand, because of Adam's sin, the argument goes, all humans now are born **totally depraved**. They do not have free will and are not able to do any good in their own power. Because of their inherent evil, they

Free will was how we could do evil, and our suffering evil [in consequence] is [God's] righteous judgment . . .

—⁂—

God is the greatest and highest good, and he has created these lesser goods. Both Creator and created are all good. Where, then, did evil come from? . . .

—⁂—

I asked what sin was, and realized it is not a substance, but a perversion of our will, bent aside from you, O God.

Augustine,
Confessions **7.5, 7.7, 7.22**

The first evil act of Adam's will . . . was a falling away from the work of God . . . not a substantive act itself . . .

The effect of that sin was to subject human nature to all the process of decay that we see and feel, and consequently to death also.

Augustine,
The City of God **14.11–12**

BIOGRAPHY

AUGUSTINE

Augustine (354–430) was born in North Africa, which was then part of the Roman Empire. For a time he taught rhetoric in Rome and Milan (Italy). But after his conversion he returned to the city of Hippo (Algeria), where he served as bishop until his death.

Before his conversion Augustine had first been a proponent of Manichaeanism, a dualistic religion that believed in two primary deities, a good one and an evil one who were equally powerful. After he concluded that Manichaeanism could not answer his questions, he turned to **Neoplatonism**, the version of Platonism popular in Augustine's day; the key originator had been Plotinus (ca. 204–270).

A key feature of Neoplatonism was its belief that evil was the absence of good. Augustine came to believe that everything God had created was good, and that the evil in the world was a result of the corruption of the good. Augustine is usually credited for articulating the free-will theodicy, which explains the existence of both moral and natural evil in the world as a consequence of Adam's bad choice.

In Milan, under the influence of its bishop, Ambrose, Augustine finally converted to Christianity. His Christian mother had long tried to steer him in that direction. In one of his most famous works, *The Confessions*, Augustine claims that the final straw was when he opened the book of Romans to 13:13: "Let us behave decently, as in the daytime, not in carousing and drunkenness, not in sexual immorality and debauchery, not in dissension and jealousy." Augustine's own guilt over his relationship with the concubine with whom he lived for more than a decade no doubt played some role in his conversion.

In general, Augustine accepted the prevalent view of his day that sex was evil. He believed that lust or "concupiscence" was the mechanism by which the **original sin** of Adam and Eve took place, thus connecting sex with the fundamental sin of human history. Augustine is the one from whom Western Christianity derived its basic understanding of this first sin, which theologians call the Fall. The Fall corrupted human nature such that humans are unable to do good in their own power. Augustine believed that the sin of Adam and Eve is passed down through the lust of sex, thus explaining why Jesus needed to be born of a virgin.

Augustine's views on these matters came principally into play in his debates with a group of Christians known as Pelagians. Pelagians believed that Adam's sin had not made it impossible for humans to choose good over evil in their own power. In response, Augustine developed his sense of human depravity, the impossibility that humans might do good or choose God in their own power. Corresponding to his sense of depravity was Augustine's understanding of predestination, that God determined who would be saved, that human will played no role in God's choice, and that God's grace was irresistible if God chose you.

In the field of ethics, Thomas Aquinas drew significantly from Augustine when formulating three criteria for starting a just war (*Summa Theologica* 2.2.40). **Just-war theory** would say that a war can only be considered just if it meets three criteria: (1) It must be waged by an appropriate authority. (2) It must be in pursuit of a just cause. (3) They must be undertaken with good motives, in pursuit of peace.

In the latter half of Augustine's life, Rome was sacked by the Visigoths (410). The fact that Rome had stood impregnable for well over a thousand years must have made this event a catastrophic shock to the empire, next to which the attack on the Twin Towers on 9-11 pales in significance. Many Romans believed the destruction was the punishment of the gods for the abolishment of all religions but Christianity in 380 by the emperor Theodosius I.

BIOGRAPHY

AUGUSTINE *(continued)*

Augustine's response was his second-most famous work, *The City of God*, in which he was the first to formulate a philosophy of history. In *The City of God*, Augustine argued that history was the story of an ongoing conflict between the city of God and the city of humanity. The city of God was made up of those who abandoned earthly pleasures and devoted themselves to God's values. The city of humanity consisted of those who had strayed from the city of God.

So the Romans should not be surprised that the cities of mortals should be destroyed, since that world was destined to pass away. The city of God and even the true church is not the visible one, but the invisible one that only God knows. Even the visible church is filled with both wheat and weeds. God will sort them out at the Judgment.

inevitably do many things that do not deserve God's favor. God is thus under no obligation to do good to anyone, and anyone God *does* "save" is saved exclusively by an act of mercy and love.

At the same time, the natural world "fell" with Adam. There were no earthquakes, tornados, or paper cuts in the Garden of Eden. These are also a by-product of Adam's free choice. Augustine thus explained the origins of natural evil by way of Adam's moral evil. Later thinkers such as John Calvin (1509–1564) and John Wesley (1703–1791) built on Augustine's system in divergent ways. Calvin passed along Augustine's thought largely as it was: God does not choose to condemn those who are damned directly, because they were already condemned by their own actions.[23] But in his love and mercy, God chooses to save some.

By contrast, Jacobus Arminius (1560–1609) and John Wesley did not believe Calvin's picture of God matched with God's character as portrayed in the Bible. A God who arbitrarily chooses some can hardly be said to love the world (John 3:16) or to want *all* to be saved (1 Tim. 2:4). So Arminius and Wesley suggested that God's grace gives us all a chance to be saved, even though we are still unable to save ourselves. We will address these thinkers again in chapter 10.

We should mention that the systems of Augustine, Calvin, Arminius, and Wesley are all thoroughly ensconced in the Western Christian tradition. The idea of total depravity, which originated with Augustine, is more a feature of Western than Eastern Christianity. Christians before Augustine, as well as the Eastern Christian tradition, did not absolutize human fallenness to quite the same degree as did the later Western tradition. In this respect, the

The Fall: the event when Adam and Eve disobeyed God in the Garden of Eden, with the subsequent entrance of death, evil, and suffering into the world.

Total depravity: the idea that humans are unable to will or do any good at all in their own power.

Original sin: for Augustine, the first sin of Adam and Eve that corrupted human nature, a corruption they passed down to all their human descendants.

Neoplatonism: the form of Platonism at the time of Augustine, whose chief founder was Plotinus. It taught that evil was the absence of good.

understanding of human sinfulness in Eastern Christianity perhaps comes closer to that of Paul in the New Testament, who thought of human sinfulness as our enslavement to evil powers in this world more than as some evil nature within us. (Some translations, such as the 1984 *New International Version*, render the Greek word *flesh* as "sinful nature," but this is more a reflection of Western theology than of Paul's thinking.) Further, Paul taught that God's Holy Spirit could free us from these powers in this life (e.g., Rom. 8:2; Gal. 5:16).

We might synthesize these thinkers into a free-will theodicy that looks something like the following: God created a universe in which it was better to be able to choose the good freely rather than be forced to choose the good. Unfortunately Satan and Adam made the wrong free-will choice. As a result, the world was corrupted both naturally and spiritually. The default state of humanity and the world is enslavement to sin.

Yet because God loves the whole world, he graciously is willing to empower all to choose the good. One day God will restore the creation to its prefallen state of complete human freedom. But in the meantime, the gracious empowerment of God's Holy Spirit makes possible the same free choice either for or against God, the same choice Adam had before the Fall.

Certainly we should not think that the free-will theodicy answers all our questions about evil. Why, for example, has God waited so long to reset the creation to its prefallen state? It cannot be so that he can save more, for time only adds individuals—both to be saved *and* to be damned. From a traditional understanding of salvation, additional time would only add to the overall number of the condemned, while diminishing the percentage of the saved.

An even more significant question is why God set the world up this way in the first place, and whether he *had* to do so. **Gottfried Leibniz** (1646–1716) thought that God's setup of the world was the best possible one. He did not think God could have created anything but the best of all possible worlds, and this world is it. He did not mean to say that the specific way life turned out for us was always the best possible scenario or that every event that took place was the best thing that could happen. What he meant was that this was the best possible *way* for God to set up the world. In *Theodicy* he wrote:

> The best plan is not always the one that tries to avoid evil. It may turn out that *the evil is accompanied by a greater good* . . . an imperfection in the part may be required for a greater perfection in the whole. In this position I have followed that of St. Augustine, who has said a hundred times that God has permitted evil in order to bring about good, a greater good. And I have followed Thomas Aquinas, that allowing evil tends toward the good of the universe . . .

The ancients called Adam's Fall a *felix culpa*, a happy sin, because it brought as a consequence the incarnation of the Son of God, who has given to the universe something nobler than ever would have come to be among creatures except for it.[24]

Leibniz's argument certainly appeals to the democratic sensibilities of the West. Would we rather marry someone who freely has chosen to love us or someone who was forced to obey us? Would we rather a robot love us because it was programmed to do so, or would we like to have someone choose us among other possibilities? Because a world of choice seems better

THEISTIC EVOLUTION AND THE PROBLEM OF EVIL

© istockphoto.com

One of the strengths of Augustine's free-will theodicy is the way that it accounts for natural evil. Why is it that, in nature, the most vicious and cunning of animals tend to thrive, while the weak tend to get eaten? Why do the most virtuous of people get cancer, die in earthquakes, tornados, hurricanes, and floods? The free-will theodicy suggests all the apparent inequities of nature are a consequence of Adam's sin.

One of the challenges for a theistic evolutionist—someone who believes God has directed the process of evolution—is to account for these sorts of things. A theistic evolutionist might believe that an Adam existed, perhaps the first *Homo sapiens* with a soul or the first human on whom God somehow imprinted his image. They might even believe that spiritual death entered the world through Adam's sin. But a theistic evolutionist will need to have millions of years of animal death, pain, and suffering long before Adam. Further, many theistic evolutionists today do not take the Adam story literally but rather as a poetic expression of the human condition.

Some of the earliest objections by Christians to evolution did not derive so much from perceived conflicts with the Bible. For example, William Jennings Bryan, who argued against evolution in the famous 1925 Scopes Trial, opposed evolution because of what seemed to him its philosophical implications. Indeed, in the decades before Bryan, some of the richest and most powerful Americans subscribed to a kind of "social Darwinism."

Following Darwin's idea of the "survival of the fittest," they took their success as an indication that nature had "selected" them. And with this view came the corresponding sense that it was perfectly appropriate for them to ignore, run over, and in general "eat" any of the weak or less powerful who got in their way. We see this same philosophy in Adolph Hitler's approach to those he considered inferior, the ease with which he eliminated the infirm, and those whom he thought corrupted the purer race.

If we assumed that the evolutionary dynamics of nature are *not* a result of human sin or the sin of Satan, then would we have to conclude that God created the world with these dynamics? Did God create a world where the fittest survive, not because they love their neighbors, but precisely because they can beat their neighbor to the food or because a male can impregnate more females than his rival, perhaps including his rival's mate? To say the least, these considerations would invite some rethinking of what good and evil are, as well as of what it would mean to say that God is love. We will discuss some of these issues further in chapter 8, "Science and Faith."

to most of us than a world of force, the free-will explanation for evil tends to make sense to us.

Yet surely God is smarter than we are. Could not God create a world where it was better *not* to have free will than one where it was better *to have* free will? And do we actually have free will at all (a question we will take up again in chap. 10)?

The question of evolution also has implications for Augustine's theodicy. If a Christian believes in theistic (God-directed) evolution, that person can hardly believe that physical death entered the world through Adam or that "natural evil" is a consequence of Adam's sin. Such individuals might still be able to account for the existence of evil caused by human (or animal?) choice. But they would need to turn to something like the soul-making theodicy to explain the existence of natural evil, if they did not feel compelled to develop a more far reaching reappraisal of what constitutes evil.[25]

6.6
CONCLUSION

The "problem of evil" is the question of why a good God would allow evil and suffering to continue in the world. Throughout the chapter, we have hinted that we ultimately must rely on our faith in God's goodness, despite what we see and experience around us. The rhetorical question Abraham put to God in Genesis 18:25 sums it up well: "Will not the Judge of all the earth do right?" (NIV). The answer for the Christian is an unequivocal yes. We have little reason to believe in the existence of a god who is not all powerful. And the alternative to believing in a good God is not a friendlier world. The person who throws out faith in God because of evil and suffering ends up with no hope at all.

Accordingly, because we believe that God is good, we must assume that everything that happens ultimately fits with his goodness in some way. Even though we often cannot understand why God does not stop evil and suffering, we assume that he is in control and loves us. Part of the solution is to recognize that our understanding of things is extremely limited. We can never see the big picture to the extent that God does.

The soul-making and free-will theodicies make sense as well, even if they do not account fully for the issue. Not all pain is bad. To some extent, we as a culture may be spoiled by the technological and pharmaceutical advances that allow us to avoid displeasure. It also makes sense that a world in which we are *free* to choose the good is a better world than one in which we *must* choose the good, which of course means that some individuals will choose to do evil. God does not always cause what happens in the world directly. Some things he more allows to happen, than specifically commanding them to happen.

None of these explanations eliminates the necessity for faith. Kierkegaard reminds us as usual that we are foolish to think we could understand all the workings of God. A quotation of Blaise Pascal from the previous chapter applies as well here:

> We can't understand anything about God's actions in the world unless we accept the principle that he wanted to blind some of us and enlighten others.

> —⁓—

> God wants to move our will rather than our intellect. Perfect clarity in understanding would help our intellect but handicap our will.

Blaise Pascal, *Pensées* **566, 581**[26]

Perhaps Pascal here assumes that human beings are more rational than they are, that they generally take the course of action that is most reasonable. Nevertheless, he highlights the fact that whatever equation we come up with to explain evil, one of the most significant elements will be faith.

KEY TERMS

- problem of evil
- process theology
- Calvinism
- God's directive will
- God's permissive will
- natural evil
- moral evil
- theodicy
- soul-making theodicy
- free-will theodicy
- Neoplatonism
- just-war theory
- the Fall
- total depravity
- original sin

KEY PHILOSOPHERS

- Epicurus
- Irenaeus
- Augustine
- John Calvin
- Gottfried Leibniz

PHILOSOPHICAL QUOTATIONS

- "Pain is His megaphone to rouse a deaf world." (Lewis)
- "What does not kill me makes me stronger." (Nietzsche)
- "God wants to move our will rather than our intellect." (Pascal)

KEY QUESTIONS

1. How would you define evil? Would you consider pain or suffering to be evil or only the will or actions of beings? What do you think it means to say that God is love?

2. Which solution to the problem of evil do you find most convincing? Which ones do you find least convincing?

3. How far do you think God's directive will extends into the things that happen in the world? Do you think God directly causes everything that happens in the world? Do you think God leaves some things to chance, to human choice, or to the consequences of natural laws?

4. What do you think about the idea that pain and suffering in nature have resulted from the sin of Adam? Do you have any suggestions for how theistic evolutionists might account for "natural evil"?

NOTES

1. Archibald MacLeish, *J.B.* (1956; repr., Boston: Houghton Mifflin, 1989), 10.
2. The quotation comes from the third-century Christian, Lactantius, in a work called *De Ira Dei*. Lactantius claims to be quoting Epicurus.
3. See chapter 8 for more on panentheism.
4. Paraphrased from the foreword of Nietzsche's book in English translation, *A Genealogy of Morals,* trans. W Hausemann (London: Macmillan, 1897), 10:4.
5. The phrase first appeared in Nietzsche's 1882 book *The Gay Science*, but subsequently became better known from the madman in his slightly later work, *Thus Spoke Zarathustra*. The quotation "God is dead" is usually taken out of context. In *Zarathustra*, a madman proclaims God's death to a group of individuals celebrating that God was no longer around to judge them. The madman tries unsuccessfully to warn them that chaos will inevitably ensue in a world where people no longer believe in God. In some respects Nietzsche was thus a prophet of the twentieth century with its Holocaust and other atrocities.
6. John Calvin, *The Institutes of the Christian Religion.* All Calvin quotations in this chapter are paraphrased from the 1845 English translation of Henry Beveridge (Peabody, MA: Hendrickson, 2008).
7. Calvin did not originate the idea of total depravity. The doctrine, rather, originated with Augustine in the early 400s. Both Calvin and Augustine believed that they had found this idea in the writings of Paul in the New Testament, especially Romans, although Paul arguably teaches universal sinfulness, not absolute sinfulness.
8. This line of reasoning is called a tautology, where a statement is true by definition and thus does not really say anything. Everything God wills is good, because good is defined as whatever God wills.
9. Only one chapter of the New Testament comes anywhere close to sounding like this perspective, namely, Romans 9; this chapter, however, has much more to do with Jews and non-Jews than with God determining what *individuals* will be saved. Paul's missionary practices assumed that anyone might be saved. See chapter 10 for more extensive discussion of this issue.
10. Not much, however, even in mainstream Calvinism. In mainstream Calvinism, God's permissive will applies only to the choice of Adam in the Garden of Eden and perhaps Satan's choice whether or not to sin.
11. All quotations from Augustine in this book are paraphrased on the basis of the translation by Philip Schaff, *The Nicene and Post-Nicene Fathers*, Series 1, 14 vols. (Peabody, MA: Hendrickson, 1994).
12. Some Christians would of course argue that the new covenant works itself out in a way that makes it always wrong to kill today. Someone might argue that it is impossible ever to kill with a right attitude and thus that Christians must not kill anyone under any circumstance.
13. Not all Christians take the story of Adam literally, although Christians have historically.
14. C. S. Lewis, *The Problem of Pain* (1940; repr., San Francisco: HarperSanFrancisco, 2001); John Hick, *Evil and the God of Love* (San Francisco: HarperSanFrancisco, 1966).
15. All quotations from the ante-Nicene church fathers in this book are paraphrased on the basis of the translation by Philip Schaff, *The Ante-Nicene Fathers*, 10 vols. (Peabody, MA: Hendrickson, 1994).
16. See n. 14. In *A Grief Observed* (1961), written after watching his wife die from cancer, Lewis seemed less enthusiastic about the answer he had given earlier.
17. Lewis, *Problem of Pain*, 91.
18. Although C. S. Lewis never states this in his books, it fairly captures his early thinking and appears in the 1993 movie *Shadowlands* written by William Nicholson.
19. Friedrich Nietzsche, *Twilight of the Idols* (1889).

NOTES

20. Hick, *Evil and the God of Love,* 256.

21. Although Augustine believed we are still free to choose evil, since evil for him was a turning from good.

22. Some debate exists over whether Augustine believed God to have predestined Satan's sin. See Hick, *Evil and the God of Love,* 64, where Hick discusses Augustine, *The City of God* 12.

23. Some of Calvin's followers became *double* predestinarians who believe that God chooses both those to be saved and to be damned. We also mentioned earlier in the chapter some who believe God predestined both Satan and Adam to sin.

24. The quotation is paraphrased from "Abridgement of the Argument Reduced to Syllogistic Form," in *The Philosophical Works of Leibnitz,* trans. G. M. Duncan (New Haven, CT: Tuttle, Morehouse & Taylor, 1890).

25. For example, someone might argue that evolution, while it involves great pain for individuals, nevertheless works toward the betterment of the living creation as a whole.

26. The paraphrases and numbering of Pascal quotes are based on the 1897 French edition compiled by Léon Brunschvicg. Cf. Blase Pascal, *Pensées* (Paris: Flammarion, 1976).

UNIT 4

PHILOSOPHY OF REALITY:
METAPHYSICS

© istockphoto.com

7.1
THE STUDY OF EXISTENCE

Although many students do not care much for math and science, the Western world as a whole has often valued science more than other fields of knowledge. High school students may sometimes call good math and science students nerds and geeks. But as adults we are all thankful for the cell phones and laptops such students go on to invent.

Certainly you can make more money in other fields. But as a culture, most in the Western world consider scientists and mathematicians some of the smartest people. Of course it is not necessarily true. The ex-jock could have a much higher IQ than the valedictorian who now teaches physics at MIT. But as a culture we *think* of science as king in the game of truth.

A **paradigm** is a particular way of thinking about a particular topic. A worldview involves a person's whole view of the world; a paradigm has to do with a person's view of just one particular piece of the puzzle. In that sense, a **worldview** is the collection of all your paradigms put together.[1]

What to Get from This Chapter

- Ontology is the study of existence.
- Materialists believe that everything that exists in the universe is made up of matter and energy.
- Idealists believe that thought is the ultimate reality, if not the only reality.
- Dualists believe the universe is made up of two basic types of substance, usually the material and the immaterial.
- Critical realists believe that reality exists, but acknowledge that our understanding of it will always be skewed to varying degrees.

Questions to Consider

- What basic answers have been given about what the universe is made out of?
- Can we really know what reality-in-itself is?

Key Words

- Ontology/metaphysics
- Natural and supernatural
- Materialism
- Idealism
- Dualism

Worldview: the lenses through which a person understands reality.

Paradigm: a particular way of thinking about a particular topic; one particular lens through which we look at one area within our overall worldview.

Sir Isaac Newton (oil on canvas), Kneller, Sir Godfrey (1646–1723) / Petworth House, West Sussex, UK / The Bridgeman Art Library

Protestant Reformation: the movement of protest against the beliefs and practices of the medieval Roman Catholic Church in the early 1500s, ultimately resulting in the more than twenty thousand other church denominations in the Western world today.

Natural: things we can explain on the basis of matter/materials and "laws."

Supernatural: things that seem to stand outside the normal rules of nature and are best explained by recourse to forces outside or beyond the natural.

Although most in the Western world may not be good at science, we tend to have elements of a scientific paradigm in our varying views of the world. For example, if we are in a thunderstorm, we do not usually ask ourselves what demon might be angry with us or if God is trying to teach us a lesson. We think of rain and snow as *natural* events rather than as "supernatural" events involving spiritual forces like angels.

By the same token, we do not ask what angel will be flying our plane to Denver this afternoon. We worry more about engines and pilot error than whether demons might try to down our plane. If something unusual were to happen, like a crash, some people would begin to inquire what purpose God (or Satan) had in mind. But we less often refer to God or other spiritual forces to explain the "ordinary" workings of our lives.[2]

This train of thought leads us to an important issue. On the one hand, we would not have all the scientific discoveries of these past years if people had not begun to look for *natural* rather than spiritual explanations for the things that happen. Isaac Newton (1643–1727) strongly believed in the existence of God. But he did not refer to God to explain the precise mechanics of gravity. He looked for a physical *law of nature* to explain it: $F = G(m_1m_2)/r^2$.

Yet as Christians we believe that God is involved in the world. Where do we draw the line between "natural" explanations for events and "supernatural" ones, if we should at all? A little more than a hundred years earlier than Newton, a young man named Martin Luther (1483–1546) interpreted a lightning strike near him as God's vocational direction: threatening him if he did not become a monk. So Luther abandoned his studies to be a lawyer and became a priest. The rest is history; he went on to lead the **"Protestant"** mass exodus from the Roman Catholic Church, resulting in the great variety of non-Catholic churches we have today.

Unlike Newton, Luther saw this storm as a spiritual rather than natural event. He did not divide the world into the categories of natural and supernatural. Rather, everything about the world was spiritual for him. If everyone had viewed the world as Luther did, we might not have all the inventions we have today; our forebears would not have looked for "laws" to explain the workings of the world.[3] In short, we would not have become scientists in the modern sense of the word.

Here we arrive at one of the main questions addressed in this chapter. Does the world around us consist of matter operating according to laws that God created and then set to run largely on their own? Is the universe a **natural** realm distinct from the **supernatural** realm of God, angels, and other spiritual forces "outside" it?

Or, on the other end of the spectrum, is our sense of matter an illusion? Perhaps the world in some sense is an extension of God. Perhaps a little deeper, beyond quarks, gluons, and dark matter, the most basic material of all is the "material" of God? Or perhaps we are all thoughts in the mind of God rather than some separate "natural" material.

In the end, most Christians today function as dualists who believe in two fundamental kinds of reality. They picture distinct natural and supernatural elements to the world right "next" to each other—for example, a human soul associated with a physical human body.

This chapter deals with these questions of **ontology**, the part of philosophy that asks what reality is made of, what the nature of existence is. Ontology is one of the two sub-branches of metaphysics, the branch of philosophy that asks questions about reality. In the next chapter we will discuss the other subject of metaphysics, the nature of the universe or cosmology.

© Kevin L. Welch

7.2
A MATERIAL WORLD?

A historic Christian believes in a God who in some sense is distinguishable or "detachable" from the creation. It is difficult to imagine at this point how a traditional Christian could be a **pantheist** who equates the world with God. And a traditional Christian could hardly be a **naturalist**, someone who believes that nature is *all* that exists. But could a Christian have a mostly **materialist** view of God's creation? A materialist believes that the universe consists *only* of matter. This person does not believe that we have a detachable soul or that reality involves some other distinct type of reality like spirit.[4]

For example, we might call a person like **Thomas Hobbes** (1588–1679) a materialist, even though he believed in the existence of God. Although he believed that God created the world, he saw the world as a kind of machine that ran according to its own laws apart from any divine intervention. His view of the creation, therefore, was entirely materialist. With regard to God, he was a **deist**, someone who believes that, although God created the world, God is not currently involved in its operations (he thus did not believe that Jesus was God).

> Life is only the movement of body parts, a movement that begins in some place inside us. Can we not say that all *automata* (machines that move themselves by things like springs and wheels—like a watch) have a kind of "life" to them? What is the heart, but a spring? And what

Ontology: the sub-branch of metaphysics in philosophy that asks what the nature of being or existence itself is.

Pantheism: the belief that everything is god, that the world equates to god.

Materialism: the belief that the universe consists only of matter and energy.

Naturalism: the belief that the natural realm is all that exists.

are the nerves, but many strings? And the joints? So many wheels, giving motion to the whole body, as was intended by their Maker.

Thomas Hobbes, *Leviathan*[5]

At this point we want to pick up the question we raised in the introduction above. To what extent can we as Christians distinguish the material and energy of the universe from God? Western philosophy has traditionally traced its beginnings back to a Greek named **Thales** (ca. 624–546 BC).[6] He is often called the father of philosophy, although this designation is very ethnocentric. It makes it sound as if philosophy originated in the so-called Western world.[7] It can make those who identify themselves as Westerners sound as if they are smarter than those in other parts of the world who do not identify themselves in this way.

As we define philosophy, however, philosophy has existed since the first human. In the first chapter, we suggested that, in one sense, we are not fully "human" unless we reflect on the world and life. By this definition, philosophy has existed since the first true human. If we take the story of Genesis 2 literally, we might suggest that Adam (or Eve) was the first philosopher.

Nevertheless, many have considered Thales the first Greek philosopher because he seemed to look for an explanation for the world apart from the gods. Thales believed that the earth around him had been generated from underlying and surrounding water. For him, water was the basic substance from which all other materials were produced. This was not a startling suggestion; several of the cultures at that time had a significant place for water in their creation myths. In the Babylonian creation story, the *Enuma Elish*, the god Marduk fashions the world out of chaotic water goddesses. Even in Genesis 1:2, we see "formless and empty" waters at the beginning of creation, before God has spoken a word.[8]

So while it puzzles many philosophers that Thales also said that "there are gods in everything," we should not be surprised. The so-called break between myth and science with Thales seems not as great as some think. Indeed, in the next chapter we will suggest that modern science is not as far removed from myth as most think.

Nevertheless, because he suggested water as the underlying basis of reality, Thales is often considered the founder of science as well as the founder of philosophy.[9] The later philosopher Aristotle and others spoke of Thales as the first of several philosophers who suggested some "element" as the basic substance out of which the world was made. For Thales it was water. For Anaximenes the most basic substance was air. **Heraclitus** thought it was a kind of fire. Some of the earliest examples of science in the Western world were thus philosophers asking what was the underlying nature of the world, the underlying material that brought continuity between things that appeared discontinuous.

© Kevin L. Welch

BIOGRAPHY

THE "NATURAL" PHILOSOPHERS

Thales (ca. 624–ca. 546 BC): Thales was born in the city of Miletus on the coast of Asia Minor (western Turkey today). Aristotle considered him the founder of Greek philosophy. Thales apparently believed that, despite the change in form that takes place, all things proceed from the same underlying substance, namely, water. He is said to have predicted an eclipse that took place in 585 BC.

Photo Credit: Thales of Miletus, from "Crabbes Historical Dictionary," published in 1825 (litho), English School (19th century) / Private Collection / Ken Welsh / The Bridgeman Art Library

Anaximander (ca. 610–ca. 546 BC): A younger contemporary of Thales in Miletus, Anaximander apparently thought that our world rises out of and returns to something he called the "Boundless." Anaximander's understanding of the Boundless seems a little like Aristotle's understanding of the First Mover. If almost everything has to have a beginning, there must be something that does not, which *is* the beginning.

Anaximenes (ca. 585–525 BC): This younger contemporary of Anaximander completes the triad of natural philosophers from Miletus in the sixth century BC. Anaximenes supposed that Thales's suggestion of water as the most basic substance did not go far enough. Doesn't rain come out of the air? So Anaximenes suggested that water was condensed air and that, in fact, air is the most basic underlying substance from which water, fire, and earth come.

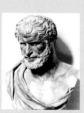

Heraclitus (ca. 535–ca. 475 BC): Not long after the three Milesian philosophers above, Heraclitus philosophized in Ephesus, also on the western coast of Asia Minor, not far to the north of Miletus. Heraclitus continued the discussion of what the most basic substance was by suggesting it was a kind of fire. Not surprisingly, this led him to say things like "Everything comes into existence through conflict, and everything is in flux, like a river." If you step into a river and then step into it again, it is already a different river because the water has changed. Heraclitus did not believe this flow was chaotic but that it was ordered by something he called **Logos** or reason.

Photo Credit: Bust of Heraclitus of Ephesus (ca. 535–ca. 475 BC) (bronze) (b/w photo), Roman / Museo Archeologico Nazionale, Naples, Italy / Alinari / The Bridgeman Art Library

Empedocles (ca. 490–ca. 430 BC): Empedocles, who unlike the philosophers above was from Sicily (an island near Italy), seems to take a major step forward in the discussion of what the underlying substances of reality are. He does not propose that everything comes from just one substance such as water. He suggests that there are four basic "roots": earth, air, fire, and water. Empedocles believed everything we see boils down to four basic elements that combine (by "love") and separate (by "strife") in various ways to form what we see. (Think in terms of the modern periodic table in chemistry, which includes some ninety elements that occur naturally.)

Anaxagoras (ca. 500–ca. 428 BC): Anaxagoras was born in Asia Minor but moved to Athens, making him the first philosopher we know in the city. Indeed, it is possible that he transported the philosophy of Asia Minor to Athens. He was eventually expelled from Athens because he did not believe in the gods. For example, he suggested that the sun was not a god but a red hot stone and that the moon only reflected light, rather than generating it. Anaxagoras rejected the underlying substance theories of Empedocles and others. Instead, he suggested that everything was made up of almost infinite smaller versions of the same thing (e.g., wood made of infinite little wood bits).

BIOGRAPHY

THE "NATURAL" PHILOSOPHERS *(continued)*

Democritus (ca. 460–ca. 370 BC): He was the first of the known philosophers born in Greece (Thrace). Democritus suggested that the fundamental building blocks of the world were very small and very numerous, differing in shape, arrangement, and position, constantly in motion. He called them *a-toms*, which means uncuttable. But unlike those before him, he saw the combinations of atoms strictly as a matter of motion and connection; he did not see some *logos* or Boundless or god directing their combination. Everything that happened was thus determined by playing out motion and shape. Democritus further believed that the "soul," the life force of a person, was made out of fine, spherical soul atoms, which simply passed back into nature as individual life-force atoms at death (not the kind of soul we speak of).

Photo Credit: Democritus (ca. 460–ca. 370 BC), Ribera, Jusepe de (lo Spagnoletto) (ca. 1590–1652) / © Collection of the Earl of Pembroke, Wilton House, Wilts. / The Bridgeman Art Library

Theism: the perspective that God created the universe, set up its rules, and continues to be involved with it.

Deism: the perspective that God created the universe and set up its rules but does not currently interact with it.

Enlightenment: period from roughly 1650 to 1800 when many intellectuals in France, England, and Germany questioned all previous assumptions and tried to rely on reason and evidence alone (not revelation) to arrive at the truth.

Determinism: the belief that everything that takes place has to happen exactly as it does because of the laws of cause and effect.

Materialism in its modern form seems to have been a by-product of the scientific revolutions of the 1500s and 1600s. People began to look for natural explanations of the world, laws that govern the way the universe works. This development led some to become **deists**, believing that God created the universe as a watchmaker makes a watch. The watchmaker makes the watch and winds it up. Then it runs on its own. Many of the minds we associate with the 1600s and 1700s, a period known as the **Enlightenment** (see chap. 14), fall into this category, including several founding fathers of the United States such as Thomas Jefferson and Benjamin Franklin.

The materialists of that time tended to be **determinists**. Determinists of this sort believe that everything that happens must happen because of the laws of cause and effect. If we think of the materials of the world as a set of pool balls in motion, we could in theory predict what all the balls would do because of the laws of physics.[10] So materialists tend to think that history is simply playing out the "bouncing" of one material "ball" against another.

Today we find some Christian materialists who are not deists. Somewhat similarly to Hobbes, these Christian physicalists believe in God and a spiritual realm. Being **monists,** they see the natural, created realm made out of one basic type of reality. Unlike Hobbes, they are not deists but **theists,** believing that God can and does act in the world today. They might believe in the possibility of miracles, for example.

Yet they would not believe that we have souls that are **immaterial**, made up of something different from the materials of the world. They would not believe in spirit as something different from matter. We will discuss these Christian physicalists in chapter 9.

> **Monism:** the belief that the universe consists of only one basic type of thing, such as matter, ideas, etc.
>
> **Immaterial:** not material, usually applied to heavenly "substances" such as the soul or that of which angels consist.

7.3
THOUGHTS IN GOD'S MIND?

Because the scientific paradigm has so influenced the Western world, it is not difficult for us to understand materialism, purporting that the creation consists of matter and nothing else. By the same token, it is difficult for most of us to imagine a different kind of monist, one who does not believe that matter is real but who thinks that everything consists of something like idea or spirit. The best-known example of this sort of monism is **idealism**, which believes that ideas are the most real type of thing or perhaps the only reality at all.

For example, **Plato** believed that the world we see and experience with our senses is not the truly real world but a shadowy copy of the world we can access through our minds. The real world is thus the world of ideas, not the physical "embodied" world around us. When Plato said such things, he was not coming up with an entirely new idea. Many will be familiar with the name **Pythagoras** (ca. 580–500 BC) from geometry. He is best known for his association with the Pythagorean theorem, which gives the relationship between the lengths of the sides of a right triangle ($a^2 + b^2 = c^2$). You might not be surprised to know that Pythagoras apparently believed that numbers were more real than the things around us we can see and feel.

> We must distinguish and ask, "What always exists and never comes into existence and what is always coming in and out of existence and never simply exists?" The answer is that the things we understand with intelligence and reason are always the same and exist. On the other hand, our opinions based on our senses apart from reason never fully exist but are always coming and going . . .
>
> The creator must have looked to the eternal . . . he framed the world in the likeness of what is understood by reason and mind and is unchangeable. The world must be . . . a copy of something.
>
> **Plato,** *Timaeus* **27d, 29a**

By the same token, the philosopher **Parmenides** (ca. 515–450 BC) is known to have said that "thought is being." Because he believed ideas are what is truly real, he could say that "nothing changes." At least nothing that is truly real changes, because the reality that underlies the world is constant. His thought had considerable influence on Plato, as well as on many of the other key figures at the beginning of Western philosophy.

A more recent and Christian example of an idealist is **George Berkeley** (1685–1753), whom we met briefly in chapter 4 as a famous empiricist. Berkeley believed that "to be is to be perceived."[11] He was an empiricist who believed we can say something is real only if it can be experienced. If you think about it, we do not actually experience the "matter" of the world. You don't crumple up each page of this book and stick it somehow in your eye or your ear. What you experience is your "sensation" of this book, your perception of it.

Because Berkeley did not believe in things you could not perceive, he suggested that matter did not exist as something different from my perception. He initially called himself an "immaterialist," in contrast to the many materialists around him. He was a monist, because he believed in only one "substance" of reality, namely, thoughts.

As counterintuitive as idealism may seem to us, it seems as impossible to disprove as it would be to prove. After all, I cannot prove that the world around me is not some sort of computer program and that I am not actually, like Neo in *The Matrix*, hooked up to wires in some cocoon somewhere. I cannot even prove that *I* am not a sophisticated computer program, with no real body anywhere. But these sorts of scenarios are mostly for the movies and for esoteric coffee conversation. We will surely function best in the world if we think of ourselves as real with bodies and the world as real with substance, whatever we are actually made of.[12]

7.4
MATERIAL AND IMMATERIAL?

In the last two sections we have discussed individuals who have been monists or who have tended toward monism. We have seen that materialists believe that the creation is nothing more than a material world; spirit does not exist as something different from matter. We have seen that idealists believe that matter does not truly exist; the true world is the world of ideas or that we are thoughts in the mind of God.

However, most Christians today are not *monists* who believe that everything is made up of one kind of reality. Most Christians today are **dualists**. A dualist believes that the universe consists of two distinct kinds of

BIOGRAPHY

FAMOUS NONMATERIALISTS

Pythagoras (ca. 580–ca. 500 BC): He was born off the coast of Asia Minor on the island of Samos but eventually established a communal, quasireligious community in southern Italy. Pythagoras and his followers believed that *number* was the ultimate reality and that everything could be predicted through mathematics. He also taught the existence of a soul that survived death and then migrated into the bodies of others (including animals; transmigration). He was the first known person to call himself a philosopher and is said to have taken advice on where to study from his elder contemporary, Thales.

Parmenides (ca. 515–ca. 450 BC): Parmenides was from Elea, a city in southern Italy, where he set up a school. Unlike the slightly older Heraclitus, who emphasized that everything changes, Parmenides believed that change was an illusion, that in fact **nothing changes**. Although our senses might make us think things differ from one another and change, our *reason* indicates that everything is one and always remains the same. He is thus the first clear example of a rationalist, someone who believes reason is the path to truth (see chap. 4). He is said to have met, at the age of sixty-five, the young Socrates in Athens and heavily influenced Plato.

Zeno of Elea (ca. 490–ca. 430 BC): A student and defender of Parmenides, he is best known for Zeno's Paradox. To get from point A to point B, you have to go half way. But to get to half way, you have to go half way to half way (a quarter of the way). Since this process goes on infinitely, one apparently cannot get to point B, indeed, one can hardly start the journey. By this and other paradoxes, Zeno attempted to show that the common sense of change and difference entails numerous contradictions. We saw this kind of argument, the reductio ad absurdam, in

chapter 3. Aristotle credits him for inventing **dialectical reasoning**: making a proposal, raising questions and pointing out problems, then modifying the proposal.

Photo Credit: Statue of Zeno of Elea (489 BC–431 BC) / Greek philosopher and mathematician. Hellenistic sculpture from 2nd century BC / Photo by Archive Photos/Getty Images.

Plato (ca. 428–ca. 348 BC): Plato believed that the most real things were the ideal patterns and "forms" accessible through the mind. The things we experience with our senses are only copies, images, and shadows of these realities. See the biography on Plato later in the chapter.

Photo Credit: Plato (429–347 BC), ca. 1475 (oil on panel), French School (17th century) / Bibliotheque de la Faculte de Medecine, Paris, France / Archives Charmet / The Bridgeman Art Library

Neoplatonists: Although the Neoplatonists did not see themselves as anything other than the true heirs of Plato, their distinct "brand" of Platonism is usually traced to Plotinus (AD 204–270). Plotinus was a monist who held everything that exists to be an emanation or projection from the "One"—from divine Light. The successive emanations of the One, however, are less and less complete, partake less and less of the One. They thus less and less truly exist until they blur off into complete nonexistence.

Photo Credit: Neoclassical statue of ancient Greek philosopher, Plato, in front of the Academy of Athens in Greece.

Baruch Spinoza (1634–1677): For Spinoza, everything that exists is "God"—or "nature"—making him both a monist and a pantheist (the universe is God). For him, thought and space are both characteristics of God rather than separate things with their own existence. God is absolutely infinite, although we cannot know much of God at all.

Photo Credit: Baruch Benedict Spinoza (1632–77) (oil on canvas), Dutch School (17th century) / Herzog August Bibliothek, Wolfenbuttel, Germany / The Bridgeman Art Library

BIOGRAPHY

FAMOUS NONMATERIALISTS *(continued)*

George Berkeley (1685–1753): Berkeley was unique in that he was not only an empiricist, but an idealist as well. He did not think it made sense to speak of some material behind what we perceive, since all we know is our perception of things. So he concluded that "to be is to be perceived," except when it came to God, for whom to be is to do the perceiving. Everything apart from God that exists is thus one type of thing—thought.

Photo Credit: George Berkeley, engraved by Bocquet, illustration from 'A catalogue of Royal and Noble Authors, Volume III', published in 1806 (litho), English School (19th century) Private Collection / Ken Welsh / The Bridgeman Art Library

Georg Wilhelm Friedrich Hegel (1770–1831): Hegel believed that reality is ultimately rational and that its structure is understood through reason. History is the evolutionary unfolding of conflicts between opposing thoughts. As one thought (thesis) comes into conflict with its opposite (antithesis), a synthesis results that integrates the best of the two. Then that better synthesis becomes a new thesis that encounters its opposite. This conflict continues until the process reaches "absolute spirit." History is thus an inevitable movement toward the better.

Photo Credit: Portrait of Georg Wilhelm Friedrich Hegel (1770–1831), 1825, Schlesinger, Jacob (1792–1855) / Nationalgalerie, Berlin, Germany / The Bridgeman Art Library

reality, usually one material and one nonmaterial or, more precisely, one immaterial. So most Christians today believe that we have a physical part, a body, and a nonphysical part, a soul. When we think of angels interacting with the world, we do not usually think of material beings but spiritual beings, made of a different sort of "stuff" than we are.

Most Christians do not realize that this particular kind of dualism is fairly recent. In fact, it is largely a by-product of the philosophy of **René Descartes** (1596–1650). On the one hand, it makes sense to speak of a dualism in the ancient world too, although perhaps not exactly in the way we now think. For example, Luke gives us these words from Jesus on the cross: "Father, into your hands I commend my spirit" (Luke 23:46). We rightly picture Jesus's body dying on earth and his spirit going on to paradise (cf. Luke 23:43).[13]

But we should not presume that the contrast between body and spirit here is between a material and a nonmaterial substance. Rather, it seems the ancients thought of spirit as material—just much thinner material, like the difference we would make between a solid and a gas.[14] So the ancient contrast was between embodied and disembodied, not between material and immaterial. We will talk more about this distinction in chapter 9.

The ancient world, and thus the biblical world, did not see spiritual beings as *super*natural in quite the way we tend to see them. Rather, there was a

Dualism: the belief that the universe consists of two basic types of "stuff" (e.g., the material and the immaterial).

BIOGRAPHY

PLATO

Although Plato (ca. 428–ca. 348 BC) was apparently present at Socrates's death, Plato was still a young man and not one of Socrates's early followers. Nevertheless, it is mainly through Plato (and Xenophon, another source of Socrates's life) that we know about Socrates and his thinking.

The writings of Plato that have survived are "dialogues," conversations between Socrates and various other individuals on different topics. Plato's earliest dialogues are probably better reflections of Socrates's own thought than his later ones, where we get much more of Plato using Socrates as Plato's own voice. Sometime in his forties, Plato founded his "Academy," so named after the man who owned the land where Plato and his students met.

Plato is probably best known today for his **theory of ideas** or "forms," captured somewhat in his allegory of the cave (see chap. 1). The **world of senses** that we perceive with our eyes, ears, touch, taste, and smell is a world of "shadows" (cf. Parmenides). The true reality is the **world of ideas** that we can know only through our minds. Any table we see on earth is only a "copy," "shadow," or "image" of the real table, whose form we can know only by thinking. The ideal table is the essence of what a table is, the "universal" table. Any "particular" table I might experience with my senses is only a representation of that ideal table. Predictably, Plato thought even less of art, it being a copy of a copy of the real.

In keeping with the tension between the mind and the senses, Plato believed humans had a soul that was more in touch with true reality than their bodies. When people learned something, they were simply remembering what their souls had known before birth. Because women as well as men could access the world of ideas through their souls, they were also capable of true thinking. Then at death immortal souls were freed from the "prison house" of the body and would eventually transmigrate to another body (cf. Pythagoras).

In ethics Plato was an absolutist, captured well in his myth of Gyges's ring (see chap. 11). He believed that if something was wrong, it was always wrong without exception. He associated the "four cardinal virtues" with parts of the body: wisdom with the head, courage with the chest, self-control with the abdomen, and justice with the proper working of all three in harmony.

The ideal society, which he presented most famously in his dialogue *The Republic*, would be run by wise philosopher kings (like the head) who ruled unselfishly. Meanwhile, the chest of society was the soldiers who showed courage. The workers were then ideally governed by self-control, like the abdomen.

The highest absolute for Plato was undoubtedly "the Good," which even stood above the gods. Asking the question, "Is what is right loved by the gods because it is right, or is it right because the gods love it?" Plato answered that the gods love the Good because it is good and, thus, that they are subject to it as well (see chap. 6). Plato apparently had a "secret doctrine" relating to the Good that he shared only with his closest followers. It apparently stands in some conflict with his public dialogues.

spectrum, a continuum of being. For pagans, the gods basically amounted to superhumans. They were like humans except with immense power and immortality. Philosophers debated whether the "stuff" of heaven was a different sort of stuff than the stuff of earth.

Since the fifth century BC—the time of Empedocles—it had become conventional for the Greek and Roman world to speak of **four basic elements** to the universe: earth, air, fire, and water. These elements were mixed and matched in various configurations to make all matter. But Aristotle suggested a fifth element, "ether," the stuff of the heavens.[15] Other philosophers associated spirits with the element of fire.

But the scientific revolutions of the 1500s and 1600s led to a different way of thinking about the spiritual realm. If the material universe operates by natural law, the spiritual realm must be something else. Science turns to things like atoms and material to explain the workings of the natural realm. So the spiritual realm becomes the realm of the *super*natural, that which cannot be explained on the basis of natural law. It becomes something different from the material world around us. It becomes *im*material.

And so the dualism of Descartes—Cartesian dualism—came into existence. The Cartesian dualist believes that the material world is one kind of existence. Then the immaterial world is another kind of existence. Most Christians today operate with this view of reality and assume it is biblical without full awareness of how their dualistic paradigm might differ from that of the biblical writers themselves. Of course this Cartesian dualism could actually be right. It does not seem unchristian in any obvious way. But it is helpful to recognize the forces at work on our thinking rather than simply being shoved around by history.

> I rightly conclude that my essence consists solely in the fact that I am something that thinks, a "thinking thing" . . . I have a clear and distinct idea of myself only as something that thinks without any thought of taking up space. On the other hand, I do have distinct ideas about my body as something that does not think and does take up space. So it is clear that "I" am absolutely distinct from my body and can exist without it.
>
> **René Descartes,** *Meditations* **6**[16]

When it comes to topics like this, it is important to recognize that the authors of the Bible expressed the truths they wrote in the categories of their day. For example, many of the biblical writers seemed to equate the breath inside them in some way with the spirit that leaves the body at death.[17] But we would no longer make that connection. We would not equate the carbon monoxide and other gases we exhale with what we call the "spirit" of a person. Science in multiple fields has thrown major new considerations into this discussion, and we ignore those considerations at the potential peril of our children's faith and the potential faith of the unconvinced around us. In chapter 9 we will discuss how many of the functions we often assign to the soul are associated with physical structures in our brains. While you will have to make up your own mind, we will look at some new suggestions for how a Christian might account for what we have called body and soul in the light of such discoveries.

As another example, modern physics no longer makes a sharp distinction between matter and energy, as Einstein's famous $E = mc^2$ indicates.[18] In fact, there is apparently little difference between a wave and a particle on the subatomic level. The quantum world—at least given our current expressions of it—is a strange place where the "laws" of nature as we have come to know them often do not apply in exactly the same ways they seem to on the "macro" world. Physicists now talk about *probabilities* rather than of the certainties Isaac Newton called "laws." At this point in time, we seem to have no way to perceive exactly what the underlying nature of reality is or how God might interact with it.

7.5
FAITH IN REALITY

The subject of metaphysics has fallen on hard times since the days of **Immanuel Kant**. In chapter 4 we mentioned Kant's conclusion that our understanding is a product of our minds and the way they organize individual impressions from our senses. The implication is that we really do not know the world as it is in itself, what Kant called *das Ding an sich*, "**the thing-in-itself**." We know the world only as it appears to us, as our minds organize the data according to our "interpreting software"—the categories built into our heads.

Kant wrote his ideas along these lines in his book titled *Prolegomena to Any Future Metaphysics*. Prolegomena are the things you need to keep in mind before you begin to talk about something. In this case Kant thought that all the metaphysicians of philosophy before him had not properly considered the role their own mind played in their theories. And with that he dismissed just about everything we have been talking about in the chapter up to this point. Many philosophers would claim that his book made chapters like this one obsolete, suggesting that we have no way to know what the ultimate "stuff" behind the world is; we know only how we experience that world outside our heads as interpreted by the physiology of our heads.

The Bible too, as we have seen in chapter 4 and will see further in the next chapter, largely gives us truth in the clothing of the paradigms of the ancient authors. God did not bypass all human categories in the act of revelation. So to look to the Bible for answers to these sorts of ontological questions is probably to ask questions it is not trying to answer. We must be careful not to mistake a human paradigm through which God spoke for the inspired point itself.[19]

Consider three basic paths we might take in the light of these considerations. Although the philosophers who take these paths would no doubt strongly distinguish themselves from one another, the three paths have some key commonalities. The first is what we might call **commonsense realism**, usually connected to the Scotsman **Thomas Reid** (1710–1796), so much so that it is sometimes called "Scottish realism." Reid was reacting to the speculations of philosophers like the skeptic David Hume and the idealist George Berkeley. Am I really a thought in God's mind? Can I really say that the hammer caused the nail to go in? Is this table really here in front of me? Many a philosophy student at this point will like Reid's style. Well, of course there's a table here! What are you, stupid?

Reid's commonsense approach to reality had a big effect on American thinking. It fit with the frontier and entrepreneurial spirit of the United States, which formed near the end of Reid's life. It is no coincidence that **pragmatism** was principally born on American soil. Pragmatism is a philosophical approach to life that largely avoids theoretical questions and focuses instead on what *works* in real life. The American **William James** (1842–1910) is often considered its founder. And the approach to education of pragmatist **John Dewey** (1859–1952) has left its imprint on the American educational system.

Pragmatic realism largely arrives at the same practical destination as commonsense realism, but it does so after grappling with the hard theoretical work of Immanuel Kant. **Hilary Putnam** (b. 1926) is perhaps the name we should most associate with pragmatic realism in its most recent form (see chap. 15). **Richard Rorty** (1931–2007) gives us a more pessimistic sense of things, suggesting that talk about the nature of reality is completely meaningless. Questions about the underlying nature of things do not make sense to him; they are nonsensical questions. By contrast, Putnam believes that reality must really exist in some way for our language to work in the first place. The truck driving toward me must be real in some sense. If not, why do I step out of the way? And Thomas Reid would say, "Of course there's a truck coming at you. What are you, stupid?"

Perhaps a more optimistic term even than pragmatic realism is **critical realism**. A critical realist would affirm by faith that reality does exist and that

Commonsense realism: an approach to reality that avoids theoretical questions and takes a what-you–see-is-what-you-get attitude.

Pragmatism: an approach to life that determines what is true by what "works."

Pragmatic realism: an approach to reality whose view of reality centers on the fact that some understandings of reality work better than others.

Critical realism: an approach to reality that affirms by faith that reality exists, even though our perception of that reality will always be skewed by the fact that we inevitably view it from a certain perspective.

We learn by doing.

John Dewey,
Schools of Tomorrow

our knowledge of it is not complete nonsense. At the same time, this person would acknowledge that we cannot help but view the world from a certain perspective; no one sees reality exactly as it is. Reality exists, but our understanding of it will always be skewed to one extent or another.

Those who might call themselves critical realists have varying degrees of confidence in our potential knowledge of reality. Some, like Michael Polanyi (1891–1976), would be quite optimistic about arriving at fairly close approximations to reality as it actually is. Others, like the author of this book, see a plausible form of critical realism more as an updating of Kant's basic position. We cannot fully know the real nature of the world, and our very affirmation of its existence is a matter of faith. We can never conceptualize its existence or operations in absolute terms, but only within human paradigms and language. Nevertheless, we can distinguish between better and worse paradigms—expressions of reality that account for the data and operations of the world. Our parabolic and storied expressions of the world can work well enough for us to deem them true.

Critical realists and commonsense realists agree that the world does actually exist. Critical realists and pragmatic realists agree to varying degrees that we can operate with a sense of truth, even though we are not in a position to evaluate rationally the reality of that truth. And commonsense realists, pragmatists, and pragmatic realists would agree that what works deserves most to be called "truth."

7.6
CONCLUSION

Christians throughout the centuries have held different ideas about the materials out of which the world is made. Some Christians have believed that the world is simply the thoughts of God. Others, while believing that God is a Spirit, have more or less seen the universe as material. Even the biblical authors may have seen spirit as a thin type of material. Since Descartes in the 1600s, it has been popular for Christians to be dualists who make a sharp distinction between the "materials" of body and soul. Arguably there is no one Christian position on this issue.

A much more important question for a Christian is the distinction between God and the creation. Historically, Christians have made a clear distinction between God as Creator and the world, as created. God existed "before" the world, whatever that statement might mean—he even created the empty space that the material world inhabits. Wherever the essence of God is, it is not in this universe. He has apparently created the universe to run by certain (natural) laws.

Accordingly, there are events that seem to follow the normal "rules" of how things happen, the rules of cause and effect. Then there are things that are out of the ordinary, things Christians call "miracles" (super-natural). Is God behind the scenes, constantly causing these things we call "laws"? Is what we call gravity really God's consistent action in the world by which things with mass attract other things? From a pragmatic point of view, it doesn't really matter exactly how it works. There are occurrences that are natural and occurrences that are out of the ordinary, which we may as well call supernatural.

KEY TERMS

- paradigm
- worldview
- Protestant Reformation
- natural
- supernatural
- ontology
- pantheism
- naturalism
- materialism
- deism
- theism
- Enlightenment
- Logos
- determinism
- monism
- immaterial
- idealism
- Neoplatonism
- nothing changes
- dialectic reasoning
- dualism
- Plato's theory of ideas
- world of senses
- world of ideas
- four basic elements
- thing-in-itself
- commonsense realism
- pragmatism
- pragmatic realism
- critical realism

KEY PHILOSOPHERS

- Thales
- Pythagoras
- Heraclitus
- Empedocles
- Democritus
- Parmenides
- Plato
- Thomas Hobbes
- René Descartes
- George Berkeley
- Thomas Reid
- Immanuel Kant
- G. W. F. Hegel
- William James
- John Dewey
- Hilary Putnam
- Richard Rorty

PHILOSOPHICAL QUOTATIONS

- "Everything is in flux, like a river." (Heraclitus)
- "Nothing changes." (Parmenides)
- "We learn by doing." (Dewey)

KEY QUESTIONS

1. To what extent would you consider yourself a friend or foe of science? Are you consistent? For example, do you think of mathematicians and scientists as some of the smartest people and yet tend to reject what they say?

2. In practice, what, if any, distinction do you make between the actions of God in the world and natural "laws" such as gravity and friction? Do you think God is pulling all the strings, even the ones scientists have captured as mathematical laws, or has God created the world to a large extent to run on its own without direct involvement? Give reasons for your opinion.

3. If you had to peg yourself as a materialist, idealist, or dualist, which one would you pick? Do we really have any way of picking between these options, or would you agree with those who say we have no way of knowing what ultimate reality is?

4. Of the three—commonsense realism, pragmatic realism, and critical realism—which do you find most attractive and why?

NOTES

1. In chapter 2 we treated worldviews as if they were monolithic, single packages that fit together neatly. Many Christian thinkers treat worldviews in this way, e.g., a naturalistic worldview, a theistic worldview. In reality, however, few of us are entirely consistent across all our paradigms, in addition to the fact that each worldview usually accommodates a good deal of variation within it.
2. Certainly some Christians do. A good example of a thoroughgoing application of divine purpose to our lives is found in Rick Warren, *The Purpose Driven Life: What on Earth Am I Here For?* (Grand Rapids: Zondervan, 2003). We saw in the previous chapter that John Calvin viewed the world the same way.
3. It is important to realize that there were Roman Catholics in the medieval period such as Thomas Aquinas (1225–1274) who, following Aristotle, had more room in their worldview for science and discovery than Luther did. G. K. Chesterton argued that the Reformation was a step backward in some respects. G. K. Chesterton, *Saint Thomas Aquinas* (1933; repr., New York: Doubleday, 1956).
4. We will wait until chapter 9 to discuss the question of the human soul.
5. Paraphrased from the Introduction written by Hobbes in English in 1651.
6. It is possible that Thales was Phoenician, but he lived in Greek territory.
7. Historians debate the extent to which it makes much sense to group together the various individual cultures we call the Western world.
8. We will discuss creation at greater length in the next chapter.
9. What then are we to make of the many others who did impressive things like the Egyptians who had built the pyramids more than a thousand years before Thales?
10. In chapter 10 we will see that this analogy does not actually work. Because of quantum physics, one cannot say today that materialism implies determinism at all.
11. Or, if you are God, to be is to do the perceiving.
12. In the next chapter, we will suggest that science does not really tell us what the universe is made of. It provides us only with models and language that work very well at predicting what we perceive to happen when we perceive certain other things to happen. Even the description of a cell under a microscope is only a description of what we perceive when we perceive ourselves to have done something. It is quite impossible to disprove Berkeley's hypothesis, as unhelpful a hypothesis as it may seem.
13. Although, in Luke's account, Jesus's spirit is reunited with his body, to the extent that Luke says that Jesus had flesh and bones again (Luke 24:39) after he rises "out of the corpses," the most literal translation of the phrase *from the dead.*
14. An excellent presentation of how the ancients understood spirit is in D. B. Martin, *The Corinthian Body* (New Haven, CT: Yale University, 1995), 3–37.
15. Thus the word *ethereal.*
16. Paraphrased from René Descartes, *Meditations on the First Philosophy with Selections from the Objections and Replies*, trans. J. Cottingham (Cambridge: Cambridge University, 1986).
17. In both Greek (*pneuma*) and Hebrew (*ruach*), the word we regularly translate as "spirit" might also be translated as "breath."
18. Einstein suggested that matter turns to energy when it is traveling at the speed of light and that the amount of energy would be the mass of the matter times the square of the speed of light.
19. More in chapter 9.

© istockphoto.com

8.1
RETHINKING MYTH

In the fictionalized introduction to philosophy *Sophie's World*, the story's fictional "tutor" says that a particular myth "tried to give people an explanation for something they could not understand."[1] In this casual definition, *Sophie's World* reflects the popular, Western understanding of ancient myths: they were basically primitive (i.e., bad) science. For example, people from Scandinavia were trying to explain why the seasons changed, so someone made up a story. A god named Thor gets his hammer stolen, and the earth turns winter cold. And the primitive people believed it!

It does seem true that many, if not most, of the ancients took these myths literally. We mentioned in the previous chapter that Anaxagoras (ca. 500–428 BC) was forced to leave Athens for disbelieving in the gods and suggesting instead that the sun was a very hot rock or that the

What to Get from This Chapter

- Myths are creative expressions of the mysteries of the world in story form.
- The scientific method moves from observation of data to hypotheses it then tests until it establishes a theory.
- Observability and falsifiability are very desirable, some would say essential, characteristics of a good scientific hypothesis.
- A paradigm is a lens through which a given set of data is processed and understood.
- Historically, Christians have believed that God created the universe, has exhaustive power and knowledge of it, and remains involved with it.
- Critical realism assumes by faith that the universe exists but recognizes that our perceptions and understandings of it are inevitably perspectivized and expressed within nonabsolute frameworks.

Questions to Consider

- What is the scientific method?
- What is a paradigm shift?
- What is a critical realist approach to truth?

Key Words

- Hypothesis
- Paradigm
- Occam's razor
- Critical realism

Image of the Canaanite god El.
Bronze with gold overlay.

© Kevin L. Welch

> The divine being is nothing other than the human being . . . All the characteristics of divine nature are, therefore, characteristics of human nature.
>
> **Ludwig Feuerbach,**
> *The Essence of Christianity* 1.2[2]

Negative theology: an approach to God that focuses on what God is not rather than on what God is.

Trinity: the classical Christian belief that, while there is only one God and that God is one in substance, God is at the same time three persons: Father, Son, and Holy Spirit.

moon simply reflected light. Anaxagoras was following in the tradition of a slightly earlier philosopher from Asia Minor, Xenophanes (570–480 BC).

Xenophanes thought that the portrayals of the gods in Homer and the poet Hesiod were deplorable. In their stories, the gods behaved little better than mere mortals. They became jealous, slept with other men's wives, murdered the innocent, and differed from ordinary humans only in that they were powerful enough to get away with it. Xenophanes concluded that people basically portrayed gods as bigger versions of themselves. If a cow could make up gods, he suggested, they would look and act like cows, only with greater power to do the kinds of things cows do. Xenophanes was thus the first person we know of to suggest that people create gods in their own image. He said, "If cattle, horses, and lions had hands, if they could draw with them and do what people do, horses would draw the gods in the shape of horses. Cattle would draw them in the shape of cattle. Each animal would give the gods bodies like their own."

Interestingly, Xenophanes did believe in a god, but to him this one god was unlike any human being. Like many of the Greek philosophers, he had a concept of an underlying power behind reality that was quite different from human beings. As Christians, we live in a tension between this tendency to picture God as being too much like us, while believing at the same time that God created us in his image (Gen. 1:27). What exactly does it mean to say that humans were created like God (cf. Ps. 8)? We will discuss this issue further in chapter 9.

An entire stream of Christian thought, however, has responded to these concerns and suggested that God is primarily known not for what he is like, which inevitably leads us to understand him in human categories, but by what he is *not like*. This approach to God is called **negative theology** or the *via negativa* (the "negative way"). This "apophatic" perspective is based on what we cannot say. So God is *not* limited in power or in knowledge or by space or time, since any attempt to portray God in terms of human power or knowledge or space and time will inevitably lead us to understand him in human categories. We might say that we know God primarily by analogy to the things we can understand but that God's *literal* ways are "beyond our understanding" (e.g., Job 36:26; Isa. 55:9).[3]

At the same time, many Christian thinkers would suggest that this way of thinking about God is not quite Christian because of several essential, positive affirmations about God. For example, can a *via negativa* account for Christian belief in the **Trinity**? Historically Christians believe that, although there is only one God in terms of his identity and being, God is nonetheless three persons. This is not an easy idea to understand; maybe it is beyond the capacity of the human mind to understand!

Belief in the Trinity claims that there is only one God; at the same time it claims that Jesus is God, and Jesus's heavenly Father is God, and the Holy Spirit who fills us and works within us is God. These three persons together comprise one God. In a way, this Christian belief has the flavor of something apophatic, for it scarcely makes sense to our human reasoning. Any attempt to explain the idea almost always ends up messing up either the idea that God is one or the idea that there are three distinct persons in the Trinity.

Many Christian thinkers would suggest that our belief in the Trinity *does* tell us what God is actually like in his actual being. In fact, the past few decades have seen Christian thinkers explore the Trinity extensively, in particular how it might serve as a model for the way we live as Christians. Is it possible, however, that some of these explorations fall into Xenophanes's trap? For example, more than one group has recently looked to the Trinity for a model of how we might order our families. Not surprisingly, those who already believe the man should "run the house" find God the Father running the Trinity. And those who believe the partners should be equal find equality in the Trinity. Perhaps even the Trinity is only an analogy for something we humans could not possibly understand on a literal level.

The past few decades have seen some reevaluation of the myths of ancient peoples. When science reigned supreme in Western culture, it was perhaps inevitable that the ancient myths would be viewed as bad science, as the poor attempts of ignorant people to *explain* the world as best they could. And, as we have mentioned, most of the ancients probably did take these stories literally.

But let us return to some of what we explored in the previous chapter. Can we really get outside of our heads, beyond our perceptions of the world to the things of the world itself? Are not my "explanations" of the world *expressions* of my perceptions of the world? By faith we take our perceptions as generally accurate; we do not have to abandon our faith in reality or truth. But it is an act of faith, not a proof. I cannot prove that I am not a brain in a vat somewhere. It is just an idea that does not "work" very well for everyday living.

If we return to the Scandinavian myth of Thor and the changing of the seasons, Thor's hammer gets stolen by another god, and winter blows in. Thor then dresses in drag and manages to get himself engaged to this other god. Then when they get together to get married, he kills the other god and spring returns.

As bizarre as this story is, it would not make a very good *explanation* for why the seasons change. After all, Thor killed the other guy. For it to be a good explanation, the guy would have to come alive every year and steal the hammer again. We wonder if, rather than being a bad explanation for why the seasons change, this story was more a fun and playful *expression* of the changing of the seasons. Considering it a poetic expression of a mystery makes more sense than thinking of it as a nonsensical explanation of weather patterns.

Jack Finegan put it nicely when he said, "A myth is not, then, in the first instance, a fanciful tale, but a symbolic or poetic expression of that which is incapable of direct statement."[4] You can see the idea even in the similarity between the word *myth* and the word *mystery*. Certainly people will use words as they use words. We saw in chapter 4 that the meanings of words are a matter of how people *use* them. So, like it or not, the most common use of the word *myth* today is in reference to something that is false.

But thinking of the myths of the ancients as "false stories" may skew how they functioned for the ancients. Ancient myths were stories that expressed the mysterious aspects of life. True, many ancients, including biblical writers, did question the veracity of these stories.[5] And certainly some of the stories expressed notions about life with which we disagree. But the fundamental shift from thinking of myths as explanations to thinking of them as expressions opens up beneficial ways for us to think about ourselves.

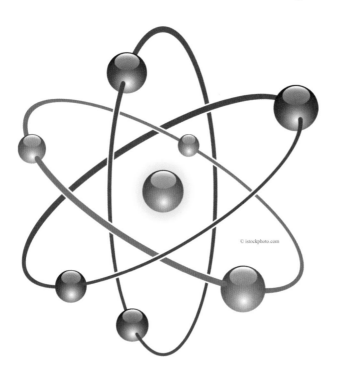

© istockphoto.com

In particular, rather than thinking of myths as bad science, this shift leads us to think of science as very finely tuned myths! What are scientific formulas, theories, and hypotheses but sophisticated attempts to express the ways in which we perceive various things in the world to operate? The myth of Demeter and Persephone expressed the fact that the seasons change from hot to cold to hot again every year. Newton's law of universal gravitation expresses the pull of gravity on a falling object.

The rise of relativity and quantum mechanics in the twentieth century has pointed out that the Newtonian "myths" were not as precise as they could be. They expressed the way things behave to a certain degree. But we needed new myths to express the way things behave on the "subatomic" level. So we have mathematical stories about characters we call photons, quarks, and gluons. These are "true myths," not insofar as they tell us the way things *really* are on the "subatomic" level, but insofar as they correctly express the way we perceive things to behave in certain situations.

8.2
PHILOSOPHY OF SCIENCE

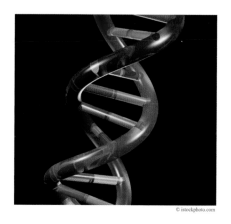

© istockphoto.com

Whether individuals could describe it or not, the **scientific method** is deeply ingrained in the consciousness of Western culture. Our teachers in middle school and high school at least tried to teach it to us. But we probably learn it more effectively from watching police and crime shows, where they gather evidence and form **hypotheses** about "who done it." They test these hypotheses against the evidence, gather further evidence, and test a hypothesis some more.

At some point they move beyond considering someone a "person of interest" and declare a "suspect" in the case. Eventually they may arrest the person and put him or her on trial. Finally, a jury will, at least in theory, weigh the evidence again to decide whether guilt is the most logical conclusion given the evidence, at least "beyond a reasonable doubt." As we have argued previously, it would often seem impossible to *prove* anything of this sort absolutely—the world of inductive thinking is a world of probabilities, not absolute certainties.

The process is so commonsensical that it hardly seems something anyone would question. After all, isn't this the way we operate in our day-to-day activities? I hear a thumping on the roof. I go and investigate. Is it a burglar? Santa Claus? Too big for a squirrel. Not sure if it was heavy enough for a person. I go upstairs and look out the window. Oh, it's a raccoon.

On the other hand, most of us are scarcely consistent. Sometimes—perhaps more often than we might admit to ourselves—we form conclusions on the basis of almost no real evidence at all. We prejudge someone or something on some irrelevant basis. This is the stuff of **prejudice**. We see a person's color, race, or gender and presume that the person must be a certain way. In chapter 2 we called this the informal fallacy of hasty generalization, with other fallacies often involved as well.

Nevertheless, even if we are not *good* inductive thinkers, most of us Westerners would likely claim in theory that we consider this method of investigation legitimate and valuable. You will remember from chapter 2 that inductive thinking is when you look at a collection of data and induce a general truth from it. We are so used to this way of thinking in science that it is hard for most of us to imagine a time when the best-known thinkers were primarily talking about truth from a *deductive* standpoint, where you start with certain assumptions and then play them out in particular details.

To be sure, we are seeing a resurgence of this older deductive approach to truth, especially since postmodernism raises questions about whether we

---

The Scientific Method

1. Observe a relevant set of data in relation to a relevant question.

2. Form a **hypothesis**, a possible rule or pattern that might explain the data and predict what would happen under similar circumstances in the future.

3. Test and retest the hypothesis against similar sets of data.

4. Establish a **theory**, a hypothesis that has proved to have significant predictive power as it has been tested and retested.

Prejudice: an attitude that tends to draw conclusions or make judgments before examining relevant information on the basis of irrelevant biases.

can really induce truth from our observations of the world.[6] We live in a climate where it is acceptable to start with large, unproved assumptions and talk about reality from there. Some Christians, such as those in the radical orthodoxy movement we mentioned in chapter 2, see this situation as a great climate for Christian faith. We do not need to do "apologetics" in defense of our faith. We can be "unapologetic" and need no rational basis for our faith at all.

Some of postmodernism's criticisms seem to be valid, as we will see later in this section. But the usefulness of inductive thinking will likely continue to predominate in the days to come. Its usefulness in expressing accurately what happens in the world, as well as in enabling us to act in the world, is too great for it to disappear. If every group starts with its own untouchable assumptions and proceeds from there, then such groups can hardly even talk to each other.

Sir Francis Bacon (1561–1626)

Historians often trace the reemergence of inductive reasoning and scientific method to **Sir Francis Bacon** in the 1500s (1561–1626). But others suggest that Bacon was riding a wave that goes further back to the theologian Thomas Aquinas in the 1200s and then beyond him to Islamic philosophers such as Ibn Sina (sometimes called Avicenna, ca. 980–1037) and Ibn Rushd (sometimes called Averroës, 1126–1198).[7] These individuals did use deductive reasoning to a significant extent. But their reasoning often began with some observation of the world, such as the fact that for something to move, it has to be pushed. In that sense, Bacon is perhaps not as completely new as he is sometimes made out to be.

Francis Bacon secured his reputation as the father of scientific method primarily on the basis of his book *New Organon*. There he suggested that when trying to arrive at a conclusion on some matter relating to the world, a person should create tables of data. One would put data relating to some factor, like heat, in one column. Then one would put data relating to the opposite, like coldness, in another. Then you would test hypotheses against the columns, to see if your understanding matched the way the data played out. This grounded the study of the world in *observation* rather than in making deductions from assumed "axioms" as a starting point.

> There are and can only be two ways of searching and discovering truth . . . The second moves toward basic truths through the senses and particular experiences, moving from these particulars in a gradual and unbroken ascent, coming to the most general truths at the very end of the process. This is the true way, even though thus far it is untried.

Francis Bacon, *New Organon*[8]

A few features of Bacon's approach are significant. First, he assumes that a person can be more or less **objective** or unbiased as he or she looks at the data. Second, he assumes that one can come to a definite and final answer to the question being posed to the data. Both of these assumptions came under serious question in the twentieth century.

One twentieth-century figure who challenged these two assumptions was **Karl Popper** (1902–1994). Popper rightly pointed out that the very questions with which we come to some set of data color the answers we will draw from that data. No one comes to a set of data without certain presuppositions or expectations. No one can look at a set of data with a God's-eye view. No one is perfectly objective.

Second, Popper seriously questioned whether we could ever come to a final answer and verify that a scientific theory was true. A claim like "all snow is white" cannot be finally verified. The very nature of inductive thinking is open ended, except perhaps in some situation where one has *all* the relevant data.[9] Thus after Europeans had thought for years that all swans were white, they came across black swans in Australia. So Popper suggested that science was based on the quest not to verify theories but to falsify them. Good theories were theories that, thus far, had resisted falsification.

In this methodology, he rejected another approach that enjoyed a brief moment of popularity in the early twentieth century, **logical positivism**.[10] Logical positivists held that only things a person could observe and verify had any real claim to being called "true." The fundamental problem with this theory is that its fundamental hypothesis is an assumption that cannot be observed or verified. It is thus incoherent on a most basic level. Popper's suggestion that the best theories are those that have not yet been falsified is at least an improvement on logical positivism, although it still assumes that with scientific theory we are basically dealing with theories that are either "true" or "false."

By far the most significant philosopher of science in the twentieth century was **Thomas Kuhn** (1922–1996).[11] In the first edition of Kuhn's *The Structure of Scientific Revolutions*, he argued that no scientific paradigm is ultimately better than another. You will remember that a **paradigm** is a way of looking at a particular subject, like the diversity of animal species. To Kuhn, what is traditionally considered to be scientific development is a kind of organized wandering from one paradigm to another, following a predictable process. In the second edition, he tempered his thinking, particularly over protests at the thought that creation science might be equally valid in comparison to evolutionary science.[12]

Kuhn's basic idea was that science operates most of the time according to a dominant paradigm, the **normal science**. So in the early 1500s, the

> Knowledge is power.
>
> **Francis Bacon**

"Normal" science: science operating under the assumptions of a dominant paradigm.

Logical positivism: an early-twentieth-century approach to truth that suggested something had to be observable to be considered true.

dominant astronomical paradigm held that the sun went around the earth. In the 1800s, the paradigm of physics was Newtonian. In the twentieth century, the dominant biological paradigm was evolutionary. These are the lenses through which a particular set of data are viewed and organized.

So you are at the Grand Canyon, and you see a set of layers of earth and rock. In the typical creation-science paradigm, you might assume that these layers were laid down over a relatively short period of time, perhaps in the aftermath of a worldwide flood.[13] Alternatively, such a person might suggest that God created the earth to have "apparent age." In other words, the earth may look like it is billions of years old, but it only appears this way because God made the earth and universe to look old. The dominant geological paradigm in these matters, of course, is that these layers represent millions of years of slow, largely uniform conditions in which layer was gradually laid down over time.[14]

According to Kuhn, paradigms change not so much because we get smarter or that science gets better. Rather, *all* paradigms leave unexplained or seemingly contradictory data. I like to call it "naughty data." After a paradigm has shifted, most "normal scientists" expend their energy trying to fit anomalous data into the new, dominant paradigm. Such operations may go for a long time without changing the current paradigm too much.

For example, evolution has been the dominant scientific paradigm perhaps for more than a century now. But it has not gone unchanged. For example, although **Charles Darwin** (1809–1882) suggested that the more complex organisms we know today evolved from less complex ones, he could not really explain how such changes took place. His version of evolution simply saw organisms gradually changing bit by bit, with nature over time selecting the bits that best helped organisms adapt and survive.

But Darwin's version of evolution, often called **Darwinism**, could not explain how the new changes came about in the first place. This element of evolutionary theory did not enter the equation until after Darwin, when the idea of mutation entered the scene. Genetic mutations are the minute alterations of an organism's DNA that take place over the course of time. Most mutations place an organism at a decided disadvantage, but occasionally a mutation results in an advantageous trait.

So in this case we have an example of "normal science" persisting with the paradigm of evolution. When encountering a problem with the theory, normal scientists did not abandon the overall idea of evolution. Rather, they modified the theory to account for some "naughty data" that did not fit.

Kuhn suggested that there will always be anomalous data in relation to a dominant paradigm. This data is the seed of a **paradigm shift**, which Kuhn predicted would inevitably take place eventually. At some point, Kuhn argued, someone would suggest a significantly different way of looking at the data—one that focused on the data that did not fit the current paradigm.

Of course normal science resists such radical rethinking. Copernicus's (1473–1543) suggestion that the earth went around the sun was not met with open arms by either the Roman Catholic Church *or* the scientists of the day.[15] Indeed, Kuhn notes that it was not *scientifically* obvious at the time that Copernicus was correct. For example, his mathematical explanations of the planets' movements did not work as well as the Ptolemaic scientists who defended the normal science of the day—that the heavenly bodies moved around the earth.[16]

But the math of the Ptolemaic scientists was much more complex than Copernicus's. So although they might account for the motions of the heavenly bodies more accurately, **Occam's razor**—the idea that the simplest explanation is usually a better explanation—was against them.

As Christians, we should take warning. We Christians have paradigms about Christianity as well. We have paradigms of interpretations, for example.

A Baptist will emphasize certain verses that fit with his or her way of thinking and tend to de-emphasize other "naughty verses" that do not fit as well. The same is true of a Methodist, a Presbyterian, or a Reformed thinker. At the same time, we find that Christians in a particular tradition may expend a good deal of intellectual energy trying to account for the passages that do not fit their paradigm as well. Often new churches and denominations are born off such naughty verses.[17]

In the case of the planets, Copernicus's **heliocentric** solar system (sun at center) did not fit all the details as precisely as the **geocentric** system (earth as center) defended by the math of the Ptolemaic scientists, but it was simpler and not far off. Less than a century later, Johannes Kepler (1571–1630) made the heliocentric math both simpler *and* more

> **Occam's razor:** the idea that the simplest explanation is usually the better explanation.
>
> **Paradigm shift:** a radical shift from one way of looking at a particular topic to a significantly different perspective.

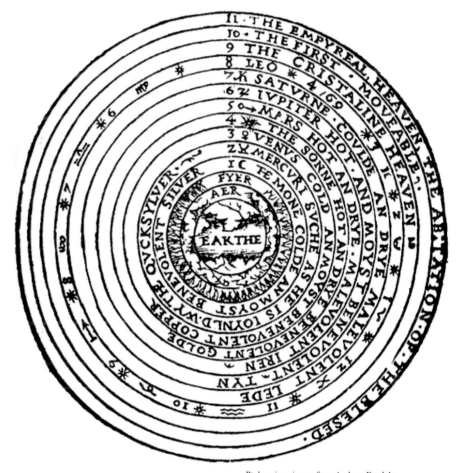

Ptolemaic universe from Andrew Borde's *The First Book of the Introduction of Knowledge*, 1542

BIOGRAPHY

THOMAS KUHN

Thomas Kuhn lived from 1922 to 1996 and is best known in philosophy for his book *The Structure of Scientific Revolutions*. Philosophically Kuhn stands between the logical positivists, who believed that only things that could be observed could be considered true in any real sense, and postmodern philosophers of science like **Paul Feyerabend** (1924–1994), who did not believe science was about reality at all but about sociology and groups of people interacting with each other.

Kuhn's central challenge to the prevalent understanding of science is his sense that scientific discovery is not strictly an ever-improving movement toward greater and greater understanding of reality. Rather, significant human elements are involved in the process that has traditionally been considered scientific development. Differing scientific "paradigms" operate from categories that are "incommensurable" or not comparable with each other. In contrast, Kuhn's critics suggest that some of the fundamental observations that paradigms interpret remain the same, meaning that differing paradigms do allow for comparison.

After criticism of his book's first edition, Kuhn distanced himself from the label of "relativist." In the second edition, for example, he suggests that a paradigm that explains a larger pool of data can be considered a better paradigm. He thus did not reject the basic idea of scientific progress.

Some overlap exists between the thought of Thomas Kuhn and the slightly earlier **Michael Polanyi** (1891–1976) such that some Polanyi devotees initially saw Kuhn as borrowing from Polanyi's thought. So in the second edition of *Structure*, Kuhn brought Polanyi into explicit conversation with his ideas. Polanyi argued that "tacit knowledge"—elements of thought that are not completely conscious or easily articulated—is involved in all knowing. This means we cannot be completely objective, because there are always hidden elements steering our thinking. (Polanyi is associated with critical realism.) Scientific development is thus not strictly an objective development; human factors are also involved.

Geocentric solar system: the view that the earth is at the center and the sun moves around it.

Heliocentric solar system: the view that the sun is at the center and the earth moves around it.

accurate by arguing that the planets moved around the sun in ellipses rather than circles. As Kuhn argued, however, what now seem to be obvious steps forward in a progression of knowledge were not at all clear at the time.

According to Kuhn, paradigms shift in a political struggle between those who support the old paradigm and those who focus on data that does not fit the old paradigm. Because normal science tries to fit anomalous data into the old paradigm, it usually resists strongly the advent of new paradigms that form around the problem data. The old-paradigm establishment may keep new-paradigm supporters from publishing or speaking at conferences or getting jobs. But if the new paradigm gets its foot in the door, if its supporters increase—usually among younger scientists—the older scientists will eventually die off.

So it was that Albert Einstein (1879–1955) never supported the radical version of quantum mechanics, developed in the 1920s, that is now the normal paradigm of physics. "God does not throw dice," he once wrote in a letter to a fellow scientist. But Einstein has been dead for more than fifty years now. And it would be hard to find a reputable nuclear physicist today who agrees with him on the nature of quantum mechanics!

Kuhn's approach to science is helpful in understanding the way all paradigms change—in any field of knowledge that involves the organization of data. We can wonder, however, if he was not too pessimistic in his sense that such paradigms are not really headed anywhere. For example, quantum mechanics—even though it may very well be superseded at some point—certainly accounts for the workings of the world on a vastly different scale than did Newtonian physics. It may still be an "expression" of what we observe in the world, a kind of scientific myth. But it is a myth that has served and continues to serve us very well. Quantum mechanics is a vastly more useful scientific approach to the world than was Newtonian physics. In that respect, surely it deserves to be called a better, even a "truer," theory than Newton's.

Gnostics: early Jewish and Christian movement that believed the material world is evil in contrast to spirit which is good.

Creation ex nihilo: creation "out of nothing," with God creating all the materials and, we might say further today, even the emptiness of space itself.

© Kevin L. Welch

8.3
CREATION AND CHRISTIANITY

Christians throughout the centuries have affirmed that God created the universe, seen and unseen. As the Apostles' Creed says, "I believe in God, the Father Almighty, maker of heaven and earth." Since at least the 200s, Christians have also regularly affirmed that God created the world out of nothing. Jews and Christians may have forged this particular belief in argument with individuals called **Gnostics**.[18] The Gnostics believed matter was evil, perhaps even created by an evil spiritual power. In response, both Jews and Christians asserted that in fact God had created the world out of nothing, creation **ex nihilo**.[19] If God created everything, including the substance of the universe, Gnostics could not blame said matter for the evil in the world.

Every spirit that confesses that Jesus Christ has come in the flesh is from God, but every spirit that does not confess Jesus is not from God.

See **1 John 4:2–3**

The Word became flesh . . .

John 1:14

Some Classical Attributes of God

Omnipotence:
God is all powerful.

Omniscience:
God is all knowing.

Omnipresence:
God is everywhere present.

Omnibenevolence:
God is entirely good.

Aseity:
God is self-sufficient.

The conviction that God created the world out of nothing brings into perspective a number of other things that Christians have usually believed. For example, if God created the world out of nothing, God apparently does not need the world to exist. God existed at a point when no world was around. God is thus self-sufficient in relation to the world. This "attribute" or characteristic of God is sometimes called his **aseity**.

Similarly, if God created the world out of nothing, then God presumably has as much "power" as he put into the world. Christians have accordingly considered God to be all powerful, an attribute called his **omnipotence**. And since God does not have any materials to begin with, God must know everything he created in every way. We thus say that God is all knowing or **omniscient**, although this line of argument seems to necessitate only that God knows all the possibilities of the creation.[20]

The Gnostics are not the only ones who have challenged the way Christians have viewed creation. For example, until the time of the Renaissance in the 1500s, Christians assumed that the earth stood at the center of the universe, with the heavenly realm (where angels and Christ lived) straight up from and the dead below the earth. It thus went against the commonly held view of the universe for individuals like Copernicus, Kepler, and Galileo to suggest that in fact the earth went around the sun, as mentioned earlier.

. . . every knee should bend,
in heaven and on earth and under the earth.

Philippians 2:10

Some thing yet of doubt remains,
Which onely thy solution can resolve . . .
How Nature wise and frugal could commit
Such disproportions, with superfluous hand
So many nobler bodies to create,
Greater so manifold to this one use,
For aught appears, and on their Orbs impose
Such restless revolution day by day
Repeated, while the sedentarie earth,
That better might with farr less compass move,
Serv'd by more noble than her self, attaines
Her end without least motion . . .

**Adam, questioning whether it is in fact the earth that moves
John Milton, *Paradise Lost* 8.13–14, 26–35**

It is easy for us to dismiss this challenge to faith today as if it was nothing significant, as if Christians should not have been disturbed at the time. Indeed, the fact that the greatest opposition came from the Roman Catholic Church makes it all the easier for Bible-oriented Christians today to dismiss the issue. Yet it seems likely that if modern-day **fundamentalists** had existed in the 1500s, they almost certainly would have joined the Roman Catholics in opposition to a heliocentric view of the universe.

Another challenge to Christian views of creation has come from voices that have either identified the world with God (**pantheism**) or have seen the world as a part of God (**panentheism**). Since neither of these views rests on scientific evidence, neither has really brought about any substantial change to historic Christian views of creation. Baruch Spinoza (1632–1677), who was Jewish not Christian, was perhaps the earliest person to suggest that we should identify God with the world. As a result he was "excommunicated" from the Jewish community in Amsterdam.

Panentheism is a more recent version of this approach to creation in which the world does not completely make up God, as it did for Spinoza. Rather, the world is a part of God, perhaps something like God's body. Charles Hartshorne (1897–2000) popularized the term when he developed an approach to God called **process theology**. Unlike historic Christianity, which sees God's nature as unchanging, process theology sees God's nature changing in interaction with an evolving world.[21]

Process theology thus brings up the most notorious recent challenge to traditional Christian views of creation, namely, **evolution**. On a most basic level, evolution is the idea that complex organisms have developed or "evolved" from less complicated organisms over time. For example, Charles Darwin suggested that all the different finches he observed in the Galapagos Islands had developed from a common finch-like ancestor over a long period of time.

Darwin did not have a good explanation for how this variety might have come about in the first place. But he did have a suggestion for how some types ended up on one island and other types on other islands. His suggestion was called **natural selection**, or what is popularly known as **survival of the fittest**. Once the variety existed, some birds were better equipped to survive on some islands than on others. Perhaps they had just the right beaks for the particular food on that island. Over time, then, the better equipped birds on each particular island—the "fittest"—came to dominate there.

Those describing evolution often give the peppered moth of England as an example of natural selection. Before the Industrial Revolution, before high amounts of soot were introduced into England's atmosphere, light-colored moths tended to dominate the English countryside. The darker or peppered moths tended to be a much smaller population if for no other reason than the fact that they stood out and birds could see them better. But after the Industrial Revolution, trees darkened from the soot and the peppered moth population flourished, while the lighter-colored moth dropped off sharply in population.

On the one hand, this level of "evolution" does not seem problematic, especially since it is common sense. It is sometimes called **microevolution**, and Christian scientists of all stripes have no problem with it. However, Darwin suggested that this process had taken place from the first life all the way to humanity, **macroevolution**, and it is this understanding of evolution that has called into question traditional Christian understandings of creation.

While Darwin could explain survival of the fittest, he had no good explanation for how the fittest came into existence in the first place. This piece of the puzzle was added later by **neo-Darwinism**. Neo-Darwinism suggests that **mutation** occasionally produces a "fitter" form of an organism

Fundamentalism: In American Christianity, a movement that arose in the early twentieth century in reaction to certain developments in biblical studies (e.g., higher criticism), science (e.g., evolution), and broader American culture (e.g., women's rights). It is thus perhaps best characterized in terms of what it opposes, often militantly, or that from which it is separated.

Pantheism: belief that the world is the same as God.

Panentheism: belief that the world is a part of God.

Process theology: a form of panentheism that sees God evolving and developing along with the world.

Evolution: the idea that complex organisms developed from less complex ones.

Natural selection: the idea that nature "selects" those organisms that are best suited to survive in a particular environment over time.

Survival of the fittest: popular way of describing natural selection—the organisms best equipped to survive in a particular environment tend to advance in competition with those less well equipped.

Microevolution: the idea that variation (such as with the peppered moth) does occur on a small scale, such as within a species or genus, but not on a larger scale.

Macroevolution: the idea that, over millions of years, complex organisms like human beings have evolved from the smallest of micro-organisms.

that eventually wins out over the earlier form of that organism. The vast majority of mutations, small changes to our genetic structure, are harmful.

But Christian scientists of all stripes would agree that mutations do occasionally benefit an organism, particularly when we are talking about micro-organisms. One of the reasons certain medicines stop working over time is because some new, mutated form of a virus or bacteria proves to be resistant. Over time, the old medicine kills off all the earlier forms, leaving the drug-resistant form to flourish. New medicines have to be developed.

It is beyond the scope of this book to engage in Christian debates over the science of macroevolution. Over the past few decades, a significant literature has emerged against it by **scientific creationists** and more recently, by those who hold to **intelligent design** theory (ID). The former group marshaled biologists, geologists, and other scientists in the 1970s to argue for a young earth, the complexion of which is best explained on the basis of the biblical flood.[22] Intelligent design theory takes a slightly different tack.[23] It suggests that certain aspects of life reflect an "irreducible complexity" that could not have evolved by chance. They attempt to demonstrate that the evolution of certain building blocks, such as proteins, is a mathematical impossibility by chance, because they are so complex. Unless they were designed, we cannot account for their existence.

At the same time, the evolutionary community has not stood still. Many evolutionists no longer hold to the gradual evolutionary model of Darwinism and now suggest that the most radical phases of evolution may take place "quickly" in various spurts (quickly meaning over thousands rather than millions of years). This process is sometimes called punctuated equilibrium.

Again, our purpose is not to examine the science involved. We can refer to a body of Christian scientific literature that makes scientific arguments against macroevolution.[24] Other Christian scientists argue for **theistic evolution**, the idea that God directed the evolutionary process.[25] When the theory of evolution first began to gain prominence, a number of "evangelical" Christians strategized to fit it within their Christian understanding. For example, some suggested what became known as the "gap theory," the idea that dinosaurs and other extinct animals might have lived in an era between Genesis 1:1 and Genesis 1:2. They suggested that Satan's fall from heaven might have caused the world of 1:1 to become the "formless void" of 1:2.

Over time, however, evolution was used as a rationale for **social Darwinism**, the idea that the rich and powerful should naturally run over the poor and powerless in society. After all, they were the fittest! It is possible that William Jennings Bryan, who argued against evolution in the famed Scopes Trial of 1925, was opposed to evolution primarily because of what he

Darwinism: the idea that evolution has taken place gradually over millions of years simply by nature "selecting" organisms better equipped to survive in particular environments.

Mutation: a change in the fundamental molecular structure of an organism.

Neo-Darwinism: a revision of Darwin's theory that understands mutation as the method by which organisms arise that are better equipped to survive in particular environments.

Scientific creationism: a Christian approach to scientific evidence that arose in the 1970s to counter belief in macroevolution. It assumes a literal seven-day creation and explains the earth's geology by recourse to a world-wide flood.

Intelligent design theory (ID): a more recent Christian approach to scientific evidence that suggests it cannot be explained adequately without recourse to an intelligent Designer, namely, God.

saw as its unchristian *social* implications, more than because it violated a literal understanding of the Bible.[26] That emphasis of scientific creationism did not become the main argument until the 1970s.

We might briefly mention the biblical texts that most come into play in such debates. The first is obviously Genesis 1, which presents creation in terms of seven "days." Theistic evolutionists take such language as figurative and poetic rather than as a literal description. Perhaps the days represent ages of history, they might say. At the same time, fundamentalist interpreters put a high premium on taking the days as literal twenty-four-hour days. Similarly, when Genesis says God made everything "after its kind," this description is taken to preclude evolution between species.

Perhaps a greater challenge to the theistic evolutionist view comes from the New Testament book of Romans. In chapter 5 Paul tells the Romans that death entered the world through sin, through the sin of Adam in particular (e.g., 5:12). Since evolution requires lots and lots of death to take place before Adam, some theistic evolutionists have argued that Paul is primarily or really talking about spiritual rather than physical death.[27] They have a foothold in the Genesis text, since it implies that Adam and Eve would naturally have died anyway without eating of the tree of life (Gen. 3:22).

Some theistic evolutionists have thus seen Adam as the first *Homo sapiens*, or perhaps the first humanoid into which God put a soul. They may see God as very involved in the process of evolution, steering it, helping it to head in the direction it went. For others, like Kenneth Miller, the Adam and Eve story might shift into the category we explored at the beginning of the chapter: a story expressing a mystery that does not refer to historical figures.[28] The Christian scientist Francis Collins has argued from his work on the human genome that the diversity of human genetic variation today could not have come from two distinct human predecessors.[29] He argues that the number had to be more like ten thousand original ancestors.

What is nonnegotiable for the historic Christian is that God created the universe, that God has all power over it and all knowledge of it. Further, God is involved in the world and through Christ will eventually set right everything that is wrong in it. Within these boundaries, we find some variety of perspective among faithful Christians. Each one will have to decide what he or she thinks is acceptable to believe. At the same time, there is surely a danger if Christianity can work only if we ignore positions held by the vast majority of those who are experts on a particular topic—especially if we are not experts and our positions are driven almost entirely from assumptions that other faithful Christians question.

Social Darwinism: the application of the idea of "survival of the fittest" to its "haves" and "have nots," justifying the domination of the powerful over society's weak.

Theistic evolution: the idea that God in some way directed the evolutionary process or at least that macroevolution is compatible with belief in God.

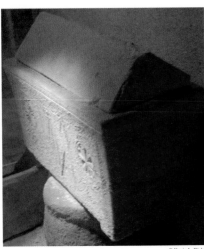

First-century ossuary. One similar to this has inscribed on it "James son of Joseph brother of Jesus." Whether it is really Jesus's brother James is debated.

8.4
FAITH AND EVIDENCE

In the final chapter of this book, we will step back and overview what we might call "postmodern" developments in philosophy, which aptly describe the state of thinking in which Western philosophy currently finds itself. However, at that point you will likely recognize that you have already seen much of its impact in the discussions of earlier chapters. We glimpsed that impact way back in chapter 2, where we looked at faith and reason. There we encountered one Christian school of thought that sees faith largely as *blind*, as something we can legitimately affirm with or without rational proof. For example, we came across "radical orthodoxy," a current Christian trend that is *un*apologetic in its affirmation of faith, believing without needing to substantiate its faith.

In this chapter we have seen the impact of what we might call "postmodern uncertainty." The chapter started with the suggestion that ancient myth was much more about *expressing* the mysteries of reality than about *explaining* how reality worked. There we wondered if in fact scientific theories today are really a kind of "myth" as well, though much more precise than ancient ones. We use our contemporary, scientific "myths" to express in great detail the mysteries of what we call the physical world. These myths express the operations of reality so well that we have been able to use them to go to the moon and build things like computers and flat screen TVs. We may not be able to say exactly what reality itself actually is, what "things-in-themselves" are made of, as we noted in regard to Kant at the end of the previous chapter. But our expressions of reality have worked astoundingly well in the age of science.

In the second section of the chapter, we saw the impact of postmodernism on the philosophy of science. We encountered Thomas Kuhn's analysis of how scientific revolutions take place. For him, scientific developments are not really developments but shifts in thinking that inevitably take place because no scientific theory can adequately account for all the data. New theories inevitably arise and take over in the attempt to account for such "naughty" data. But in his view, these new paradigms are just as doomed to fail as the ones they replace. According to Kuhn, scientific revolutions have as much to do with the personalities and sociology of the people doing science as they do with anything like truth or real progress in understanding.

At this point, many Christians will want to bring in God as a Guarantor of certainty, a *deus ex machina*, like the "god of the machine" that sometimes arrived in the nick of time in ancient plays to rescue the hero from a hopeless situation. Indeed, philosophers such as René Descartes, John Locke, and Immanuel Kant did bring in God at exactly such points of uncertainty in their philosophies. Someone might want to bring in the Bible as the direct revelation that removes what would otherwise be uncertainty without the possibility of resolution. Someone else might suggest that God has given us clarity through the church.

But as we saw in chapter 4, we cannot get outside our heads to read the Bible or play out the teaching of the church apart from human reasoning and thought. And indeed, the words of the Bible themselves, as well as all the creeds and traditions of the church, were understood within the categories of their original authors and audiences. In the end, whether by God's original design or as a result of human sin, all human understanding seems to involve interpretation, and interpretation would always seem to involve human paradigms and categories.[30]

As we conclude this chapter on science and faith, we would like to suggest a "critical-realist myth" that (1) is full of faith yet (2) takes adequate account of the limitations of human understanding and (3) allows us to continue to benefit from the scientific paradigm. You will remember from the end of the previous chapter that critical realism (as we define it) is an approach to reality that (1) affirms by faith that reality exists and that there are better and worse conceptualizations of it yet (2) recognizes that we can never get a bird's-eye or God's-eye view of it, that we are stuck in our heads, and that our understandings of reality inevitably take place from a limited and ultimately skewed perspective.

© Kevin L. Welch

First, apart from our affirmation of existence itself, every single thing we believe about every topic and matter involves and ultimately comes down to faith. Descartes believed that because he thought, he must exist: "I think; therefore, *I* am." But in actuality, his thinking proved only that whatever we might call "thought" exists. It does not prove that "I" exist, nor does it prove that what I am calling "thought" is accurately or best understood as thought. My thought could be a sophisticated computer program or something I could not possibly conceptualize.

We operate in this world overwhelmingly by faith, faith that the things around us are real, faith that I am real. We cannot prove these things. Nevertheless, faith in reality works really well. "I think; therefore thought exists" is all we can say with absolute certainty. Everything else involves a hefty dose of faith.

The opposite of faith is thus not reason but proof. In science, it has to do with the way we glue together the evidence or data at hand. It has to do with the way we fill in the blanks between the evidence, not to mention our basic apprehension of the evidence itself. In logic it has to do with the premises or presuppositions we assume in making an argument. Whether or not faith is "blind" depends on how much glue we have to supply to make our paradigms work and how well our assumptions fit the evidence we seem to have.

In a postmodern world, blind faith is not necessarily irrational, especially if we are up-front and honest about the apparent lay of the evidence. A person's thinking can be incoherent, and we can still call that kind of thinking "irrational." But in a world where virtually everything is a matter of faith, there is a way in which we can affirm ideas that do not seem to fit the evidence we have or that do not seem to work very well, *and we can do it rationally and logically*. The main thing is that we are honest about it. Radical orthodoxy is thus a rational and coherent approach to Christian faith, even though it has no interest in justifying or defending itself rationally.

At the same time, we wonder what the longevity of such an approach to truth will be, beyond its initial adherents. In Christian thinking, such an approach fits well with the ideas of the most significant theologian of the twentieth century, Karl Barth (1886–1968). For him, the beliefs of Christianity were not based on evidence at all but purely on God's revelation. Truth is revealed, not discovered or proven. Accordingly, Barth had no interest in questions asking whether history might prove Jesus's tomb was empty on Easter Sunday or whether archaeology supported the historicity of the Bible's stories. If Barth were still alive, he would certainly affirm those who say that Christianity is *un*apologetic about its beliefs.

One potential problem with this line of thinking is that it leaves no *reason* to believe in Christianity. For thinkers in the Calvinist tradition, this is not a problem, because they believe God orchestrates faith anyway. The only ones who will believe are those God has chosen to believe. But for those who think God makes it possible for humans to choose or not choose him, this approach is more problematic. Barth and the radically orthodox give the unconvinced no basis to adopt a Christian understanding. For them, it is largely irrelevant whether Christianity seems to make sense to anyone except those to whom God makes it make sense.

In the end, if the claims of Christianity are not basically reasonable, if they do not at least generally fit the data of the world, we wonder what sense it makes to say it is a religion of truth. We are not suggesting that "the evidence *demands* a verdict" or that faith is provable—not at all. We are suggesting that it would make little sense to say God is a God of truth if Christianity did not fit the data in at least some general way. Our normal thought processes get us through life well most of the time. What would it say if they did not work when it came to our Christian beliefs?

Any interpretation of the world involves (1) faith that the world exists

It would make little sense to say God is a God of truth if Christianity did not fit the data in at least a general way.

and (2) a recognition that our interpretations of the world are exactly that—interpretations from a point of view that is not exactly God's point of view. God knows all the data of the world, and God knows it all in proper relation to all the other data of the world. By contrast, we know the smallest, infinitesimal portion of the data, and we know it in only the most partial of relationships to the other data. A little reflection on these last two sentences should be humbling to all of us, including textbook writers. How strange it is for us to think how little we know in relation to what can be known.

At the same time, given the current lay of evidence at any given time, there would seem to be better and worse interpretations of reality. If we return to the three tests for truth we mentioned way back in chapter 3, a *better* interpretation is one that (1) relates well to the data we have (correspondence), (2) is logical and does not contradict itself (coherency), and (3) works well in the "real" world, the world in which we live and operate (pragmatic). From these basic tests, we can suggest reasonable criteria for distinguishing between more and less likely interpretations of evidence, given whatever evidence we have.

First, *the more data, the more evidence, we have, the more certainty we can afford the hypothesis or theory.* The social sciences speak of having enough data to constitute a "valid sample." You cannot really say that a certain pattern applies to millions of people if you have seen the pattern only in ten.

True, it is difficult to speak of "data-in-itself," of evidence that does not already involve interpretation. In his book *Beyond Good and Evil,* Friedrich Nietzsche, the famous skeptic, once suggested that "there are no facts, only interpretations." There does seem to be some truth to this idea. Nevertheless, by *evidence* we simply mean the most basic of things, like an object with a certain apparent size and shape, mass, etc. In historical research, we might be speaking of a primary text, a document that says such and such a thing in such and such a language. The Bible is also a text written in certain languages saying certain things.

Second, *the theory that accounts for the most data in the simplest or most "elegant" way is the better hypothesis or theory.* Again, it may well be that the more complicated theory is the right one. We cannot prove it isn't, and a person can believe in a less likely theory by faith and be rational. But the more of the picture that has to be drawn outside the "dots" of data we have, the less reliable the theory is, given the evidence we have. We can consider such a hypothesis a worse hypothesis on the basis of the evidence. We encountered this rule earlier in the chapter, Occam's razor. The simplest explanation for a set of evidence is the more likely explanation.

© Kevin L. Welch

Cuneiform tablets. Clay was softened and shaped, then, using a triangular shaped reed, the tablets were written on while still wet.

A Critical-Realist Hermeneutic

1. The more data, and the more data accounted for, the better the hypothesis.
2. The simplest and most elegant explanation is the better one.
3. A logically coherent hypothesis is better than an incoherent one.
4. A hypothesis that predicts future data while accounting for past data is much to be preferred.

Third, the rules of logic would seem to be as certain as anything we can know in the world. *A theory that does not contradict itself is a better theory than one that is logically inconsistent or incoherent.* The quantum world of physics has made it clear, however, that we must be careful even here. The various formulas of quantum mechanics do not fit with each other. They currently contradict and are not consistent with each other. In their cases, the rules of logic apply to a *part* of physics, but not to all of it. Thus we return to our suggestion at the beginning of the chapter: that even in science we are dealing more with *expressions* of reality than with explanations of the way the world actually is.

Finally, *a theory or hypothesis that seems to predict what will happen or account for what did happen is better than one that requires us to explain away past and future events that do not fit our theory.* In short, a better theory is one that seems to work in the unfolding of events, whether past or future. The more exceptions we have to account for, the less helpful the hypothesis. And as we saw in the previous section, such "naughty data" is the stuff of paradigm shifts.

When it comes to Christian faith, then, or even interpretations of the Bible, these rules would seem to apply. We can rationally believe in things that do not seem to fit the current lay of the evidence as best we can tell. After all, *all* of our beliefs, except the affirmation of existence itself, require varying degrees of faith. What is more important, we think, is that we are honest with the lay of the evidence.

8.5
CONCLUSION

We have become more and more aware in the last few decades that science is not purely objective. It has been very successful, mind you, at manipulating reality. The scientific method has been incredibly fruitful. You look at a set of data and formulate a hypothesis that accounts for some phenomenon as simply as possible without oversimplifying. You return to the data and test your hypothesis. You refine your hypothesis as necessary until it is dependable enough to be considered a workable theory, and the process continues. The scientific method has brought us the comfort of life that the modern world so much enjoys. We would be foolish to dismiss any scientific theory without really good reasons.

At the same time, science is about workable theories more than about reality itself. Science operates on the basis of paradigms, ways of looking at

© Kevin L. Welch

Ancient scroll of the Torah, the first five books of the Old Testament, written on vellum, animal skins.

the evidence and organizing it in our minds. These paradigms historically have changed over time. They influence what data scientists consider significant and where they look for it, confirming that science has a significant element of subjectivity in it. This chapter argued for a "critical realist" approach that affirms the reality of the world, but recognizes that our sense of it is always partial and usually skewed in ways of which we are never fully aware.

On the other end of the spectrum, myths were not some primitive, bad version of science. They were far more expressions of the mysterious than anything we would consider to be explanations today. And, in a sense, our scientific explanations today are also expressions of reality. It is only that they are far more precise and minute in the way they express the fundamental mysteries that they attempt to describe.

KEY TERMS

- negative theology
- Trinity
- scientific method
- hypothesis
- theory
- prejudice
- objective
- logical positivism
- paradigm
- normal science
- Darwinism
- paradigm shift
- Occam's razor
- geocentric
- heliocentric
- Gnosticism
- ex nihilo
- aseity
- omnipotence
- omniscience
- omnipresence
- omnibenevolence
- fundamentalism
- pantheism
- panentheism
- process theology
- evolution
- natural selection
- survival of the fittest
- microevolution
- macroevolution
- mutation
- neo-Darwinism
- scientific creationism
- intelligent design
- social Darwinism
- theistic evolution

KEY PHILOSOPHERS

- Francis Bacon
- Charles Darwin
- Michael Polanyi
- Karl Popper
- Thomas Kuhn
- Paul Feyerabend

PHILOSOPHICAL QUOTATIONS

- "Knowledge is power." (Bacon)
- "There are no facts, only interpretations." (Nietzsche)

KEY QUESTIONS

1. What is the author's definition of myth? In that light, do you agree or disagree that scientific theories are a kind of very detailed myth? Why or why not?

2. To what extent do you agree with Kuhn that science is as much about social movements and personalities as about truth? Explain.

3. Do you think a theory needs to be verifiable or falsifiable to be meaningful?

4. Do you think that evolution and Christianity are potentially compatible? Why or why not? What about process theology or pantheism? Why or why not? What do you think are the bottom-line Christian beliefs on the issues of creation? Explain.

5. Evaluate the author's proposal for a critical-realist hermeneutic. With what points do you agree or disagree and why?

NOTES

1. Jostein Gaarder, *Sophie's World*, trans. P. Møller (1991; repr. New York: Berkley Books, 1996), 25.

2. Paraphrased from the English translation, Ludwig Feuerbach, *The Essence of Christianity*, trans. G. Eliot (1841; repr., New York: Harper Torchbooks, 1957).

3. *Literal* refers to words being used in their ordinary sense. So to say that someone is "a dog" is not to use the word *dog* in its normal sense. To say that we cannot speak of God in literal terms is to say that our normal use of words is not adequate to describe him.

4. Jack Finegan, *Myth and Mystery: An Introduction to the Pagan Religions of the Biblical World* (Grand Rapids: Baker, 1997), 15.

5. We also have to be careful when we translate the Greek word *mythos* in the New Testament, because it can mean simply a story. Second Peter 1:16 uses the word to say that the Transfiguration was not a "cleverly devised *story*." First Timothy 1:4 and 4:7, as well as 2 Timothy 4:4 and Titus 1:14, refer to false stories, but they are not Greek but apparently Jewish stories of some kind.

6. Interestingly, string theory in nuclear physics is currently raising most of the issues covered in this chapter. It is thus far unverifiable and unfalsifiable. It is a beautiful assumption but not one to which scientists have been led because of evidence. Those who support it use their power to squelch those who disagree with their paradigm. See Lee Smolin, *The Trouble with Physics: The Rise of String Theory, the Fall of a Science, and What Comes Next?* (New York: Spin Networks, 2007).

7. G. K. Chesterton suggests something of this sort in his playful minibiography of Aquinas, *Saint Thomas Aquinas* (1933; repr, New York: Doubleday/Image, 1956), 45–73.

8. Francis Bacon, *New Organon.* Paraphrased from the nineteenth aphorism of the first book of Bacon's 1620 work in English.

9. Even in such a case, the kinds of questions one asks of this data may be "skewed" by your perspective.

10. Rudolf Carnap (1891–1970) and A. J. Ayer (1910–1989) are perhaps the two best-known positivists.

11. See Thomas Kuhn, *The Structure of Scientific Revolutions*, 3rd ed. (Chicago: University of Chicago, 1996).

12. "Creation science" here refers to those Christian scientists who argue for a relatively young earth with only a minimal amount of evolution around the level of individual species or orders.

13. We will mention this paradigm again later in the chapter. It is called catastrophism, the idea that the earth's geology is best explained on the basis of worldwide catastrophes, particularly a worldwide flood.

14. A paradigm we might call uniformitarianism. Certainly mainstream geology also would allow for major earth catastrophes as well. A common theory for why the dinosaurs went extinct involves a rather large asteroid hitting the earth and changing its climate.

15. We should point out that the Roman Catholic Church today actually has scientists on retainer and could not be described accurately as being against science. For example, Roman Catholic thinkers would more likely engage themselves with questions of how evolution might connect to Christian faith than with attempts to disprove evolution.

16. Ptolemaic here refers to the Greek astronomer Ptolemy (AD 90–168), who argued that the planets, sun, and moon moved in perfect circles around the earth.

17. The Seventh Day Adventist Church is a great example of a church formed around "naughty" verses. This church worships on Saturday because the Sabbath in the Bible always refers to Saturday. They have noticed verses in 1 Corinthians 15 and 1 Thessalonians 4 where Paul speaks of death as sleep and so do not believe we are conscious between death and resurrection.

NOTES

18. One famous Gnostic Christian around AD 150, Marcion, believed that the God of the Old Testament, since he was creator of the evil, material world, was an evil God and not the Father of Jesus Christ.
19. Christians ever since have generally heard the idea of creation out of nothing in biblical texts like Genesis 1:1–2 and Hebrews 11:3. Certainly some scholars disagree with this historical analysis and would argue that the idea of creation out of nothing was in fact the original meaning of Genesis 1:1–2. E.g., see Victor Hamilton, *Handbook on the Pentateuch* (Grand Rapids: Baker, 1982), 17–56.
20. As we will briefly discuss in chapter 10, the idea that God knows every *possible* outcome (in distinction from every actual outcome) is called "middle knowledge" or Molinism.
21. Process theology is not the same as open theism, although the two are often mistakenly equated. In process theology, God's nature changes. In open theism, God as an act of his will intentionally limits his knowledge so that humans can have free will.
22. E.g., Henry M. Morris, *Scientific Creationism* (Green Forest, AR: Master, 1974).
23. E.g., Michael J. Behe, William A. Dembski, and Stephen C. Meyer, *Science and Evidence for Design in the Universe* (San Francisco: Ignatius, 2000).
24. In addition to nn. 22–23, we might also mention Michael J. Behe, *Darwin's Black Box: The Biochemical Challenge to Evolution*, 2nd ed. (New York: Free, 2006). For the spectrum of positions Christians have taken on this issue, see Gregory Boyd and Paul Eddy, *Across the Spectrum: Understanding Issues in Evangelical Theology*, 2nd ed. (Grand Rapids: Baker Academic, 2009), 70–96.
25. E.g., Kenneth Miller, *Finding Darwin's God: A Scientist's Search for Common Ground between God and Evolution* (New York: Cliff Street, 1999).
26. See Mark Noll, *The Scandal of the Evangelical Mind* (Grand Rapids: Eerdmans, 1994), 189.
27. David Snoke, *A Biblical Case for an Old Earth* (Grand Rapids: Baker, 2006).
28. See n. 25. This solution of course then removes for us Augustine's "free will" explanation for worldwide evil and natural calamity. We would have no human parent on which to pin the "Fall." The recent work of Francis Collins is perhaps better known than Miller's. Francis Collins, *The Language of God: A Scientist Presents Evidence for Belief* (New York: Free, 2007).
29. Collins, *The Language of God*, 206–10.
30. Some have suggested that there is such a thing as preverbal apprehension of reality, a kind of blunt, brute knowledge of the world as it is in itself prior to human conceptualization (e.g., Arthur Schopenhaur [1788–1860]).

Unit 5

Philosophy of the Psyche:
Psychology

CHAPTER 9
WHAT IS A HUMAN BEING?

What to Get from This Chapter

- While we are much more than biological machines, we are biological machines like other animals.
- We inherit the majority of who we think we are from the categories of the cultures and subcultures to which we belong.
- Existentialists emphasize that we have to create our own identity; my body exists long before *I* truly exist.
- Descartes shifted the understanding of the soul radically, from a life principle to a distinct and autonomous center for the individual self, where thinking and the will are centered.
- Perhaps the best current Christian way to think of human beings is as being the image of God, intrinsically valuable.

Questions to Consider

- What is a human being?
- Where does meaning come from in life?
- What does it mean for a human being to be created in the image of God?

Key Words

- Culture
- Existence
- Essence
- Image of God

© shutterstock.com

9.1
A BIOLOGICAL MACHINE

Christians believe that a human being is *much more* than a biological machine. But we are nevertheless biological machines. We have bodies that work when they have the appropriate fuels in the appropriate environments. They break down, they need repairs, they cease to function altogether.

Ecclesiastes expresses somewhat pessimistically that humans "can see for themselves that they are no better than animals. For humans and animals both breathe the same air, and both die. So people have no real advantage over the animals. How meaningless! Both go to the same place—the dust from which they came and to which they must return" (3:18–20 NLT). In a different context, Paul contrasts the truly spiritual person from the "natural" person (1 Cor. 2:14), a word notoriously difficult to translate.[1] A literal translation might be a "soulish" person. A strong argument can be made that Paul here is alluding to the part of the human soul we share with the animal realm, while our spirits are different.[2] So you might say that some people are merely animal, not spiritual—even some Christians!

We need to be very careful not to take this language as God's literal view of the human makeup. The Bible expresses truths about human beings using more than one picture of how we mortals are put together, revealing truth in the categories of those to whom God was speaking at the time. As we will see in this chapter, the Old Testament does not use the word *soul* the same way that we do. The New Testament comes closer occasionally, but still with slightly different assumptions than we have. Those who try to break down the parts of the human psyche using biblical language inevitably end up with a very strange mixture indeed, made up of ancient language, contemporary psychology, and even some seventeenth-century philosophy![3]

Nevertheless, as long as we do not take the distinction between our animal part and our spiritual part too literally, the distinction is helpful.[4] We may share a great deal more with the animal world than many of us imagine. Certainly we all recognize that we need to eat, sleep, keep warm, and engage in other animalistic activities. **Abraham Maslow** (1908–1970) famously categorized human drives in terms of a "hierarchy of needs" in the form of a pyramid.[5] At the base of the pyramid were basic needs like breathing, food, water, sex, sleep, and excretion. If you do not have most of these things, you will die.

Self-actualization

Self-esteem and respect needs

Social and belonging needs

Safety and security needs

Physiological & body needs

But we share much more with the animal world than these basics. Maslow suggested that when our physiological needs are met, we will focus on higher "needs." For example, once we have food and our most basic bodily needs met, we might next focus on safety and security.[6] Then he placed our social needs—including our drive for love, belonging, and family—on the next-higher level. Once we feel safe in our environment, we focus on these social concerns. Above that level he placed our longing for self-esteem and respect. Finally, on the highest level, he placed something he called **self-actualization**, by which he meant reaching one's highest potential as an individual, to be all a particular individual can be. Maslow thought of self-actualization as something different for each person, something relative to who one is as an individual.

Subsequent psychology has picked apart the particulars of Maslow's theory, questioning such a fixed hierarchy in relation to some of these "needs." His idea of self-actualization also seems dubious, and Christians believe that regardless of what personal peace or fulfillment one might feel, God is the one who has determined *the* appropriate goals for human life. But Maslow does get us thinking about some of the basic longings and drives we as humans share with other animals. Certainly we share very similar physiological needs with other animals. Humans often seem little different from animals in their inability to control their sex drives.

The best-known vices and human sins show us to be slaves to our desires just as much as any other animal. For example, it would be hard to find an animal in the wild as prone to obesity as the American *Homo sapiens*. How many humans are able to rise above the herd mentality of so many species to treat groups other than their own fairly or view their own objectively? How many examples of attempted genocide has history left us? How many humans show mercy when they sense weakened prey on which to pounce? We are, in so many instances, little different from other predatory animals.

© istockphoto.com

We share other longings and drives with the animal kingdom. We have a drive for security, as other animals, and we can become vicious when cornered. On the other hand, anyone who has had a dog or cat recognizes that they, like humans, can recognize their belonging to a family and long for attention and affection. Some animals can even demonstrate a kind of selflessness and self-sacrifice that many humans would not offer under the same circumstances.

Most of us humans are easily manipulated and can be trained. We obviously try to train up our children in the way they should go (see Prov. 22:6). We "reinforce" positive behavior and often use a "punishment" model to discourage behavior we do not want. When we become adults, we often think we are free and no longer being trained, but most of us continue to be herded and "conditioned" by the media, politicians, and countless cultural forces and trends throughout our lives.

Some of the language of the previous paragraph comes from the work of the atheist **B. F. Skinner** (1904–1990), perhaps the most significant psychologist of the twentieth century. He is best known as the originator of a system of training or "conditioning" others—especially children—called **behavior modification**. While we strongly disagree with his assumption that humans are only highly evolved animals, it would be difficult to deny that you can steer the behavior of humans in very similar ways to how we might steer the behavior of other animals like rats and pigeons.

Skinner's terminology has made its way into popular language. When we talk about **positive reinforcement**, we are referring to the rewarding of a person or animal for an action or choice that we want them to do. **Negative reinforcement** is thus when one withholds or withdraws reward or something desired to discourage a particular choice or action.[7] Skinner notoriously used this method with success in relation to lower animals, and it usually works with human animals, unless one of the more unique features of humanity kicks in, namely, our ability to reflect on ourselves. If someone realizes he or she is being manipulated, that person will normally stop cooperating with the manipulator.[8]

It is clear that many parts of the human brain perform similarly to the brains of other animals. For example, the brains of lower animals are basically like our brain stem, which keeps us alive by controlling functions such as breathing or body temperature without our even thinking about it. The more complex the animal, the more similarity between their brains and ours. Thus reptiles have not only a brain stem, but also a cerebellum like ours that helps regulate movement and balance.

Then mammals like ourselves have a neocortex similar to ours in the cerebrum, the outer part of our brains. Theirs are not as developed as ours, but they share certain features. At the core of the human cerebrum is the limbic system, where basic emotions such as fear and aggression seem to originate. We share these basic structures with other mammals, and it seems that we share many of the same basic drives associated with them.

Behavior modification: the shaping of behavior by associating reward or withholding of reward with certain choices (also called "operant conditioning").

Positive reinforcement: incentive for certain behaviors by connecting them with reward or positive consequences.

Negative reinforcement: the demotivation of certain behavior by withholding or withdrawing reward or desired consequences.

primary sensory area
primary motor area
secondary motor and sensory area
anterior speech area
(Broca's area)
posterior speech area
(Wernicke's area)
secondary
visual area
primary auditory area
primary visual area
secondary auditory area

Diagram of the lateral view of the human brain, showing the functional areas (motor, sensory, auditory, visual, and speech). / Encyclopaedia Britannica / UIG / The Bridgeman Art Library

Our brains are unique in the outermost parts of our brain, the parts that seem to be able to control and moderate our aggression and emotion—in other words, our reasoning parts.

Certainly as Christians we believe that humans are much more than biological machines. But we are biological machines as well, perhaps far more than most people realize. There are locations in our brains involved in everything from our memories to our personalities to our spiritual experiences. Change the structure of our brains, and we become different people—fundamentally different! Having said that, as Christians we believe that a "spiritual" realm exists in addition to the merely "physical," even if we cannot say exactly what these words are *literally* referring to. Nevertheless, we believe they refer to something real that makes us much more than animal.

9.2
SOCIALLY CONSTRUCTED IDENTITY

Open air market in Old Jerusalem.

We are often unaware of the degree to which we are different from other individuals until we really get to know someone different from us. In the meantime, we might assume that other personalities are inferior or deficient simply because they are not like ours. We might assume that someone who does not plan out his or her future in detail is irresponsible or, vice versa, that someone who plans things out in detail is boring and inflexible. The truth is that both personalities have their strengths and weaknesses, and neither should look down on the other.

What is true of individuals is also true of culture. Cultures as a whole can take on personalities, although we must always be careful not to stereotype or prejudge an individual's identity or probable behavior simply because of where he or she is from. Having said that, cultures usually do have different norms, ideas, and practices. And you often cannot see the idiosyncrasies of your own culture until you live awhile in another and can see your own as if you were looking in from the outside.

One of the benefits of intercultural experience is to realize that most of these differences are not a matter of right or wrong; cultures are just different from each other. This realization is especially important when it comes to reading the Bible. Do Christian women today need to veil their heads when they pray or prophesy in worship (1 Cor. 11:5)? Do Christians need to abstain from pork (Lev. 11:7)? Must the husband be the head of the household in the twenty-first-century United States (Eph. 5:23–24)? These are all issues raised by instructions given in various books of the Bible, instructions that were very relevant to the cultural situations of their day. At the same time, they all seem far removed from contemporary Western culture. So do they still apply?

Our identity, thinking, and behavior as human beings are far more "socially constructed" than we might at first imagine. One of the ground-breaking books of this dimension of human existence was Peter Berger and Thomas Luckman's *The Social Construction of Reality*, in which they write, "to be given an identity involves being assigned a specific place in the world."[9] One grows up with experiences of how one is treated by parents and others, and eventually one makes general assumptions about how "everyone" should act and be treated. This becomes a part of our sense of who we are—the "internalization of society as such and of the objective reality established therein, and, at the same time, the subjective establishment of a coherent and continuous identity."[10]

We thus absorb much of our understanding of what a human being is from our environment growing up. These understandings are some of the most basic ways we think about ourselves and others around us—and some of the elements of our thinking about which we tend to be most unreflective. In the West, for example, children are often raised to be individualists who can sharply distinguish themselves from their families and their starting point in life. We often think of ourselves as free to determine who we are, whom we marry, and what we want to be.

But this understanding does not seem to be the default way in which most human beings think about themselves. The majority of cultures, both past and present, have not tended to think of themselves in this way. The West cherishes the freedom of individuals to determine their own identity and to have individual influence on society at large. But historically in most cultures individuals have valued remaining true to one's inherited identity and societal structure, with certain select individuals destined to lead the vast majority of "lessers." The contrast between these two perspectives—both largely unreflected upon—has been particularly evident when the West has tried to "help" other cultures in the area of freedom and democracy without clearly taking the distinctions into full account.

The distinction also comes into play for Western Christians when we read the books of the Bible, which were written in what are sometimes called **collectivist cultures**, cultures in which a person's identity is primarily embedded in the groups to which that person belongs, particularly race, family, and gender.[11] Westerners will tend to read simple words like *I* and *you* with all the assumptions they make when they use these words in reference to

Collectivist culture: culture in which your identity is largely a function of the groups to which you belong, especially family, ethnicity, and gender.

Individualist culture: culture in which individuals largely determine their own identity apart from their inherited status, ethnicity, or gender.

themselves and others as individuals. We live in an **individualist culture**. But many of these assumptions will not hold true for what biblical authors and audiences were thinking.

In collectivist or *group* cultures, individuals have more what is called dyadic personality. A person defines him- or herself primarily in terms of external relationships and the perceptions of others rather than by personal self-identification. Men are a certain way, and women are another. Jews are one way, and Greeks are another. Wealthy people are this way, and poor people another.

In reality, as previously noted, people and people groups are much more complex than simple stereotypes. But most human brains can differentiate things only by way of a relatively small number of distinctions. We inevitably learn things and process the world by categorizing things, by putting things into "boxes."[12] In group cultures, these boxes are relatively large and sanctioned by culture and "tribe." We tend to ignore the things that don't fit in our boxes—or label such people as deviant—while highlighting those things that fit with our preconceived categories. Such boxes thus have an inherent tendency to skew reality, despite the fact that we cannot think without them.[13]

The biblical texts are filled with reflections of the group orientation of their authors and audiences. Christians affirm Israel as God's chosen people in the Old Testament, and yet the relationship God has with Israel has a number of characteristics that fit with the way other ancient peoples understood their relationship with their chief god. For example, the most likely original wording of Deuteronomy 32:8 pictures Israel's God as "God Most High" who is assigning the lesser gods to the other nations of the world.[14] Different peoples had different gods as their special patrons. Their gods were part of their identity, went to war with them, and so forth.

The fact that the Egyptians detested shepherds who herded sheep (Gen. 46:34) suggests that ways of life and the foods that went along with them could be part of ethnic distinction in the ancient world. In that sense, eating lamb can distinguish one people from another that eats pork. It is quite possible that the Old Testament prohibition against pork was as much a matter of ethnic identity as anything else, despite the common claim that it had to do with health issues.[15] The surrounding Philistines, Moabites, and Ammonites ate pork; Israelites in the central plain did not. Because gods were part of this identity, to eat pork was indirectly to associate with the gods of the surrounding peoples. When the Prodigal Son of Luke 15 finds himself feeding pigs, a Jewish audience would have immediately recognized that he had left Israel and, by implication, Israel's God.

© Kevin L. Welch

The New Testament also reflects group-embedded identity, although much of it undermines traditional groupings. Titus reinforces the stereotype that "Cretans are always liars, evil brutes, lazy gluttons" (1:12 NIV). Today we would want to emphasize that every individual from a place like Crete should be allowed to determine by personal actions whether he or she is a liar. We would call such a statement prejudicial. But it is typical of collectivist, us/them, thinking.

The household codes of Ephesians 5–6, Colossians 3–4, and 1 Peter 2–3 largely embody stereotypically ancient roles for men and women, slaves and free, parents and children. Passages like Galatians 3:28 are far more distinctive and unique in the ancient world: "There is neither Jew nor Greek, slave nor free, male nor female" (NIV). Of course the ancient world also allowed for "deviants." Aristotle, for example, can speak of certain women who are a "departure from nature" in their fitness to lead others.[16] Again, today in the Western world we would recognize that such boxes are as much a matter of culture as of nature and would argue that an individual should be defined by his or her actions and intentions rather than by presuppositions of how someone will act or think because of the groups to which that person belongs.

A group culture is oriented around external honor and shame more than internal guilt for violating one's own values. Westerners tend not to notice biblical statements like "I am not ashamed of the gospel" (Rom. 1:16), Jesus scorning the *shame* of the cross (Heb. 12:2), God crowning humanity with *glory* and *honor* (Ps. 8:5), or sexual relations with an aunt serving to uncover the "nakedness" of an uncle (Lev. 18:14). Even the "blesseds" of the Beatitudes in Matthew 5 are about receiving honor from God despite the shame or apparent foolishness of earthly peacemaking or poverty. We have changed the meaning when we read them in terms of individual happiness.

So what is a human person, as far as most of the world in most times and most places throughout history is concerned? The predominant answer has been that there are different types of people depending on their grouping—their social location. Ancient Jews divided the world into Jews and non-Jews (Rom. 1:16). Greeks divided the world into Greeks and barbarians (Rom. 1:14). There are slaves and free individuals. There are men and women. There are the rich and everyone else. We would argue that the default understanding of the human person,

© Kevin L. Welch

The Western Wall, also known as the "Wailing Wall," is the only portion of Herod's Temple complex still standing.

insofar as how people understand people, has historically been to define them externally in terms of the key groups to which they belong.

That is not to say, however, that we do not find expressions of common or universal personhood, especially in wisdom or proverbial literature.

> All people are like grass
>   and all their faithfulness is like the flowers of the field.
> The grass withers and the flowers fall,
>   because the breath of the LORD blows on them.

Isaiah 40:6–7 NIV

Or consider the words of Confucius: "Man is born for uprightness. If a man lose his uprightness and yet live, his escape from death is mere good fortune." Yet even in the ancient proverbial wisdom, we generally find people divided up into types, say, the "righteous" and the "wicked," with little sense of the possibility for someone to change from one to another or little allowance for mixture.

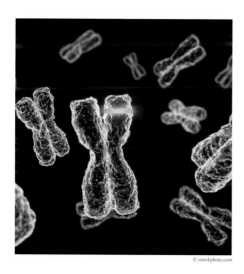

© istockphoto.com

9.3
EXISTENTIALISM AND IDENTITY

Friedrich Nietzsche (1844–1900), one of the best-known atheists and skeptics of the 1800s, is often quoted for his line, "God is dead."[17] But Nietzsche's point in saying this was not so much to argue for the nonexistence of God as to show what he thought the implications were.[18] The twentieth century saw a proliferation of atheism, and we may very well be witnessing a further decline in Christianity in North America already this century as well.[19] Many of those who adopt an atheist position do so with the same ignorance that Nietzsche himself talked about more than a hundred years ago. In that respect, Nietzsche is sometimes called a prophet of the twentieth century. Popular atheism failed to recognize the potentially disastrous consequences of what a world without God might look like, potentially justifying things like holocausts and world annihilation.

In his 1882 book *The Gay Science*, Nietzsche depicts a madman coming to a marketplace where a group of people seem to be celebrating the death of God. The madman tries to make them realize what they have done in killing God, but they are uninterested. He finally goes away. They just do not see what will follow. In particular, the madman claims that we will have to become like gods to be worthy of having killed God. What Nietzsche meant is fairly clear from his other writings, not least his novel *Thus Spoke Zarathustra*.

If God is dead, Nietzsche argued, then we are entirely responsible for who we are and what we do.[20] Echoing Fyodor Dostoevsky, who did believe in God, Nietzsche would write that if God does not exist, then "Nothing is true; everything is permissible."[21] Nietzsche thus developed his understanding of the "superman," the person who has a strong enough will to create him- or herself. As ordinary people, "men" need God to tell them who they are and what they can and cannot do. If God is dead, then "men" must either become "supermen" and create their own identities, or they must follow and obey those who do have such a "will to power."[22]

Nietzsche's philosophy thus stood at the end of a long deterioration of theism while also trying to find meaning in a meaningless world.[23] In chapter 7 we looked at some of the changes in Western culture that led from a world in which almost everyone believed that God existed and was actively involved in the world (theism) to the Enlightenment where many believed God had created the world but was no longer involved (deism) to a worldview in which everything could be explained on a purely natural and scientific basis (naturalism). Nietzsche effectively predicted that a world in which God does not exist to give meaning is a **nihilistic** world that lacks any intrinsic meaning or purpose. If God does not exist as a Guarantor of meaning and right and wrong, then everything is ultimately meaningless.

At the same time, Nietzsche anticipated a twentieth-century movement called **existentialism**. "Everything is meaningless" represents a glass-is-half-empty view. The corresponding glass-is-half-full view considers everything as equally meaning*ful*. If there is no real or intrinsic meaning to the world, then any meaning I adopt and make my own is just as meaningful as anything else. The existentialists of the mid-twentieth century thus taught that we create our own identities. We make ourselves what we are. An existentialist would say that we are whatever we will ourselves to be. A human person is a creator of identity, and identity is self-constructed.

Probably the best-known existentialists of the twentieth century are **Jean-Paul Sartre** (1905–1980) and **Albert Camus** (1913–1960; "Al-BEAR Ca-MOO"). Sartre keenly captures existentialism, particularly atheistic existentialism, in his motto "Existence precedes essence." **Existence** relates

Nihilism: the philosophical view that sees no intrinsic meaning to the world.

Existentialism: the philosophical view that sees meaning as self-created, created as a matter of individual human will and choice.

BIOGRAPHY

FAMOUS EXISTENTIALISTS

Søren Kierkegaard (1813–1855): The Danish Kierkegaard is sometimes retroactively called the "father of existentialism" for his focus on the centrality of human choices over ideas and the cognitive. He held that a "leap of faith," one that could not be based on reason, was essential for a life with meaning. Although he was a Christian who talked of this leap of faith in terms of Christian faith, the subjective nature of such leaps makes him the father both of theistic and atheistic existentialism. See chapter 2.

Photo Credit: Portrait of Soren Kierkegaard (1813–55) 1922 (engraving), German School (20th century) / Private Collection / The Bridgeman Art Library

Friedrich Nietzsche (1844–1900): Whether we consider the German Nietzsche a proper existentialist or not, he clearly laid the groundwork for the twentieth-century movement with this name. Atheistic existentialism starts with the inherent meaninglessness of things and argues that any meaning we impose on the world is as valid as anything else. Nietzsche is the starkest in his presentation of such nihilism, and he equally focuses on the human "will to power" as the human drive to force our choices to be the right ones. If we do not retroactively consider him an existentialist, we must certainly see him as its most important forerunner.

Photo Credit: Friedrich Wilhelm Nietzsche (1844–1900) 1873 (b/w photo), French Photographer (19th century) / Private Collection / The Bridgeman Art Library

Martin Heidegger (1886–1976): Although Heidegger (who at least initially supported Hitler) did not self-identify as an existentialist, he was a significant influence on Sartre and those who did. In *Being and Time*, Heidegger rejected Descartes's attempt to separate oneself as a thinker from the world one is thinking about. Rather, one is inseparable from the world, and one's fundamental existence is *Dasein* (being-in-the-world). Authentic existence is when in the midst of our caring deeply about our situation as part of the world we nonetheless make a decision to take responsibility for the situation into which we are thrown and resolutely shoulder our inherited burden.

Photo Credit: Martin Heidegger (1889–1976) (b/w photo), French School (20th century) / Archives Larousse, Paris, France / Giraudon / The Bridgeman Art Library

Rudolph Bultmann (1884–1976): The German Bultmann was perhaps the most influential New Testament scholar of the twentieth century, even if most scholars would today reject his best-known interpretations. On the other hand, many who are sympathetic to Christianity but who struggle with faith still find his existentialist agenda attractive. Bultmann famously did not believe that it was possible to "use electric light and the wireless . . . and at the same time believe in the New Testament world of spirits and miracles."[24] Instead, he believed that if we "demythologize" the New Testament, we would find that its core teaching is existentialist. Resurrection is the call to authentic existence in the face of death.

Jean-Paul Sartre (1905–1980): We might consider the French Sartre the true father of modern existentialism, particularly atheistic existentialism. As mentioned in this chapter, Sartre taught that "existence precedes essence," meaning that we have to come up with "what we are" (essence) long after our bodies are born (existence). According to Sartre, we are "condemned to be free." We have no choice but to choose who we are, but we are free to choose any "who we are." The classic treatment of his existentialism is his 1943 *Being and Nothingness*.

Photo Credit: Jean-Paul Sartre (1905–80), portrait from the notice board of his literature class at the Ecole Normale Superieure, 1924 (b/w photo), French Photographer (20th century) / Ecole Normale Superieure, Paris, France / Archives Charmet / The Bridgeman Art Library

BIOGRAPHY

FAMOUS EXISTENTIALISTS *(continued)*

Simone de Beauvoir (1908–1986):

In contrast to Sartre's difficult *Being and Nothingness*, Simone de Beauvoir's, *The Ethics of Ambiguity* is a much more readable presentation of French existentialism. She was Sartre's lifetime partner, and together they were activists for mid-twentieth-century socialist and communist causes. Her *The Second Sex* is a major piece of secular feminist literature and captured the spirit of existentialism well when she wrote that "one is not born, but rather becomes, a woman."

Albert Camus (1913–1960):

As mentioned in the chapter, the French Camus was known for the "theater of the absurd," a school of art that portrayed things we experience as very significant in insignificant ways. In *The Stranger*, for example, a series of casual decisions and accidental occurrences end in murder and subsequent capital punishment, a consequence Camus portrays as rather inconsequential. His essay "The Myth of Sisyphus" portrayed life like the fate of Sisyphus, who in Hades eternally pushes a boulder up a hill only for it to roll back down as he reaches the top. So Camus would have us believe that life is truly meaningless, but we nevertheless start each day all over again as an act of rebellion.

to whether or not we exist—*that* we are. By contrast, our **essence** is *what* we are. Our essential characteristics are the things that, if changed, would make us someone different. Sartre himself put it this way:

> What do we mean by saying that existence precedes essence? We mean that man [and woman] first of all exists, encounters himself, surges up in the world—and defines himself afterwards . . . Thus, there is no human nature, because there is no God to have a conception of it. Man simply is. Not that he is simply what he conceives himself to be, but he is what he wills, and as he conceives himself after already existing—as he wills to be after that leap towards existence. Man is nothing else but that which he makes of himself. That is the first principle of existentialism.
>
> **"Existence Is a Humanism"**[25]

Sartre was basically saying the same thing as Nietzsche. Humanity has no objective identity, no "what it really is" and no "what it should be." We are born; we come into existence. But *we* are the ones who have to decide what we are, what our essence will be. "Man [sic] is condemned to be free.

Condemned, because he did not create himself, yet is nevertheless at liberty, and from the moment that he is thrown into this world he is responsible for everything he does."[26] For Sartre, therefore, none of us has a destiny. We have to determine who we are.

At the same time, it does not matter to the atheistic existentialist what we choose to be. One identity is as legitimate as any other. Albert Camus is known for saying, "There is but one truly serious philosophical problem, and that is suicide."[27] Behind this comment was the idea that life itself has no objective meaning. It does not matter whether we live or die. Camus wrote a number of dramas in the genre of the **theater of the absurd**. In novels like *The Stranger*, he portrayed matters of life and death as taking place by pure chance and happenstance, and matters we experience as incredibly serious he treated casually and as insignificant. In effect he was saying that things we might consider absurd are really no different from things we consider significant.

For Camus, any reason we find to live, to go on, becomes valid. Why have you not committed suicide? Any reason you have to live is as legitimate as it is absurd. Go with it. Do you love to help the needy and liberate the oppressed? Wonderful! You have found a reason to live. Do you love collecting rocks or stamps or repeatedly seeing how many times you can hop on one leg? Great! Go for it. You have found a reason to live.

While we might most associate existentialism with atheism, we can also speak of a certain Christian existentialism. Indeed, **Søren Kierkegaard** (1813–1855), whom we have met before, has as much claim to be the founder of existentialism as anyone else. As we saw in chapter 2, Kierkegaard is the one who promoted a "leap of faith" or "blind faith." For him, we cannot find any compelling rational basis for our faith. Therefore, our faith is a matter of our choice. We take a leap of faith into Christian faith. The problem with Kierkegaard's approach is that it gives us no compelling reason not to jump just as well into Hinduism or Islam or atheism.

Nevertheless, some of the imagery of existentialism can fit with certain forms of Christianity. Existentialism emphasizes the importance of identity as a matter of individual choice. While Christians do not believe the nature of this identity is a free-for-all or a matter of individual determination, many Christians do believe that a person can be "born again" as a new person, a new creation by a choice for Christ. The New Testament itself uses the imagery of moving from death to life (e.g., 1 John 3:14). Thus many Christians might say that we take on our true identity when we make a choice to have faith.[28]

> A man [or woman] can live with any *how*, if he has a *why*.
>
> **Victor Frankl**

> One is not born a woman, but becomes one.
>
> **Simone de Beauvoir**

> Every man [or woman] is born as many men and dies as a single one.
>
> **Martin Heidegger**

Existence: that something is.

Essence: what something is.

Theater of the absurd: dramas of the mid-twentieth century that were meant to portray the meaninglessness and irrationality of human existence.

9.4
A Soul in a Body

© istockphoto.com

When Christians affirm what is known as the Apostles' Creed, we confess our belief in the "forgiveness of sins, the resurrection of the body, and the life everlasting." Popular Christianity often misses the meaning of Christian faith in "the resurrection of the body." It is an affirmation that, one day in the future, God will transform our dead corpses (or whatever is left of them) into new bodies, and we will come back from the dead, possibly on an equally transformed earth. The "resurrection of the body" is thus something distinct from the "immortality of the soul"; the two ideas do not necessarily contradict each other. The idea that "you die and go to heaven or hell" is thus slightly different from what most Christians in the past have believed. Most Christians in history have traditionally believed that one dies and goes to a place of reward or torment *to wait* for the final resurrection and judgment, *after which* one will go to eternal life or condemnation.

So where does the idea of the soul come in? We do find some language in the New Testament that may relate to "disembodied" existence between our deaths and our resurrections—whether for eternal life or death. But we ironically find very little language in the Bible that speaks of "souls" in this way. The idea that we have a detachable soul, which comes into existence at our conception (from the creation?) and continues to exist forever arguably came into Christian tradition as much from the influence of Greek philosophy as from the Bible itself.[29]

Most Christians throughout the centuries have believed that we have immortal souls and that we will one day receive resurrection bodies. When the vast majority of Christians have believed something for so long, we should be cautious about drawing a different conclusion. Those of us who are Protestants have room for "reformation," particularly when the tide seems to have deviated from the founding principles and practices of earliest Christianity. But some extrabiblical developments from New Testament times seem like appropriate extensions or refinements of first principles and practices, even clarifications of tensions or ambiguities within the earliest church. So we can neither dismiss out of hand historic elements of Christianity nor dismiss the possibility of reformation or development.

At the same time, we human beings cannot remove our thinking completely from the categories of our times and places. Maybe our idea of the soul itself is not as important as our faith that we continue to exist after death. True, the idea of the soul is helpful to explain other things. For example, it might provide explanations for our individual identity and even our free will. For some, it might provide an argument against abortion. After all, an embryo has no blood or breath—the biblical images of life. It has no nerves to feel pain; it has no thought. Some might suggest that it is wrong to destroy an embryo because it has a soul. But if we could argue for personal identity, free will, and sanctity of life in other ways, would that not be equally acceptable? Is it essential to believe in a detachable soul or a particular version of human psychology if one still believes the things for which the soul stands?

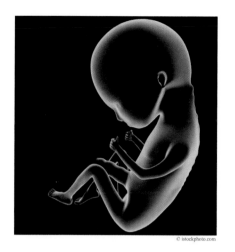

© istockphoto.com

At the time of Christ, most people in the Roman world did not believe in a meaningful, personal afterlife for individuals. If the acronym RIP is somewhat well known today ("rest in peace"), a common Roman epitaph translates as "I was not. I was. I am not. I care not." When we read the ancient Greek epics of Homer and the Latin *Aeneid*, we primarily find an underworld where shadows wander mindlessly, lacking the flesh and blood necessary for them to have much of a meaningful or thoughtful existence.[30] This is presumably the same sense of the afterlife we find in the Old Testament when we find statements like:

> But when people die, their strength is gone.
>> They breathe their last, and then where are they? . . .
> people are laid to rest and do not rise again.
>> Until the heavens are no more, they will not wake up
>> nor be roused from their sleep . . .
> They never know if their children grow up in honor
>> or sink to insignificance.

Job 14:10, 12, 21 NLT

And yet even in Homer's *Iliad* we find hints of a place among the dead for very special people, the Elysian Fields.[31] The idea that the dead might return to the living in some way seems to have emerged in the 500s BC.[32] One of the oldest-known Greek philosophers to think something of this sort was **Pythagoras** (ca. 520 BC), who is best known for his theorem in geometry.[33] He believed in a form of reincarnation. A famous anecdote tells that "once when he passed a dog being mistreated, Pythagoras pitied the animal and told the person, 'Stop! Don't beat him! He is the soul of a friend I recognized immediately when I heard his voice.'"[34]

A little over a century later, Plato also held to this **transmigration of the soul**. For Plato, a fixed number of souls were in existence, and they made their ways into various human bodies. While Plato did not think the body was evil, he thought of it as a "prison house" or tomb of the soul, from which the soul was freed at death.[35] At death we drink from the river of forgetfulness (Lethe), and eventually our souls return to enter different bodies of various animals.

For most Greek thinkers, the soul was not completely distinguishable from the more animal part of a person, particularly whatever life force keeps us alive. For example, **Democritus** (ca. 460–ca. 370 BC) taught that a person's soul was made up of "soul atoms" that disintegrated with the body at death. He thus believed in a soul, *but he did not believe in an afterlife*! The soul was simply that which gave your body life, and it dissolved at death like the rest of you. It was material that after death blended back into the elements of the world just like skin or hair.

Democritus highlights a very important realization: just because the Bible or some other ancient source uses a word similar to one we use, this does not mean it had the same meaning.[36] Indeed, the Old Testament in particular *never* uses its word for *soul* (*nephesh*) in the sense we do. *Soul* in Hebrew never refers to a detachable part of us. It refers to a living being in its entirety, both body and breath of life within it. So Adam becomes a "living soul" when God breathes into the dust (Gen. 2:7).

In fact, Genesis uses the same word for "living souls" of sea creatures (Gen. 1:20) as it does for Adam becoming a living soul. And even though the Old Testament speaks of the breath (*ruach*) inside living things, it never thinks of this spirit as the container of our personhood. It is simply the breath of life within us, and animals have the same breath we do (cf. Eccl. 3:19). In general, the Old Testament has little sense of a meaningful, personal afterlife. Indeed, scholars across the board can generally agree on only one Old Testament passage that actually refers to a meaningful life after death: Daniel 12:2–3.

The New Testament also can use the word *soul* in this way. First Peter 3:20 uses the Greek word for soul (*psyche*) when it speaks of "eight souls in all" being saved on the ark. Translations usually translate the word as "eight people" so we do not get confused. Jesus uses this word in Matthew 16:25 where he says that whoever "loses his *soul* will find it." English translations rightly translate the verse as "whoever loses his *life*." We cannot assume, therefore, that the word *soul* in our English translations of the New Testament always means the same thing as we do when we use the word *soul*. And when New Testament authors *do* use the word similarly to the way we do (e.g., Matt. 10:28), they may not have as much invested in the language as we do. I can talk of "being on cloud nine" without believing that clouds are numbered literally.

© istockphoto.com

Nevertheless, a number of New Testament authors do seem to use either *soul* or more often *spirit* in relation to a part inside us that is separable from the body. In 2 Corinthians 12:2–3 Paul is unsure whether he has had an "out-of-the-body" experience. In 1 Corinthians 15 Paul so strongly assumes that we will have a resurrection body that it is probably hard for him to imagine life without a body. But he seems at least open to the possibility in

2 Corinthians 12.[37] Philippians 1:23 also seems to imply continued existence at death in heaven in some way, prior to the resurrection (cf. Phil. 3:11). Revelation 6:9 speaks of the (disembodied) "souls" under the altar of heaven. These are individuals who were martyred, perhaps beheaded, while they were alive (Rev. 20:4). They apparently receive resurrection bodies and return to the living at the first resurrection (Rev. 20:6).

Because the Bible gives us varied pictures of human psychology and of the afterlife, we probably should not consider any of these pictures absolute. Clearly the New Testament teaches that believers will continue to exist in eternity, and several passages even point to continued existence immediately at death. The Gospel of Luke, for example, has its Parable of the Rich Man, who awakes in torment after death. His brothers are still alive, so he has not yet awakened after the resurrection.[38] He has not risen from the dead like Jesus, for Abraham denies him that option (Luke 16:31). He is thus conscious in an "intermediate state" between death and resurrection. But the rich man does not apparently have a resurrection body—a body that Luke pictures having flesh and bones (cf. Luke 24:39). We should probably infer the same state for Jesus and the thief on the cross between their deaths and resurrection (cf. Luke 23:43).

These are pictures, put in the categories of the ancients so that the original audiences of these texts could understand them. The books of the Bible give us differing images of human makeup and the particulars of the afterlife. These things relate to another world, another dimension, another universe. And just as Christians generally have not speculated much about what God is made of in his substance, what "Spirit" really is, probably we should sit loosely to our language of *soul* and *spirit* more as pictures and metaphors than as literally something(s) we could understand on this side of death.

Our current understanding of the soul has as much to do with **René Descartes**, the father of modern philosophy, as with the Bible or historic Christianity. Prior to Descartes the soul was principally the seat of *life*, the life force. After Descartes the soul principally becomes the center of our *thinking*. The soul becomes the part of me where my "I" most truly resides. It becomes like a little escape pod with the real me in it, the part of me that detaches from my body at death and survives with my personality and memories intact. The shift was so profound that it is sometimes likened to Copernicus's claim that the earth goes around the sun, rather than the other way around, a "Copernican revolution" in the way we think of ourselves.

The Rich Man in Hell, illustration for 'The Life of Christ', ca. 1886-94 (w/c & gouache on paperboard), Tissot, James Jacques Joseph (1836-1902) / Brooklyn Museum of Art, New York, USA / The Bridgeman Art Library

We mentioned in chapter 7 that people in the 1600s increasingly viewed the world as a machine that ran on its own according to natural laws. Before this time people often saw the spiritual world as a material world like the physical world—the difference being that it was made up of much thinner material like ether or fire. So Descartes practically invented the distinction between the natural and the *super*natural when he wrote the following:

> I am talking about "nature" in a narrower sense than when it means the total of everything God has given me. In that meaning, nature includes things that only have to do with the mind alone … (and I am not including those things when I use the word *nature*).

René Descartes, *Meditations* 6[39]

Nature for him did not include the things of the mind or the soul, only the "narrower" sense of the machine of the world, governed by laws God had built into the world. The supernatural thus referred not to these sorts of *material* things but to *immaterial* things like God, angels, and the soul.

The core elements of Descartes's understanding of the soul may look familiar to us, even though they are largely foreign to the Bible. For him the soul is the part of me that is truly me, the part that thinks, has my personality, holds my memories, and survives death. Other aspects of Descartes's view will seem a little more bizarre. For example, he thought the soul largely engaged the body at the small pineal gland in the brain.

However, as our understanding of the brain has advanced, we have found a physical basis for every element in Descartes's soul. As evidenced with Alzheimer's disease, for example, the physical ganglia of the brain is closely connected to memory. Tangle those neurons, and the memory goes away. Most psychology courses mention Phineas Gage (1823–1860) as an example of how closely related the front part of our brain is related to our personalities. Gage was apparently a hard-working and responsible individual prior to an accident in which a rod penetrated the front of his brain. Afterward, he was rude and profane, showing little self-control.

In other words, researchers can identify various parts of the brain involved in everything from emotions, to choices, to memories, to thinking, indeed to religious experiences. The fact that these parts of the brain affect such faculties does not necessarily mean that we do not have a soul. It is simply to say that it is not clear that we need to resort to a soul to explain these things. Further, we know that messing with the brain also messes with our thinking, feeling, choosing, and so forth. What role a soul might play in these functions is unclear.

© istockphoto.com

9.5
THE IMAGE OF GOD

Thus far in the chapter we have looked at the human person from four different angles. We started with those who have viewed us as biological machines. Certainly we are such machines, but it is not nearly the whole picture from a Christian perspective.

Then we looked at the extent to which human identity is socially constructed, that is, the degree to which we draw our identities from the social groups and contexts in which we grow up and live. Again, Christianity would historically see more to human existence than the mere constructs of particular societies. Further, Christianity's understanding of salvation sets us on a trajectory that tends to transcend visible social groupings and group-embedded identity. Since being a Jew or a Greek, a male or a female, a slave or a free person—or any visible indicator—cannot indicate that a person is part of the people of God (Gal. 3:28), the usual external indicators of identity become quite inadequate.[40]

The third angle was that of personal choice, existentialism. Existentialism focuses on the potential for each of us to create our own identity for ourselves, to make ourselves into anything we want to be. Again, while Christianity can certainly accommodate a view that sees individual choice as essential to becoming a Christian, historic Christians would not believe that *truly authentic* existence is something anyone can create from any or every chosen direction. We believe that there are right and wrong choices; no matter how much one might invest oneself in making choices, some choices are better than others.

Finally, we looked at the traditionally Christian view that we have souls or spirits within us that survive death. The idea that the soul is the primary container of our identities dates largely to Descartes. Still, Christians have long associated the soul or spirit with the part of us that survives death until the resurrection when we are reunited with a transformed body. In the previous section, however, we saw that much of what we think about the soul today is a modern innovation that is questionable from a number of angles, including that of the Bible itself.

In this final section, we want to think about humans as being made in the image of God and suggest that this view is the best way for Christians to think about human beings today. Yes, we are biological machines whose self-understanding derives significantly from our social context. Yes, a privilege of Western society in particular is the freedom to determine who we are in many more respects than afforded to people at other times and places. Yes, whatever the mechanism, we believe that all humans continue to exist at death and that we will eventually be re-embodied. But more basic than anything else, a human is a reflection of God. A human person is an image of God.

As with the soul, the idea of the image of God has shifted over the centuries. As Western culture after Descartes became more individualistic, so the image of God became increasingly understood as something inside of me as an individual.[41] This was a crucial shift. Prior to Descartes, the image of God was something *about me* that reflected the divine order of things. Humans reflect part of what God is. God is Ruler of the universe. So God created humanity as his image to rule the created order.[42] Other aspects of humans often thought to reflect characteristics of God and the order of the world were rationality and the potential for moral righteousness. Referring to Genesis 1:26–27—God creating man and woman in his image—John Wesley drew out an explanation:

> Not only in his *natural image*, a picture of his own immortality, a spiritual being, endued with understanding, freedom of will, and various emotions. Not merely in his *political image*, the governor of this lower world, having "authority over the fishes of the sea, and over all the earth." But primarily in his *moral image*, which, according to the Apostle, is "righteousness and true holiness."
>
> **John Wesley, "The New Birth"**[43]

Reformers from the time of Martin Luther increasingly looked at the image of God as something almost completely destroyed by Adam's sin in the Garden of Eden.[44] It became something we largely do not have in the present but that Adam and Eve had in the past. Reformers focused primarily on the "moral" image as something completely lost in the Fall of humanity. Yet another view, now popular in some circles, focuses on the image of God as something greater than anything Adam and Eve had in the past but that we are destined to have in the future, at the time when God restores all things.

All of these views go well beyond anything in the Bible. Genesis is not very specific as to what the image of God in humanity might be, although

BIOGRAPHY

RENÉ DESCARTES

René Descartes (1596–1650; "day-CART") is rightly considered the father of modern philosophy. He also had a massive impact on mathematics, inventing the Cartesian coordinate system of x's and y's that every high school student learns. He was a devout Roman Catholic, although the church of his day condemned his physics and philosophy. He was French but did most of his work in the Netherlands, most importantly a work called *Discourse on Method*. At the time of his death he was a tutor to Queen Christina of Sweden.

All philosophers to some extent give expression to the struggles and spirit (zeitgeist) of their time. The most famous thinkers are those whose expressions and solutions most resonate with their age or some later one. That to which Descartes gave expression was a sense of uncertainty and a thirst for something solid and true. The Protestant Reformation and the Renaissance had generally eroded the assumptions of a thousand years; in particular, that the things Christians had heard and believed through the Catholic Church were correct. Those who were convinced that charismatic leaders such as Martin Luther, John Calvin, or Huldrych Zwingli had correctly interpreted the Bible might switch the source of their certainty. But what had been an unquestioned assumption (Christian belief is self-evident and universally agreed) now had to be argued for.

The beginnings of the scientific revolution would become yet another source of questioning assumptions. In chapter 8 we discussed Francis Bacon (1561–1626) and his attempts to place the quest for knowledge on an experimental basis. One gathers evidence and tabulates the data, eventually drawing the conclusion that best fits the evidence. Again, he represents a move from assumption of truth to the need to justify it.

In this context, Descartes begins to look for a place of absolute certainty from which to establish a firm basis for truth. Unlike Bacon, he is a rationalist (see chap. 4). He searches for truth first in reason. He questions everything he can question and finds he can doubt everything except for the fact that he is doubting. His conclusion is *cogito ergo sum*, "I think; therefore, I am." From this point of certainty, he then proceeds to try to reconstruct certainty on all the things people of his day took for granted, including the existence of God.

Despite how certain Descartes himself might be of his conclusions, he sowed a doubt that had not been there before, much as the Reformation did. All the ordinary truths about the world—that I am really sitting somewhere reading this book—now have a question mark over them. He creates a new sort of human identity. "I" am the most certain thing I can know, and the rest of the world is the object of my knowledge. I may still believe in God, but it is *I* who is doing the deciding and believing. The order of the world, all the truths that I had once assumed without question, are now truth claims that *I* am forced to make decisions about. Even faith becomes an inevitable choice *I* have to make as an individual, instead of an assumption. The shift seems inevitable. I can still believe everything I believed before about God, faith, and the world, and I can believe them ferociously. But I am now keenly aware that *I* am the one doing the believing.

The impact of this shift—this turn of focus of truth from something "out there" inherent in the world to something I have to make judgments on inside my head—has been massive. This sense of a human individual as a rational being who makes decisions about what is true eventually empowered everything from the scientific revolution to the birth of capitalism to the notion of social contracts between individuals, the basis for the U.S. system of government. Descartes

BIOGRAPHY

René Descartes *(continued)*

inadvertently gave birth to the "autonomous individual," a sense of a human person as someone who can make objective decisions about the quite distinct world outside of oneself.

Descartes's sense of nature and of the soul fit hand in glove with his other ideas. He makes a sharp distinction between the natural world and the now *super*-natural world. Nature is no longer *everything* that God created but only the physical, material part of it. Descartes does not include in what he calls "nature" things of God, angels, or spirits, or things having to do with the mind. These now "immaterial" things are far more certain to him than what would become the world of science. He thus inadvertently prepares the way for deism, which sees the world as a machine God created but with which God no longer needs to be involved.

Descartes also shifts the soul from being the life principle of a person to being the immaterial container in which the self resides. It is where the "I" can think about the world in a detached and objective fashion. It is where the human will is located. It is the part of the person that survives death, like an escape pod.

The current climate is rather negative toward Descartes, and clearly we can point out any number of extremes in his thinking. Martin Heidegger (1886–1976), more than anyone, has shown that we cannot detach ourselves from the world around us. Almost everyone today would recognize the impossibility of complete objectivity. Nevertheless, we should not forget that most of the greatest cultural developments in the Western world these last few centuries can be traced back to Descartes more than to any other single individual.

in 1:27 it seems to relate to men and women governing the world. Indeed, Paul and others in the New Testament seemed to relate this position of honor in the creation to Psalm 8:4–8:

> What are human beings that you are mindful of them,
>   mortals that you care for them?
> Yet you have made them a little lower than God,
>   and crowned them with glory and honor.
> You have given them dominion over the works of your hands;
>   you have put all things under their feet,
> all sheep and oxen,
>   and also the beasts of the field,
> the birds of the air, and the fish of the sea,
>   whatever passes along the paths of the seas.

God has granted humans as his image a position of honor in the world that is a reflection of his own honor. In this view we see no sense of human rationality or even morality. We simply reflect God. The place God holds over everything is the place God has assigned humanity over the earth. Paul notes that a man should not cover his head when he prays because his head reflects God (1 Cor. 11:7); to see the honor of a man is to see the honor of God. Similarly, James says one should not harm an innocent human, because one would be harming the image of God (3:9). These are all pictures, but we can easily synthesize them into a Christian way of thinking about what we are as human beings created in the image of God.

First, even if one looked at humans only as biological machines, we are clearly the dominant beings on the planet, at least as far as we can see.[45] The idea that humans "rule" in the animal kingdom—even if we are poor rulers at times—seems beyond question. We hold a position of honor in the created order that reflects the role God has in relation to the entire creation. Part of that high position does include a higher rational and moral capacity than the rest of the creation, which reflects our sense of God as the perfect thinker and absolute standard of goodness. In this sense, Christian thinkers throughout the ages have fastened on legitimate aspects of what we are as humans, even if they read much more into the image of God than any biblical author was thinking.

Sculpture of Jesus reinstating Peter.

But perhaps what is more important for us today is to recognize that humanity in the image of God is implicitly valuable and meaningful. Prior to Descartes and the Reformation, the value of humanity as a whole was as a reflection of the very order of things, of the world. The value of an individual human might have been more connected to the social class to which the person was born. There was no sense of development. It was assumed that a person who turned out to be great must have always been great.

After Descartes, thinkers no longer assumed an intrinsic order to things. A person's choices might show that person to be great; a person might start from nowhere and rise to greatness. The late 1800s saw **Sigmund Freud** (1856–1939) and the birth of psychoanalysis, by which events in a person's childhood were viewed as formative influences that combined to make a person what he or she became. The nature/nurture controversy began: is what we are more a function of our genetics or the environment in which we grew up?

With this background, we can return to the thinking of the Christians of the ages by considering how *God* thinks of humanity. If humanity—if indeed all the creation—is important to God, then it becomes a moral offense to mess with any of God's "stuff" and especially with humanity, which Scripture has declared to be the image of God in a way that the rest of the creation is not. *God's* view of us makes us inherently valuable, despite the fact that we might *also* be biological machines that think and make moral choices.

9.6
CONCLUSION

What are human beings? Certainly we are biological machines. We are, at the very least, animals. But we are also much more than animals. We are able to make choices on a level no other animal can make. For this reason, we can both define ourselves more fully than any other creature—as well as consider our lives meaningless in a way other creatures cannot.

As Christians, however, we believe that God does not consider our individual lives to be meaningless. We believe that God has created us "in his image," with characteristics analogous to his own. We not only can think but we can make moral judgments. He has empowered us to make decisions for good, so that we are not simply doomed to do evil.

Most importantly, the fact that he loves every one of us means that we are all valuable. Woe to the person who harms another person. Such individuals are harming someone who is a reflection of God, someone valuable to God. For Christians, no one's life is meaningless.

KEY TERMS

- self-actualization
- behavior modification
- positive reinforcement
- negative reinforcement
- collectivist culture
- individualist culture
- nihilism
- existentialism
- Dasein
- existence
- essence
- theater of the absurd
- transmigration of soul

KEY PHILOSOPHERS

- Pythagoras
- Democritus
- René Descartes
- Sigmund Freud
- B. F. Skinner
- Abraham Maslow
- Søren Kierkegaard
- Friedrich Nietzsche
- Martin Heidegger
- Rudolph Bultmann
- Jean-Paul Sartre
- Simone de Beauvoir
- Albert Camus

PHILOSOPHICAL QUOTATIONS

- "God is dead; we have killed him." (Nietzsche)
- "Existence precedes essence." (Sartre)
- "Man is condemned to be free." (Sartre)
- "A man can live with any *how*, if he has a *why*." (Frankl)
- "One is not born a woman, but becomes one." (de Beauvoir)

KEY QUESTIONS

1. One theme in this chapter is the degree to which we can correlate thinking, emotions, the will, memory, personality, even spiritual experiences to particular regions of the brain. Alzheimer's disease and physical accidents can fundamentally change all of these faculties, showing a strong connection between our brains and these functions that since Descartes have often been attributed to the soul. In this light, what role do you think the soul might play in human personhood? Do you think belief in a detachable soul is an essential Christian belief? What do you believe about the resurrection of our bodies and how would you relate this event to the human soul?

2. What aspects of the way you think about yourself and others around you come from your cultural and family background? How distinct would you say your sense of yourself is from that of those around you? Take into consideration the fact that we can also create ourselves as a kind of "anti-self" to those around us; here our context is still creating us, only in reverse. What legitimate role, if any, might stereotyping or prejudging play in our sense of ourselves and others?

3. What do you make of existentialism? To what extent would you say this movement that emphasized choice influenced the spirit of the late twentieth century—or is existentialism itself a reflection of a broader zeitgeist? To what extent would you say that contemporary atheists are aware or unaware of the meaninglessness and nonexistence of moral norms that seem to follow logically from their position?

4. What do you make of the shifts that flowed inadvertently from Descartes's "Copernican revolution" in which he turned the focus of truth from "out there" to inside our heads? Do you think the impact of this inward turn can be avoided, once the issue of certainty is questioned? Do some research on the many voices out there that currently decry Descartes.

5. How do you think you would live, act, even vote differently if you took this as your fundamental conception of the human person: someone created in the image of God, a neighbor whom God expects you to honor, respect, and love, whether near or far?

NOTES

1. KJV: "natural"; NRSV: "unspiritual"; NIV 1984: "man without the Spirit"; NLT: "people who aren't Christians."
2. Thinking here of the Jewish interpreter/philosopher Philo who thought that the spirit was the "soul's soul" but that the rest of the soul was that which humanity had in common with the animals. (*Allegorical Laws* 1.11; *Who Is the Heir?* 55).
3. Namely, René Descartes's understanding of the soul.
4. Many scholars believe that Paul's language in 1 Corinthians 2 is using the language of his opponents. For a brief exploration of this passage in the light of Philo's writings, see my *A Brief Guide to Philo* (Louisville, KY: Westminster John Knox, 2005), 76–79.
5. Abraham Maslow, "A Theory of Human Motivation," *Psychological Review* 50, no. 4 (1943): 370–96.
6. Including security, employment, health, resources, morality, etc.
7. Not to be confused with punishment. Skinner believed that punishment trains a person to avoid punishment rather than to avoid a particular choice; he is well known for his opposition to corporal punishment. While it is possible he was more correct than wrong on many of these ideas in theory, many parents will likely conclude there is still a legitimate role for punishment to play as a deterrent to certain behaviors. We will discuss the question of punishment versus formation in chapter 12, "Living Together in Societies."
8. Unless, of course, the manipulator is using reverse psychology, and the goal is actually to get you to do the opposite of what he or she seems to be trying to get you to do.
9. Peter Berger and Thomas Luckman, *The Social Construction of Reality: A Treatise in the Sociology of Knowledge* (New York: Doubleday/Anchor, 1966), 132.
10. Ibid., 133.
11. See, e.g., Bruce J. Malina, *The New Testament World: Insights from Cultural Anthropology* (Louisville, KY: Westminster John Knox, 1993).
12. Cf. Jean Piaget's theory of learning.
13. See chapter 15 about postmodernism.
14. One of the Dead Sea Scrolls, written in Hebrew, has confirmed that the ancient Greek translation of Deuteronomy 32:8 was actually closer to the original Hebrew than the Hebrew texts we had prior to 1947. The Greek (and the Dead Sea Scroll) refers to God separating "the sons of men" . . . "according to the number of the sons of God" (NRSV). Later Hebrew and most English translations refer to the separation as being according to "the number of the sons of Israel." Ronald S. Hendel, "When the Sons of God Cavorted with the Daughters of Men," in Hershel Shanks, ed., *Understanding the Dead Sea Scrolls* (1992; repr., New York: Random House/Vintage, 1993), 170.
15. Cf., e.g., Israel Finkelstein and Neil Silberman, *The Bible Unearthed: Archaeology's New Vision of Ancient Israel and the Origin of Sacred Texts* (New York: Touchstone, 2002), 119–20. While Finkelstein is a minimalist who should be read very guardedly, he may be correct on this issue. We know that eating pork distinguished Israel from its ethnic neighbors, while the Holiness Codes of Leviticus say absolutely nothing about health in relation to the food laws.
16. Aristotle, *Politics* 1.1259b.
17. Nietzsche makes this statement both in *The Gay Science* (1882) and *Thus Spoke Zarathustra* (1883–1885).
18. That is to say, Nietzsche concluded early in his life that God did not exist. His writings were not arguments to advance the idea that God did not exist but rather his sense of what the implications of God's nonexistence were for morality and human identity.
19. A book to consult here is Philip Jenkins, *The Next Christendom: The Coming of Global Christendom*, 3rd ed. (Oxford: Oxford University, 2011).
20. Another key work of Nietzsche here is *Beyond Good and Evil* (1886).

NOTES

21. *Thus Spoke Zarathustra*, part 4, "The Shadow." Nietzsche and Dostoevsky apparently reached similar conclusions independently about what is true if God does not exist. However, Dostoevsky did so with faith that God actually did exist. His novel *Crime and Punishment* (1866) is an apt expression of his understanding.

22. It is generally argued that Nietzsche would not have thought of Hitler as such a "superman," even though Hitler himself did.

23. An interesting book that aims at tracing the philosophical deterioration of faith in God over the past few centuries is James Sire, *The Universe Next Door*, 5th ed. (Downers Grove, IL: InterVarsity, 2009).

24. Rudolph Bultmann, "The New Testament and Mythology," originally a 1941 lecture, later published and then translated into English as *The New Testament and Mythology and Other Basic Writings* (Minneapolis: Augsburg Fortress, 1984).

25. Jean-Paul Sartre, "Existence Is a Humanism," a lecture given in 1946. Paraphrased from *Existentialism from Dostoevsky to Sartre*, W. Kaufman, ed., trans. P. Mairet (New York: Meridian, 1956).

26. Ibid.

27. Albert Camus, *The Myth of Sisyphus and Other Essays* (New York: Vintage, 1991), 3.

28. The zeitgeist or spirit of the age has in fact often taken Christians too far. Historically Christianity has not believed that I can decide to have faith in my own power. Orthodox Christianity believes that it is only by God's gracious empowerment that anyone can make a choice for God.

29. The church father Origen (185–254) believed that God created all the souls of humankind when he made the world. He thus believed that our souls preexisted our conception. He also believed that, since all souls were good, all humans would be good after they were freed of their bodies. He is thus the earliest known Christian "universalist," someone who believes everyone will be saved in the end. For this reason he was posthumously excommunicated several centuries after his death.

30. In the *Odyssey*, e.g., Odysseus has to give blood to the "shade" of the prophet Tiresias so that he can think and speak to him.

31. E.g., *Odyssey* 4.561; cf. also Virgil's *Aeneid* 6.630, where many more of the dead will find delight.

32. Although it seems currently impossible to know exactly when it arose, many think that the idea of resurrection first arose in the Persian religion known as Zoroastrianism. The problem is that the Persian texts that have survived are all from much later than the Bible.

33. $a^2 + b^2 = c^2$.

34. Diogenes Laertius attributes this quote of Pythagoras to Xenophanes in his *Lives of the Philosophers* 8.36. This particular quotation is paraphrased from the collection of Xenophanes fragments (fragment 7) by J. H. Lesher, *Xenophanes of Colophon: Fragments* (Toronto: University of Toronto, 1992), 19.

35. E.g., Plato, *Cratylus* 400C.

36. For a fuller exploration of this topic, see Joel Green, *Body, Soul, and Human Life: The Nature of Humanity in the Bible* (Grand Rapids: Baker, 2008).

37. Some (but not most) scholars suggest that Paul underwent a development on his thinking on this subject. They suggest that Paul started in 1 Thessalonians 4 and 1 Corinthians 15 with a strong sense that we sleep until a point at the end of history when we are re-embodied as part of the resurrection. Then they suggest that he switched to see us being re-embodied immediately at death in 2 Corinthians 5. Perhaps the most famous exponent of this interpretation was F. F. Bruce, *Paul: Apostle of the Heart Set Free* (Grand Rapids: Eerdmans, 1977).

38. I have heard the ingenious suggestion that eternity is outside the time of our current universe and thus that the rich man could have been raised at the resurrection and still be

NOTES

"now" in relation to human time. He would thus be raised much later in regard to human time, but resurrected already in relation to otherworldly time. This suggestion is ingenious, but hardly something that the author of Luke would have been thinking.

39. Paraphrased from the English translation, *Meditations on the First Philosophy with Selections from the Objections and Replies*, trans. J. Cottingham (Cambridge: Cambridge University, 1986).

40. Although to be sure, visible Christianity soon developed its own set of visible indicators so that group-embedded identity has continued to dominate the history of Christianity as well, another indication that *Homo sapiens* is a herd animal.

41. In what follows I am highly dependent on Charles Taylor, *The Sources of the Self* (Cambridge, MA: Harvard University, 1989).

42. This would seem to be the primary sense of the image of God in Genesis 1:27.

43. Paraphrased from the original English of the sermon. See *The Works of John Wesley*, 3rd ed. (Peabody, MA: Hendrickson, 1986), 6:66.

44. The late Stanley Grenz spoke of a shift to a "relational" view of the image of God in the Reformation, followed by a more "dynamic" view as something God wants to restore in us at the time of Christ's return. See *Theology for the Community of God* (Grand Rapids: Eerdmans, 2000), 168–73.

45. Leaving the spiritual realm out of consideration for the moment.

CHAPTER 10
FREE OR FATED?

© istockphoto.com

10.1
WHAT IS FREE WILL?

On one level, the question of whether or not we are free is relatively easy to answer. No one physically forced me to get out of bed this morning. No one physically forces you to do the vast majority of the things you do. From this standpoint, you "freely" do most things. Even though someone is likely "motivating" you to read this book, no one is physically forcing you. You might flunk a course if you *choose* not to read, but you are still "free" not to read.

Having said that, there are many contexts in which people are forced in some manner to do things. Someone might physically force you to do something "against your will." Unfortunately history is full of rape, torture, and slavery. Even someone who accidentally bumps you in a hallway might push you somewhere you do not want to go.

What to Get from This Chapter

- Our desires, wills, and actions are far more determined than we might think they are.
- Determinists think that we cannot possibly act or choose differently than we do.
- Free-will libertarians think that our choices are not determined by the forces at work on us.
- Compatibilists believe that while our actions and choices are ultimately determined, we experience ourselves as freely choosing beings if we are free to act in accordance with what we want to do.
- Indeterminists commonly believe that events are random and unpredictable.
- The ancient and New Testament world was fatalistic.
- Calvinists and Arminians disagree on whether God's foreknowledge determines our choices.
- Regardless of the determinism or indeterminism of our wills, we experience our choices as free.

Questions to Consider

- To what extent are our lives free?
- Does God directly plan every detail that happens in the world?
- To what extent is the future uncertain?

Key Words

- Free will
- Determinism
- Calvinism
- Wesleyan-Arminian

We all also have various physical, intellectual, and social gifts and limitations. The vast majority of us are simply *not* "free" to run, swim, or play well enough to be in the Olympics. Most of us are not "free" to get A's on calculus tests or get elected president of the United States. The motto "You can do anything you put your mind to" is noble, inspiring, and patently false.

Drugs and alcohol also cause people to do things they would never do under normal circumstances. People who are drunk or high may not be "free" to stop themselves from saying or doing things they normally would not say or do. A person who is addicted to heroin might steal or even kill to get more, something he or she might not otherwise even think of doing. It is the very nature of addiction to limit or take away a person's freedom in certain ways.

Cultural and environmental conditioning also tend to enslave us to ways of thinking and behaving, usually without us realizing it. The term *generational poverty*, for example, is used to refer to a cycle of poverty where children and grandchildren know no other way of life. They might live off government welfare with no thought of ever aiming at something better. Such individuals may not be free to change, without outside intervention. They may not be free to get an education or a job, because their minds have been conditioned to a certain way of life over the course of generations. They might be surrounded by all sorts of job or educational opportunities and not be free to take them.

One of the difficulties of talking about **free will** is that different people mean different things by the expression. For some philosophers, free will means little more than the freedom *to act* according to your will. In this sense, free will basically means that I do not have anything keeping me from doing what I want to do. So no one is physically keeping me from doing it, and I am not impaired by drugs or some psychological disorder.

We might also distinguish between what we think of as *self* and what we think of as forces "outside" oneself. Free will would then be the freedom to do what your *self* wants to do regardless of the "outside" forces at work on you. Of course then we run into the question of what we mean by our "selves" and what we mean by "outside." My brain is at least a part of my mind, and some would say my mind is nothing more than my brain or that my mind is a projection of my brain. As we saw in the last chapter, despite one's perceptions, it is not entirely clear the extent to which one can distinguish one's "self" from one's physical brain!

How then could we neatly distinguish "outside" and "inside" forces? Clearly someone egging me on is an outside force. But is a tendency to be competitive, built into the very structure of my brain by genetics and/or upbringing, an inside or an outside force? Usually those who believe in free

© istockphoto.com

Generational poverty: a cycle of poverty passed on from generation to generation to the point that it becomes a conditioned way of life.

will allow that at least sometimes we are free to choose differently from the way our genetics or upbringing might drive us, in interaction with forces outside our bodies.

But some philosophers are even more radical in their belief in free will. They would argue that free will is the capacity to do something other than what you are being pushed to do by the sum total of all the forces involved in a decision. This more radical **libertarian** view of free will argues that you have the capacity to make choices undetermined by all the forces at work on you. It might be considered as the freedom to will what you want ex nihilo, as it were, "out of nothing." For example, someone might suggest that God can empower, or perhaps to some extent has empowered, the soul to create decisions out of nothing.

The fields of psychology and sociology have made it increasingly clear that our "will," our desires, are far more determined by various forces than we realize. The old nature/nurture debate highlights these forces. Do we become who we are more because of our genes or because of our upbringing? Many people go through their whole lives without realizing that they act in various ways because of the forces of their genetics or environment. In that sense, they may be free to act according to their wills. But they are not meaningfully free in these areas, since they are not even aware of the forces leading them to want what they want.

> **Free will (libertarian view):** the capacity to make choices undetermined by all the forces at work on you.
>
> **Free will (compatibilist view):** the capacity to make choices undetermined by forces perceived to be outside your "self."
>
> **Determinism (hard):** the idea that we cannot help but will and act the way we do.

We often underestimate the psychological and sociological forces at work on us. Those who are abused by their spouses are often "not free" to leave them. An outsider might look at her and think, "It's her own fault. She could leave him." But the research indicates otherwise. Her will may be so beat down that only intervention from the outside can rescue her.

Similarly, we have heard of instances where a child is kidnapped and raised by his or her kidnapper. Some become unsympathetic and suggest the child could have just walked away at some point. It is important to realize what can happen to a person's will when he or she has been abused, tortured, or brainwashed over time. Such individuals are often not free to want out of such situations. Those of us who live "normal" lives simply cannot imagine the impairment of will that comes from such conditions.

One of the benefits of studying philosophy, mentioned in chapter 1, is that philosophy can make a person freer. When individuals are aware of the forces at work on their wills—their cultures, their histories, the flow of ideas in which they find themselves—they are freer to choose something other than what they would otherwise choose without knowing why. The vast majority of humans are slaves of this sort; in theory such freedom is the primary objective of a liberal arts education.

But some would argue that such knowledge only moves the **determinism** to a different level. Determinism is the idea that we cannot help but will and act the way we do; if we knew all the elements in the equation, we could predict exactly how everything would unfold for the rest of our lives and, indeed, for the rest of the history of the universe. Determinists would say that we can become more aware of ourselves and various courses of action; even so, the choices we make are still inevitable. This was a common position in the 1600s and 1700s with the rise of modern science, where the world seemed to be ruled by predictable laws.

> **Indeterminism:** the idea that reality is fundamentally random and unpredictable.

If anything, the quantum physics of the twentieth century has shifted the spirit of the age to one of **indeterminism**: the idea that reality is fundamentally random and unpredictable, that the course of future events is not determined by God, our wills, or the laws of nature. On the quantum, subatomic level, events seem to happen unpredictably and randomly. Such apparently random events have immense consequences on the macrolevel. This chapter addresses some of the basic positions that thinkers and Christians have taken on these sorts of issues.

© Kevin L. Welch

10.2
ANCIENT FATALISM

It is no coincidence that modern Western culture, with all its technological developments, tends to emphasize human freedom. The Western world is a democratic world, where people at least think they have a voice in their future. Medical and technological advancements are coming at such a rapid rate it can almost seem for a time that we are physically invincible. It is quite possible to live out full lives with maladies that would have been fatal even ten or twenty years ago.

At the same time, it is understandable that ancient cultures and less-developed countries have a much greater sense of fatedness. Imagine a world where hurricanes come ashore without warning and where what we consider trivial sicknesses might kill you the day after you exhibit the first symptoms. It is no coincidence that most cultures in the past viewed their gods as whimsical beings whose anger needed continuous placating.

Fatalism is an attitude that does not think human choices affect what will happen in the future: "*Que sera, sera.*" What will be, will be. When it's your time to go, it's your time to go. Everyone has a destiny, and there's no point in fighting it. A person with a fatalistic attitude does not feel in control of his or her "fate," of what is going to happen in life or death.

Fatalism is more of an attitude toward life than a developed philosophy. It was the pervasive attitude of the Greco-Roman world, as a number of ancient myths reflect. Aeschylus's *Prometheus Bound*, for example, makes it clear that even the king of the gods, Zeus, was ultimately subject to the whims of the Fates. The popular Disney movie *Hercules* depicted the Fates as being unable to cut the thread of Hercules's life because he had become immortal at just the right moment. But in Greek thought, Hercules could become immortal only if in fact the Fates themselves had willed it.

Another well-known ancient story is that of **Oedipus**, famously dramatized in three plays by the Greek playwright Sophocles.[1] At birth, it is prophesied that Oedipus will grow up to kill his father and marry his mother. In an attempt to thwart his fate, Oedipus's father "exposes" him as an infant, leaving him for dead in the middle of nowhere. Yet someone rescues him, and he grows up thinking that he is the son of a different king in a different city-state. When Oedipus grows up and discovers the prophecy—that he will kill his father and marry his mother—he flees his home, thinking his adopted parents are his real parents.

Then to no one's surprise, he runs into his biological father. Fatedly, they cross paths while traveling and get into an argument in which Oedipus kills his father, unbeknownst to him. He then "happens" to come to his mother's city; after rescuing the city from a monster, Oedipus marries his mother as a reward. All the parties involved have done their best to flee their fates—and in the process they fulfill it!

Some aspects of this story may be helpful for understanding some of the things Paul says in his writings. The Oedipus story seems to affirm both that Fate determines the ultimate outcome of events and that the individuals involved make many unfated decisions to get there. There is no attempt to reconcile the two aspects to the story. The idea is not that everything they do is fated. Rather, their destiny seems to fulfill itself mysteriously without Fate necessarily directing every action along the way.

The ancient **Stoics** may be even more helpful. One of their famous sayings was that we should have *amor fati*, "love of fate." It would be foolish, they taught, to resist the destiny that the **Logos**, divine Reason, had in store for you.[2] Inside you was a little "Logos seed," an "implanted word" (cf. James 1:21; 1 John 3:9). You should follow its direction and have *apatheia* about it, a nonemotional acceptance of your situation. As Paul says in Philippians 4:11–12, you should be content with your circumstances.

It is interesting that one could, in fact, resist one's fate at all. There was apparently some wiggle room alongside one's fate. On the one hand, the Stoic sense of fate focused mostly on things that were givens in one's life, circumstances that had already happened and that one could not change. The

Fatalism: an attitude toward life that sees the future course of events as inevitable.

Stoicism: ancient philosophical school that emphasized rationality and accepting one's circumstances. One should have *amor fati*, "love of fate," with *apatheia*, nonemotional acceptance.

The Thinker, 1881, Rodin, Auguste (1840–1917) / Musee Rodin, Paris, France / The Bridgeman Art Library

Stoic response was to accept one's circumstances without emotion; after all, one cannot change what has already happened. In terms of the future, certain courses of action were "logical" (Logos), rational and reasonable, going forward. It was absurd to follow a path of emotion since reason, the Logos, would inevitably win out.

We find this same tension between language of determinism and language of freedom in the New Testament. Like the Oedipus story, the New Testament never works out the details of how God can have chosen the "elect" (those "chosen ones" who believe in Christ) and yet affirm that the Good News is for anyone, that God would prefer for everyone to respond favorably to him (e.g., 1 Tim. 2:4). In terms of human reasoning, these two claims are contradictory. It is a simple syllogism:

1. If God determines who will respond positively to him and
2. God wants everyone to respond positively to him,
3. then everyone will respond positively to him.

But the New Testament assumes throughout that only some respond positively to God. So it is no surprise that later Christians have tried to solve this logical puzzle. Some traditions such as my own (Arminian) deny the first premise, that God forcibly predetermines who will respond positively to him. Others, including the Calvinist tradition, attack the second premise, that God wants everyone to respond to him. Still another might accept the third point, the conclusion, and become a universalist, someone who believes that God will save everyone. Focus on one set of passages, and you might not believe that God allows humans to decide their fate. Focus on others, and you might think God leaves it up to us to choose.

The ancient world may help us gain perspective if we consider the possibility that language of destiny may have functioned primarily as "after-the-fact" language. The fate of the Stoics dealt primarily with things that had already happened. We know our fate after it happens. How we got to this "destiny," on the other hand, is mysterious. We proceed freely through life, apparently making free choices along the way, but where we end up is where we were supposed to be. In that sense, the ancients were often unreflective "compatibilists" of a sort who affirmed both free will and determinism without really trying to reconcile the two.

For example, Paul in the New Testament occasionally refers to believers in Jesus as "the elect" (e.g., Rom. 8:33). He even goes so far as to say that God "has mercy on whomever he chooses, and he hardens the heart of whomever he chooses" (Rom. 9:18). This statement seems harsh, but when we look at Paul's reported actions and what his expectations are in relation to other people, we have to conclude that he does not connect the dots philosophically. The meaning of words is in what they *do* more than in what they *say*. When I say, "How are you?" I may simply be saying, "Hello." I may be "doing" something social rather than really asking a question.

In the same way, when Paul says that God has chosen those who believe or that those who are in the church are the "elect," he is arguably doing at least two things. First, he is affirming that God is in control, that God is **sovereign**, that God is king. Second, he is doing something **affective**, something that has to do with his audience's emotions, sense of belonging, and sense of God's hand working in their lives. So we are not surprised to find in Romans 11 that some of those whom Paul has implied are predetermined to be condemned can get right with God if they stop their unbelief (v. 23). Similarly, the position of those who are currently elect can change too, since too much pride on their part could result in God ultimately rejecting them (vv. 20–21).

In short, Paul does not seem to use predestination language in a straight-forwardly literal way. When he refers to individuals as "chosen" (e.g., Rom. 16:13), he does not intend the kinds of things that would follow if he meant such language on a fully literal level. He does not mean, for example, that such an individual is certain to continue into the kingdom. He suggests at more than one point that even his own eternal destiny is not yet secure (1 Cor. 9:24–27; Phil. 3:10–14). Second Peter 1:10 reveals this dynamic well when it exhorts its audience to "be all the more eager to make your calling and election sure" (NIV). If election was purely a matter of God's choosing, one's actions would hardly have anything to do with making it certain. Predestination language seems to be after-the-fact language: you are elect and chosen because you are here. But your actions can apparently change whether or not you stay here. As I mentioned in chapter 6, the way my tradition maintains God's sovereignty without affirming predestination is to distinguish between God's **directive will** and God's **permissive will**. For God to be sovereign, he must "sign off" on everything that happens. He must be completely in control so that nothing happens without his permission—without his "permissive will" allowing it. At the same time, this setup would not mean that God explicitly commands everything that happens to happen; it would not mean that his "directive will" makes every single thing happen exactly the way it does. I personally believe that God has set up the universe with certain laws that he lets run on their own and that he empowers human will on some level to make choices independently of his direction. The result is that God allows everything that happens, but that he only occasionally directs specific happenings. God thus allows actions or situations, such as murder and epidemics, but he may not directly cause them.

Sovereignty: in relation to God, absolute authority and control over everything.

Affective: the emotional, feeling dimension of human life.

God's directive will: God's active and explicit command to make certain things to happen.

God's permissive will: God's allowance for things to happen that God does not actively determine.

10.3
Calvin and Arminius

The old comic strip "Calvin and Hobbes" was not randomly named. **John Calvin** (1509–1564) and **Thomas Hobbes** (1588–1679) lived in the same general period, at the beginning of the scientific revolution. It is probably no coincidence that both were determinists of a sort who believed that at least certain aspects of the future were already decided by forces beyond one's control. Despite the significant differences between these two thinkers, they both are good examples of the **zeitgeist** of their time—the "spirit of the age."

We will look more at Hobbes and the zeitgeist of the 1600s in the next section. Here we look at the Christian determinism of John Calvin and his heirs. **Calvinists** are Christian groups, especially Reformed and Presbyterian traditions, that are heirs of John Calvin's thinking in one respect or another. To a lesser degree, Calvin's thought has also influenced other traditions, including Baptist, Anglican, and Methodist.

Calvin largely took up and developed the thinking of Augustine (AD 354–430). According to Calvin, humanity was completely "depraved" as a result of Adam's sin in the Garden of Eden. No human is capable of doing any good at all in his or her own power. As a result, if anyone is to be saved, Calvin suggested, God must choose and empower him or her. Eternal life is thus entirely a matter of God's "election."

Accordingly, Calvin believed that the only people who will be saved are those whom God has determined to be saved. God in his complete control of the universe has arbitrarily (at least from our perspective) chosen to elect some to be saved. The others are already damned, so God does not determine their fate; it was already determined by Adam's choice.

Calvin's thinking was later summarized by his opponents with the acronym **TULIP**, the "five points" of Calvinism:

Total depravity: no human can do any good in his or her own power.
Unconditional election: God has chosen who will be saved with us playing no part in it at all.
Limited atonement: Christ died only for those God has chosen, not for everyone.
Irresistible grace: if God has chosen you, you are chosen; you can do nothing about it.
Perseverance of the saints: if you are chosen, you will make it.

> **Zeitgeist:** the spirit of the age.
>
> **Calvinism:** Christian school of thought derived from John Calvin, in particular the idea that God chooses those who will be saved from hell.

By the time of Hobbes, Calvin's "single" **predestination** had become "double predestination," in which God not only actively determined who would be saved from hell, but also who would be damned. Today some "hyper-Calvinists" even believe God caused Satan and Adam to sin.

Not everyone within Calvin's Reformed tradition agreed fully with the way he worked out his theology. In Holland, **Jakobus Arminius** in particular (1560–1609) objected to the idea that God's "election" of those who would be saved did not involve any human element. He suggested that God predestined those who would be saved because God foreknew—knew ahead of time—what their free-will choices would be.

Arminius's view raises one of the classic philosophical conundrums. Does the fact that God *knows* the future—his **foreknowledge**—imply that God *determines* what will happen? The line of thinking usually goes something like this: If God knows what I will do, then I cannot possibly do anything different. But if I must do what God knows, then I am not free to do anything else. Thus, so the argument goes, God's foreknowledge and omniscience are incompatible with free will, with my ability to choose or reject God without being forced to do so. Either God knows the future and we are not free, or we are not free and God does not fully know the future.

A good number of Christians find this argument persuasive. The Calvinist, for example, ends up rejecting free will in the libertarian sense in favor of God's foreknowledge and omniscience. Another recent approach, called **open theism**, suggests that God intentionally suspends his foreknowledge so that we can be free. According to this camp, God could know the future and indeed does know every possible course of events. However, God freely chooses not to access this knowledge of what we will specifically do so that we can have free will.[3]

It is not surprising that some Old Testament scholars are sympathetic to this view, for the Old Testament by and large does not present God as omniscient. Just before God causes the Flood, for example, he says that he is sorry that he created humanity in the first place (Gen. 6:6). But an all-knowing God would have known what was going to happen before creating humanity. God cannot thus literally "be sorry" for anything if he is omniscient.

Indeed, the very idea that God might have emotions seems to imply that he reacts to things and thus that he lacks foreknowledge of what will happen. While we as humans often distinguish between head knowledge and experiential knowledge, omniscience for God means that he has *all* knowledge. If he created everything from nothing, then there is no distinction of this sort for him. If we believe in omniscience, therefore, we have to take language of God getting angry or being sorry as anthropomorphic language, language that pictures God in human terms, language we should not take literally.[4]

> **Foreknowledge:** God's prior knowledge of the future.
>
> **Predestination:** God's prior determination of the future, usually, in particular, whether or not we will be saved from his judgment.

> **Open theism:** the view that God intentionally suspends his foreknowledge of what we will choose so that we can be free to choose.

The Old Testament thus presents God as changing his mind on more than one occasion. God sends the prophet Jonah to Nineveh with the prediction that God is going to destroy them. But then God changes his mind and does not do so. Again, if we are to believe that God is omniscient, we must take language like this as somewhat figurative, the Bible expressing God's actions in anthropomorphic terms.

We wonder, however, if the supposed contradiction between foreknowledge and free will is flawed. For example, let us say you are present at a football game that you videotape to watch with your friends. When you later watch the game, you might be able to predict everything that happens. But certainly your "foreknowledge" of what will happen does not determine what will happen on the video.

If God in some way is "outside" time, as Christian philosophers like Boethius (ca. 480–524) and Thomas Aquinas (1225–1274) suggested, it is possible that he knows the future because he has, in a sense, already seen it. What seems to be foreknowledge from our perspective amounts to past knowledge on God's part. It would thus not follow that foreknowledge equals determinism. We are not in a position to say how God knows what God knows.

> The sun does not shine because I know it. I know it because it shines. My knowledge presupposes that the sun shines, but it does not in any way cause it. Similarly, God knows that humans sin, because he knows everything. Yet we do not sin because he knows it, but he knows it because we sin. His knowledge presupposes our sin, but does not in any way cause it.
>
> In a word, God, looking on all ages as a moment—from the creation to the consummation—and seeing at once whatever is in the hearts of all the children of mortals, knows every one that does or does not believe, in every age or nation. Yet what he knows, whether faith or unbelief, is in no way caused by his knowledge. We are as free in believing or not believing as if he did not know it at all.
>
> **John Wesley, "On Predestination"**[5]

At the same time, the argument that God is outside time does not answer the question of whether God gained knowledge when he created the universe. **Luis de Molina** (1526–1600) was a Spanish Jesuit who wrestled with the issue of God's foreknowledge and human free will at about the same time as Calvin and Arminius. He introduced some important distinctions into the discussion that have been adopted by some contemporary philosophers such as Alvin Plantinga and William Lane Craig.

© Kevin L. Welch

Statue of John Wesley

Molinism, the approach to God's knowledge started by Molina, is best known for its belief in what it calls **middle knowledge**. According to Molina, God has three kinds of knowledge. His first type of knowledge is knowledge of what must be true, what is logically true, for example. His third kind of knowledge is knowledge of what will happen depending on how he acts in the world. Middle knowledge is his knowledge of what will happen depending on *human* will.

God having middle knowledge thus means that God knows every *possible* thing that might happen. If God is outside of time, however, his knowledge of what could happen is also knowledge of what will actually happen in this universe.[6] When God creates time and the universe, he comes to know everything that will happen without determining it. Of course, after we have had this entire discussion, we must admit that we have no real way of knowing how knowledge works for God. God may have ways of knowing that do not imply determinism, ways that we could not possibly comprehend.

John Wesley (1703–1791) built further on Arminius's objections to Calvinist predestination. His theology is sometimes called **Wesleyan-Arminian** theology. Like Calvin, Arminius, and Augustine, Wesley agreed that humans were totally depraved and could do no good in their own power. However, like Arminius, he denied that God elected humans unconditionally, with no element of human will involved.

To use an analogy: Calvin viewed God's election somewhat like an on/off switch. Either God turned the light on or he left it off. If God turned his grace on, you would be saved. If God did not, you would remain damned. For Wesley, on the other hand, God at some point turned the lights up for everyone so that *they* could choose or reject his grace. In other words, Wesley believed that God offered everyone the opportunity to be saved. It was entirely God's power that made this choice possible, but God offered it to everyone, not just to a few whom he had arbitrarily chosen.

> **Middle knowledge:** knowledge of all the possible outcomes depending on human choice.
>
> **Molinism:** the perspective that holds God knows the definite outcome of what must be true and of how he will act, but that he has only middle knowledge of the outcome of human choices.
>
> **Wesleyan-Arminian theology:** the perspective that holds that God potentially empowers everyone to be saved from judgment if he or she responds favorably.

> There is no one, unless someone has quenched the Spirit, who completely lacks the grace of God. No one alive is entirely lacking what is popularly called "natural conscience." But it is not natural. It is more appropriately called "prevenient grace." Everyone has a greater or lesser measure of it, which does not wait for us to call for it. Everyone, sooner or later, has good desires, although most people stifle them before they can take deep root or produce fruit of any significance. Everyone has some measure of that light, some faint glimmering ray, which, sooner or later, more or less, enlightens everyone who comes into the world.
>
> **John Wesley, "On Working out Our Salvation"**[7]

Belief in predestination is alive and well today. It largely follows the lines laid down in the debates of the 1500s and 1600s. "Five-point Calvinism" has experienced somewhat of a revival, including some hyper-Calvinist forms we have mentioned. At the same time, Arminianism has enjoyed a prominence among some of the most significant Christian philosophers of recent times.

Your sense of human freedom usually has immense implications for other areas of your life. Say you believe God predetermines whether or not you will believe. You might also believe God determines many if not most other things that happen to you.[8] You might emphasize the absolute authority and sovereignty of God, along with justice and punishment as key features of God's nature. Conversely, a person who believes in free will might tend to see love as the primary way God relates to the world currently, with an emphasis on helping us grow and come to make the right choices.

While none of us is completely consistent with our ideas, these views of God will tend to play themselves out in the details of our lives, such as how we raise our children or how we vote.[9] A person who views God's justice in rigid terms may tend to respond to a child's disobedience with a wrathful response, focusing on punishment of wrongdoing. The person for whom God's mercy is focal may see disobedience as the child inflicting harm on him- or herself and respond accordingly to effect a "teaching moment."

Similarly, the person who emphasizes God's justice may see it as a duty to try to make the laws of the land mirror as much as possible divine law. Such a person may emphasize "preaching against sin," seeing sin as an effrontery to God's justice. The person who believes in free will, on the other hand, may not feel as much compulsion to force the rest of the world to follow God's will. If such a person believes God created a world in which we can choose to disobey him, that person may focus more on influencing others for good than in trying to force it.

Hands of the Puppeteer, 1929
(b/w photo), Modotti, Tina (1896–1942)
© Galerie Bilderwelt / The Bridgeman Art Library

10.4
COMPATIBILISM AND INDETERMINISM

Not long after John Calvin died in Geneva, Switzerland, Thomas Hobbes was born in England. Hobbes lived at the beginning of the Baroque period, which many have seen as a very pessimistic time in Europe's history. It was the time of the Thirty-Years' War (1608–1648) that decimated Germany and Austria. It was the time of the English Civil War, involving the unprecedented execution of an English king (1649) and the harsh but short-lived rule of the Puritan Oliver Cromwell.

BIOGRAPHY

THOMAS HOBBES

Englishman Thomas Hobbes (1588–1679) lived in a turbulent time in which England rose to political dominance. During his life Hobbes navigated the rough political waters of the English Civil War. Hobbes supported King Charles I and spent eleven years in Paris, when the royalists lost power. Charles himself was executed (1649). But some of Hobbes's writings would later anger royalists as well.

It was also a time when some of the most foundational developments in modern science were taking place. Hobbes was a materialist who disagreed with the dualism of soul and body, as taught by René Descartes. Indeed, the two knew each other and corresponded while Hobbes was in Paris, just a few years before Descartes's death. Although he was accused of being an atheist later in life, Hobbes affirmed the key creed of the church, the Nicene Creed. Nevertheless, he did believe that the normal course of history was determined on the basis of the (materialistic) laws of motion.

His work *Questions concerning Liberty, Necessity, and Chance* was part of an exchange with the Arminian-believing bishop John Bramhall and perhaps the first clear expression of psychological determinism, purporting that our thoughts are ultimately determined by the forces on us. But Hobbes is better known as a compatibilist, someone who believes determinism and free will are compatible. By free will, Hobbes meant that we are free to act according to our wills, not that our wills are somehow undetermined by the forces at work on us.

Hobbes is best known for his political philosophy. In *Leviathan* he compared the state to the fantastical monster of the Bible (e.g., Ps. 74:14). Humans form the state because of their need for protection and then dissolve it as their passions lead to strife. In general, it is a defense of the absolute power of kings on the basis of a "social contract" between a king and his people.

If people were completely in a "state of nature," it would be everyone for himself and the result would be a "war of all against all." For this reason, people make implicit or explicit contracts with sovereign powers like kings for protection. In return they surrender absolute power to the sovereign in all areas, in civil, judicial, military, and even church matters. Even if the sovereign abuses these powers, the people cannot take the authority back.

Photo Credit: Thomas Hobbes (oil on canvas), Fuller, Isaac (1606–72) (circle of) / Burghley House Collection, Lincolnshire, UK / The Bridgeman Art Library

It was also the time of Shakespeare, whose lines sometimes capture the spirit of the age. In *As You Like It*, Jaques says,

All the world's a stage,
    And all the men and women merely players:
They have their exits and their entrances;
    And one man in his time plays many parts.

William Shakespeare, *As You Like It* II.7

William Shakespeare

The lines have a clear fatalism to them. We do not write our "script" in life. We merely read the lines and play the role that the world has already assigned to us. *Macbeth* has the same feel:

Life's but a walking shadow, a poor player
    That struts and frets his hour upon the stage,
And then is heard no more; it is a tale
    Told by an idiot, full of sound and fury,
Signifying nothing.

William Shakespeare, *Macbeth* V.5

With the rise of scientific explanation, people had a greater sense that the world was a big machine. God may have created the machine, but people increasingly thought of things happening because of natural laws rather than divine intervention. The world is like a pool table. God "broke" with his divine cue stick, and now the balls are in motion. If you knew the math and physics, you could predict exactly where all the balls would end up.

Thomas Hobbes is a good example of this type of thinker from that period. He was a materialist who rejected Descartes's dualism of soul and body.[10] For him, the world was only matter, so what happens in the world is strictly a matter of the laws of cause and effect. If we knew everything about that matter and all the laws that govern it, we could predict everything that would happen from now until the universe goes cold.

Whatever happens, happens of necessity, for whatever happens has had a sufficient cause to produce it, or else it would not have happened. Therefore, voluntary actions also take place of necessity . . .

[But] the ordinary definition of a free agent is incoherent, namely, that a free agent is one who, when everything necessary to produce an effect is present, nevertheless does not produce it. This idea is nonsense because it so much as says that the cause is . . . necessary, and yet the effect does not follow.

Thomas Hobbes, *Liberty and Necessity*[11]

For Hobbes, freedom is not the ability to want whatever we want to want; our wants are strictly a product of the math. Freedom is the ability to do what we desire, freedom to act according to our desires rather than the freedom to determine our desires undetermined by all the forces at work on us.

At the same time, Hobbes did use language of free will. He was a **compatibilist**. A compatibilist believes that we can be free to act in accordance with our wills even though, truth be known, our wills are ultimately determined.[12] Such forces can include the laws of cause and effect, human sinfulness, or God's will at work on us. The psychologist-philosopher **William James** (1842–1910) called this position **soft determinism**, because it "abhors harsh words . . . and says its real name is freedom."[13]

Some philosophers have seen no need to speak of free will at all. For example, the **Baron d'Holbach** (1723–1789) was a prominent figure of the French Enlightenment just before the French Revolution. A stream within his writings, many of them anonymous or written under pseudonyms, was against Christianity and in favor of a materialistic view of the universe. However, he is perhaps best known for his **hard determinism**, his refusal to speak of human freedom in any meaningful sense at all.

We have already mentioned that William James coined the term *soft determinism* in relation to compatibilists. He himself believed we had insufficient evidence to conclude definitively one way or another on the free-will question, although he did not deny the massive forces at work on our wills. He argued strongly that we do not experience the world with a deterministic attitude. If we think of human actions in deterministic terms, we find it difficult to argue that we *ought not* do certain things. The murderer had to kill his wife, so why do we find fault?

> I cannot understand the belief that an act is bad without regret at its happening. I cannot understand regret without the admission of real, genuine possibilities in the world . . .
>
> —⁂—
>
> The great point is that the possibilities are really *here*. Whether it be we who solve them or he [God] working through us is no matter. At those soul-trying moments when fate's scales seem to quiver, when good snatches the victory from evil or to the contrary shrinks from the fight, what is important is that we acknowledge that the issue is decided nowhere else than *here* and *now*. That is what gives the palpitating reality to our moral life and makes it tingle.

William James, *The Will to Believe* [14]

James claimed that a deterministic outlook does not cohere well with our lived experience of the world. We experience the world as if we have choices and as if those choices matter. From the standpoint of "right" and "wrong," it matters to us whether we think we have a choice to steal or not to steal, to kill or not to kill. Regardless of the math—something James pointed out we simply cannot know—it is important for us to frame life as if we have choices and that those choices matter.

Compatibilism: the philosophical position that sees determinism and free will as logically compatible, if free will is defined as the freedom to act in accordance with what you want to do.

Soft determinism: compatibilism, the view that while everything we do is ultimately determined, we at least experience life as having free will.

Hard determinism: the idea that we cannot help but will and act the way we do, that humans are not free in any meaningful sense.

We mentioned in the first section of this chapter that quantum physics has led science away from determinism and toward a radical indeterminism, where the course of future events is completely random and unpredictable. In other words, it is not determined by God, science, us, or anything at all. The future is entirely random. Indeed, perhaps even the majority of quantum physicists at present believe that quantum reality itself involves situations where two contradictory states of things are for all intents and purposes true at the same time. An electron might, in one sense, be at two different places at the same time.

Ernst Schrödinger (1887–1961), one of the founding intellects of modern physics, depicted this school of interpretation with a famous thought experiment known as **Schrödinger's cat**.

A cat is penned up in a steel chamber, along with the following device (which must be secured against direct interference by the cat). In a Geiger counter, there is a tiny bit of radioactive substance, so small that perhaps in the course of the hour, one of the atoms decays, but also, with equal probability, perhaps none. If one of the atoms decays, the Geiger counter discharges, and through a relay releases a hammer that shatters a small flask of hydrocyanic acid. If one has left this entire system to itself for an hour, one would say that the cat still lives if no atom has decayed in the meantime. The psi-function [quantum physics equation] of the entire system would express this situation by having the living or dead cat (pardon the expression) mixed or smeared out with equal parts.

Ernst Schrödinger, "The Present Situation in Quantum Mechanics"[15]

If we are to accept the **Copenhagen interpretation** of quantum mechanics, the view that came to prevail, the implication of Schrödinger's experiment would mean that the cat is both dead and alive at the same time in the box, at least prior to anyone opening the box. Strangely, the cat would not be one or the other until you opened the box to look. Then *you* would force the cat to be one or the other. Schrödinger's point was that the Copenhagen interpretation could hardly be correct because in reality, this cat would either be dead or alive, whether anyone observed it or not.

Nevertheless, quantum physics at present has no clear solution to the problem of nuclear indeterminacy, and when we couple it with the **butterfly effect**, the indeterminacy of reality becomes an acute issue. The butterfly effect is the recognition that small changes in one place in a string of causes and effects will often have major impact on the course of later events. So the flapping of a butterfly's wings in Brazil might alter the air in such a way as to effect a tornado in Texas. **Chaos theory** is a contemporary area of mathematical study concluding that complex behaviors can result from randomness. While it is not probable that any one instance of complexity would come about randomly, it is mathematically probable that *some* instance of complexity would arise over time from sheer randomness. The long and short of it is that even the smallest amount of indeterminacy on the nuclear level would likely have massive consequences in the macroworld in which we live.

Quantum physics does not have these issues resolved, so it remains to be seen how philosophers will debate free will in the years to come. As physics continues to wrestle with these sorts of issues, I propose that we give serious consideration to William James's **phenomenological** approach: we start with the way things appear, the way we experience things, rather than with the question of how things actually are behind the veil of what we do not know. For example, no one knows for sure where quantum physics will be in fifty years, let alone a hundred years. What we know is that we experience the world as if we are "selves" who are distinct from the rest of the world, and we experience the world as if we are free to choose between various options in our behavior. In that sense, we have free will at least phenomenologically, and it makes sense to live in the world as if we have free will.

10.5
CONCLUSION

In this chapter we have looked at the age-old debate over whether we as human beings are truly free. Many readers may be surprised to find out that our actions are far more determined than we might think. Our desires are formed not only by the genes we inherit from our biological parents but also from the culture and environment in which we were raised. Would I be a Christian if I had been born in a different time and place?

This question flows naturally into some of the debates Christians have had about predestination. Does God decide who will be saved? Back in the 1700s when Christians began to send missionaries out, some argued that it was pointless because if those "heathen" were predestined they would have been born in a Christian country. Another approach sees God giving light to everyone who comes into the world (see John 1:9), so that everyone at least has a chance. If God evaluates people on the basis of the light they have, then even those who have never heard of Christ have the opportunity to respond to God to some degree.

In the end, we all have to live as though we have free will. Even if you believe that God, determinism, or chance is ultimately a decider, none of us should live that way. We have to live as though we are free and take responsibility for our actions. Otherwise there would be no basis for moral accountability, and society as we know it would disintegrate. We have to live as though we are making our own choices.

KEY TERMS

- generational poverty
- free will (libertarian)
- determinism
- indeterminism
- fatalism
- Oedipus
- Stoicism
- *amor fati*
- Logos
- *apatheia*
- sovereignty

- affective
- directive will
- permissive will
- zeitgeist
- Calvinism
- TULIP
- predestination
- foreknowledge
- open theism
- Molinism
- middle knowledge

- Wesleyan-Arminian
- free will (compatibilist)
- soft determinism
- hard determinism
- Schrödinger's cat
- butterfly effect
- Copenhagen interpretation
- chaos theory
- phenomenological approach

KEY PHILOSOPHERS

- John Calvin
- Thomas Hobbes
- Jakobus Arminius
- Baron d'Holbach

- Luis de Molina
- John Wesley
- William James
- Ernst Schrödinger

KEY QUESTIONS

1. What do you make of the claim that many who are generationally poor or who are in abuse situations are not free to will themselves out of that situation? Would this idea change your attitudes toward such individuals?

2. Which of the following positions best fits your sense of human freedom: hard determinist, compatibilist, free will libertarian, or indeterminist? Why?

3. Take a position in the Calvinist-Arminian debate and argue for it biblically and philosophically. Evaluate the author's argument that the apostle Paul's predestination language was after-the-fact language. What do you make of the author's argument that foreknowledge need not imply predestination?

4. Are you consistent in your view of predestination and free will? Do you think your sense of punishment and discipline or your sense of government and legislating ethics fit together? Defend your position.

NOTES

1. *Oedipus the King*, *Antigone*, and *Oedipus at Colonus*.
2. About the time of Christ, a number of thinkers in Alexandria, Egypt, mixed the Stoic Logos with some of Plato's thinking about ideal patterns and earthly copies and created a philosophical trend sometimes called middle Platonism. For example, the Jewish thinker Philo extensively interpreted Scripture using these categories. The Logos was divine, a mediator between God and humanity. The Logos was the instrument through which God created the world. The Logos was the image of God.

    One can argue that the earliest Christians drew on this Jewish Logos imagery when it sought to describe the significance of Jesus. "In the beginning was the Logos," John 1:1 says before going on to say that God's Logos became flesh in Jesus (1:14). God created the world through the Logos (John 1:3), through Christ (Col. 1:16; Heb. 1:3). Christ is the "image of the invisible God" (Col. 1:15), like the Logos. While most Christians take this language straightforwardly, the earliest Christians may have intended a rich message that Jesus embodies God's very purpose and direction for the cosmos.
3. Open theism should not be confused with process theology, as it often is. Process theology believes that God is evolving, that God doesn't know everything because he is evolving with the world. Open theists believe that God intentionally suspends his omniscience so that we can have free will.
4. Perhaps it would be more technically correct to call it anthropopathism, the ascription of human feelings to nonhuman entities.
5. Paraphrased from the original English of the sermon. See *The Works of John Wesley*, 3rd ed. (Peabody, MA: Hendrickson, 1986), 6:227.
6. It is of course possible (if Leibniz is wrong about God being able to create only the best possible world) that God also knows what will happen in other possible universes as well, where human will makes other possible choices.
7. Paraphrased from the original English of the sermon. See *The Works of John Wesley*, 6:512.
8. Many of those who believe in predestination do not believe that God predetermines *everything*. Many believe he determines only one's ultimate salvation. Popularly, however, many Christians believe that God orchestrates even little things in our lives to give them direction and purpose.
9. Not to mention other areas of our belief system. For example, Calvinists tend to emphasize the idea of "penal substitution": because God's justice is so absolute, God must exact the precise amount of penalty for any sin. God cannot simply have mercy on someone. For Calvin, Christ not only took our punishment, including his descent into hell; Christ experienced the exact amount of punishment justice demanded of every individual God predestined for forgiveness.

    Others see such a mathematical sense of God's justice as absurd. God is God, and in the parables, Jesus presents a God who has the authority to forgive sins simply on his own authority. For example, Joel Green and Mark Baker point out that the Parable of the Prodigal Son says nothing about the father having to arrange someone to pay for the debts of the younger son. The father has the authority to forgive the son, with no payment made at all. Joel Green and Mark Baker, *Rediscovering the Scandal of the Cross: Atonement in New Testament and Contemporary Contexts* (Downers Grove, IL: InterVarsity, 2000), 148.
10. See chapter 7, "What Is Reality?"
11. Paraphrased from the original English, par. 31 and 32. See Vere Chappell, ed., *Hobbes and Bramhall on Liberty and Necessity* (Cambridge: Cambridge University, 1999), 38–39.
12. A good resource here is William Hasker, *Metaphysics: Constructing a World View* (Downers Grove, IL: InterVarsity, 1983). Many thanks to Scott Burson of Indiana Wesleyan University for his feedback on compatibilism.
13. William James, *The Will to Believe and Other Essays in Popular Philosophy, and Human Immortality* (1897; repr., Seaside, OR: Watchmaker, 2010), 76.
14. Ibid., 88, 91.
15. Ernst Schrödinger, "The Present Situation in Quantum Mechanics," *Proceedings of the American Philosophical Society* 124 (1935): 323–38. It later appeared in J. A. Wheeler and W. H. Zureck, eds., *Quantum Theory and Measurement* (Princeton, NJ: Princeton University, 1983), part 1, sec. I.11.

UNIT 6

PHILOSOPHIES OF VALUE:
AXIOLOGY

Family

Time

Popularity

Fortune

Knowledge

Job Friends

Money

Values

Nation Fame Possessions

God Work

© Elizabeth Welch

© istockphoto.com

11.1
SETTING PRIORITIES

Ethics is the area of philosophy that has to do with how to live in the world.[1] Hardly any area of philosophy is more directly applicable to "real life" than ethics, because it deals with the kinds of decisions we have to make both in the long and short term. Should I do something that benefits me but hurts others? Should I live for the pleasure of the moment, or should I focus more on long-term happiness or on being a good person in general?

We can approach ethics from two basic perspectives. Probably the more widely used approach in the Western world today is **act-based ethics**. Act-based approaches to ethics predictably focus on *doing*—what we should or should not do, how we should act. The other approach is more interested in *being*—what sort of people we should be or become. **Virtue-based ethics**, as it is called, is more focused on things like

What to Get from This Chapter

- Ethics is the field of philosophy that asks about how best to live in this world.
- Act-based ethics is oriented around what we should *do* or not do.
- Virtue-based ethics is oriented around what sort of people we should *be* or not be.
- Duty-based ethics asks what actions are universally right or wrong.
- Utilitarian ethics looks to consequences and asks what action will bring about the greatest good for the greatest number.
- Egoist ethics looks to consequences and asks what action will bring about the greatest benefit for me.
- Few duties can be absolutes, because we have to prioritize our values, and values play themselves out differently in different contexts.
- A Christian ethic is primarily virtue based, focusing on love of God and neighbor.

Questions to Consider

- Which duties in life are absolute and which relative?
- In what circumstances does the end justify the means?
- What constitutes a "good life"?
- What is the most fundamental Christian ethic?

Key Words

- Ethics
- Golden Rule
- Golden Mean
- Happiness

Ethics: a branch of philosophy that asks how we best live in the world.

Act-based ethics: ethics oriented around what we should *do* or not do.

Virtue-based ethics: ethics oriented around who we should *be* or not be.

Duty-based ethics: an act-based approach to ethics that focuses on acts that are universally right or wrong in themselves (e.g., lying, stealing).

Utilitarianism: an act-based approach to ethics that looks to consequences and focuses on what will bring about the greatest good for the greatest number.

Egoist ethics: an act-based approach to ethics that looks to consequences and focuses on what will most benefit me.

Axiology: the study of what is valuable, another way of viewing ethics.

character, motives, and true happiness rather than on whether specific actions are right or wrong.

Virtue-based and act-based approaches to ethics are not completely unrelated to each other. Some would argue that consistently choosing to act in a certain way is precisely what it means to "be" virtuous. Indeed, is not consistently acting in a certain way precisely what it means to "be" something? And a person's actions usually say something about a person's character or happiness. So which approach we take is more a matter of emphasis than a choice of one to the exclusion of the other.

We also find at least three different kinds of act-based approaches to ethics. (1) **Duty-based ethics** focuses specifically on actions that are universally—some would say intrinsically—right or wrong.[2] Such things are wrong in themselves whether or not they cause something else bad to happen. (2) By contrast, **utilitarianism** focuses primarily on the consequences of actions.[3] The right course of action is what brings about the "greatest good for the greatest number." (3) **Egoist** approaches to ethics ask, what's in it for me? The "right" course of action is what will most benefit me. In many respects, the egoist approach would seem to be the current default ethic of the West, whether consciously or unconsciously. As we will see in chapter 12, it is the fundamental theoretical basis of the American economic system and any capitalist society.

The problem with all ethical theories is the complexity of life. Life is filled with no-win situations. For example, what happens when two different duties come into conflict with each other? What were those who hid Jews during World War II to do when Nazis searched their homes? Should they lie or surrender the Jews? What if someone is trying to harm your family and will almost certainly succeed unless you harm him? Is it okay to kill when your life is in danger or when someone else's life is in danger?

Axiology is the study of what is valuable in life. It actually covers not only ethics but the philosophy of art and everything in this section of the textbook. Real life necessitates that we prioritize our values so that we know what to do when our values come into conflict with each other. We have no other option. It simply is not possible to consider every right or wrong an absolute, as something we must do or not do without exception. Whether we realize it or not, we all operate with a certain "hierarchy of values," so that when two of our values come into conflict with each other, we trump one with the other.

Christianity has always been concerned with both who a person is and what a person does. To be sure, different groups throughout history have leaned in one direction or the other, some toward the importance of the heart and others toward the importance of proper action. Yet only the most extreme

Christian groups would deny either "faith" or "works" entirely as a part of Christian life.

On balance, Christianity has historically placed a greater emphasis on "who you are" than on "what you do." Even the Roman Catholic Church of today sees faith as the primary element in our relationship with God, despite the faith-versus-works debate of the Reformation in the 1500s.[4] Both Jesus and Paul seemed to focus more on the heart than on one's concrete actions, and those books of the New Testament that do put significant emphasis on works (e.g., Matthew and James) do so within the context of the heart. When Jesus was asked what the greatest commandment was, he replied,

> "You shall love the Lord your God with all your heart, and with all your soul, and with all your mind." This is the greatest and first commandment. And a second is like it: "You shall love your neighbor as yourself." On these two commandments hang all the law and the prophets.
>
> **Matthew 22:37–40**

This teaching in Matthew is echoed in Paul (Rom. 13:9; Gal. 5:14), James (2:8), and 1 John (4:7–8). It has echoed throughout Christian history as the essence of a Christian ethic (e.g., in Augustine). The "love God and neighbor" command is thus the bedrock of a Christian ethic. These twin commands are the most absolute of Christian duties, for no conceivable situation would create an exception where it was not appropriate to love God or one's neighbor. Similarly, these two values can never come into conflict if they are properly understood.

These two Christian absolutes thus trump all other Christian values, as we will see in the next section. For example, Jesus himself made an exception to the rule not to work on the Sabbath in the light of his disciples' hunger (Mark 2:21–28). When his opponents questioned him, he did not reinterpret the Sabbath rule, as if plucking grain were not really working. His argument is rather that the situation calls for an exception to the rule not to work on the Sabbath.

With a basic sense of what the Christian priorities are, we are set to look at the main ethical theories we have just mentioned. The next section looks at duty-based ethics from a Christian perspective, followed by a more in-depth discussion of the scope of human duty. Which Christian duties are absolute? Which ones are universal but have exceptions? Which ones are relative to culture and personal conviction? The fourth section of the chapter examines utilitarianism and when "the ends justify the means," if ever. Then we briefly look at egoist ethics and the extent to which we should live for our own advantage. The last two sections end with a look at virtue-based ethics and what Christian virtue might look like.

© istockphoto.com

11.2
DUTY-BASED ETHICS

Duty-based ethics focuses on actions that are universally right or wrong—some would say intrinsically right or wrong. For example, most cultures consider it *wrong* to kill for no reason those within your group. Most would also consider it wrong to steal from your family, even if it would be to your own personal advantage.

Most cultures consider it *good* to help those closest to you when they are in need. The word *duty* might seem inappropriate for such actions, since we often want to act in this way. One would hope it is a pleasure to act lovingly toward those close to you. Nevertheless, in philosophy we can call such behavior "duties," because we are asking if it would be morally wrong for us to do otherwise. In Christian theology we speak of **sins of commission**, when we do something wrong, and **sins of omission**, when we do not do something good that we should do.

The bigger philosophical question is *why* these are duties. Is it simply a matter of culture? Is it only that our cultures find it abhorrent to steal from parents or harm someone who has nurtured and protected you? Or is there something that makes values like these universal or even exceptionless absolutes? For example, is it something biological, something about the way we evolved as animals? Is it something God created inside us, inside our "souls" or perhaps something within our brains?

Some would argue that core rights and wrongs are **absolutes**. An absolute right or wrong is one that is *always* right or wrong *without exception*. At the same time, many Christians use language of absolutes in an imprecise way. People often call something an *absolute* when they really mean that something is *definitely* right or wrong.

But if you can think of an exceptional situation to some principle or action, even one, then by definition it is not an absolute. For example, many Christians are opposed to abortion, *except* in the case of rape or when the life of the mother is in danger. By definition, therefore, these Christians are not "absolutist" when it comes to the issue of abortion.[5] Similarly, when Jesus made exceptions to the fourth commandment on keeping the Sabbath, he showed that he was not an absolutist in relation to that command.[6]

Several famous philosophers have been absolutist when it comes to ethics. For example, Plato believed that if something was morally right or

Sins of commission: wrongs a person does by doing something.

Sins of omission: wrongs a person does by *not* doing something (see James 4:17).

Absolute: in ethics, a principle of action that applies in every situation, time, and place.

Relative: in ethics, a principle of action that varies depending on the situation, time, or place.

wrong, one must always either do or not do it. The most memorable illustration of Plato's ethic is the story of **Gyges's ring**.[7] Gyges was a shepherd who found a ring that could make him invisible. So he placed himself among certain delegates to the king and then proceeded to have an affair with the king's wife, who then plotted with him and killed the king. The question posed in Plato's story is whether we should do the right thing even when we will not get caught.

Plato's answer is that we should. His reasoning is that a person is happy only when the whole person is healthy and each part—soul and body—is doing what it is supposed to do. Plato thus did not believe that a person like Gyges would be truly happy. The person might not have any physical consequences for such actions, but he or she would not be soul healthy for doing them.[8]

Immanuel Kant (1724–1804) is certainly one of the best-known absolutists in history. You might remember from chapter 4 that Kant believed we had certain built-in categories of thinking that help us process the content of our senses. He believed that this reasoning "software"—to use a contemporary metaphor—could also help us determine right and wrong.

Just before Kant, **David Hume** (1711–1776) had argued that there was no clear connection between facts (things that happen in the world) and values (the moral values we assign to those events). Kant's idea of built-in categories was his attempt to deal with Hume's argument. Kant acknowledged that we have no basis *in our experiences* for saying that happenings are right or wrong. We can say only that some events or actions bring us more or less pleasure, more or less pain. But if it gives someone pleasure to cause someone else pain, we have no experiential basis for saying the inflictor *should* not gain personal pleasure in that way.[9]

Kant's "mind software" is his solution to Hume's **fact-value problem**. In our minds we can reason to universal law, to what is "categorically" necessary for us to do or not do. This is Kant's **categorical imperative**. An imperative is a command, something that you *must* do, that is your *duty* to do or not to do. The word *categorical* means that these imperatives are absolute, without exception; it applies to everything in that category. For Kant, if something is right or wrong, it is always and without exception right or wrong.

Kant's attempt to put his categorical imperative into words proved to be a struggle over the years. His best-known formulation translates something like the following:[10]

> Only put into practice that ethical principle that you at the same time would consider to be a universal law.

Kant's Categorical Imperative

> **Fact-value problem:** the difficulty of finding an intrinsic connection between the "facts" of the world and the "values" we assign to them.

Categorical imperative: Kant's idea that if something is a "must do," an imperative, then it is always something you must do, without exception.

An end in itself: if we say something is an end in itself, we do it or value it regardless of whether it causes something else good or bad to happen. It is good for its own sake.

The ends justify the means: the idea that the goal we are moving toward is so good or valuable that it does not matter how we achieve it, even if we have to "break a few rules" in the process of getting there.

Intrinsic good: something that is an end in itself, good for its own sake.

Instrumental good: something that is good only because it leads to something else that is good.

© istockphoto.com

What Kant is saying is that a "maxim," an ethical statement, is truly an imperative only when it is always and everywhere an imperative. In other words, if something is right or wrong, it will always be right or wrong.

Countless ethicists have raised questions about such a sweeping sense of ethical absolutism, and they did in Kant's day as well. Indeed, Kant himself tried more than once to restate what he was saying in more acceptable terms. For example, at one point he said that his categorical imperative amounted to treating people as "ends in themselves."

What did he mean? If something is a "means to an end," it is a stop on a journey to somewhere else. It is an **instrumental good**. For example, nurses have to study chemistry at some point. But for them the study of chemistry is not an **end in itself,** an **intrinsic good**, despite how much they might enjoy blowing things up in a lab. Nurses study chemistry in hopes that it will make them better nurses, that they will have some background context for understanding how one aspect of the human body works. Studying chemistry is thus a means to an end.

It is usually considered problematic in ethics if someone believes that **the end justifies the means.** A person who believes that the end justifies the means believes that if the goal is good, it does not matter what path one takes to get to that goal. For example, World War II may have ended earlier than it would have because we dropped an atomic bomb on the cities of Hiroshima and Nagasaki. One might argue that fewer people died by dropping the bomb than if we had not.

But in this case, did the "end" (the goal of ending the war) justify the "means" (destroying two cities and thereby killing men, women, and children who were simply going about their daily business and not actively fighting the United States). It is a matter of debate. Are those uninvolved in the fighting of a war "guilty" because they are associated with the enemy? Was it appropriate for the Allied forces in World War II to "carpet bomb" German cities not only to destroy factories, but to demoralize the Germans as a people, killing thousands of women and children who were not involved in the fighting?

When Kant said that people are ends in themselves, he implied that you must not harm or do wrong to a person as a means to achieve some other end. And he suggested that this principle basically defines his categorical imperative. But does it, really? For example, we might argue that Kant's absolutism, because it does not allow for exceptions, actually makes "rules" more important than people. You might argue that in Kant's ethic, his *rule* is an end in itself, and people are merely a means to that end.

Let us say that you lived in Holland during World War II and were hiding Jews in your apartment. Then let us say that some Nazi soldiers came to your door and asked if you were aware of any Jews hiding on your block. Kant's categorical imperative would seem to say that, if it is wrong to lie, then it is always wrong to lie under any circumstances. Kant would seem to say that you cannot lie about the Jews being hidden.

Some believe that this is the case. However, it is difficult to see how following this maxim categorically makes people an end in themselves. If you tell the truth, "Yes, I know of Jews hiding on this block," you will likely find that both you and any Jews hiding in your apartment are about to suffer quite dramatically, perhaps even die. So Kant's ethic seems to make the maxim the end in itself rather than people.

In another attempt to clarify his categorical imperative, Kant said that it amounted to the **Golden Rule**: "Do to others what you would have them do to you."[11] Again, it is hard to see that this is anything like an accurate representation of Kant's ethic. If I were a Jew hiding from Nazis, I might be quite happy for you to lie to the Nazis at your door about my whereabouts, and I might do the same for you.

In the end, is it far more virtuous to consider the majority of ethical maxims as universally true, *but with possible exceptions*? Certainly the two great ethical commands are exceptionless absolutes: love God and love neighbor. It is difficult to imagine any situation where the right thing to do would be *not* to act in a manner consistent with love of God or love of neighbor. But the New Testament norm, as well as the norm in Christian history, seems to consider ethical norms as being universal and timeless, yes—but not as being exceptionless and thus not as being absolutes.

The topic of lying is a good case study. Most Christians would be comfortable with the idea that it is wrong to lie no matter when or where you have lived in history. However, we can question whether this ethical maxim is an *absolute*, that is, whether it is an imperative to which we should never under any circumstances make an exception. The Bible does not treat this ethic as exceptionless. You might remember the logical fallacy from chapter 3 called "circular reasoning." Circular reasoning is where you assume your conclusion in your argument. Some arguments that treat biblical teaching as exceptionless commit this fallacy.

Take the following argument:

How do you know that it is always wrong to lie without exception?

Because the Ten Commandments say, "You will not bear false witness."

We will leave aside the fact that this commandment was originally about perjury rather than lying in general.[12] Nevertheless, this answer does not

> **Golden Rule:** Do to others what you would have them do to you.

address the issue. The question we are asking is whether these commandments were meant to be *absolutes*. We are asking about the *scope* of the command, not whether the command is a command. The commandment itself says nothing about this question, about whether there would be exceptional situations where God would want you to bear false witness.

We do find instances of lying in the Bible. Certainly we must be careful not to assume that a biblical narrative's description of an action of a biblical hero corresponds to a divine or scriptural *endorsement* of that action. Nevertheless, the book of Joshua seems to look favorably on the prostitute Rahab because she lied to protect the Israelite spies at Jericho (Josh. 6:25). In other words, in this particular case, Joshua seems to consider it not only allowed but commendable to lie. Old Testament stories like this one must be read in the light of all Scripture and not simply applied straightforwardly to today, but here we have an instance where the biblical text seems to consider it better to lie than not to.[13]

Our point in this chapter is not to commend lying—not at all! Almost all Christians would agree that truth telling is a universal value that applies in all times and all places (cf. Col. 3:9). We are suggesting that this ethic is a good candidate for a maxim that is universally valid *but not exceptionless*. Lying is universally wrong, but not an absolute in situations where a higher value conflicts with it, such as when a life is at stake. Most lies are self-serving, and the Bible gives no justification for that kind of lie.

11.3
WHEN CONTEXT MATTERS

As we have argued, many use the word *absolute* in reference to values that we would more accurately call **universal rights and wrongs** that have rare exceptions. Far more biblical commands operate on this level than as exceptionless absolutes, and many even address specific situations. The books of the Bible were not written to be philosophy textbooks but to address particular audiences with their particular concerns.

For example, Paul's letters are not in the form of legal documents, with his ethical charges written so that there are no exceptions. In 1 Corinthians 6, he says that it is a shame for Christians to take other Christians to a secular Roman court and that it would be better to lose out than to do so. But did he mean this as a timeless absolute, to where there would never be any situation in history where a Christian might appropriately take another Christian to court? We can at least wonder whether he intended his words to have that sort of scope.

Another example of an ethical position that is universal in scope, but not exceptionless, is the imperative that "Let every person be subject to the governing authorities" (Rom. 13:1). This value is universal, but it is not absolute. So we find Peter and John deliberately disobeying the Jerusalem Sanhedrin, saying, "Whether it is right in God's sight to listen to you rather than to God, you must judge" (Acts 4:19).

These two passages are easy to fit together from a Christian perspective. It is universally a Christian principle to obey those in authority over you, *unless* that authority commands you to do something that contradicts a higher Christian value. So if the conflict is between obeying God and obeying the higher authority, you should obey God.

We find similar misconceptions on a popular level about what ethical or **moral relativism** is. For example, people commonly define relativism as not believing in *any* right or wrong. But that position is actually called **moral nihilism**. A relativist *does* believe in right and wrong. They simply believe that it is relative to either the person or culture.[14]

It is important to recognize that *everyone* is relativist on some issues, just as everyone makes exceptions on some issues (even Kant, no doubt). Christians are absolutist on the two love commands, and they have a universal ethic on many other issues. But we will surely find other issues on which each individual Christian must form his or her own *convictions*, his or her own sense of what God requires of the individual. Convictions are instances of relativism.

A "relative" in this context is a position that you affirm as definitely right or wrong *for you* but not necessarily for someone else. We can identify two levels. **Cultural relativism** is the view that right or wrong is determined by the culture in which you are located. **Personal relativism** is the view that right or wrong is determined by you as an individual.

When Christians oppose relativism, they are usually opposing the idea that *all* right and wrong is a function of culture or the individual, even though a relativist position will be the correct one on some issues. The individuals with whom Socrates debated, the **Sophists**, were generally cultural relativists, and at least in one place the earlier Greek historian Herodotus (ca. 484–25 BC) points in this direction. Many cultural anthropologists today lean in this direction, because they are aware of the great diversity that exists among cultures.

Herodotus tells a story about the Persian king Darius asking a group of Greeks what he would have to pay them to get them to *eat* the bodies of their dead fathers.[15] The Greeks said they would not do it for any amount of

Universal rights and wrongs: as we are defining them, ethical duties that are universal and timeless, but not exceptionless.

Moral nihilism: a position that holds that "right and wrong" does not truly exist.

Cultural relativism: the idea that right and wrong is a function of the culture in which you are located.

Personal relativism: the idea that right and wrong is a function of one's individual values and convictions.

money. Then Darius asked a group from India called the Callatians what he would have to pay them to *burn* the dead bodies of their fathers. They were appalled and begged him not even to say such a thing. They of course *ate* the bodies of their dead fathers.

At the end of his tale Herodotus reaches the conclusion that "custom is king over all," quoting a poet named Pindar. In other words, he was claiming that what you believe is right or wrong is mostly a matter of where you are from and what the customs of your location are. In fact, the word that is usually translated "law" in the New Testament also had the meaning of "custom" in the original Greek.

> Custom is king over all.
>
> **Herodotus, quoting Pindar**

Although we may hear people talk about some universal sense of right and wrong that all people have built into them, the list of common ethical customs among the peoples of the world is not very long. Almost all cultures have customs about how to treat one's children and parents, as well as about incest. It is generally considered wrong to murder an innocent person within one's particular group or family.

But beyond this short list, we find immense ethical diversity. For example, it used to be the practice of Eskimo culture to let one's elderly parents starve to death, because of the scarcity of food. The ancient Spartans and the Dobu tribe today encourage stealing among their own group to develop survival skills. Polygamy is not only acceptable in much of Africa today; it is even a sign of prosperity.

So they would not be lonely in the afterlife, wealthy Egyptian men used to have their wives and pets buried alive with their dead bodies. Similarly, it used to be the practice in India that a new widow was burned to death on the same funeral pyre as her husband, the practice of suttee. Previously in Japan, a wife accused, not necessarily guilty, of infidelity was expected to commit suicide to save her husband from the shame of the accusation.

Even in the Bible, we find instruction that most Christians would consider relative to the times and places of the Bible, but not applicable to us today. For example, we find the practice of levirate marriage in the Old Testament (e.g., Deut. 25:5–6): If an older brother dies without a son, the younger brother is to marry the wife of his dead brother to raise up seed for him. Since polygamy was fully allowed at this time in Israel (e.g., Deut. 21:15–17), we should imagine the brother adding her as an additional wife rather than taking her on as his first wife.

In the New Testament, it seems that Paul is telling the women of the Corinthian congregation to wear a hair veil in public worship when they are praying or prophesying (1 Cor. 11:5). Part of the reason is perhaps so that they show proper respect for their husbands in the presence of other males, including putative "males" such as angels (11:10) and God "himself"

BIOGRAPHY

FAMOUS MORAL DOUBTERS

Diogenes the Cynic (4th century BC): While Diogenes had his own clear sense of right and wrong, his values stood in stark contrast with those of Greek society around him. He made it a point to scorn social values he considered obstacles to happiness. According to legend, he once urinated on another person and defecated in the theater. These sorts of antics won him the title "the dog" (*kynē*). The **Cynics**—a group that advocated a simple life without possessions and considered most of society's rules unnatural—thus trace their origins largely to him. The word has changed its meaning to where today a "cynic" is someone who questions everyone's true motives.

Photo Credit: Diogenes (ca. 412–323 BC) with his Lantern, ca. 1720–40 (oil on canvas), Petrini, Giuseppe Antonio (1677–ca. 1758) / Gemaeldegalerie Alte Meister, Kassel, Germany / © Museumslandschaft Hessen Kassel / Ute Brunzel / The Bridgeman Art Library

Pyrrho the Skeptic (ca. 360–270 BC): Pyrrho was the alleged starting point for the **Skeptics** of ancient philosophy. His fundamental philosophical principle was that we cannot know anything for certain. Equal arguments, he said, can always be made for opposing sides in an argument. This sort of "noncognitivism," when applied to ethics, leads to moral skepticism: we cannot know whether moral claims are true or false. The word *skeptic* has also changed meanings and today refers to someone who doubts the truth of something.

Nicolò Machiavelli (1469–1527): Machiavelli probably held more moral values than one might think from his most famous work *The Prince*, dedicated to a Medici prince. This book is known for the way in which it advocates a political realism that flew in the face of the political idealism that preceded him. In *The Prince*, Machiavelli suggests that a new prince may have to act immorally, using his power and deception to secure his position. In other words, "might makes right" and "history is written by the winners," two sayings that do not come from Machiavelli, but aptly summarize some of his advice.

David Hume (1711–1776): Hume largely believed that our passions and emotions were what stood behind our moral statements. He did not believe that reason had anything to do with our morality; he believed that "facts" and "values" were completely different kinds of things. As such, he is a significant precursor to what would become "emotivism," the idea that moral statements are really statements of emotion. "You should not kill me" really means "I don't want you to kill me" or "I fear you killing me."

Friedrich Nietzsche (1844–1900): Nietzsche was a moral nihilist. He did not believe that evil truly existed. It was rather an idea that slaves came up with to keep their masters from exerting over them the power that in reality was theirs. The masses may need some sense of morality, but the "Übermensch," the "superperson," would always create their own right and wrong.

J. L. Mackie (1917–1981): Mackie is perhaps the most notorious moral skeptic/nihilist of recent times. He famously stated that "there are no objective values" and thus that ethics is something we invent rather than discover.

Michel Foucault (1926–1984): Although Foucault was notoriously resistant to any label, his sense of morality was basically that it changes over time. For him, power and knowledge were intimately connected. The power structures of a particular time and place create what is true for that time and place. He thus largely played out Nietzsche's perspective in the examination of the history of things like madness, crime/punishment, and sexuality. In his view his examination of these shifts itself was an exercise of power rather than a search for what was historically true.

Photo Credit: Michel Foucault, AFP / AFP / Getty Images

© istockphoto.com

(11:13).[16] Some groups do follow practices today such as women wearing prayer bonnets or putting their (uncut) hair up in a bun. But it is questionable whether these practices function the same way that veiling did at Corinth. In short, most Christian women by their very practices infer that 1 Corinthians 11 is a teaching relative to ancient Mediterranean culture.

Interestingly, Paul in the New Testament seems to have a relativist approach to one of the Ten Commandments: to remember the Sabbath day by keeping it holy. Christians over the centuries have reconceptualized the Sabbath law in terms of Sunday and have generalized it to mean setting aside a day of worship to God. But the original meaning of this commandment focused on the Israelites not working on Saturday, the Jewish Sabbath.[17] Paul's writings, however, do not consider this Sabbath legislation binding on non-Jewish Christians (Rom. 14:5; Col. 2:16). If Paul considered it still binding on Jews, but not on non-Jews, then he by definition considered obedience to the fourth commandment relative to one's ethnicity.

Are there some issues on which Christians are *appropriately* relativist today? It would seem likely. For example, Arab Christian women in the Middle East should probably cover more of their bodies in their cultural context than North American women would need to in order to be modest.[18] Similarly it seems likely that North American Christian women should cover more of their bodies than Christian women from parts of New Guinea or Africa. Few Western missionaries return from these parts of the world without reaching these sorts of conclusions.

Many Christians also have "personal convictions" that they do not consider binding on other Christians. In other words, they believe that something is right or wrong for them as a Christian individual but not necessarily for other Christians. For example, many Christians believe that it would be wrong for them to drink any form of alcohol. At the same time, many of these same believers would affirm that there are other Christians who drink moderately and are no less spiritual for doing so.

These are instances of personal relativism, where a person considers something right or wrong on an individual basis. When we have a proper understanding of what absolutism and relativism really are, we can have ethical debates that are much more productive. Some Christian ethical discussion in the past has taken place with the assumption that if a person does not take an absolutist position on an issue or if a person takes a relativist position on an issue, that person is automatically right or wrong respectively.

But Christian ethics is not as simple as absolutism versus relativism. Christians will be absolutists on some principles. Christians will be relativists on other issues. On many principles Christians will see a universal value that can have exceptional situations. One cannot simply dismiss a perspective by labeling it as relativist, and one cannot prove a perspective as Christian simply by labeling it as absolutist.

Labeling a position really says nothing about whether it is right or wrong. This way of thinking—"death by labeling"—exemplifies a number of the logical fallacies from chapter 3. For example, it can be a fallacy of diversion, where we change the subject from the real issue to an associated issue. It can be an example of the fallacy of composition, where because we find one example of "bad" relativism, we illogically generalize and say that all instances of relativism are bad. In the end, reaching sound ethical conclusions requires informed, intelligent arguments in which we weigh core principles against each other and consider the consequences of different courses of action.

Weighing ethical values requires us to get a sense of priorities, to establish a kind of hierarchy of values. For example, for the Christian, loving God and loving neighbor stand at the top of any such list as true absolutes. But below those absolutes are many universal values we hold that have exceptions: showing mercy, helping our family, telling the truth, submitting to those in authority, doing our best, and so forth. In practice, we must weigh values against values, also taking into consideration the potential consequences of an action.

> Labeling a position as "absolutist" or "relativist" proves nothing about the issue. Reaching sound ethical conclusions requires informed, intelligent arguments in which we weigh core principles against each other and consider the consequences of different courses of action.

11.4
CONSEQUENCES: UTILITARIANISM AND THE GREATER GOOD

The previous two sections looked at duty-based approaches to ethics. These are approaches that view ethics primarily through the lens of do's and don'ts. We should do certain things, and we should not do other things. Where do those duties come from? For Christians, the most important ones come from divine revelation; God has revealed certain things as right and certain things as wrong. For others, those duties might exist for some other reason. Whatever their origin, a duty approach to ethics is an act-based ethic that formulates the right course of action in the interplay between potentially competing moral values.

However, as we saw at the beginning of the chapter, there are other approaches to ethics. For example, if duty-based ethics focuses on our obligations and moral *duties*, another approach to ethics focuses on the *consequences* of various courses of actions. In reality, we take a mixture of these factors into account when trying to decide what to do.

At the beginning of the chapter, we mentioned two approaches to making ethical decisions based primarily on the potential consequences of those decisions. Utilitarianism asks what course of action is most likely to bring about the greatest pleasure or good for the greatest number. Egoism asks what course of action is most likely to bring about the greatest pleasure or good for me.

Jeremy Bentham (1748–1832) was the father of modern utilitarianism. Certainly he was not the first utilitarian. For example, in the 400s BC, Mo Tzu in China argued that we should live in a way that advances the happiness of others, challenging the more passive virtue of Confucianism and Taoism. Nevertheless, in more recent times, especially in the Western world, we look to Bentham as the strongest and most influential proponent of utilitarianism as an ethical philosophy.

The 1700s were a time of social transition in Europe, culminating in the American and French revolutions. It was also the beginning of the Industrial Revolution, where those who used to work the land steadily migrated to cities to work in factories. We would consider the living and working conditions of such workers, including the use of child labor, abhorrent today. For example, children worked in coal mines, where their smaller size enabled them to get into smaller spaces. Children as young as four years old were compelled to work from before dawn to after dusk for a small fraction of normal wage, and they often did not reach adulthood.

BIOGRAPHY

JEREMY BENTHAM

Jeremy Bentham (1748–1832) was born and died in London. His form of utilitarianism led him to several striking positions on social and political issues. He favored the complete equality of women and the abolition of slavery. But his philosophy also led him to champion animal rights, since he considered all pain and pleasure equal, whether that of a human or an animal.

He opposed the death penalty and was among the first to suggest that prisons might be used to reform individuals rather than to punish them. His writing published posthumously advocated loosening laws against homosexual practice. At the time, such individuals were arrested and imprisoned.

Photo Credit: Engraving from 1837 featuring the British Philosopher, Jeremy Bentham. © istockphoto.com

Bentham's primary concern was to find a "scientific" way of formulating law and social policy. He devised a utilitarian theory based on what might bring the greatest pleasure to the greatest number of people. For him, pain and pleasure was what ethics was all about. He and others like him were frustrated with what they saw as the artificial values of British society.

Bentham saw superstition and ignorance as the primary obstacles to putting a more rational system of law into place. For example, he was instrumental in founding the University of London, which was fully secular and admitted academically qualified students whether or not they were members of the Church of England. Upon his death, as part of his fight against what he saw as superstition, he bequeathed his estate to the university on the condition that his dead body be dressed in his clothes and be present for all university board meetings. After all, why be afraid of death when, in his opinion, there was no hell to fear? One can still see his body on display there today.

Bentham was quite calculating in the system he created. First, all that mattered was pleasure and pain. He invented the "hedon" as a single unit of pleasure. His goal was thus to quantify pleasure and pain, to turn experiences of pain and pleasure into numbers so that you could actually weigh one course of action against another. If you have a choice between two courses of action or two laws and have good reason to think that one course of action will bring about a greater total amount of pleasure in society than another, that is the course of action you should take.

In the calculation he insisted that all pleasures must count exactly the same. In fact, his system was later mocked as "pig philosophy," with the idea that the pleasure of a happy pig wallowing in the mud might count the same as the pleasure of helping someone in need or thinking an insightful thought. "Better the pig satisfied than Socrates dissatisfied," his position was caricaturized.

For Bentham, therefore, creating the laws of the land and making political decisions was a matter of adding up the total pleasure a decision would make for the populace, subtracting the total pain it would bring, and then comparing the result of the calculation with the other potential decisions. The pleasure and pain of every individual in the populace counted the same, from child to woman to lord to king. He lived long enough to see the Reform Act of 1832 passed in England, which significantly extended the right to vote in England, as well as the parliamentary representation of the large cities of the Industrial Revolution.

At the same time, we can raise a number of questions about Bentham's system in any pure form. For example, what if the total amount of pleasure and happiness of a country would increase if you were to kill off an entire

> The single goal that a legislator should have in view is the happiness of the individuals of which a community is composed, their pleasure and their security.
>
> **Jeremy Bentham,**
> *Principles of Morals and Legislation*[19]

Embalmed body of Jeremy Bentham as exhibited at University College / University College Museum, London, UK / The Bridgeman Art Library

BIOGRAPHY

EPICURUS

Bentham drew some of his inspiration from the Greek philosopher Epicurus (341–270 BC). For Epicurus, good and bad correlated directly to pleasure and pain, with pleasure being the highest good. However, Epicurus was quite clear that pleasure was not simply a matter of sensual indulgence (e.g., sex, gluttony), and temporary pain can lead to much greater long-term pleasure. Pleasure for him was mostly about a peace that comes from the absence of pain and suffering.

Epicurus built on the atomist philosophy of Democritus (see chap. 7), meaning that he believed everything breaks down into small particles and that we simply disintegrate at death. He thus taught that death is nothing to be feared. Death is the end, and the gods do not reward or punish you after death. Although he believed in the gods, he did not believe they were interested in humanity and thus were not to be feared. We saw his formulation of the problem of evil in chapter 6.

Epicurus is known for a number of other key teachings, one being the so-called "ethic of reciprocity," a form of the Golden Rule. Do no harm to others, and they will do no harm to you. He was an egalitarian and admitted women and slaves to his school as equal members, not as exceptions.

Questioning whether a person could be truly happy in the troubles of society, he advocated removing oneself from political life. (He was thus quite the opposite of Aristotle, who taught that humanity was a "political animal.") His followers met in his garden and became known as the garden philosophers.

At the time of the New Testament, Epicureanism and Stoicism were the two strongest philosophical schools; both emphasized ethics and how to have a good life. Many are familiar with the famous phrase of Horace, an Epicurean: "carpe diem" (seize the day). Interestingly, Paul in 1 Corinthians 15:32 is not quoting an Epicurean but Isaiah 22:13: "Let us eat and drink, for tomorrow we die." Some Old Testament scholars wonder if the book of Ecclesiastes was influenced by Epicurean thought, although this would require a rather late date for the book.

Words related to Epicureanism have taken on different meanings today, as have the words *cynic* and *skeptic*. An epicure is someone with a very sophisticated taste for fine food and wine. And someone who has epicurean tastes loves to eat fine food and drink fine wine.

Photo Credit: Bust of Epicurus (341–270 BC), Greek philosopher, founder of the school known as the Garden (306 BC), marble De Agostini Picture Library / G. Dagli Orti / The Bridgeman Art Library

segment of the population? Chances are that the tribe or group you would kill is already unhappy, right? So could not Bentham's "utilitarian calculus" be used to justify genocide? What if a new show called *Torture of the Week* brought immense happiness to a viewing audience, despite the immense displeasure of the tortured individuals?

It is also very difficult to know all the consequences of a future decision. A particular solution may generate its own problems and unintended consequences. For example, those who implemented "**communism**" in Russia and Eastern Europe in the early 1900s no doubt thought that a system where the state controlled how work and resources were distributed would create a happier society than one where people competed with one another for goods and services. But their historical experiment seems to have produced incredibly unhappy societies that started to turn around only after a more capitalistic system was reintroduced, based on competition.

Just after Bentham, **John Stuart Mill** (1806–1873) offered some critique and modification to the utilitarian system of Bentham, as well as to Adam Smith (1723–1790), the founder of capitalism. Mill was the son of a close friend of Bentham's, James Mill; together they had started a political group they called the Philosophical Radicals. From John's birth, James raised his son to carry on the torch of utilitarianism into the next generation. John could not associate with any children other than his own brothers and sisters. He started learning Greek at the age of three. He started Latin at eight. Throughout his teens he conversed and socialized with the leading economic minds of his day.

John Stuart Mill, 1873 (oil on canvas), Watts, George Frederic (1817–1904) National Portrait Gallery, London, UK / The Bridgeman Art Library

This first phase of John's life culminated in a nervous breakdown at the age of twenty. When he emerged from this crisis, he had become his own man and could no longer accept Bentham's utilitarianism without some modification. For example, Mill rejected the notion that all types of pleasures should count the same when one is trying to determine what course of action will have the greatest benefit. It is better to be an unhappy Socrates than a happy pig, Mill argued, meaning that some forms of happiness should count more than others.

Accordingly, Mill modified the greatest-happiness principle of Bentham. For Bentham, the principle strictly had to do with pleasure, and all pleasure counted the same. But for Mill, happiness is something more sophisticated than Bentham's idea of pleasure. For example, Mill disagreed that the pleasure of playing the game of push-pin counted the same as the pleasure of reading poetry.[21] To Mill, those who had experienced the pleasures of art and music usually recognized that these were more significant than more simple pleasures like playing a child's game. He even supported the idea that university graduates should have a greater vote, because they usually had a better idea of what was in the best interest of society as a whole than those without such an education.

> It is better to be a human being dissatisfied than a pig satisfied; better to be Socrates dissatisfied than a fool satisfied.
>
> **John Stuart Mill**, *Utilitarianism*[20]

As questionable as this idea sounds to us today, Mill's goal was to open the doors for any person—rich or poor, man or woman—to get an education. He was not in any way trying to perpetuate the class system of earlier days. Although he disagreed with Bentham's sense that all pleasures counted the same, he was playing out Bentham's sense that lack of education stood in the way of the greater good for society as a whole. The happiness of every individual counted the same, but he did not believe that every individual was equally informed about what was in his or her own best interest.

Utilitarianism has deeply impacted the modern world and in many respects seems like common sense to us today. We might assume that elected leaders and representatives in government should make decisions based on what will result in the greatest good for the greatest number, with everyone counting alike. But we also know that, in practice, politicians, political parties, states, regions, counties, and cities make decisions based on what is in their own best interest rather than in the best interest of others. Accordingly, systems of government usually try to balance out the competing interests within a society, as we will begin to see in the next section.

Also in the mix of modern governance are certain ideas concerning "ethical duties" such as those we have already discussed in this chapter. Many of them are embodied in our laws and constitutions. The Bill of Rights sets down certain ethical principles that provide boundaries that utilitarian considerations cannot cross. For example, no matter how much pleasure we might receive from grabbing and punishing someone we think committed a crime, the law of the land demands that we consider all individuals innocent until proven guilty. We are obligated to give suspects a fair trial, and the punishment cannot be cruel and unusual.

11.5
IS SELFISHNESS A VIRTUE? CONSEQUENCES AND EGOISM

© istockphoto.com

Is selfishness a virtue? One hopes the immediate response of a Christian to this question is "no, of course not." Did not Jesus and Paul say that the law was captured in the command to "love your neighbor as yourself" (Matt. 22:39; Rom. 13:9)? Did not Paul tell the Philippians to "do nothing from selfish ambition" (2:3)? How could we entertain such a thought for even a moment?

Of course, as we try to live out this idea of loving our neighbor as we would love ourselves, we might encounter some complications. Most of the world does not live by this ethic. The more common manifestation of human nature tries to get as much as it can for itself, without regard for others.

Indeed, we unfortunately would find many who call themselves Christians who have little impulse to give to others. The much more common drive is to get as much as you can. If we do not take our own interests into consideration at all, others are likely to reduce us to nothing.

Further, we find some Christians who do not "love" themselves at all. To be sure, Jesus was not addressing a "low self-concept" when he made the command to love your neighbor "as yourself." The idea of "low self-esteem" is a fairly recent and Western psychological notion. But he probably was assuming you would want to be treated nicely. We do find many people who do not "feel" as if God loves them or that anyone could truly love them. As Christians, we believe God would have such people give higher value to themselves and their own interests!

It is only in this spirit that we as Christians can consider there to be any value to the ethical approach known as **egoism**, an approach that makes decisions based on what will bring about the greatest benefit *to me as an individual*. Like utilitarianism, it is an act-based ethic that focuses on the *consequences* of an action, rather than on ethical duties or principles. Its best-known proponent was **Ayn Rand** (1905–1982), whose book *The Virtue of Selfishness* has provided us with the title of this section.[22]

Rand supported an ethical approach sometimes called *universal ethical egoism*. This is the idea that everyone should always do what is in his or her best interest. For example, Rand considered altruism, giving to others when it brings you no clear advantage, to be immoral. Having immigrated to the United States from Russia in 1926, Rand was all-too familiar with the principles of communism, and she thoroughly rejected them, moving to the opposite "libertarian" extreme. In true communism, people work for the greater good rather than for their individual benefit.

Rand's egoism is thus based on the fundamental principle of **capitalism**: if everyone acts in his or her own self-interest, a system will evolve that maximizes the personal benefit to *all* individuals. Those with resources will get as much as they can from those who want them. At the same time, those who need resources will not pay any more than they must. If everyone acts in his or her own best interests, so the theory goes, the various self-interests will cancel each other out, and an optimal situation will develop for everyone.

As far as economic systems go, history seems in general to have vindicated the capitalistic system over the attempts at communism in the twentieth century in Russia and Eastern Europe. In reality, those experiments in communism were never even able to become fully communistic, because their governments had to orchestrate the system (i.e., they were socialist rather than truly communist). Human nature being what it is, most people

Communism: in theory, "from each according to his ability; to each according to his need," a system in which everything is held in common, where everyone contributes as much as he or she can to society and takes only what he or she needs.

Capitalism: an economic system by which individuals compete for resources; those with resources sell them for as much as they can, while those acquiring them pay as little as they must.

simply are not wired to work for the good of others. In our default state, we are much more motivated when we are working in our own best interests than when we will not see any personal benefit from what we are doing.

However, it is equally clear that the idea that we should do only what is in our own self-interest is unchristian to its core. The fundamental Christian ethic is love, which by definition involves giving to others with no promise of personal benefit. Universal ethical egoism may be a good starting point for an economic system, not because it is God's ideal, but because default human nature is not what it is supposed to be. It is "fallen," corrupted, enslaved to sin (Rom. 6:17; 7:5).

Christians thus find themselves in an awkward position. We as individual believers must love our neighbors and enemies, which means we must reject the values of ethical egoism. Acts 2:44–46 gives its ideal picture of Christian community, where "All who believed were together and had all things in common; they would sell their possessions and goods and distribute the proceeds to all, as any had need. Day by day, as they spent much time together in the temple, they broke bread at home and ate their food with glad and generous hearts." Yet we live in a world where few are motivated if they are not going to see any personal benefit to what they do, and most will take anything they can get from us if we will give it.

We thus seem forced to look out for our own interests to survive while valuing more the chance to give away as much as we can. We may make some concessions to egoism when it comes to certain economic systems, but it can never be our individual ethic. That is, we may make some concessions to *universal* ethical egoism, but we cannot be *individual* ethical egoists who treat the world as if everything in it should be in our individual best interest. As Christians, our bias is supposed to be oriented around the interests of others more than around ourselves.

> Let each of you look not to your own interests, but to the interests of others.
>
> **Philippians 2:4**

> Earn all you can. Save all you can [meaning, don't spend more for things than you have to]. Give all you can.
>
> **John Wesley,
> "The Use of Money"**[23]

© Kevin L. Welch

11.6
VIRTUE AND A HAPPY LIFE

Because they are act-based ethics, all the approaches we have discussed so far in the chapter have focused on *doing*. For example, duty-based ethics focuses on things we must or must not do because they are forbidden or required. Utilitarianism and egoist ethics focus on making choices based on the potential consequences of our actions.

By contrast, virtue-based ethical approaches focus on *being* and what we should be. In other words, the focus is on our character and our motives. On the one hand, we should not think that virtue-oriented ethics are completely unrelated to act-based ethics. Surely a person demonstrates character by the way he or she acts. But a duty-based ethic is *oriented* around laws, around external do's and don'ts, while a virtue-based ethic looks more for what is "inside" a person, leading that person to act in certain ways.

Similarly, like utilitarianism, virtuous motives often involve certain goals, not least the greater good. So good consequences can also be an element of virtue-based ethics. Utilitarianism focuses almost *entirely* on consequences. It is a "consequential" or "teleological" kind of ethic. By contrast, a person of virtue might act in a certain way regardless of the consequences, perhaps in the name of honor itself.

> *Eudaimonia*: happiness.

Ethics in the ancient world generally operated on the assumption that if a person was virtuous, he or she would be happy. By happy, they did not mean flippantly happy, but satisfied, at peace, fulfilled. They called it **eudaimonia,** the "good life," "the art of living well." To be sure, ancient philosophers disagreed on some aspects of happiness and virtue. For example, some suggested you could not be fully happy unless you lived in a just society (Plato, Aristotle). Others believed you could be happy in any situation (Stoics).

As we've previously discussed, for Plato, a person was made up of three basic parts: a head, a chest, and an abdomen. Each of these three corresponded to a virtue. The virtue of the head was wisdom. The virtue of the chest, the location of the heart, was courage. Then the virtue of the abdomen, the location of the bowels, was self-control. The virtue of all three working in proper relationship to one another was justice or righteousness.

> **The Four Cardinal Virtues**
>
> **Wisdom:** knowing the right thing to do.
>
> **Courage:** being willing to do the right thing, despite obstacles.
>
> **Self-control:** controlling passions that would lead to doing the wrong thing.
>
> **Justice:** doing the right thing at the right time.

These four—wisdom, courage, self-control, and justice—were known as the **four cardinal virtues** in the ancient world. For Plato, you could be truly happy only if you had these virtues in proper relationship to one another. People with *eudaimonia* would thus have the wisdom to know the right thing to do in each situation. They would have the courage to do what they knew they should do, regardless of the obstacles that stood in the way. They would keep passions in control that might lead them astray and thus would act with justice in the world, doing the right thing at the right time.

> Virtue is a result of habit.
>
> **Aristotle,**
> *Nicomachean Ethics* 2.1[24]

Aristotle basically invented the word *ethics* in his work called the *Nicomachean Ethics*. Ethics for him was about developing a virtuous character that could lead to *eudaimonia*, true happiness. For him, the path to happiness begins with doing the right thing, with action. First, good teachers train you to do the right things. If we continue to do the right things, those actions will become habits. So becoming virtuous is about establishing good habits in how we live. Psychologists today tell us that he was actually on to something. As the saying goes, "motion brings emotion."

This is a great insight. Perhaps we do not feel like forgiving someone but we know we need to. Perhaps we have stopped feeling love for a spouse, but we want to rekindle our marriage. If we play out the very actions of forgiveness and love, we may experience those feelings—if those patterns of behavior become a habit. There are no guarantees, but it often works.[25]

So Aristotle believed that doing the right thing could lead to the habits of virtue. The habits of moral virtue, then, could lead to truly virtuous character, in which you did virtuous things by choice. Character for Aristotle meant that we consciously choose to do the right thing. Then character in turn leads to *eudaimonia*, happiness.

Happiness for Aristotle was the summum bonum, the highest good. All the other things you might desire, he claimed, you desire because you instinctively sense they will lead to your happiness. You pursue pleasure for this reason, because you believe it will make you happy. Aristotle also thought happiness comes from us living together in good communities as good citizens. He believed that humans are "political animals," so we cannot be happy outside of living together in just societies. However, in the end he believed the greatest path to happiness was the contemplation of truth.

Another key idea that Aristotle espoused was the **Golden Mean**: "moderation in all things." Unlike the Stoics, Aristotle did not believe emotions were bad or needed to be eliminated. Rather, our emotions and passions should be held in moderation. This insight is also very helpful advice for living. We humans tend to go to extremes. Aristotle suggests that the ideal is usually somewhere in the middle.

In chapter 12 we will see neither Plato nor Aristotle believed people could be fully happy unless they lived in a just society. For Plato, a government should mirror a properly ordered body. It should be ruled by philosophers directing courageous soldiers and a worker populace. For Aristotle, humanity is a "political animal," built to live together in cities. A person could be happy in several different forms of state if its leadership was benevolent.

In contrast to Plato and Aristotle, the Stoics believed a person could be happy under any circumstances. The key was to eliminate all your emotions and passions. They called this state of mind *apatheia*, which was not "apathy" in the modern sense but being "passionless." They believed that you should "love your fate" because the world was under the direction of a logical mind, the Logos.

As mentioned in the previous chapter, if the world is directed by Reason itself, by the Word, the Logos, then each one of us has inside a little seed of

Golden Mean: moderation in all things.

I have learned to be content with whatever I have. I know what it is to have little, and I know what it is to have plenty. In any and all circumstances I have learned the secret of being well-fed and of going hungry, of having plenty and of being in need. I can do all things through him who strengthens me.

Philippians 4:11–13

Logos, the "implanted word" (cf. James 1:21). The Stoics believed we have freedom to fight against the reason inside of us. But it is foolish to do so. We need to submit to the reason inside of us and accept the order of the world, to accept the direction of the divine Mind that orders everything. The Stoics thought contentment came through a process they called *oikeiosis*, coming to view your circumstances as your "home," being content with the way things are.

Recent times have seen a shift in many circles back toward a more virtue-based approach to ethics. Alistair MacIntyre, in a landmark book called *After Virtue*, argued that the Western world has lost its ethical way. "We have—very largely, if not entirely—lost our comprehension, both

> God's Logos is a shadow of him. By it he made the world, using it as an instrument.
>
> **Philo, *Allegorical Laws* 3.96**

> In the beginning was the Logos, and the Logos was with God, and the Logos was divine. This Logos was with God in the beginning. Everything came into existence through it. And without it, not even one thing came into existence.
>
> **John 1:1 Author's Translation**

BIOGRAPHY

THE STOICS

At the time of the New Testament, Stoicism was the most influential of the Greek philosophical schools. In keeping with the fact that God incarnated the truth of the Bible in understandable categories, some of Paul's ethic may reflect Stoic influence. The school itself was founded by Zeno of Citium (ca. 334–ca. 262 BC). His group became known as the Stoics because it met in the colonnade called the Stoa Poikile, in the Greek agora (marketplace).

The key idea of Stoicism is love of fate (*amor fati*). The universe is governed by divine Logos (Word). It is the Reason or Mind that orders everything. You can resist it, but it is pointless because the Logos determines what will happen. We all have seeds of this overall Logos inside of us, *logoi spermatikoi*. This is the "divinely implanted word" (see James 1:21).

The ideal is thus to live in accordance with the reason that is inside of you. The Stoics believed that emotions were the enemy of reason and thus that a person should strive to eliminate all emotion, to achieve *apatheia* or an emotionless state. Similar to Paul, a person should be content with whatever circumstances come (Phil. 4:12).

We should strive for *oikeiosis*, to accept the situations of our lives as our true home. Another contribution of Stoicism to moral discussion is the idea of *adiaphora*, things neither good nor bad, things that are neither appropriate nor sins.

Cicero (106–43 BC), in the century before Christ, and Seneca (ca. 4 BC–AD 65), at about the same time as Paul, were very influential Roman Stoics. A mixture of Stoicism with Platonism, called middle Platonism, may stand behind much of the New Testament's use of the word *Logos*. It may have influenced the way early Christians talked about Christ before he came to earth (e.g., John 1:1; 1 Cor. 8:6; Col. 1:15; Heb. 1:2).

Already in the chapter we have seen how the words *cynic*, *skeptic*, and *epicurean* have changed their meaning over time. The word *stoic* today actually remains similar to the ancient Stoics and refers to someone who is very disciplined and rational, without much emotion. On the other hand, the word *apatheia* did not mean what the word *apathetic* means in English. To be apathetic in English has a negative sense, while Stoic *apatheia* implied no feeling at all.

theoretical and practical, of morality."[26] For MacIntyre modern morality is a collection of incoherent, fragmented pieces that have managed to survive the virtue-oriented tradition of Aristotle.[27] Whether you agree with MacIntyre or not, he highlights key questions: Are good and evil real? Are virtues something real and "intrinsic" to life, built in to reality, if you would? Or are they simply a matter of human feeling or cultural perception?

Earlier in the chapter, we mentioned David Hume's sense that an uncrossable gulf existed between "facts" and "values." How do we get from "you killed someone" to "you *should* not have killed someone"? MacIntyre points out that a lot of ethical theory in the early twentieth century amounted to "you shouldn't kill people because we don't *feel* good about such things," a theory of ethics called emotivism.

Christians believe that virtue and vice, good and evil, are bigger than simply how people feel. Some may say goodness and virtue derive from God's nature. Others may say they come from God's command.[28] Whatever the precise basis of significance, Christians believe that virtue and goodness are indeed significant. The final section of this chapter will try to flesh out even more what a Christian orientation toward virtue might look like.

© istockphoto.com

11.7
CHRISTIAN VIRTUE

Of the three main types of ethical theory—duty based, consequence based, and virtue based—we will not be surprised to find that the New Testament is primarily virtue oriented. We are not surprised because, as we have seen, ancient ethics in general was primarily virtue based. It is not that we do not find ethical duties in the New Testament—"Avoid sexual immorality" (1 Thess. 4:3 NIV), for example. It is not that we do not find interest in consequences— "Make every effort to do what leads to peace and to mutual edification" (Rom. 14:19 NIV). It is only that the primary ethical interest is in virtues such as faith, hope, and love (e.g., 1 Cor. 13:13).

Accordingly New Testament ethics tends to focus more on a person's character and motives than on his or her specific actions or the consequences of those actions. To be sure, we find enough commands and prohibitions in the Bible that some Christians do focus more on duties than character. For example, many Christians today focus heavily on exceptionless, ethical absolutes and despise any thought of ethical relativisms. By emphasizing such things, these forms of Christianity tend more toward a duty-based approach to ethics than a virtue-based one.

Another example of duty-oriented Christian thinking is when Christians process the death of Jesus primarily in legal terms. They think God is so bound by duty to punish wrongdoing that he *himself* could not possibly forgive any wrong against him unless someone from the guilty party pays him in full. Accordingly, Jesus *must* become human because a human *must* pay God back, and Jesus *must* suffer the full punishment of every single sin for which he atones.

Of course, the benefit is that we as individuals are forgiven our sins, so an underlying "duty-based" sense of God turns into a picture of God as very merciful and gracious. Because Jesus has paid the debt in full, believers are no longer judged at all on the basis of their actions. God's judgment of us in his divine court is based solely on his consideration of Jesus. Nevertheless, the underlying thinking is still duty based. It is just that God assesses Jesus rather than us.

A more virtue-based approach might focus on God's character as one of love, graciousness, and faithfulness.[29] It might invoke the Parable of the Prodigal Son as a better illustration of the character of God (Luke 15). In this story, there is no legal exchange or act of atonement. The father has the authority to forgive his son of his recklessness, not to mention the insult of asking for his inheritance before his father had even died. The father forgives because he loves the son and waives off justice—which of course greatly disturbs the older brother.

Indeed, although there is clearly duty language within the New Testament, the primary orientation of Jesus and Paul seems around a person's heart and intentions. In Mark 7:18–23 Jesus says,

> "Do you not see that whatever goes into a person from outside cannot defile, since it enters, not the heart but the stomach, and goes out into the sewer?" (Thus he declared all foods clean.) And he said, "It is what comes out of a person that defiles. For it is from within, from the human heart, that evil intentions come: fornication, theft, murder, adultery, avarice, wickedness, deceit, licentiousness, envy, slander, pride, folly. All these evil things come from within, and they defile a person."

This is a vice list, the opposite of a virtue list. Jesus is basically saying that virtue and vice flow out of a person's character. To be clean or unclean is not so much a matter of external actions but a matter of what is inside a person.

Similarly, Paul speaks of the fruit of the Spirit being "love, joy, peace, patience, kindness, generosity, faithfulness, gentleness, and self-control. There is no law against such things" (Gal. 5:22–23). This is a virtue list, and Paul says these things flows naturally from God's Spirit being inside us. When Paul comes close to defining sin, he says that "whatever does not proceed from faith is sin" (Rom. 14:23). His sense of what sin is for a believer is thus not primarily a matter of violating a law but of a life that does not reflect the right character.

The New Testament does encapsulate the entirety of human duty into two commands, as we said earlier in the chapter: love God and love neighbor. These two duties indicate the appropriate motivations of a Christian's character. The heart of a Christian should be one that is oriented around helping and not hurting all others in every way. In terms of God, the heart of a Christian should be one that does everything "for the glory of God" (1 Cor. 10:31).

Here many will try to sneak back in a more duty-oriented framework. Loving God, some might say, involves keeping this list of laws for their own sake. Perhaps so, but some strong cautions are in order. First, loving God never contradicts loving our neighbor or enemy. It is not—"I must love my neighbor unless he is a homosexual, for love of God requires me to hate homosexuals." The love of God does not work this way but reinforces the love of my neighbor and enemy. It hopes for the redemption of my enemy even if my enemy is seeking to harm me.

Love of God also contradicts an inordinate focus on myself. It requires me to shift from myself being the focus of all my actions to God and his desire for the greater good. I cannot excuse selfishness or actions done in private simply because they do not harm my neighbor or enemy. A heart oriented toward God is a heart that is not oriented around myself.

11.8
CONCLUSION

In this chapter we looked at various forms of act-based ethics, as well as virtue-based ethics. Virtue-based ethics looks at what a person should *be* in order to be a happy, satisfied human being. Act-based ethics are of two basic types. Duty-based ethics is focused on rights and wrongs, the actions a person should or should not do. Utilitarian and egoist ethics focus on the consequences of a person's actions, whether it be what brings about the greatest good for the greatest number or the greatest good for me, respectively.

However, in the end we suggested that a virtue-based, character-oriented approach to ethics fits most naturally with both Scripture and historic Christianity. The most fundamental absolutes of Christianity are a matter of the heart and of intention, namely, that we love God with all our heart and our neighbor as ourselves. Jesus and the New Testament tell us that if a person will love both neighbor and enemy, then that person will have met all the requirements of Scripture.

In that light, the clearest path to a fulfilled life is a life fully surrendered to God and a life in which we look out for the true benefit of others. It is not a life of jealousy or getting ahead by harming others. The "end" does not "justify the means" when our path to accomplish something brings harm to others or undermines our service to God. But in most other circumstances, the goal of truly loving God and others will often cause us to make exceptions to other rules. Love is the absolute. The way it plays out is relative to context and circumstance.

KEY TERMS

- ethics
- act-based ethics
- virtue-based ethics
- duty-based ethics
- utilitarianism
- egoist ethics
- axiology
- sins of commission
- sins of omission
- absolutes
- fact-value problem
- Gyges's ring
- categorical imperative
- instrumental goods
- intrinsic goods
- end in itself
- ends justify the means
- Golden Rule
- universal rights and wrongs
- moral nihilism
- moral relativism
- cultural relativism
- personal relativism
- communism
- egoism
- capitalism
- *eudaimonia*
- four cardinal virtues
- Golden Mean

KEY PHILOSOPHERS / MOVEMENTS

- Sophists
- Cynics
- Skeptics
- Stoics
- Epicureans
- David Hume
- Immanuel Kant
- Jeremy Bentham
- John Stuart Mill
- Ayn Rand

PHILOSOPHICAL QUOTATIONS / IDEAS

- "Custom is king over all." (Herodotus)
- "Might makes right." (Machiavelli)
- Virtue is a habit. (Aristotle)

KEY QUESTIONS

1. Toward which of the three main ethical approaches (duty based, consequence based [utilitarian], virtue based) do you most lean? To what extent are you egoist in your approach to life?

2. What do you see as the normal "scope" of ethical duties? Do you think most ethical duties are absolutes, universal with exceptions, relative, or not really a matter of right and wrong at all (*adiaphora*)? Can you think of one issue on which your position falls into each of these categories? If so, describe.

3. Create a list of your "hierarchy of values." If "saving a life" and "telling the truth" come into conflict, which is higher on your list of priorities, for example? Compare your list with someone else's.

4. Look at your own life. Are there any patterns of behavior that you recognize as vices? Strategize how you might turn this area of your life into a virtue by forming the right habits. Do you believe that virtue can be a habit?

5. Is there anything in this chapter about which you have serious questions or to which you take major exception? Investigate it and discuss it with others.

NOTES

1. Along with aesthetics (study of the beautiful), it is a branch of axiology, which more broadly asks questions about what is truly valuable.
2. Also called deontological approaches.
3. Also called a teleological approach.
4. See in particular the *Joint Declaration on the Doctrine of Justification by the Lutheran World Federation and the Catholic Church* (Grand Rapids: Eerdmans, 2000). The declaration was made in 1999.
5. An absolutist might argue that removing the unborn from the womb to save the life of the mother is not an abortion if one does not actively kill the unborn but removes it to save the mother's life.
6. As we will see below, we would probably classify Paul better in the New Testament as a relativist when it comes to the Old Testament Sabbath law, because he did not consider the Sabbath law binding on all people in all times and all places.
7. Plato's *Republic* 359b–360b.
8. Plato's ethic flowed naturally from his sense that behind the shadowy world we see around us with our senses is a more real world of ideas we can access with our minds. This world of ideas is unchanging and is thus a realm of absolute truth. Accordingly, our actions should line up without exception to these truths.
9. This is my extension of Hume's point.
10. A more formal translation of his German would be "Act only on that maxim that you can, at the same time, wish to be a universal law."
11. A form of the Golden Rule appears in Jesus's Sermon on the Mount in Matthew 7:12.
12. Discussion of the Ten Commandments frequently generalizes these commandments in ways that alter their original meaning. For example, the third commandment not to take the name of the LORD in vain was originally about keeping oaths that one had made by swearing by YHWH, the name of God. If we take it to be about cursing or swearing, we have changed its meaning from what it originally was, probably without even knowing it.
13. Interestingly, some very early copies of John 7:8 have Jesus tell his brothers that he is not going to the feast in Jerusalem, after which he then goes secretly.
14. A person who believes in universal rights and wrongs but believes there may be exceptional *situations* is not a relativist. The position we presented above with regard to lying, for example, is not a relativist position, because it believes that lying is wrong in all times and places. It simply argues that there are exceptional cases.
15. Herodotus, *The Histories* 38.
16. God is of course not literally male, for literal maleness requires male sexual organs, which God does not have. God has no body; therefore, male language in reference to him is metaphorical de facto (by the nature of the situation).
17. The Jewish Sabbath has always been from sundown on Friday to sundown on Saturday, as we see in the pattern of creation in Genesis 1: "And there was evening and there was morning, the first day" (Gen. 1:5).
18. It is ironic that many American Christians equate Israel with Christian and Arab/Palestinian with non-Christian. There are arguably far more Arab and Palestinian Christians than Jewish Christians living in the Middle East.
19. Jeremy Bentham, *Principles of Morals and Legislation* (1780), chap 3. Paraphrased from the original work in English.
20. John Stuart Mill, *Utilitarianism* (1861), chap. 2.
21. The actual quotation by Bentham is "Prejudice apart, the game of push-pin is of equal value with the arts and sciences of music and poetry." Jeremy Bentham, *The Rationale of Reward* (London: Robert Heward, 1830), 206. Mill summarized Bentham's position as "Push-pin is as good as poetry." John Stuart Mill, "Bentham," in *Dissertations and Discussions* (London: Parker, 1959), 1:389.
22. Ayn Rand, *The Virtue of Selfishness* (New York: Signet, 1964).

NOTES

23. These are the slightly paraphrased main points of John Wesley's sermon, "The Use of Money." See *The Works of John Wesley*, 3rd ed. (Peabody, MA: Hendrickson, 1986), 6:126, 131, 133.

24. All quotations of Aristotle in this book are paraphrased on the basis of *The Complete Works of Aristotle*, ed. J. Barnes, vols. 1–2 (Princeton, NJ: Princeton University, 1984).

25. You may wonder how this idea fits with the Christian sense that we cannot do any good in our own power but only by God's power. It is indeed a mystery how our wills work together with God's will. But most of us do not sit around and wait for God to feed us miraculously! We seek out food and eat it. Similarly, to say that acting virtuously can facilitate the desire and feelings of virtue does not deny in any way that God might be working behind the scenes in us.

26. Alasdair MacIntyre, *After Virtue: A Study in Moral Theory,* 2nd ed. (London: Duckworth, 1985), 2.

27. Ibid., 257.

28. See chapter 6.

29. See Joel B. Green and Mark D. Baker, *Recovering the Scandal of the Cross: Atonement in New Testament and Contemporary Contexts* (Downers Grove, IL: InterVarsity, 2000).

© Kevin L. Welch

12.1
THE DEVELOPMENT OF GOVERNANCE

By most accounts, the earliest forms of human society involved bands of extended families.[1] At some point, these groups collected together in tribes. We see a snapshot of these dynamics in the origins of Israel in the Old Testament. Abraham seems somewhat nomadic and wanders across the land. The family of Jacob becomes over time the tribes of Israel.

It may take some effort for modern Westerners to get their heads around how recent an invention the **nation-state** is in human history. Some historians would argue that nations as we now conceive them are perhaps less than two hundred years old. The default way of human thinking is local and "tribal," and it takes some effort for diverse social groups spread out over a wide area to

What to Get from This Chapter

- Social and political philosophy tries to ascertain the best (and worst) ways we might live together.
- The simplest forms of human society involve bands and tribes. For most of recorded history, societies have focused around city-states. The nation-state is a relatively recent development.
- History has seen a number of different forms of government including theocracies, monarchies, aristocracies, democracies, and anarchies.
- A social contract is an implicit or explicit agreement between the members of a society.
- Capitalism arose as an economic system in the 1700s and aims at the free exchange of goods and services in accordance with the laws of supply and demand.
- Karl Marx argued that capitalism was inherently unstable and inevitably oppressed workers.
- The New Testament world had a sense of "limited good" and thus viewed wealth negatively because one person's accumulation was seen to imply another person's loss.

Questions to Consider

- To what extent are nationalities "social constructs"?
- What do you think is the best way to structure a government?
- How do people "contract" to live together, both formally and informally?
- What do you think is the best way to structure an economy?

Key Words

- Nation
- Democracy
- Social contract
- Capitalism

think of themselves as a single group with a central point of governance that they embrace as their own rather than as an imposition of power on them.

Which came first, a nation or its people? Arguably the people always come first. The idea of a nation is a **social construct**, a way of looking at a collection of people that is not intrinsically based on who those people are.[2] It is a way of looking at a collection of people that cultures "create" and then put into effect by way of certain structures. It is a set of glasses through which a people views itself, when it is quite possible that individuals within the nation might view themselves in a different way. It is a social construct that does not exist unless a group of people owns and thus creates it.

That is not to say that there is no concrete element involved in the formation of the modern "nation." Location, language, common customs, common enemies—all sorts of concrete reasons exist that allow a group far beyond the local to consider itself to have a singular identity. In previous times, of course, the formation of social groups large enough to be called "empires" took place by way of war and military conquest, led by strong autocratic leaders. In such situations it is clear that the leaders are exercising power from the outside and are "other." Nations as we are speaking of them are identities embraced from within rather than forced from without.

As we look back, we tend to assume these sorts of constructs were the norm throughout history. It thus requires some cognitive effort on our part to think of ancient Israel more as a tribal collection, an amphictyony, than as a nation per se. For example, we should not think of the judges of Israel as being some kind of centralized leaders over Israel as a single entity. These were rather ad hoc charismatic leaders that some portion of the Israelite tribes gathered around primarily in times of military engagement.[3]

In the past Western history was taught in a way that led many of us to think of Greece and Rome as islands of civilization in the middle of the barbarian world that surrounded them. Of course this is how the Greeks and Romans viewed themselves. We even find traces of this way of constructing reality in the New Testament, such as in Romans 1:14 where Paul follows the convention of dividing the non-Jewish world into "Greeks and barbarians."

The result is that we often think of places like ancient Greece and Rome in the same way we look at nations today. But if we dig a little deeper, we find that the Greek and Latin words for places like Athens and Carthage are plural. These cities were originally collections of tribes. The city of Athens was originally hundreds of individual clans combined to form ten tribes in 508–507 BC. The city of Rome similarly consisted of numerous tribes.[4] In the year 242 BC, there were officially thirty-five tribes in Rome.

In the times before empires, prominent cities usually had their own kings—thus the idea of **city-states**. The ancient norm for a long time

Social construct: a way of understanding something not intrinsic to the thing itself but generated by a social group.

Nation-state: the modern sense of nations where a relatively large group of people in a significant space embrace a common identity and governance.

City-state: cities as the unit of independent governance in the ancient world, usually with each city having its own king.

involved cities ruled independently of one another. These cities were surrounded by lands with smaller villages, which they subjected to their power. And cities and alliances of cities would try to conquer other cities and alliances (see Gen. 14:1–11). Kingdoms and empires were born. Conquered cities paid tribute to the chief city—until they were either powerful enough to conquer back or could switch their allegiance to the enemies of their conquerors.

Again, reading the history in the Bible with its original connotations will require us to make some paradigm shifts. We tend to think of ancient Israel as a single entity, but the kingdoms of David and Solomon were much more a collection of loosely associated tribes. Certainly Jerusalem was not the obvious center of any identity; it had not even been Israelite until David himself conquered it. The tribes of Israel bound together under a king so that they could defend themselves against the Philistines, something the mere tribal alliance they had before was no longer able to do.[5]

When the Assyrians invaded Palestine in the late 700s BC, they conquered all the cities of Israel and Judah except one—Jerusalem. But this was the key city, the "city-state" that ruled all the other cities of so-called Judah. As long as it remained intact, the "kingdom" of Judah remained intact. By contrast, because the "city-state" of Samaria had fallen in the north, the "kingdom" of Israel fell. The borders of kingdoms and empires at that time were a matter of what cities you conquered, which cities paid tribute to which cities. In the period between the testaments, Jerusalem was part of various kingdoms, depended on which it was currently paying tribute to—whether Persia, Egypt, Syria, or, finally, Rome.

The point of this brief historical tour is to highlight that the way we view ourselves as a group of people living together may not be as self-evident as we suppose. We live together within certain social paradigms and assumptions that could be markedly different. For example, most of us in the Western world assume the "obvious" superiority of democracy over other forms of government. Many people thought that, when the United States set out to remove Saddam Hussein from power in 2003, the people of Iraq would welcome the opportunity for democracy. What we found was a group-oriented, tribal society that Britain had artificially spliced together in 1920. Several years of intense civil strife and hostility to the United States ensued.

This chapter is about **social and political philosophy**. It asks questions about how humans might live together in the best (and worst) ways. In a sense it is the field of ethics on a societal scale. As chapter 11 on ethics focused on how *I* should live or how I might achieve a good life, this chapter will ask more about how *we* might best live together. The two subjects are not distinct from each other, and we have already dipped a little into this chapter's issues in chapter 11.

Social and political philosophy: that branch of philosophy that tries to ascertain the best (and worst) ways we might live together.

BIOGRAPHY

THE EXAMPLE OF GERMANY

The history of Germany these past two hundred years illustrates how the self-understanding of a society can change dramatically in a rather short period. If we turn back to 1800, what we now call Germany was part of a collection of some three hundred relatively independent states spread out over present-day Germany, Austria, Switzerland, Belgium, etc. (the Holy Roman Empire).

The almost one-city countries of Luxembourg and Lichtenstein are leftovers from that period. Interestingly, even today the German cities of Berlin, Hamburg, and Bremen have a somewhat independent "city-state" status unlike any other German cities. These small states are artifacts of an age when rule was localized and city oriented under kings and kinglike rulers.

Who ruled what was more a matter of inheritance and marriage than a bounded area of land. For example, the king of England in the 1700s and early 1800s was also the ruler of Hanover in Germany. Governance thus was less about *where* a place was as *who* its ruler was. Marriage was a way of unifying kingdoms. Catherine the Great of Russia (1729–1796) was German, as is the current ruling family of England.

Meanwhile, in 1800 there were other forces going on in the world that were also working in Germany. Both France and the United States had seen revolutions that strongly pushed the right of the "common man" to govern himself (literally) without kings in charge, a fairly new idea in history, even if the Greeks had briefly explored it a couple of millennia ago. At this same time, the German Johann Gottfried von Herder (1744–1803) apparently invented the word *nationalism* and argued that a people's identity grows best out of its geography and language (not its rulers). He urged people living in the Holy Roman Empire to stop speaking French and speak their more natural language: German.

Herder's fairly innocuous ideas on history had an immense impact on German history through others who built on his ideas. Johann Gottlieb Fichte (1762–1814) made his *Addresses to the German Nation* in which he pointedly made it clear that the French and the Jews were not German and did not belong. They did not trace their ancestry and language to the Germanic peoples mentioned as far back as the second century by the Roman historian Tacitus. Of course those tribes had long since moved on. What we are seeing here is the invention of the German "nation" as a social construct.

The Brothers Grimm began to write down German folk tales that were meant to reveal authentic German identity. This was the era of Romanticism (see chap. 13), and in part it played itself out in Germany with music like that of Richard Wagner (1813–1883), who celebrated an idealized (i.e., socially constructed) German past. Georg W. F. Hegel (1770–1831) spoke of a zeitgeist, a "spirit of the age" that can reach a critical mass when a people comes to determine its place in history (see chap. 14). These forces climaxed of course in Adolf Hitler's (1889–1945) attempt to reunify all the areas he believed were German into a single people, as well as to expunge these lands of those he did not consider to be truly German.

The period since Hitler has been a rocky one for Germany. After World War II, Germany was divided into two countries, east and west, with the east under the influence of communist Russia. Two quite different understandings of society pervaded in the two parts of Germany. The west adopted the democratic structures of the West and prospered. The east adopted a modified version of Karl Marx's (1818–1883) understanding of history (see chap. 14), where the end goal of society is for all property to be held in common—communism.

With the decay of the Soviet Union, the two parts of Germany were reunified in 1990. All of Germany is now a democracy and one of the key players in the European Union, a collection of countries in Europe. This unified Europe is no doubt creating a new sense of identity for Germany, complicated not only by the fragments of so many different earlier perspectives, but also by a massive immigration from the east that will soon take over the population of the country.

12.2
WAYS TO GOVERN SOCIETY

If we look at different societies from the standpoint of who is in charge, certain basic options emerge to structure the governance. We can find examples of each option in history, as well as philosophers who have favored each. In recent years the dominant form of government—the constitutional democracy—somewhat combines the strengths of the varying options and thus tries to maximize the benefits of each.

Engraving of Moses receiving the Ten Commandments.

Theocracy (Rule by God or Gods)

A very old option, and one that we see in play in parts of the world today, is that of a **theocracy**, in which God or gods are said to rule. We like to think of ancient Israel as somewhat of a theocracy from Moses to the time Israel got a king. John Calvin ran the city of Geneva in the 1500s something like a theocracy. When Muslim groups strive to bring their countries under sharia law, they are striving toward a relatively theocratic form of governance.

The problem with a theocracy, of course, is that the gods rarely come down to govern in person. In ancient India, for example, the will of the gods came through the caste of priests who claimed to know what they wanted. We find no record of a theophany—a visible appearance of God—in Calvin's Geneva. Theocracies turn out generally to be rule by priests or by central religious figures. All scriptures have to be interpreted by someone, and issues always arise that such scriptures do not address. Rule by God or gods thus usually turns out to be rule by one or by a few who can convince everyone else that they know what God or the gods want.

The question of a theocracy does, however, raise important issues for Christians to consider in terms of how they should relate to the broader societies in which they live. To what extent should Christians strive to make the laws of their lands a mirror of their Christian understanding? The same question applies similarly to Muslims today. To what extent should predominantly Muslim countries enact laws based on a particular understanding of the Qu'ran?

H. Richard Niebuhr, in his book *Christ and Culture*, suggested five basic ways in which Christianity has related to its surrounding culture throughout history.[6]

Theocracy: rule by God or certain gods.

1. **Christ against Culture**

   In this model Christianity sees itself in hostile conflict with the secular culture around it. From an aggressive perspective, the goal might be to eliminate the secular and make the world conform to Christianity. Alternatively, this approach might lead a group to remove itself from the broader culture and isolate itself. Christ and culture are seen as adversaries.

2. **The Christ of Culture**

   At other times Christianity has seen the progress of culture as the unfolding of God's will in the world. Accordingly, cultural developments *are* Christian developments, and so the movement of secular culture is the movement of God. In this model the distinctiveness of Christian faith blurs into the broader worldview of the host culture. Classical Christian liberalism might illustrate this approach.

3. **Christ above Culture**

   This perspective synthesizes culture with Christianity and is best illustrated today by the difficulty some people have distinguishing their patriotism from Christianity. An American flag on a pulpit may hint that a congregation has a hard time distinguishing nationalism or a specific political party from Christian faith.

4. **Christ and Culture in Paradox**

   Some Christians have found it difficult to reconcile their Christian beliefs with their participation in secular culture, but they have nevertheless participated in that broader culture by thinking and acting one way in the secular realm and another way in the church. They may recognize that these two ways of thinking and acting are incompatible, but they consign this paradox to the time before God sets all things aright.

5. **Christ the Transformer of Culture**

   The approach to culture that does not eliminate pagan culture but seeks to win it over to Christ, to convert it. It accepts the distinction between Christ and culture but strives to see the culture won over to Christ.

Your sense of which of these options best fits with a Christian approach to culture may connect strongly with your particular theological tradition. For example, the Lutheran tradition functions largely within the fourth model where Christ and culture are two irreconcilable realities that will always exist side by side until the end, two kingdoms coexisting next to each other. Even the life of an individual Christian for Luther was "at the same time sinner and righteous, always penitent."[7] In a way, a person belongs to both kingdoms at the same time.

The Calvinist model has often viewed secular culture as something to be taken over for Christ. In Puritan New England, for example, the entire culture was expected to conform to the Christian understanding of its leaders. The Calvinist tradition emphasizes God's sovereignty to the exclusion of human freedom and so understandably has often been oriented around eliminating actions and beliefs in its surroundings that do not conform to its understanding of God's will.

Other traditions, such as the Arminian one in which this book stands, believe that God in his sovereignty has made it possible for humans on this earth to decide whether or not to serve him. He will eventually administer final verdicts on such choices, but in this world he has more often than not "given over" the world to the consequences of its choices (e.g., Rom. 1:28). It thus would lean to Niebuhr's fifth option, with an emphasis on winning the world over to Christ rather than forcing the world to conform, conforming to the world, confusing the church with the world, or isolating oneself from the world.

Monarchy (Rule by One)

If we look back through recorded history, the dominant form of government has no doubt been that of a **monarchy**, rule by one sovereign individual. Plato and Aristotle both considered this form of government to be the best, assuming that a king was just. Aristotle also thought it would be the worst if a tyrant rather than a benevolent ruler became king.

Plato wrote about what he considered to be the ideal society in his long "dialogue" known as the *Republic*.[8] Basically Plato's dream of the ideal society ran parallel to his sense of the virtuous person (see chap. 11). Just as he believed a person would be happy if all the parts of his or her body were doing what they were supposed to do, so in the ideal society each person would do the kinds of things that he or she was most suited to do.[9] So the wisest in a society should lead, just as the head should govern the body with wisdom. He saw such leaders as "philosopher kings," monarchs who ruled not because of ambition or greed, but because they were the wisest and had the best interest of society in view.

King Henry VIII of England reigned from 1509 to 1547.

> Until philosophers are kings over nations, or the current kings and rulers take philosophy seriously . . . there will be no end of troubles for our cities or the human race.
>
> **Plato, *Republic* 473c–d**

The warriors and the workers in a society corresponded for Plato to the chest and abdomen of the body. The warriors defend and fight for the state with courage (the "chest" of society). The workers are then controlled for the good of the body, like the head controls the passions in our guts (the "abdomen" of society). With everyone in his or her proper place, such a republic would be a place of peace and happiness. Interestingly, because Plato believed that this physical world was not the most real world—truth is found with the mind (see chap. 4)—Plato believed women could rule just the same as men.

Like Plato, **Aristotle** did not believe a person could be fully happy unless that person was in a good society. "A human is by nature a political animal," he said.[10] To him, the best government was a monarchy: rule by a single king who had the best interests of his people in mind. By the same token, the worst form of the state was a tyranny: rule by a single individual who ruled oppressively and only in his own interest.

Aristotle was a brilliant thinker, but some of his views clearly reflected the age in which he lived. For example, though Plato thought that the material world was a copy of the ideal world, Aristotle believed that everything was made up of form and substance. The form was the shape you could see or the essence of something you could abstract with your mind. The substance was some unseen, underlying material you could not see.

When it came to the process of conception and birth, Aristotle believed that women provided only the substance of a child, the form was purely a matter of the man. Women were like the soil in which the man's seed was planted. He provided the organization of the material. As far as the children themselves, Aristotle saw women as unfinished men. Unlike Plato, he did not believe that women could rule over society in the vast majority of cases, although he strongly distinguished them from slaves.

Although Aristotle believed a benevolent monarchy was best suited for the happiness of a people, he considered rule by an "aristocracy" or a "democracy" as potentially good societies. Rule by an aristocracy here refers not to rule by the rich or upper class but rule by a group of the best men. Aristotle considered it the second-best form of government, with its dark equivalent, rule by a collection of bad leaders (oligarchy), the second worst. Finally, he believed a democracy could be the third-best form of government if the people voted in the best interests of the whole. Conversely, democracies could become mob rule, where everyone voted selfishly in a way that caused the society to implode.

In the 1600s in France and England, the notion of the **divine right of kings** was dominant. According to this theory, God was the only one who had the authority to question the actions or authority of a king. The theory made significant use of passages such as Romans 13:1–7, which says that "those authorities that exist have been instituted by God. Therefore whoever

> A human is by nature a political animal.
>
> **Aristotle, *Politics* 1253a**

> A husband and father rules over his wife and children, with them as free individuals [not slaves], but the way he rules is different in each case. He rules over his children like a king. He rules over his wife like a city leader leads its citizens. Although there are exceptions to the order of nature, the male is by nature better equipped to command than the female.
>
> **Aristotle, *Politics* 1259b**

> Wives, in the same way, accept the authority of your husbands . . . Thus Sarah obeyed Abraham and called him lord . . . Husbands, in the same way, show consideration for your wives in your life together, paying honor to the woman as the weaker sex.
>
> **1 Peter 3:1, 6–7**

resists authority resists what God has appointed, and those who resist will incur judgment." Perhaps the best embodiment of this concept was under Louis XIV, who made his rule the final authority in all matters—even supplanting the pope's authority in religious matters in France.

The public philosophy of Thomas Hobbes (1588–1679) in relation to kings reflects the spirit of that age. For him, although kingship derived in theory from a social contract between the people of a kingdom and a sovereign ruler, the people did not have the right to question the authority of a king. Without kings, the default state of humanity was "every man against every man."[11] Because of this, people surrendered the entirety of their rights to the king in exchange for his guidance and protection. Once surrendered, the people had no choice but to submit, even if the king did not seem to keep up his end of the deal.

> **Divine right of kings:** the idea that since kings are appointed by God, their authority cannot be questioned or undermined.

Aristocracy
(Rule by a Few)

The word *aristos* in Greek means "best." In theory, therefore, the **aristocracy** are the best of a society, and rule by

Cicero in the Senate Accusing Catiline of Conspiracy on 21st October 63 BC, 1889 (fresco), Maccari, Cesare (1840–1919) / Palazzo Madama, Rome, Italy / Ancient Art and Architecture Collection Ltd. / The Bridgeman Art Library

an aristocracy is in theory rule by the best. Most of us today of course would reject this idea, since the word *aristocracy* has come to mean the wealthy of society. We have long since rejected the idea that the most powerful and the "upper class" are necessarily any more virtuous than the common person. Indeed, we are more likely to have serious suspicions about the virtue of the privileged of society.

Rule by a "few good men" has often been a key form of leadership in tribal societies. In the Old Testament, we hear of trials being held at the gates of a city by its elders (Josh. 20:4). In the New Testament, it seems local gatherings of Christians had a group of elders who were overseers of that community of faith (e.g., Titus 1:5–7). These forms of governance fit in well with the cultures of the time, so we should not think that we must imitate the same form of church governance today. What makes for effective leadership at one time and place may not be as effective in another.

Before the time of the Roman emperor Augustus (63 BC–AD 14), Rome was ruled by a senate, which comes from a Latin word that meant "elder." From the pool of these older and supposedly wiser men, two rulers (consuls)

> **Aristocracy:** in theory, rule by the most virtuous in a society. In recent centuries, the word has come to refer to the "landed gentry," those with inherited status in a society and often wealthy.
>
> **Oligarchy:** rule by a few individuals, sometimes with a pejorative sense.
>
> **Direct democracy:** rule by the people where individuals directly make a community's decisions.
>
> **Representative democracy:** rule by the people where individuals elect representatives to make most of the direct decisions for them.

were elected each year by the citizens to run the Roman republic. Only when both consuls agreed was their decision enacted. The United States drew its idea of "senators" from the Roman model. U.S. senators were thus meant to be noble, wise individuals who held office longer than the population-based House of Representatives. Two are elected from each state, no matter how big or small, on the assumption that such individuals should be statesmen who can think about the benefit for the whole, beyond the interests of a specific population.[12]

Because modern nations are too large for every citizen to vote on every issue, almost all modern democracies are **representative democracies** rather than **direct democracies**. The people elect individuals to represent their interests in a parliament or congress. The ways in which those houses represent the populace varies from country to country, sometimes parties as much as specific individuals being elected.

Ancient Greece provides us with two examples of an **oligarchy**, another word for rule by a few. A group of wealthy Athenians in 414 BC overthrew the democracy of Athens and for four months ruled as "the Four Hundred." This group was known as an oligarchy, as was the later one-year rule of "the Thirty," an oligarchy that the Spartans, after winning the Peloponnesian War, put in place in Athens in 404 BC. While these oligarchies were brief, they no doubt were principal examples for Aristotle of how rule by a few could play out as a bad form of government.[13]

Signing the Declaration of Independence, 4th July 1776, ca. 1817 (oil on canvas), Trumbull, John (1756–1843) / Location Unknown / Photo © Boltin Picture Library / The Bridgeman Art Library

Democracy (Rule by the Majority)

The idea of democracy—that a people would govern themselves, with its members voting on individual decisions—is very rare in the history of the world. It existed for almost two centuries in the ancient city-state of Athens (508–322 BC), although briefly interrupted by the oligarchies mentioned above. Even then, women, slaves, foreigners, and of course children were not allowed to vote. Direct democracy is really only practical in relatively small settings, such as the town hall meetings of New England, some of which have taken place continuously from the 1600s till today. In these, the citizens of relatively small towns constitute the local government and meet together to make the primary decisions of government themselves.

Democracy did not reemerge as a significant option for government until the 1700s with the rise of the Enlightenment's focus on individual rights and the idea that government derives its authority from those governed. Technically speaking, however, the form of government put into place in the United States after the American Revolution is a **republic**, because the majority is limited by its Constitution in what it can do by basic rights afforded to those in the minority. The United States is thus a constitutional, representative democracy, as we might consider most modern nations.

An improvement on democracy from the times of the Greeks is the inclusion of women and individuals of all races among those who get to participate in democracy. For example, the Fifteenth Amendment to the United States Constitution made former male slaves and men of every race eligible to vote. Interestingly, it was not until 1920 that a similar amendment, the nineteenth, afforded women the right to vote.

A constitutional democracy tends to combine the strengths of the other forms of government, while mitigating their weaknesses. For example, the strength of a monarchy is the efficiency of focusing power in a single individual. Things get done. The weakness is when that single individual is bad, he or she can do immense harm. A constitutional democracy usually has a single individual as its chief executive, whether a president or a prime minister, but this person is elected and limited in what he or she can do.

This is the idea of a **balance of powers** or a system of **checks and balances**. For example, the U.S. government has three branches: the executive, legislative, and judicial. Each counterbalances the power of the others. The Congress in the United States, like the parliaments of other countries, is made up of representatives of the people elected by the people to make decisions on their behalf. The advantages of rule by the people in a democracy are thus combined with the advantages of rule by a few.

Republic: a form of representative, democratic government in which individual rights are protected from the whims of the majority.

Balance of power/checks and balances: where the power of one entity is held in check or balanced by the power of another, so that no one power has absolute authority or can abuse its power.

Anarchy (Rule by No One)

Occasionally a group will arise that claims people do not need to be governed by anyone. If you take the word **anarchy** apart, it means "without rule." But we all know that in reality the word *anarchy* refers to chaos and mayhem, sometimes involving violence. Needless to say, we have to look quite hard in history to find communities that did not have some kind of clear leadership. The few we find, utopian societies like the ones in the 1800s in Oneida, New York, or Shakertown, Kentucky, were relatively small and generally short lived.

Karl Marx (1818–1883) also had a vision for a society that was "stateless." He believed that **capitalism**, the economic system in which individuals accumulate wealth by selling resources for profit, inevitably led

Anarchy: chaos, the absence of order.

Capitalism: an economic system in which individuals and companies accumulate wealth by selling their resources for profit.

Proletariat: the workers of a society.

Bourgeoisie: members of the managerial, business class of a society who control the production and distribution of goods.

Marxist communism: utopian vision of a classless, stateless society in which all resources are held in common by a people.

Socialism: economic system in which the state owns everything and directs the production and distribution of goods.

Marxist-Leninism: an approach to communism that saw socialism as a necessary transition to a classless society, led by a professional class of revolutionaries.

to the oppression of the people who did most of the work. He believed that people by nature liked to work but that the capitalist system "alienated" them from their true selves. Eventually, he believed the workers of such societies (the **proletariat**) would overthrow the company owners and managers (the **bourgeoisie**) and a "classless" society would develop. In this **Marxist communistic** system, all the resources of a state would be held in common by everyone, and there would be no need for the state to control things.

Vladimir Lenin tried to implement communism in Russia after the 1917 Bolshevik Revolution he led. In his **Leninist** version of communism, he believed a strong group of leading revolutionaries would be needed to bring about the transition. First, the state would need to take over all property and direct all the production and distribution of goods (**socialism**). But more than seventy years later, the failure of his experiment was obvious. Marx's vision for communism never actually emerged from any of the states that aimed for it.

Events of the twentieth century cast immense doubt on the likelihood of Marx's dream. The communist experiment in Russia and Eastern Europe ended in economic failure and the eventual dissolution of the Soviet Union in 1991. Communist China has also recently moved toward a partially capitalistic system. Far from empowering the people, these experiments resulted instead in heavy-handed rule both by single individuals (e.g., Stalin in Russia, Mao Tse-tung in China) and strong oligarchies.

12.3
SOCIAL CONTRACTS

© istockphoto.com

Social contract: an implicit or explicit agreement among the members of a society to abide by certain common rules for everyone's mutual benefit.

A **social contract**, as we will discuss it here, is an implicit or explicit agreement among the members of a society to abide by certain common rules for everyone's mutual benefit. Philosophers like **John Locke** (1632–1704) and **Jean-Jacques Rousseau** (1712–1778) set down the most important features of the Enlightenment concept. Later thinkers like **Thomas Jefferson** and James Madison would use its basic understanding of society when setting up the government of the United States. The Preamble to the U.S. Constitution is a clear introduction to the American social contract:

> We the people of the United States, in order to form a more perfect union, establish justice, secure domestic tranquility, provide for the common defense, promote the general welfare, and secure the blessings of liberty, to ourselves and our posterity, do ordain and establish this Constitution for the United States of America.

Fundamental to a social contract is the idea that the individuals in a society have certain basic rights. Jefferson spoke of these rights as "inalienable." For Locke, every man had fundamental rights to his property, which included his "life, liberty, and estate," a familiar concept that **Thomas Jefferson** put into the American Declaration of Independence with the line, "We hold these truths to be self-evident, that all men are created equal, that they are endowed by their creator with certain inalienable rights, that among these are life, liberty, and the pursuit of happiness."

Of course Locke and Jefferson both were thinking in terms of free men, not women or slaves. And when Jefferson said that the right to life was inalienable, he did not mean that a person could not be executed for certain crimes. Over the course of the past two centuries, the Western world has come to believe that all adults, men and women of all races and ethnicities, should have these default rights. We also believe that while various circumstances might limit the voice a person has—children, for example, are not mature enough to make many decisions—all individuals should have certain basic rights.[15]

The Bill of Rights was thus the first ten amendments to the original Constitution of the United States. These were meant to lay certain ground rules and clarify certain basic rights that individual citizens had under law. Interestingly, the states did not originally interpret these rights to bind them. For example, a number of states had a particular form of Christianity as their state religion at first. It was not until the Fourteenth Amendment in 1868 that the door was definitively closed on the states limiting individual rights in ways the Constitution did not allow Congress to do.

For most thinkers of this sort, social contracts involved a relatively new idea in the history of the world, namely, that governments should rule with the "consent of the governed." Throughout the overwhelming majority of history, rule has been imposed on people largely without their agreement. Kingdoms and empires rule until someone overthrows them and becomes the new king or emperor. The **Magna Carta** of England in 1215 was thus an astounding document at the time simply for saying that the king did not have

> The default state of a person in nature is governed by a law of nature which binds everyone. Reason, which is that law, teaches everyone . . . that since everyone is equal and independent, no one is allowed to harm another in his life, health, liberty, or possessions.
>
> **John Locke,**
> *Second Treatise of Government* 2.6[14]

SEPARATION OF CHURCH AND STATE

A very controversial issue in American politics is the idea of the "separation of church and state." The First Amendment to the Constitution says in part, "Congress shall make no law respecting an establishment of religion, or prohibiting the free exercise thereof." This basic right is usually referred to as "freedom of religion."

However, there are today differing interpretations of the "establishment clause." For some, it means that the government cannot be involved in anything religious at all. Accordingly, those who interpret the clause in this way believe it illegal for any Christian symbols to be present in the houses of government (e.g., the Ten Commandments in a courthouse) or for prayer to be present in public schools.

The other interpretation is that the government cannot endorse any specific religion. When interpreted this way, the key is that no one religion or religious viewpoint be taught exclusively. Ten Commandments can be present in public forums if they represent traditions of law rather than an endorsement of Jewish or Christian religion. Prayer can take place as long as it is generic or as long as prayer is offered from more than one faith. Certainly if children in the schools want to pray, it would violate their freedom of religion to prohibit it, unless their prayer was proving disruptive.

Religious neutrality on the part of the government fits well with the notion of the Constitution as a social contract. All individuals have the right to practice their own religions as long as the practice does not harm others. The government thus serves as moderator rather than proponent of specific religious beliefs (while protecting certain more basic ethical standards). This perspective traces its heritage in part to colonies like Rhode Island and Pennsylvania, which afforded their citizens extensive religious freedom.

the authority to do whatever he wanted with the people. Although it had limited immediate impact, it became an ideal that would echo in later times, such as in the unprecedented trial and execution of King Charles I of England in 1649.

One of the first to move in this direction was the Dutch thinker **Hugo Grotius** (1583–1645). He wrote, "One of the things unique to humanity is its desire to form societies, the inclination to live together with others of its kind. Humans desire community, not just in any way, but in peace and with rules that fit its understanding of things."[16] He goes on to disagree with the idea that humans inevitably act in ways that are for their own individual advantage. The very idea of society involves forgoing some things that might be to our short-term advantage for the greater benefit of living together in peace.

For example, we agree not to steal one another's property. We agree to punishments if we do not follow the rules.[17] Grotius considered these principles part of the law of nature and something that all could understand

BIOGRAPHY

THOMAS HOBBES AND SOCIAL CONTRACTS

Thomas Hobbes was one of the first to use the expression "social contract" in his political work *Leviathan* (see chap. 10). Like so many social contract theorists, he began with consideration of humanity in a "state of nature," hypothetical humans who consider whether to join together into a society. However, in his work, the question was one of agreeing to submit to the rule of a king. The contract for Hobbes was to submit to the king's absolute authority in exchange for the king's protection. Unlike most social contract theorists, he saw this as an absolute agreement. Once they have entered the contract, so to speak, the subjects of a king are bound to obey the king whether or not the king is just and keeps his end of the deal.

for themselves. Grotius thought these laws would be true even if there were no God—a thought considered wicked at the time. But most controversial about his thinking was the idea that a ruler was accountable to these laws of society and that individuals could in theory hold such rulers accountable. Countries were even accountable to nature and God for the way they went to war.

John Locke presented the basic principles of such social contracts in a clearer form than Grotius.[18] Governance is based on the agreement of those governed to be governed. As the Declaration of Independence puts it, "to secure these rights, governments are instituted among men, deriving their just powers from the consent of the governed." Jefferson goes on to proclaim boldly that if a government undermines basic human rights, the people have the authority to alter or abolish it.

Locke believed that the rules of a social contract were a matter of the majority. When the majority votes for something we do not like, we either have to submit to the decision or go somewhere else. He thus taught something he called **tacit consent**. If you live and remain in a particular place, you agree to abide by the social contract established by its majority.

Jean-Jacques Rousseau put it quite differently. For him, the position of the majority was the **general will**, and those who initially disagreed with the majority agreed to conclude they were wrong when they were outnumbered. This obscure idea was used by the likes of Maximilien Robespierre during the French Revolution's "reign of terror" (1793–1794) to justify the slaughter of those who disagreed with the course the revolution had taken. Robespierre would enforce the freedom of the majority!

Death of Robespierre on guillotine
Universal History Archive / UIG
The Bridgeman Art Library

BIOGRAPHY

© istockphoto.com

JEAN-JACQUES ROUSSEAU

Jean-Jacques Rousseau (1712–1778) believed that the ideal social contract would involve a direct democracy on the level of a city-state, where all the citizens could vote on decisions. He opposed the idea of a representative democracy, where citizens elect individuals to make decisions for them. He is often wrongly said to have believed that the default state of humanity was the "noble savage" (that humanity in its "state of nature" is fundamentally good). While he opposed Hobbes's view that humanity in a state of nature was "every man against every man" (*Leviathan* 13), Rousseau believed part of the goal of a social contract was to take the morally neutral default state of humanity and make us virtuous.

Photo Credit: Close up of the statue of Jean-Jacques Rousseau on the Rousseau Island, Geneva, Switzerland. This sculpture was created by James Pradier sculptor in 1835. © istockphoto.com

Certainly we can critique many aspects of this Enlightenment form of thinking about social contracts. For example, Grotius, Locke, Rousseau, and Jefferson, among others, liked to speak in terms of a law of nature and of certain intrinsic rights. The history of the world certainly suggests that such intrinsic rights are, at the very least, hard to observe. We can also question the helpfulness of all their discussions about some hypothetical "state of nature." None of us find ourselves in such a state and never will. Locke's notion of citizens simply going somewhere else if they disagree with the majority is also a highly unlikely option for most.

Nevertheless, the idea of society involving a kind of social contract among its members remains a helpful way of conceptualizing the tension between individual freedom and the corporate benefits of a society as a whole. Both biblically and historically, Christians believe that all human beings are loved by God and are thus significant and valuable. And even from a secular standpoint, societies that consider all individuals within them to be meaningful members of their social contracts seem to prosper far more than those that repress or ignore some groups or portions. Historically these ignored groups tend to revolt and exact their revenge on those who ignore them, often subjugating the others in turn.

We remember that this era of European history also produced utilitarianism, the idea that governments should strive to enact what brings about the greatest good for the greatest number. In the light of social contract theory, we can modify this proposal to say that the people of a nation would ideally set down a relatively limited number of common rules with the goal of bringing about the greatest good for the greatest number without unduly sacrificing the freedom of other individuals within the contract. How these basic principles play out varies significantly within those governments that practice this sort of social contract (e.g., will it include universal health care?). But today some variation on this form of government has become the ideal standard worldwide, the "constitutional democracy."

© istockphoto.com

12.4
CAPITALISM AND COMMUNISM

Economic philosophy is a subtopic of social and political philosophy. For the past two thousand years, Christians have rarely had the opportunity to decide how their goods would be produced and distributed. In the United States, a few groups like the Shakers (1700–1900s) and the Oneida (New York) Community (1800s) formed small communes where goods were shared in common. Today the Amish live in close community, although they individually own property. But throughout Christian history, Christians have had little choice but to live within whatever political and economic structure they were born into.

Before the industrial revolutions of the modern age, most **economies** were agrarian, as in biblical times. People produced goods off the land, consumed some of them, and perhaps traded some with others for things they did not produce themselves. However, we should not think that everyone owned land. In medieval times in the Western world, a king or "lord" owned the land, which was farmed by others who owned no land at all. Those who worked the land might be the slaves of those who owned the land, or they might be "serfs" of one kind or another who worked in return for protection, basic sustenance, or some pittance of pay.

The Industrial Revolution of the 1700s and 1800s in the Western world massively transformed the economies of everything in its wake, leading to the **industrialization** of the East in the twentieth century as well.

© istockphoto.com

Industrialization is the process of becoming a society that functions off of manufactured products rather than farm products. When we speak of developing countries in the southern hemisphere, we are referring to countries that are only now undergoing this process of transformation.

Before the rise of industry, power in Western society lay primarily with landowners and kings; the owners of the farms produced the means of living. The powerful were the long-standing, land-owning aristocracies, the "best" of society. This "landed gentry" gained increasing power even as the power of kings declined.

But the 1700s and 1800s saw a shift in power to those who possessed and controlled **capital**, rather than just land. Capital is all the resources a person has at his or her disposal for production and exchange, including money, equipment, products, and of course land. The rise of railroads and steamships facilitated this exchange over distances previously impractical. Into this world came **Adam Smith** (1723–1790), the father of capitalism, who wrote his classic work *The Wealth of Nations*. Capitalism is an economic system in which individuals and companies own capital that they use to compete against each other to make a profit off the buying and selling of goods and services. The background of Smith's economic theory was the utilitarian philosophy of Jeremy Bentham, discussed in the previous chapter.

If you remember, the goal of utilitarianism was to make a more equitable society by basing laws on what would bring about the greatest pleasure for the greatest number. For Bentham, everyone counted the same. The pleasure of a king counted just as much as the pleasure of a child working in a coal mine. The utilitarians thus wanted to build a society in which everyone's interests were taken into account.

Adam Smith formulated an economic model based on this general goal and idea. Here is a famous passage from *The Wealth of Nations*. The passage is talking about importing goods from other countries, but we can see in it the basics of Adam Smith's economic theory.

> The annual revenue of every society is always the equivalent of what it is able to exchange from what its industry produces. It is exactly the value of its products that it can exchange. Every individual, therefore, tries to use his capital to support domestic industry, so that the amount that is produced adds up to the greatest value possible. Every individual also works so that the annual revenue of the society is as great as he can make it.
>
> Of course, it is not that this individual was actually intending to promote the public interest, nor does he know how much he is promoting it. When he prefers supporting domestic rather than foreign

---

Economy: the system of producing and distributing goods in a society.

Industrialization: the process of becoming a society that functions off of manufactured products rather than farm products.

Capital: all the resources a person has at his or her disposal for production and exchange, including money, equipment, products, and land.

industry, he is only thinking about his own security. By making his industry produce the greatest value possible, he is only thinking of his own gain. But in this as in many other cases, he is led by an invisible hand to promote an end that was not a part of his intention.

Nor is society always the worse because it was not his intention to benefit it. By pursuing his own interest he frequently promotes that of the society more effectively than if he really was trying to promote it.

Adam Smith, *Wealth of Nations* 4.2[19]

Smith's basic theory is that as we each pursue our own economic interests, we will often find that, as if "led by an invisible hand," society as a whole will benefit, including the other individuals in that society. On an individual level, let's say that I have some goods I want to sell to you, and you are interested in buying them. Let's say further that the government allows you and me to agree on the price, rather than telling me what to charge or you what to pay.

Here's what Smith says will *often* happen. As a seller looking out for my own interests, I will try to get as high a price for my goods from you as I can. Meanwhile, you are also looking out for your own interests and will try to pay me as little as you can. The result is that you and I will meet in the middle with a price that maximizes the benefit to *both* of our interests.

This sort of "deregulated" approach to economics, where the government allows you and me to rankle over prices, is called **laissez-faire** capitalism, which is French for "to allow to do." Laissez-faire economics favors letting the business markets rankle over prices and rules rather than some government setting the boundaries for such things.

Another name for this school of thought is **classical liberalism**. Today, the word *liberal* is more often associated with opposition to capitalism, but we should remember that the word basically means "free." The **free-enterprise system** and laissez-faire economics were thus termed *liberal* originally because they believed individuals and companies should be *free* to set prices and the terms of trade without governmental intervention. Ironically, therefore, the economic "conservatives" of today come closest in philosophy to the classical liberals of the 1700s and 1800s.

Another noteworthy principle of capitalism is the **law of supply and demand**: as the supply of a certain product goes up, the price will generally go down, because people

> **Free-enterprise system:** an economic system that allows individuals to start their own businesses in which they set their own prices and the terms of trade, with limited governmental intervention.
>
> **Laissez-faire capitalism:** "to allow to do," another name for free-enterprise systems.
>
> **Classical liberalism:** in economics, another name for the approach that favors a free-enterprise system.
>
> **Law of supply and demand:** the basic pattern that prices go up when supply is low or when demand is high.

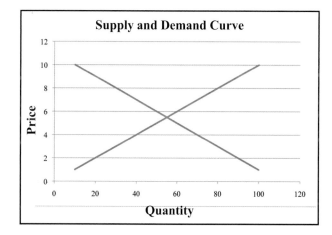

Law of supply and demand: as the supply of a certain product goes up, the price will generally go down.

have more venues from which to get it and thus there is more competition among sellers. When the price of oil goes down significantly, sometimes oil-producing nations agree to decrease the amount of oil they are producing, so the price will go back up.

Similarly, the U.S. government in the late twentieth century paid certain farmers not to put their grain on the market so that the price would not bottom out from too much supply.

Another example: as the demand for something goes up, the price will generally go up. This dynamic is especially apparent in a crisis, such as when a natural disaster interrupts the normal flow of a commodity such as gas to a particular area. Sellers of things in such high demand are sometimes accused of "price gouging" or setting a price ridiculously high because there is high demand and no competition around, so that buyers have little choice but to pay the exorbitant price.

In these sorts of exceptional situations, economists debate how free the market should be and whether some government regulation might be necessary to keep the overall system functioning the way it is supposed to function. Adam Smith's laissez-faire theory was formulated when firms were small and run by individual owners, not in a global economy with industry on a massive scale.

We saw in the last chapter that **John Stuart Mill** (1806–1873) suggested some significant modifications to the utilitarian philosophy of his father and Bentham. The same was no less true of Adam Smith's economic theory. For one thing, Mill recognized that you cannot always count on people knowing or doing what is in their best interest.

Even in the early 1800s, Mill argued that the "authorized representatives" of society would need to intervene when the interests of the buyer were jeopardized:

> As a general rule, the business of life is better conducted when those who have an immediate interest in it are left to make their own course . . . Industry is generally the best equipped to choose the path in its best interest. But can we affirm with the same universality that the consumer or person served is? . . . Is the buyer always qualified to judge the commodity?
>
> If not, then letting competition in the market run its own course does not apply. And if it is a very important commodity in which society has much at stake, it may be preferable to have some degree of intervention, by those who are the authorized representatives of the collective interests of the state.

John Stuart Mill, *Principles of Political Economy* 5.11.7[20]

When a person does not know what is in his or her own best interest, then certainly the basic principles of free enterprise play into the hands of the other person, who is following the principle of self-interest to get the best deal he or she can. In fact, it is—at least in the short term—in the best economic interest of a person to try to deceive or manipulate the other person if he or she can get away with it. Of course it may not be so in the long term, for if customers come to recognize that you are a shady dealer, they will tell others and then your business will drop sharply.

© istockphoto.com

In a global economy, however, where buyers and sellers do not live together, knowledge of the trustworthiness of the other party becomes a critical issue. Adam Smith and his compatriots could not have imagined a world where people buy things over the Internet or where the seller is so far removed from the buyer. By the late 1800s, the loopholes in a purely laissez-faire approach to economics had become all-too apparent to the average U.S. citizen. Government agencies such as the Interstate Commerce Commission and the Food and Drug Administration have evolved over time to ensure that industry is honest in the way it presents its products to consumers.

Mill addressed a second problem with Smith's economic theory—the tendency of individuals to follow their habits rather than their self-interest:

> When it comes to individual property, the way products end up being distributed is the result of two determining factors: competition and habit . . .
>
> Political economists generally . . . are used to putting their entire stress on competition . . . and to take little account of the other conflicting principle: what people are in the habit of doing . . . Because the habits of people resist competition to such a significant extent, . . . even when the competition is the greatest, we can be sure that where people are content with smaller gains and find more pleasure in things other than monetary gain, competition will not allow you to calculate what they will buy . . . Customers are sometimes used to higher prices and they acquiesce in it.

John Stuart Mill, *Principles of Political Economy* 2.4.1, 2[21]

The basic thrust is that people do not always operate in their best economic self-interest. What this fact means is that although economics is a science, you cannot predict what the markets will actually do.

It is important to realize that these founders of capitalism really had the overall betterment of society in view. The capitalistic system was not an end in itself. It certainly was not a system set up to create and reward some new aristocracy made up of the cleverest merchants of industry, while punishing the person who was not adept enough to compete. It certainly was not some evolutionary scheme set up for the survival of the fittest. Indeed, Adam Smith himself had this comment to say about how the wealth of the rich might be used to the betterment of the poor in society:

> The poor spend most of their money on the necessities of life . . . Meanwhile, the rich spend most of their money on the luxuries and vanities of life. So it is not ridiculous to suggest that the rich might contribute to the expense that the public spend on the poor, not only in proportion to their income, but even proportionally more than their income.

Adam Smith, *Wealth of Nations* 5.2

Capitalism has proved to be far more complicated than Smith, Bentham, and Mills could have imagined. We have already mentioned earlier in the chapter the strongest voice against what they had set in motion: Karl Marx, the father of communism. Ironically, some of his basic goals for society were similar to those of Smith and Bentham, even though the systems they proposed were dramatically different. But for all of these individuals, the fundamental goal was to see economic systems in place that would maximize human happiness across the board. They just saw drastically different ways of bringing it about.

When Marx arrived on the scene, the First Industrial Revolution had been in motion for the better part of a century in Europe. He could see the results of capitalistic principles as they were playing out in real time. Indeed, the very same year that he and Friedrich Engels published their *Communist Manifesto*, revolts broke out throughout Europe in dozens of countries (1848). His critiques of capitalism fall into two basic categories. First, he believed that capitalism inevitably oppressed those who actually did the work. Second, he believed that the system itself was unstable and would inevitably result in economic crisis and failure.

We now have the hindsight to see that his own proposals were far worse failures than those of Adam Smith. We will have opportunity to look in more detail at Marx's failed theory of history in chapter 14. Nevertheless, his critiques of unbridled capitalism may have some merit. What he did not envision is that capitalism might be supplemented by various protections to keep it steered in the direction it was originally meant to take.

For example, no worker who lived in the throes of the Second Industrial Revolution of the late 1800s would question the powerlessness of the worker over and against the great industries of steel and rail. No worker could start

Portrait of Karl Marx (1818–93) ca. 1970 (chromolitho), Chinese School (20th century) / Private Collection / Archives Charmet / The Bridgeman Art Library

Workers of the world unite.

Karl Marx,
The Communist Manifesto

Marx's Critique of Capitalism

Marx's critiques fall broadly into two categories:

1. He believed that capitalism debased workers and resulted in a widening gap between business owners and those who did most of the work.

2. He believed that capitalism was unstable as an economic system and would inevitably result in financial crises and collapse.

up a business to compete against the great oil monopoly of the Standard Oil Trust of 1882. There were no protections to keep the company from firing a worker who got hurt or filed a grievance. There were plenty more people to hire.

Upton Sinclair's 1906 novel, *The Jungle*, portrayed the situation of workers in the meat-packing industry in Chicago. In one memorable scene, a worker falls into a vat and no one notices he is gone until whatever remained of him had been packaged and sent out as lard. In research for the novel, Sinclair himself had spent seven weeks incognito gathering information. Although many considered his novel an exaggeration, the tentative conclusion of those sent into these factories by President Theodore Roosevelt was that the novel was largely accurate. The long-term effect was the founding of what would eventually become the Food and Drug Administration in 1930. These sorts of conditions of workers were exactly the sort of things that Marx believed would inevitably lead to bloody revolution.

However, the twentieth century saw a number of protections come into play that limit the extent to which a company can, in the interest of greater profits, abuse or neglect those who work for it. For example, the early 1900s already saw the rise of child-labor laws, which significantly restricted the way industries like coal had been abusing children for cheap labor. Most modern countries also have a legalized minimum wage. Companies can no longer immediately fire a worker because of an injury or because a woman needs to take a leave of absence to give birth. The mid-twentieth century saw the rise of labor unions, which were very powerful at the time and provided a strong balance between the interests of employers and the interests of workers.

Breaker boys working in Ewen Breaker of Pennsylvania Coal Co. 1908
Universal History Archive / UIG / The Bridgeman Art Library

To be sure, these sorts of counterbalances reduce the profits of business. But they also arguably forgo the kinds of consequences Marx believed were inevitable for a capitalistic system. From a social contract perspective, these safeguards are appropriate protections of the basic rights of those within a society. From a constitutional perspective, such regulations "promote the general welfare." From a Christian perspective, they embody our sense that the employees of a business are as significant in God's eyes as the business owner who stands to make a profit.

A recent complication is the increasing globalization of business. To avoid the kinds of regulations that developed nations put on businesses in relation to their employees, many companies have placed factories in countries such as Mexico and China where labor laws are not as strict, if they exist at all. In one scenario, however, this inequality is transitional until such time as the entire world is industrialized and such safeguards apply to the entire global economic system.

The second basic critique that Marx had of the capitalistic system was that it was inherently unstable and would lead to financial crisis and collapse. The Great Depression of the 1930s and the recent economic crisis of the 2000s at least seem to support his point. Interestingly, the precise causes of the Great Depression remain a matter of debate among economists. We find several different perspectives, many of which correspond directly to perspectives on the more recent crisis.

12.5
CONTEMPORARY ECONOMIC DEBATES

John Maynard Keynes (1883–1946) was perhaps the most influential economist of the twentieth century, and his perspective was that the government frequently needs to intervene into economic matters to avert or alleviate financial crisis.[22] For example, President George W. Bush and President Barack Obama of the United States largely followed the advice of **Keynesian economists** when they spent massive amounts of money in the 2008 world economic crisis, to keep major banks and businesses from failing, while also pumping money into the system. Although not all economists agree, most also believe that the New Deal projects of Franklin Roosevelt along similar lines helped speed the American recovery from the Great Depression.

Friedrich Hayek (1899–1992) is often placed at the other end of the economic spectrum, although Hayek and Keynes did not disagree on everything.[23] He and the "**Austrian school**" of economics reflect a minority position among economists, but nevertheless one that has had significant impact. While Keynes advocated intense involvement of government during times of economic crisis, Hayek was more likely to blame governmental involvement for economic crisis in the first place. For Hayek, a key cause of the Great Depression was the Federal Reserve (the central bank that coordinates the supply of money in the United States) in the 1920s artificially allowing more money into the market than it should have, leading to an inevitable contraction later. While Hayek's theories have occasionally had great influence, the Austrian School is generally considered to be "heterodox" or outside the mainstream.

Keynesian economics: an approach to economics that focuses on governmental intervention to make sure that the total spending of the private and governmental sectors is in equilibrium with the total demand for goods and services.

Austrian school: a heterodox school of economics that opposes using mathematical models for understanding economies (macroeconomics) and strongly opposes governmental regulation of economies (central planning).

Monetarism: a mathematical approach to economics that sees equilibrium between the money supply and the gross domestic product of a nation as the key to economic health. It otherwise opposes governmental attempts to manipulate an economy.

Along with Keynesian economics, the other main approach to economics is the monetary approach, with **Milton Friedman** (1912–2006) as its founding proponent.[24] **Monetarism** can be seen both as a development and critique of the Keynesian approach. For Keynes, the key factor in a stable economy is ensuring that the total of governmental and private *spending* are in equilibrium with the total *demand* for goods and services at any particular time and price level. When the private sector stops spending, the government has to pick up the slack, even when it causes deficit spending.

By contrast Friedman (like Hayek) thought governments more often than not compounded problems when they intervened in economic crises. He believed in governmental involvement in the economy, but it was largely to make sure the *money supply* always kept in equilibrium with the gross domestic product (GDP—the total value of the goods and services produced in a nation). In his view this policy would keep prices relatively stable. Since this approach is purely mathematical, it requires no value judgments on the part of people. Nothing special should be done in an economic crisis, because the system would eventually reach equilibrium on its own.

These perspectives remain highly debated and a basic philosophy book has little hope of resolving them. We might suggest that the capitalistic system has not remained static. While a vocal minority continue to favor a completely libertarian approach to economics, the vast majority see the importance of key governmental regulations and processes to ensure that the basic laws of supply and demand continue on a stable course. For example, the Sherman Antitrust laws of 1890 were passed to make sure that competition remains a major element in the market. Capitalism requires competition to work, so if a single company takes over an entire product or service, little stands in the way of that company charging whatever it wants to charge. Antitrust laws are a key feature of modern capitalism, as are price-gouging laws that keep a business from charging exorbitant rates in a time of crisis.

These protections no doubt help keep capitalism functioning in the way Adam Smith originally envisioned. Whether one is a Keynesian or a monetarist, the two primary economic theories at the moment, one sees a role for governments to play in making sure the regular ups and downs of economic cycles do not become catastrophic, as Marx predicted they would. The economic crisis of 2008 has highlighted new issues that Adam Smith could not have imagined, issues like the bundling and selling of debt on a massive scale and banks that, while not monopolies, are "too big to fail." We can imagine that a whole generation of economic theory will be affected, as it was after the Great Depression of the 1930s.

Adam Smith's goal was not to make a few business owners very, very rich—which is what happened in the late 1800s and which continues today.

The goal was to create a system that improved the economic state of *all* society. Occasionally we can lose sight not only of the virtue of this original goal, but of the fact that such a goal is fundamentally Christian.[25] Today economic systems are incredibly complex and require vast expertise. As Christian philosophers we can see with clarity that the best economic systems will be those that benefit the most people rather than those that invest the majority of resources and power into the hands of a few. The latter kind of world is not unlike the days of kings and aristocracies, though the names have changed.

© istockphoto.com

12.6
THE BIBLE AND MONEY

We in the Western world are so used to money that it is hard for us to picture the way most societies in the history of the world have primarily functioned, namely, by trading goods. For this reason, Christians may actually misread certain Bible passages without even realizing it. We see words like *money*, *poor*, or *rich*, and we read them in terms of what they mean in our world, without recognizing the dynamics they had in the various cultures to which the books of the Bible were written.

In the Old Testament, Israelite families gave a tithe or tenth of their crops to the priests (e.g., Lev. 27:30; Num. 18:21). They did not give a tenth of their *income*, in the manner of our modern economy. They would rarely if ever have used money. Old Testament societies were *agrarian* economies, in which goods were produced and consumed directly off the land. Such land was passed along in families and, according to the book of Numbers, was returned to these families every fifty years in the Year of Jubilees—if the family had somehow lost the land during that time.

Coinage, or money, was mostly associated in the ancient world with kings and political powers beyond the normal daily operations of most people. It is thus no surprise that the New Testament has virtually nothing good to say about money. When someone asked Jesus whether he believed in paying taxes, he gave the well-known response, "Give to Caesar what is Caesar's and to God what is God's" (Mark 12:17 NIV). He probably was not saying simply to pay your taxes. He may have been dismissing Roman coinage itself as having nothing to do with the people of God or the coming kingdom of God. It is also possible that the original audiences of Revelation

© istockphoto.com

Roman silver denarius with Domitian

might have understood the mark of the beast, without which they could not buy or sell, as an allusion to the coinage of Domitian, on which it was written that he was "Lord and God."

First Timothy 6:10 may have traveling teachers in mind when it says that "the love of money is the root of all evil" (KJV), and the letter of James lambasts the rich throughout. "It is right that the brother in humble circumstances should glory in being lifted up, and the rich in being brought low. For the rich will last no longer than the wild flower" (1:9–10). Similarly, "Well now, you rich! Lament, weep for the miseries that are coming to you" (5:1). James's assumption is that such rich individuals have treated their workers unfairly: "Can you hear crying out against you the wages which you kept back from the labourers mowing your fields? The cries of the reapers have reached the ears of the Lord Sabaoth" (5:4).

When we read passages like these, we have to remember that agrarian economies in the ancient world tended to think in terms of a limited number of resources, a **limited good**. Accordingly, if one person has more, the implication is that others have less. It would be as if twenty people in a room were each given one apple, but when they left the room some people had several apples and others had none.

> **Limited good:** the sense that only a certain amount of materials or goods exist and therefore that for one person to have more, another must have less.

It is thus no surprise to hear of the ancient Arab proverb that said that "every rich person is a thief or the son of a thief."[26] With this sort of background, it is no surprise that Jesus would tell a rich young ruler to go sell his possessions and give to the poor (Mark 10:21). If the rich were thought to have taken resources that should go to others, the poor were understood to be individuals who had lost resources that they should otherwise have had. Poverty was thus more about getting knocked out of one's inherited status than about not having money.

Luke and Acts seem to operate with these basic assumptions as well. One of the special emphases of Luke is Jesus's ministry to the poor and disempowered. For example, Luke uniquely has the Parable of the Rich Man and Lazarus, where a poor beggar, Lazarus, finds himself in a place of reward after death. Meanwhile, the rich man, at whose gate Lazarus used to sit and wait for doles from the servants, finds himself in a place of torment after death.

And while the Beatitudes of Matthew have "Blessed are the poor in spirit" (Matt. 5:3), Luke bluntly has "Blessed are you who are poor" (Luke 6:20) and the added rejoinder, "Woe to you who are rich" (6:24). In Acts 2, the early Jerusalem church brings everyone back to his or her normal economic state by redistributing the excess of some to the poor in the community. This sharing is probably not strictly communal living, but a bringing of everyone to a similar amount of possessions.

We should point out that the apostle Paul does not have as negative a view of those with significant resources as do other New Testament writers. Indeed, he may have been born into a family with some status and wealth. Only a very small number of people in the ancient world were Roman citizens as Paul was. And Paul speaks of working with his hands as if it were a kind of lowering of himself (1 Cor. 4:12; 9:6).

As a trader of leather goods in the marketplace, Paul might have had some strikes against him among some of the earliest believers. James has strong words to say about the merchant who makes plans to travel and make large amounts of money (4:13–17), and no doubt some of Paul's enemies found it easy to stereotype him in this way. Paul's thinking is rather that God sometimes blesses one part of the body of Christ and at other times other parts. Those who are blessed are to share with those who are not, so that, when the circumstances are reversed, they will share in return (2 Cor. 8–9).

We see that what is most important today is the attitude of believers toward their possessions and toward each other, while the specific economic structures of the Bible relate directly to the cultural forms of its days. We are thus to focus not only on our own interests, but also on the interests of others (Phil. 2:4). This shared interest certainly includes the material needs of others (e.g., 1 John 3:17; Matt. 25:31–46). And we are to see our possessions as belonging to God and as thoroughly unnecessary to who we are (e.g., Matt. 6:19–21).

12.7
CONCLUSION

Throughout history people have lived under various forms of government. While many of us are privileged today to live in places where we can participate in our own governance, most throughout history have had little say in how they were governed or about the rules of society. We can argue that the representative democracies of today are perhaps the best form of governance for large numbers of people even though this form of government did not exist in biblical times. For this reason we can't say it is a biblical form of government—indeed, almost all forms of government can be run in a Christian way. But the way a representative democracy tries to "love" every individual, give each person certain basic rights, and take everyone into consideration not only fits with the core principles of the Bible and Christianity in general; it probably fosters those values as strongly or more strongly than any other form of government.

The Enlightenment sense of a social contract seems very helpful and a very Christian way to conceptualize how we live together with one another in a society today. Every individual is part of a society, and everyone should be taken into consideration when formulating the rules of that society. God does not show favoritism to people because of their social status, gender, or race (Gal. 3:28), and so everyone needs to be afforded certain basic rights. This translates into the love command, since "love does no wrong to a neighbor" (Rom. 13:10).

Within this framework, a society that is structured in such a way as to bring about a maximum amount of true happiness is a better one than a society that only leads to the happiness and pleasure of a few. Your understanding of God can come into play here. If you believe as I do that God wants people to choose him freely, then you will resonate with an approach to society that allows its individuals extensive freedom—even to live life unwisely—except when it hurts or impinges on the rights of others. But the tension between individual and societal happiness will always be a matter of give and take, following the whims of a nation at a given time. While a Christian might favor individual freedom when it does not affect others, Christians will surely err more on the side of helping the many than defending the self-oriented freedom of a few.

The idea of bringing about maximal happiness for a society was a founding principle behind capitalism as an economic system when it began in the 1700s. This is why a Christian can potentially support such a system, because of the principle of loving one's neighbor. But it is also easy to lose sight of the reason why we can support a capitalistic system. The New Testament sounds very strong warnings about how money can work against fundamental Christian values. Money brings a power that, given human nature, is more likely to oppress others than to work for their benefit. We can cautiously endorse capitalism if we believe it will bring about a greater good for a greater number. While its foundational orientation around one's individual self-interest is fundamentally unchristian, we as Christians can support it when it is working in *everyone's* best interest.

KEY TERMS

- nation-state
- social construct
- city-state
- social and political philosophy
- theocracy
- monarchy
- divine right of kings
- aristocracy/oligarchy
- direct democracy
- representative democracy
- republic
- balance of power

- checks and balances
- anarchy
- capitalism
- proletariat
- bourgeoisie
- Marxist communism
- Marxist-Leninism
- Socialism
- social contract
- Magna Carta
- tacit consent
- general will

- economy
- industrialization
- capital
- laissez-faire
- classical liberalism
- free-enterprise system
- law of supply and demand
- Keynesian economics
- Austrian School
- monetarism
- limited good

KEY PHILOSOPHERS / MOVEMENTS

- Plato
- Aristotle
- Hugo Grotius
- Thomas Hobbes
- John Locke
- Jean-Jacques Rousseau
- Thomas Jefferson

- Adam Smith
- John Stuart Mill
- Karl Marx
- Vladimir Lenin
- John Maynard Keynes
- Friedrich Hayek
- Milton Friedman

PHILOSOPHICAL QUOTATIONS / IDEAS

- "Until philosophers are kings . . . there will be no end of troubles for our cities." (Plato)
- "A human is by nature a political animal." (Aristotle)
- "Workers of the world unite." (Marx)

KEY QUESTIONS

1. In the light of this chapter, what do you think the ideal form of government would be? Would it be different for a Christian than it would be for someone who is not a Christian?

2. What do you make of the relationship between a person as a Christian and a person as a citizen? Do you agree with Richard Niebuhr's categorization of the different options? Which one of the options—or one of your own making—do you favor? What do you see as the proper relationship between church and state?

3. How do fundamental Christian or human values impact a person's sense of how economic theories should play out in a society? Critique both capitalism and communism from a Christian perspective. Critique both from a utilitarian perspective.

4. In what ways should we take into account the difference between the way economies worked at the time of Christ and the way our economies work today? How do these differences influence the way Christians apply biblical thinking and instructions about money and wealth?

NOTES

1. See, e.g., William A. Haviland, Harald E. L. Prins, Dana Walrath, and Bunny McBride, *Cultural Anthropology: The Human Challenge*, 12th ed. (Belmont, CA: Thomson Wadsworth, 2007), 271.

2. Peter L. Berger and Thomas Luckmann, *The Social Construction of Reality: A Treatise in the Sociology of Knowledge* (New York: Doubleday/Anchor, 1966).

3. An excellent resource for seeing the history of Israel in this period in terms appropriate to its day, see John Bright, *The History of Israel*, 4th ed. (Louisville, KY: Westminster John Knox, 2000). For more about Israel's tribal confederacy, see 162–68.

4. In fact, the very word *tribe* comes from the Latin word for "three," because three tribes originally made up the city of Rome.

5. See Bright, *History of Israel*, 185.

6. H. Richard Niebuhr, *Christ and Culture* (New York: Harper & Row, 1956). For an argument that Niebuhr's typology—his breakdown of the various options—does not fit what is becoming a "post-Christian" West, see Craig A. Carter, *Rethinking Christ and Culture: A Post-Christendom Perspective* (Grand Rapids: Brazos, 2006).

7. E.g., you can find the idea in Luther's *Lectures on Romans*, trans. H. C. Oswald, *Luther's Works* (St. Louis: Concordia, 1972), 5:434; in the original German, *Weimarer Ausgabe* 56:442 (Stuttgart: Böhlaus, 2000). Cf. also *Lectures*, 267 (*Weimarer Ausgabe* 56:280).

8. Plato's treatises are called dialogues because he wrote out his philosophy in the form of conversations between Socrates and various other characters. They are thus like little philosophical plays. These dialogues are quasi-fictional, although Plato's earliest writings are likely based on memories of real conversations Socrates had with others. However, as time went by, Plato's dialogues are probably much more his own compositions and ideas than those of Socrates.

9. Interpreters of Paul have often noticed the similarity between Paul's thought on the various roles of the parts of the body of Christ and Plato's sense of a well-ordered society (e.g., Plato's *Republic* 462c–d).

10. Aristotle, *Politics* 1253a. Paraphrases of Aristotle are based on *The Complete Works of Aristotle*, ed. J. Barnes (Princeton, NJ: Princeton University, 1984).

11. Thomas Hobbes, *Leviathan* 1.13.

12. The House of Representatives by contrast represents citizens on the basis of population. In theory, the House of Lords in Great Britain is meant to serve a role similar to the U.S. Senate.

13. See Aristotle, *The Athenian Constitution* 37.

14. John Locke, *Second Treatise of Government* (1690). Paraphrased from the wording of the original publication in English.

15. So even a person on death row has the right not to be executed by way of a "cruel and unusual punishment" (U.S. Constitution, Eighth Amendment in the Bill of Rights).

16. Paraphrase based on Hugo Grotius, *The Rights of War and Peace*, trans. J. Barbeyrac (1625; Indianapolis: Liberty Fund, 2005). Preliminary Discourse 6.

17. Ibid., Preliminary Discourse 8.

18. See especially Locke, *Second Treatise on Government*.

19. Adam Smith, *An Inquiry into the Nature and Causes of the Wealth of Nations* 4.2. Paraphrase of the original English of the 1776 publication.

20. John Stuart Mill, *Principles of Political Economy,* 7th ed. (1871). Paraphrased from the original wording in English.

21. Ibid.

22. John Maynard Keynes's key work is *The General Theory of Employment, Interest and Money* (London: Macmillan, 1936).

23. Friedrich Hayek's key work is *The Road to Serfdom* (Chicago: University of Chicago, 1944).

NOTES

24. Milton Friedman's key work here, which he cowrote with Anna Schwartz, is *A Monetary History of the United States 1867–1960* (Princeton, NJ: Princeton University, 1963).

25. We can also forget that money is a feature of an economic *system* and is thus not the same as a straightforward possession. If I take away your watch for no reason, I am stealing something that is yours. But taxing your income may not be stealing, not only because you get something in return (e.g., police protection, public school education, paved roads), but also because taxation is part of an overall money system that involves factors including how much money is printed, how much an overall economy produces, and what the rules are for how money is exchanged. The value of my money—and how much I should get—is not something independent of the overall economic system in which it is enmeshed.

26. See especially Bruce J. Malina, *The New Testament World: Insights from Cultural Anthropology*, 3rd ed. (Louisville, KY: Westminster John Knox, 2001), 81–107.

© Kevin L. Welch

13.1
A QUESTION OF VALUE

In chapter 1 we mentioned that philosophy divided into three major areas. Metaphysics deals with questions of reality, including God and the origins of the world. Epistemology deals with questions of knowledge, including logic. Finally, the third major topic is called axiology, which deals with questions of what is valuable.

Questions of value fall basically into one of two categories. First, ethics asks what is valuable in relation to how we live; social and political philosophy ask the same question on the societal level. The second "value" category is **aesthetics**, the branch of philosophy that asks questions like what it means to say something is beautiful or ugly, what art is, and what constitutes good or bad art. This chapter is about the philosophy of art and beauty. What are we really saying when we say something is beautiful?

What to Get from This Chapter

- Aesthetics is that branch of philosophy that asks what the nature of beauty and art is.
- For Plato and Aristotle, whether art was good or bad depended on its ability to lead its audience to rational truth: good art was a good representation.
- For the Romantics, good art was the expression of feeling, intuition, and imagination by an artist possessed of genius.
- For Leo Tolstoy, good art was infectious and led individuals to love their neighbors.
- For Herbert Marcuse, art is good if it frees artist and audience from the repression inflicted by oppressive social forces.
- For Oscar Wilde, art did not need to do anything but was valid simply because it was art.
- From a Christian perspective, we can judge art as good or bad depending on what it expresses in the heart of the artist and the effect it creates.

Questions to Consider

- What makes something beautiful or valuable?
- What roles do rationality and feeling play in art?
- To what extent is art personal?

Key Words

- Value
- Beauty
- Art

Aesthetics: that branch of philosophy that asks what the nature of beauty and art is.

Subjective: a matter of personal or group perspective rather than "fact," pertaining to the observer rather than the thing observed.

Objective: a matter of fact rather than opinion, pertaining to things that would be true even if no person was involved.

In our chapter on ethics, we saw that some philosophers do not believe that ethical statements are anything more than expressions of our feelings. When I say, "It is wrong to take my dessert," I am really saying, "I don't want you to take my dessert." We find the idea that value is **subjective** even more in the area of aesthetics. "Beauty is in the eye of the beholder," the saying goes.

Is this the case? Is beauty simply a personal matter? Are there not certain features, such as symmetry or the coordination of colors, that have at least some "real" basis that would lead most people to consider something beautiful? If so, would such common human delight in something be a chance product of human evolution, where there is still nothing **objectively** beautiful about something but only the chance delight of a particular species' physiology?

And what is art? If I string up paint cans over a canvas and run around randomly knocking paint out of them, is the resulting canvas art? Is pornography art? If someone takes a picture of a crucifix in a glass filled with urine, is that art?

Is there good and bad art? Is some art "better" than other art and, if so, by what standard? Is there moral and immoral art, to the point that some art should be banned? If so, by what criteria? These are just some of the questions that are part of aesthetics, the philosophy of art. The rest of the chapter addresses some of the significant answers different individuals throughout history have given to these sorts of questions.[1]

© istockphoto.com

13.2
ART AND RATIONAL TRUTH

Both **Plato** and **Aristotle** assumed that art would be either good or bad, depending on whether it led someone toward or away from rational truth. In general Plato concluded that art was bad because it led you away from the truth and played on your emotions. By contrast Aristotle thought art was good because it led you toward truth. The key issue for both was thus *representation* or imitation.[2] Art was the attempt to represent reality in a medium like sculpture or in drama such as Greek tragedy or comedy. Aristotle also recognized an emotional element to art, but thought it could be positive.

For Plato, art was bad because it was a copy of a copy of a copy. You will remember from chapter 4 that Plato believed that true reality was something one could access only with one's mind. The things we see and touch around us, the things we experience with our senses, are shadowy copies of the true realities in heaven that we can only contemplate. A sculpture of something is a copy of something physical. And since that physical thing is only a copy of some ideal reality, the sculpture proves to be a copy of a copy of a copy. For Plato, it thus is leading us further away from the truth rather than toward it.

Similarly, Plato did not see writing as ideal. Instruction in person from a philosopher was far more likely to lead one to truth, which one ultimately can access only through one's mind. Once one had been "out of the cave," one could remember truth from one's past. By contrast, writing for Plato was not a true engagement with the eternal ideals but engaging someone else's memory of truth. It was "reminding" rather than "remembering." It was not direct engagement with the truth but, like art, indirect engagement.

Ironically Plato was a pretty good artist of sorts. What we have of his philosophy has largely come down to us through pretend dramas in which Socrates, the main character, engages various individuals whose ideas differed from his. While one can question the answers Socrates gives to their questions and issues, Plato expresses these other ideas fairly. Indeed, at times we may find ourselves more convinced by Socrates's opponents than by his own arguments! Most Plato scholars believe that, while Plato's earlier dialogues preserve some of Socrates's original voice, Plato's later works increasingly attributed Plato's own thoughts to the mouth of Socrates. Plato's dialogues were thus genuine artistic creations.

In keeping with Aristotle's philosophy, he disagreed with Plato on the value of art. If Plato thought art moved a person away from an accurate understanding of truth, Aristotle believed that art could actually help a person better understand the essence of something.

If you remember, the essence of something for Aristotle was its "form." In the physical things we see around us, form and substance are bound and mixed together. Art, Aristotle thought, can lead a person closer to the truth, because art tends to abstract the form or essence of something independent of substance. In other words, art might very well help us recognize what it is that really makes an apple to be an apple, because the representation of an apple has to focus on the essentials of what an apple looks like.

Aristotle also disagreed with Plato on the role of emotions in art. For Plato, art was dangerous because it could play on a person's emotions. It could bypass reasoning and move one to actions and thoughts that, in reality, were not right or beneficial. It could lead one to do things one would not do on the basis of normal ways of thinking. No doubt Plato was correct to recognize the power that art has along these lines, both positive and negative.

For example, consider the story of King David having an affair with someone else's wife, Bathsheba, and then having her husband, Uriah, killed because she was pregnant (2 Sam. 11). The prophet Nathan goes to David

> Painting is just imitating all the living things in nature with their colors and designs, to portray them just as they are in nature.
>
> **Giorgio Vasari, *Lives of the Most Excellent Painters, Sculptors, and Architects*[3]**

> If people learn writing, it will lead to forgetfulness in their minds. They will not use their memory because they will rely on what is written. . . . You have invented a recipe for reminding, not for remembering . . . Your students will seem to know many things, when for the most part they will know nothing.
>
> **Plato, *Phaedrus* 275a–b**

© Kevin L. Welch

and tells him a story about a rich shepherd who steals the one sheep of a poor man (2 Sam. 12). The story infuriates David, until he realizes that *he* is the rich man and the sheep he has stolen is the one wife of the murdered Uriah. By using a story, a form of art, Nathan was able to get past David's normal defenses and expose his guiltiness. Clearly art can be a powerful force in revealing our hidden assumptions or in moving us to take the right course of action.

By the same token, movies can make us feel sorry for murderers. They can make us enjoy watching people do things they should not do. Art can glamorize vice and demean virtue. It is no surprise that dictators and moralists alike have wanted to censor, even burn, various forms of art. Art often has a power, be it good or bad. It can motivate people to eliminate injustice, or it can motivate them to act unjustly.

Aristotle believed that art was positive because it can be cathartic; it can give us the opportunity to purge emotions so that we can go back to thinking clearly. Some people need a good cry every once in a while. There is even a widely used form of rehabilitation known as art therapy. Interestingly this way of thinking anticipates some of what Sigmund Freud would say about "sublimating" repressed feelings. We will see later in the chapter how Herbert Marcuse used Freudian categories to formulate his philosophy of art.

One area of debate today asks whether certain forms of art fuel a person's passions rather than cleanse a person of emotions. Do violent video games make people want to be violent, or do they allow people to work through violent urges so they do not need to act out aggression on real people? Do pornographic movies make a person want to go have sex, or do they allow a person to work through sexual urges so that person doesn't need to have actual sex? These are issues to which we will return later in the chapter.

13.3
ART AND FEELING

For Plato and Aristotle, the key question for evaluating art was the extent to which it imitated and *represented* rational truth or perhaps cleared the mind to allow one to think cogently. No doubt many individuals today would

© Kevin L. Welch

Sculpture of Jesus after his arrest.

still evaluate a piece of art by whether it is a good representation of whatever it is meant to portray. Having said that, most of us probably do not think of artists as rational, philosophical types. We've been influenced by the Romantics of the late 1700s and 1800s.

Romanticism was a movement that reacted strongly against the rational focus of the Enlightenment, as well as the cold, impersonal feel of the Industrial Revolution. Although the modern word *romantic* ultimately derives from that period two hundred years ago, we will understand Romanticism better if we forget the way we use the word now. Romanticism was a movement in art and culture that emphasized feeling, imagination, and intuition over reason. It is from the Romantics that we get the picture of an artist as a misunderstood genius, possessed of some higher power the rest of us could not possibly understand.

Ironically, many Romantic poets and philosophers drew inspiration from Plato, so much so that they are often called Neoplatonists. They reach back into Plato, not for his disparaging words against art in his most famous work, the *Republic*. They reach back to some things he says about artists in another dialogue, the *Ion*.[4] In the *Ion*, Socrates suggests that some artists can be possessed by the gods so that they have more-direct-than-normal access to the truth. Some of the Romantics seized on this idea of art as direct access to a higher realm of truth—bypassing the mind—and ran with it.

With the Romantics, art turns away from *representation* and toward *expression* of some higher truth. Since an artist may see him- or herself as possessed by a higher muse, genius, or power, art moves in the direction of the highly individualized. The work of the artist is something that others may not understand, especially those who do not have access to the muse, who are not possessed of genius.

> A poet is a light, winged, and sacred thing. He is unable to speak forth until he is first inspired and beside himself, and his mind is no longer in play.
>
> **Plato,** *Ion* **534b**

> In Roman culture a *genius* was a spirit, a god that possessed and protected an individual, a place, or an object (perhaps the origin of the idea of a guardian angel). In the Romantic Age, it became more of a possession beyond the mere powers of reason. Consider these quotations:
>
> You can often inherit talent, since it comes from understanding. You rarely or never inherit genius—it comes from reason or imagination acting.
>
> **Samuel Coleridge,** *Table Talk,* **May 21, 1830**

> Talent is when someone is able to hit a target no one else can hit. Genius hits a target no one else can even see.
>
> **Arthur Schopenhauer,** *The World as Will and Representation* **1.3**[5]

Our birth is but a sleep and a forgetting:
    The Soul that rises with us, our life's Star,
Hath had elsewhere its setting,
    And cometh from afar:
Not in entire forgetfulness,
    And not in utter nakedness,
But trailing clouds of glory do we come
    From God, who is our home:
Heaven lies about us in our infancy!
    Shades of prison-house begin to close
Upon the growing Boy . . .

William Wordsworth, from "Intimations of Immortality from Recollections of Early Childhood"

To be sure, many Romantics wanted to say that this sort of truth was universal, even that everyone potentially had access to some portion of this higher knowledge. In keeping with Plato, some Romantics wanted to see childhood as a time of purity when their souls might almost remember the universal truths they knew before inhabiting their bodies (see chap. 9). They were turning away from a cold and increasingly complex world to the imagined simplicity of childhood and an imagined past filled with primitive instincts. The effect was to foster rebellion against societal and religious norms and to celebrate the supposed genius of the idiosyncratic artist.

Leo Tolstoy (1828–1910) reacted against the individualist and inevitably rebellious orientation of Romanticism. He shared with Romanticism a sense that the key to art was feeling rather than thinking (over and against Plato and Aristotle). But the kind of feeling that art properly conveyed was feeling we all share in common. Consider the following quotations, the first by Novalis, a Romantic poet, and the second by Tolstoy:

> The more a poem is personal, local, and specifically related to its own time, the closer it is to the heart of poetry.

> **Novalis**[6]

> Art is a human activity that consists of intentionally . . . passing on to others feelings you have experienced so that other people are infected by these feelings and experience them as well.

> **Leo Tolstoy, *What Is Art?***[7]

In the first, Novalis (1772–1801), a Romantic, pictures art as something local and particular to a time and place. By contrast, Tolstoy sees art as something that communicates the universal—not universal truths of reason, but universal experiences and feelings.

In his 1897 essay "What Is Art?" Tolstoy evaluates the worth of a piece of art in part by its "infectiousness." Good art is not something only the artist can understand or appreciate. It is something that excites interest among others because they can relate to it. Tolstoy tended to see all people as one, with us all sharing a common identity and humanity. If artists express themselves genuinely, especially their personal experiences, their art will be infectious because others will relate to those same experiences.

Good art thus had a universal quality by expressing feelings that everyone has everywhere. Tolstoy also thought that good art had a religious dimension.

Tolstoy was a deeply religious man, although in his later years he had serious questions about traditional Christian beliefs. He wrote in his

BIOGRAPHY

ROMANTICISM

The Starry Night by Vincent van Gogh

Romanticism was a movement in art and culture in the late 1700s and early 1800s that emphasized feeling, intuition, and imagination. It was a reaction to the Enlightenment emphasis on reason (the Age of Reason), as well as to the cold, impersonal direction of the Industrial Revolution.

If the scientific revolution of the 1600s had made the world seem to be a mechanical, unfeeling place, the Romantics felt their way to something deeper and more mysterious about human life. If God had seemed more distant and less certain by reason, they recognized the possession of the artist by a higher power. If Kant had suggested we cannot know the world as it actually is, they responded that they *could* access the world as it really is through intuition. If the "neo-classical" art of the Enlightenment had reached back to the classical world of the Greeks and Romans for examples, the Romantics reached back into the Middle Ages for shadowy tales of Arthur, Robin Hood, and the stories of the Brothers Grimm.

No doubt the popularity and influence of Romanticism derived from the fact that the common person could identify with it. It certainly had its elite leadership, such as **Johann Wolfgang von Goethe** (1749–1832) in Germany and Samuel Taylor Coleridge (1772–1834) in England (although Goethe denied being a Romantic). But the staying power came from the fact that anyone could identify with its values and themes. Paintings were less and less about *representing* truths—less about Jesus, Mary, biblical scenes. Now they were *expressions* of feeling and imagination, ranging from scenes of everyday life to less-than-reverential treatments of religious themes.

Romanticism was thus an expression of cultural insecurity, a kind of escape from the "real world" to some other supposedly more real world. It is no surprise that fear was a primary emotion expressed, and the modern horror film finds its origins in the Romantic Age. This is the age that gave birth to Mary Shelley's Frankenstein (1818). The movement that birthed it in Germany was called *Sturm und Drang* (storm and stress). In Goethe's *Faust*, a genius has studied everything imaginable ("unfortunately theology as well") and being at the end of reason sells his soul to Satan.

Individualism in its modern form owes much to the Romantic Age. It is true that Descartes turned the lens of philosophy toward self as an individual *thinker*, but Romanticism glorified individual *feeling*. It was the age of the French and American revolutions, where any individual could disregard the time-honored roles and rules of society. (This in part explains Shakespeare emerging as a hero.) "Who am *I* as an individual and what do I *feel* about who I am?" became a question the elite asked, while common people felt empowered and embraced a common identity as a people (nationalism). These developments would set the stage for Freudian introspection at the end of the 1800s.

> The goal of art is to make the feeling of brotherhood and love of your neighbor—which is now only attained by the best members of society—the normal feeling and instinct of all humanity.
>
> **Leo Tolstoy, *What Is Art?*[8]**

Confessions that the most significant words in one Christian service he attended were "Love one another in unity." But he then ignored the words "we believe in the Father, Son, and Holy Spirit," claiming he could not understand what they meant.

Tolstoy was thus a good example of the "liberal theology" of the late 1800s and 1900s leading up to World War I. "Liberal theology" in this context is not liberal the way we use the word today but a school of thought that had little time for beliefs such as the virgin birth or the divinity of Christ;

BIOGRAPHY

PROTESTANT LIBERAL THINKING

© istockphoto.com

Although many speak today generally of something being liberal in a broad sense, liberal theology was the formal name of a stream of Protestant thinking especially in the late 1800s and early 1900s (not to be confused with the economic liberalism of the previous chapter). Friedrich Schleiermacher (1768–1834) was the father of liberal theology when he sought to protect Christianity from the challenges of the Enlightenment by defining religion in terms of religious experience: "Religion is neither thinking nor acting but intuition and feeling," he wrote in *On Religion*. In this regard, the influence of the Romantic era on him is unmistakable.

The height of Protestant liberal theology came in the late 1800s and early 1900s, prior to World War I. Albrecht Ritschl (1822–1889) built on Schleiermacher's sense that religion was about experience rather than knowledge, but he sought to give that experience a more objective basis in the origins and history of Christianity. He also saw it more as a lived-out experience in community (ethics) than did Schleiermacher, whose focus was on an individual experience of complete dependence on God.

Ritschl found part of his objective basis for Christian experience in his idealized picture of Jesus as the

supreme moral example of all history, a demonstration of the perfect human relationship with God lived out in community. He did not believe Jesus was divine, even if he had been in a class by himself. Part of the job of the theologian for him was to strip the authentic substance of Christianity from its later accretions, such as the creeds.

Protestant liberalism would then reach its peak at the beginning of the twentieth century, before World War I dashed its optimistic view of humanity to pieces. Adolf von Harnack (1850–1930) saw the essence of Christianity as "the fatherhood of God and the brotherhood of humanity." The essence of Christianity was thus to love your neighbor and what came to be known as the "social gospel," where the overwhelming focus of Christian faith is on helping others rather than on saving souls from damnation.

In many (though not all) cases, the key figures in Protestant liberalism did not view Jesus as truly divine. Even Charles Sheldon, the pastor who started the slogan "What would Jesus do?" saw Jesus as a moral example more than as divine or as Savior. Nevertheless, it is important to recognize that what was defective in the Protestant liberalism of that time (or of the neoliberalism of our day) is not the focus on loving our neighbor, imitating Jesus, or promoting social justice. Its defect was what it did *not*, rather than what it did, teach.

it focused on loving one another and giving to those in need. Accordingly, Tolstoy gave away vast amounts of his personal fortune to the poor in his later years. The religious dimension of art was thus about art that infected you with the desire to love your neighbor as yourself, while leading you away from the kinds of things that pitted people against each other.

Before we end this section on "Art and Feeling," it seems appropriate to mention another philosopher of art, **Herbert Marcuse** (1898–1979).[9] We briefly mentioned Sigmund Freud (1856–1939) in chapter 9, but we did not go into any detail about **psychoanalysis**, the school of psychology that he started.[10] Herbert Marcuse was especially interested in how art might relate to what Freud called **repression**, the tendency for people to suppress internally feelings and desires, such as anger, the drive for sex, and fear, without acknowledging or working through them. For Marcuse, art was an excellent way for repressed feelings and desires to express themselves.

Freud pictured a person's will in terms of conflicting influences. Simplistically explained, he used the term *superego* to refer to the part of us that makes us feel guilty if we do not do the "right thing." The term *id* refers to our animalistic drives. Our *ego* for him was the arbiter of these two other forces. The problem of course is that society—and frankly reality—does not let us act out our animal drives without restraint.

© istockphoto.com

When we are children, our parents often stop us from doing what we want to do, whether it be stepping into oncoming traffic or screaming in a restaurant. As adults we may have strong desires for someone who will not give us the time of day. We may be held against our wills or not have the money to buy something we desperately want. When we do not or cannot follow through on these basic drives and desires, the result is what Freud called repression.

Freud believed that repressed feelings could not be contained forever. Have you ever had someone react completely out of proportion to what you said or did? There is a good chance that you have hit a sensitive area in that person's life—an issue with a history. Sometimes the expression of such feelings is fairly mild. **Rationalization** is when you make up excuses for something because your mind does not want to face something or accept the blame. **Projection** is when you accuse others of things for which you yourself subconsciously feel guilty. A **Freudian slip** or parapraxis is when something comes out of your mouth from your subconscious that you did not consciously intend to say.

Psychoanalysis: the school of psychology Freud founded that tries to bring forces of the unconscious to the conscious mind to deal with them.

Subconscious/unconscious: the forces of one's human mind of which one is not completely aware.

Repression: suppressed drives or desires.

Defense mechanism: a way of protecting one's conscious mind from repressed feelings and drives.

Rationalization: making excuses so someone does not have to face something or accept blame.

Projection: accusing others of things for which someone subconsciously feels guilty.

Freudian slip/parapraxis: when words someone did not intend to say slip out of his or her subconscious.

Sublimation: repression that is redirected and expressed in a healthy way.

The **subconscious** or **unconscious** is key to Freud's theory. We often are not aware that we are doing these things—repressing, rationalizing, projecting. They are dynamics lying beneath the surface of our conscious thinking. To Freud more than to anyone else we owe the recognition that the most powerful forces behind what we think and feel lie beneath the surface of our awareness. Our conscious minds are like the tip of an iceberg.

For Freud these sorts of **defense mechanisms** shield our conscious minds from things we do not want to deal with. One can function fairly normally in society with such subconscious forces as long as they do not become extreme. However, such forces can become so strong that they manifest themselves in physical sickness or an inability to function normally in society (e.g., those suffering from posttraumatic stress disorder).

According to Freud the best way to process repression is by way of **sublimation**, redirecting such energies in a healthy direction. First, of course, it helps to become aware of underlying, driving forces. We also owe to Freud the insight that events we faced in childhood influence our adult patterns. Freud also believed that dreams could reveal what is going on in the subconscious. He recommended free-association games where one says the first thing that comes into one's mind, before the conscious mind has a chance to quash it.

Some of us intuitively find ways to cope with these sorts of repressed emotions. We take a cold shower when that girl will not go out with us. We go shopping. We gorge ourselves on snacks. We go out back and chop some wood. Journaling has often functioned this way, and psychologists sometimes recommend writing letters to those who are causing us pain—even if they are dead or if we never send the letters. These are all examples of sublimation.

Herbert Marcuse took these psychological insights and applied them to art. Repression results when the "pleasure principle" comes into conflict with the "reality principle," when our id could not be satisfied for whatever reason. To be sure, Marcuse—similar to the ancient Cynics—thought that most of the repression caused by society was made up, artificial. Our superegos were formed more by our environment than anything else. He was strongly influenced by Karl Marx as well as Freud, so he saw many of the rules of society as an imposition of the bourgeoisie on the common person. Art could thus be a revolutionary tool, a venue through which the common person could fight against the repression of the powers that be. Art for him was a tool of rebellion.

Most of us are not likely to identify with these aspects of Marcuse's thought. Nevertheless, he may have hit on an important function that art can have, one that we have already noted in Aristotle. Art can be cathartic. Art can be a mechanism through which our pent-up emotions are sublimated in a healthy way. The enviable artist can create art as an expression of such feelings. But as responders the rest of us can also find emotional release through their work.

When we are sad, art can help us express our sadness. We can cry as we listen to music or watch a sad play. We can express feelings of love as we read a love story. We can vent our anger as we watch justice played out in a movie. The key is for the art to help us release these emotions rather than feed them. We do not have to accept the negative aspects of Marcuse's theory to see that he recognized a powerful function that art has.

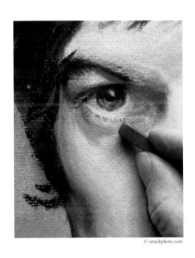

© istockphoto.com

13.4
WHAT IS ART?

Although we have not discussed it directly, all the perspectives we have mentioned thus far in the chapter have some implicit sense of what art is and what the highest purpose of art might be. For Plato and Aristotle, art was about representing truth and imitating life. This view was the prevailing function of art in the Middle Ages. Biblical or Christian-history scenes dominated art, giving the audience lessons in virtue or vice. Even in the Renaissance in the 1400s and 1500s, the content of art broadened, but the function of presenting truth remained. The scenes might have depicted ancient Greece or Rome as much as the biblical narrative, but the viewer still learned something about virtue and vice.

> **Affective:** having to do with feelings and the emotional dimensions of humanity.

The freedom of artists to express themselves in their art grew after the Renaissance. Art as individual expression thus began to become a greater and greater feature of art in the centuries that followed. Renaissance painters, even though they were commissioned to paint, often put themselves into the paintings they made for others as an element of personal expression.

And surely we who seek out art do so largely because we enjoy it. Art serves the purpose of bringing pleasure to the viewer. The intellectual stimulation brings pleasure to some, while the more emotional or **affective** sides of art may bring pleasure to even more. And of course many who commissioned their own portraits received pleasure from looking at themselves.[11] Any account of what art is must surely take into account the

Recent studies have explored the neuroscientific dynamics of how humans engage art.[12] For example, the psychological dynamics of emotion might shed light on how readers of fiction can relate to characters that are not "real." Appreciation of music relates to sense perception, as well as one's own musical ability. Neuroscience can also study the way in which visual arts impact an observer, linking specific visual features with specific neurological effects. Some of these effects may relate directly to certain features of the human visual system, especially the eye.

Waterlily Pond, 1899 (oil on canvas), Monet, Claude (1840–1926) / National Gallery, London, UK / The Bridgeman Art Library

pleasure of those of us who look at it, as well as the expression of the artist who creates it.

Perhaps no one has captured this very personal dimension of art better than the playwright **Oscar Wilde** (1854–1900), even if his thoughts were often over the top. In his essay "The Decay of Lying," Wilde presents his sense that art should not be "about" anything. Art does not need to represent anything or teach a truth. Art is valid simply because it is art—"art for art's sake." In fact, Wilde believed that the recipe for bad art was precisely in trying to make it imitate life, to represent things as they are. Rather, "lying, the telling of beautiful untrue things, is the proper aim of art."

Wilde tries to turn the typical thinking about art on its head. "Life imitates art far more than art imitates life," he argues. Where might you actually see fogs rolling down a London street such that it blurred the buildings around you? We all know the image, but it did not come from life. It is a picture we have all learned from English poets and painters. Certainly Wilde is at least right to say that art has a way of influencing the real world in this way. Would we have cell phones that flip open if the television series *Star Trek* had not created "communicators" that worked similarly?

Nevertheless, most of us would not want to restrict art in this way. Surely art can imitate life if we want it to do so, just as life can imitate art. Art is not an "intrinsic" good. We make or appreciate art because it does something else, even if that something else is merely pleasure. So art is not simply for art's sake, but perhaps for the sake of pleasure or expression or, if we want it to do so, for the purpose of representing truth.

We are now in a position to try to synthesize the various perspectives on art in this chapter. We might start by addressing art in form and art in function.

In form, art is a matter of the human senses: sight, hearing, taste, touch, and smell. So when we think of art, we think of things like paintings, sculptures, architecture, drama, novels, music, and good cooking. These all involve our senses—often combinations of senses.

However, for such things to be art in function, someone must perceive them to be art. In that sense, something can be art to me that is not art to you. Something can be art to its creator and not to anyone else. The key is that someone finds in something created by someone an embodiment of meaning or skill that is not literal or mechanical.[13]

Art is often a function of human emotion or pleasure. The artist may express feelings about something. An audience may have emotions as it experiences a piece of art. Art can also communicate rational truth, but it does so in a nonliteral or symbolic way. The painting represents a truth rather than simply telling it. A novel creates a world that embodies truths or feelings without presenting the literal world.

Someone may consider something a work of art because it embodies skills that not everyone has. Something evokes pleasure in the perception of the skill it embodies. There can be an art to writing even when a person is writing about math or science. The idea of a skill was in fact the original meaning of the word **art**. We might thus define art as the expression of something meaningful to someone in a skillful or nonliteral way in the form of something perceived by the senses.

Beyond this definition, are there criteria by which we might evaluate the *value* of art, especially as Christians? Is beauty only in the eye of the beholder? Certainly by our definition we cannot deny any individual the right to define something as art that only he or she finds to be art.

Yet as Tolstoy said, there is also something significant about art that has an infectious quality, though we acknowledge that the kind of art that is infectious in one time and place may not be in another. What one generation or culture finds appealing and desirable another may not. Abraham Lincoln's Gettysburg Address, admired today for its brevity and clarity, was not acclaimed in a day when more embellishment was the norm. William Shakespeare's plays were considered unsophisticated to the elite of his day. And Paul in the New Testament reveals that according to the style of his time, "his speech [is] contemptible" (2 Cor. 10:10).

But it is by no coincidence that centuries of individuals have found the works of Michelangelo (1475–1564) and Leonardo da Vinci (1452–1519) to

© Kevin L. Welch

Art: the expression of something meaningful to someone in a skillful or nonliteral way in the form of something perceived by the senses.

The Last Supper, 1495–97 (fresco) (post restoration), Vinci, Leonardo da (1452–1519) / Santa Maria della Grazie, Milan, Italy / The Bridgeman Art Library

be art at its best. Is it because they have captured something about the order God placed into the world? Is it because they have expressed some common dimension of the human psyche? Is it because they were able to do things none of us could imagine doing? Perhaps it is a bit of all these things.

Most Christians believe in the enjoyment of beauty or (appropriate) pleasure for its own sake. While many Christians throughout the ages felt the need to make Song of Solomon into a metaphor for Christ and the church, it was originally poetry about sex and love, plain and simple. We find acrostic poetry in Lamentations and Psalm 119, where the first word of each verse intentionally begins with a different letter of the alphabet. Lamentations 1, 2, 4, and 5 have 22 verses, one for each letter of the Hebrew alphabet. Lamentations 3 goes through the alphabet three times.

These and other artistic expressions in the Bible do not aim to teach us some lesson. They are purely a function of beauty and artistry. Many of the psalms are expressions of sadness or thanksgiving or anger. The purpose of such psalms was not to communicate information; they do not give a proposition to evaluate. They are expressions of God's people with which we can identify. We can thus agree with Oscar Wilde that art does not always have to have a purpose other than enjoyment or an expression of meaning. Art most often falls in the category of **adiaphora**—things that are morally neutral.

Yet from a Christian perspective, art can also have both positive and negative moral dimensions. We can say with Tolstoy that art that tends to promote virtue in its audience has a positive moral dimension. We can say with Aristotle and even Marcuse that art can be cathartic in a way that purges us of unhealthy emotions so that we can think or act with greater clarity or virtue. For this reason, art that embodies sadness or anger is not clearly negative in effect. But we can also say with Plato that art can be used to manipulate in a negative direction. And we can find Marcuse's sense of art dangerous when it is the expression of an evil heart. Art is an embodiment of evil when it is an expression of an evil heart, and art is negative when it embodies or promotes vice and evil in those who perceive it.

Most of us live in a culture where freedom of expression is highly valued, but freedom is never absolute. In secular American culture, I am free to express myself in speech or religion *if* such things do not lead to violence or a violation of the rights of others. Even from a secular perspective, there are limits to freedom of expression.

The limitations you want to put on others from a Christian perspective will differ in keeping with the view you have of how Christians should relate to the society around them, as we saw in chapter 12. Christians who see the world through a deterministic lens may want to force the rest of society to conform to their Christian values. Christians who believe God has given us

> **Adiaphora:** things that are morally neutral, being neither morally positive or negative.

286

free will, by contrast, will lean toward allowing others to express themselves in negative ways, as long as it does not harm the innocent.

13.5
CONCLUSION

In this chapter we have looked at the philosophy of art, a second order discipline that asks metaquestions like what art is and what makes good art. Often in the history of art, visual art has been judged by how good a representation it was of an object. Plato thought art was bad because it led away from the truth, while Aristotle thought it was good because it helped us see the essence of the thing it pictured. In the Middle Ages, art primarily functioned to teach moral lessons by picturing religious scenes from the Bible.

Still others have judged art by the feelings it evokes rather than by some rational dimension. Aristotle thought that art could have a cathartic effect on the emotions that cleared the mind for rational thinking, but the Romantics of the 1700s and 1800s saw emotion as the actual path to the transcendent. The ideal artist was a lone genius, often misunderstood because he or she was in touch with another realm. By contrast, Leo Tolstoy saw artistic feeling as most legitimate when it led to universal feelings of love for one another, when art had a "religious" dimension.

It is perhaps not surprising that the twentieth century saw art that was much more controversial in content. Herbert Marcuse used Freudian categories to argue that art was good when it helped a person vent repressed frustrations or when it tore at the (artificial) values of society and religion. Meanwhile, Oscar Wilde argued that art does not have to do anything to be good art—"art for art's sake." By contrast, still other contemporary schools have demonstrated that there frequently is a quantifiable correlation between certain features of art and a positive psychological response.

In the end, we suggested that a Christian will evaluate art on the same basis as Christians determine value in general. Jesus and Paul both made it clear that virtue is primarily a matter of one's heart and intentions. In that regard, art is positive on the part of the artist when it expresses a good heart or at least does not express an evil heart. God created beauty, so the pleasure experienced both by artist and the person who enjoys art can glorify God simply because they are rejoicing in what God has created and made possible. But, secondly, art can be evaluated in terms of its effect on the virtue of others. Art that has a negative effect on others can thus be considered of questionable value.

KEY TERMS

- aesthetics
- subjective
- objective
- psychoanalysis
- repression
- rationalization
- projection
- Freudian slip
- subconscious/unconscious
- defense mechanism
- sublimation
- affective
- art
- adiaphora

KEY PHILOSOPHERS / MOVEMENTS

- Plato
- Aristotle
- Romanticism
- Goethe
- Leo Tolstoy
- Herbert Marcuse
- Oscar Wilde
- Liberal theology

PHILOSOPHICAL QUOTATIONS / IDEAS

- "Life imitates art far more than art imitates life." (Wilde)

KEY QUESTIONS

1. Given the content of this chapter, how would you answer the question, what is beautiful? How would you respond to someone who disagreed with you?

KEY QUESTIONS

2. Do you agree with the author's definition of art near the end of the chapter? How would you critique it?

3. Do you think there is a distinction between good and bad art? What criteria would you use to decide? Do you think a Christian should try to do something about bad art of a certain kind?

4. Does it matter whether art is highly individualistic or if it appeals to a broad audience? Is art better or worse depending on the extent to which it "teaches" something or rouses emotion?

5. Has Romanticism shaped how you look at the world, especially in ways you may not have realized?

6. This is the most extensive presentation of Freud's psychology in this book. How helpful do you think his notion of repression is in explaining human behavior? Can you think of examples of his defense mechanisms from real life? How well do you think his theories apply to art?

NOTES

1. I am greatly indebted in what follows to the excellent organization of this topic in Robert Paul Wolff's introductory philosophy textbook, *About Philosophy*, 11th ed. (Upper Saddle River, NJ: Prentice Hall, 2011).

2. See the sidebar quotation by the first historian of art, Giorgio Vasari, who, in his 1550 work *Lives of the Most Excellent Painters, Sculptors, and Architects*, first used the term *renaissance* to describe the "rebirth" he saw in the arts. He did not, however, use the term to describe a historical period. See chapter 14.

3. Paraphrase based on Giorgio Vasari, *The Lives of the Artists*, trans. J. C. Bondanella and P. Bondanella (1550; Oxford: Oxford University, 1991), 101

4. One wonders if the *Ion* represents more of Socrates's view than Plato's, with Plato's later writings expressing his own views more explicitly through Socrates's mouth.

5. Paraphrase based on Arthur Schopenhauer, *The World as Will and Representation*, trans. E. F. J. Payne (1819; Indian Hills, CO: Falcon's Wing, 1958), 2:391.

6. Paraphrase based on Novalis, *Philosophical Writings*, ed. and trans. M. M. Stoljar (Albany: State University of New York, 1997), 161 (Last Fragments, no. 38).

7. Paraphrase based on Leo Tolstoy, *What Is Art?* trans. R. Pevear and L. Volokhonsky (1897; London: Penguin, 1995), 40, in sec. 5.

8. Paraphrase, ibid., 166.

9. Herbert Marcuse's key work here is *Eros and Civilization* (London: Routledge & Kegan Paul, 1955).

10. Freud's seminal work is *The Interpretation of Dreams*, trans. J. Strachey (1899; New York: Basic Books, 1955).

11. It is also true that a significant social function of art comes from impressing others that you have it. Many of the wealthy throughout history have bought or commissioned art to show how great they were. But this dynamic has less to do with what art is than with the social function art can play.

12. Many thanks to Frank Ponce for referring me to A. P. Shimamura and S. E. Palmer, *Aesthetic Science: Connecting Minds, Brains, and Experience* (Oxford: Oxford University, 2012), especially chapter 2.

13. We can of course by extension speak of God as the consummate artist in his creation of the world. And we can always make metaphors of such things, e.g., our dog is an artist in the way she arranges her food around the kitchen floor.

Unit 7

Philosophy and the Future

What to Get from This Chapter

- The philosophy of history asks questions like what history is, what historians do, and what they should do.
- Herodotus is often called the "father" of history because of his use of sources, his taking into account contrasting perspectives, and his minimal recourse to gods as causes of events.
- Ernst Troeltsch laid down principles for historical interpretation, including the expectation that events in the past played out like those in the present and to account for an event by way of natural causes and effects.
- Michel Foucault emphasized that the prevailing sense of history will always involve the use of power and that history is told by the winners.
- Linear views of history see history moving toward certain ultimate events, as opposed to cyclical views.
- The idea of "Western civilization" and its history usually involves significant impositions on the data of history as part of a myth of progress.
- Christians agree on the beginning, middle, and end of the story of history, but sometimes differ on how much God intervenes, whether things are getting better or worse, and whether God primarily acts in love or justice.

Questions to Consider

- What makes something a "history"?
- What is the best way to investigate history?
- To what extent is history-telling subjective?
- Is history moving in a particular direction?

Key Words

- History
- Sources
- Thick description
- Linear view

© istockphoto.com

14.1
PHILOSOPHY OF HISTORY?

In the first chapter, we noted that a number of areas in philosophy ask questions about other subjects, such as science and art: what are or should they be about? These are metaquestions, second-order questions about the first-order questions asked by these other fields of study. We have looked at several of these subcategories of philosophy: chapters 5 and 6—the philosophy of religion; chapter 8—the philosophy of science; chapter 13—the philosophy of art.

Here we look at the **philosophy of history**, which asks what history is, what historians do, and what they should do. It looks at **historiography**, the genre of literature that writes about history and people writing about history. The philosophy of history analyzes what people in the

The **philosophy of history** asks questions like what history is, what historians do, and what they should do.

Historiography: the genre of literature that writes about history and people writing about history.

© Kevin L. Welch

The Sennacherib Stele that recounts the campaigns of the Assyrian King Sennacherib.

past have thought history was and tries to analyze and evaluate the assumptions they have had.

For example, the ancient philosopher Cicero (106–43 BC) once called the Greek historian **Herodotus** (ca. 484–ca. 425 BC) the "father of history."[1] The philosopher of history might ask: Why did Cicero think Herodotus was different from the others before him who recorded events from the past? Have others agreed with Cicero—why or why not? What assumptions did Cicero bring to the issue that we might question? What was Herodotus's distinct contribution to history writing, if any?

We begin to investigate. The context in Cicero is a distinction between the genres of poetry and history. History is supposed to be about truth, while poetry is more about pleasure. Herodotus is the father of history because he wrote about things that actually happened, although Cicero acknowledges that some things in Herodotus's *Histories* are legendary. By contrast, poets (presumably like Homer) wrote more about gods and legends—more for pleasure.

So the standard Cicero seems to be using for "history" is that someone is writing about what actually happened rather than about legends and myths. Indeed, other ancient writers devalued Herodotus by the same standard. He has sometimes been called the "father of lies" in addition to being called the father of history. The Greek writer Plutarch (ca. AD 46–120) wrote an entire treatise called *The Malice of Herodotus*, which frequently refers to what he considered to be lies in Herodotus's *Histories*.

As we look at other writers from the ancient world, we find more confirmation of this basic standard for history writing. In his book *How to Write History*, the satirist Lucian of Samosata (ca. AD 120–190) says the job of a historian is "to tell the story as it happened."[2] **Thucydides** (ca. 460–ca. 395 BC) later in the same century as Herodotus may allude to him when he says he is not going to include any "fables" in his history; his aim is to present what truly happened and might happen again.[3] Because Thucydides does not include the gods as actors in his history, because he seems to have been more scrupulous in his use of sources, sometimes *he* is called the father of history—or at least the father of critical history.

The philosopher of history examines the assumptions of these ancient writers and of those historiographers—writers about history—who have followed. For example, is it possible to write about "what really happened" or is all history selective and told from a perspective? Did these ancient writers believe that legend was *completely* inappropriate in a history? Was their idea of truthfulness the same as ours? Should we question the assumption that good historical explanation will not include the action of God or gods? Is the significance sometimes given to Herodotus a "regional"

BIOGRAPHY

REFLECTING ON HERODOTUS

© istockphoto.com

The ancients did not consider it wrong for there to be nonhistorical material in a book about history. Cicero himself acknowledged many legends in Herodotus.

Thucydides told his audience up front that he composed some of the speeches in his history. In his *History of the Peloponnesian War,* he says that when his sources were not sufficient to recall exactly what was said, he created material he thought would have been appropriate for the occasion. Clearly the rules for writing history in ancient times were different from the factual criteria of today.

There is a certain "regional" element to this focus on Herodotus. The Romans inherited him from the Greeks. The Renaissance then started in Italy and venerated the ancient Greeks and Romans. Other places clearly told about their past before Herodotus, not least in the Old Testament—and even in Greece itself, although their works have not survived as extensively. We will revisit some of these issues later in the chapter.

bias that forgets about other places in the world, including earlier writers of history in the Old Testament? These are the kinds of questions that a philosopher of history will ask.

14.2
APPROACHES TO HISTORY

There are some features of Herodotus that do seem to make him a good starting point for a discussion of what history is, including the fact that his work survived.

First, he does not present the point of view of his people only. Indeed, one reason for Plutarch's criticism may have been Herodotus's lack of bias in favor of the Greeks. Herodotus included the perspective of the Persians, the enemies of the Greeks.[4] Is history writing better when it incorporates multiple points of view and at least tries to be objective? Many historians have thought so, although we will examine this assumption later in this section.

Second, Herodotus researched other sources in preparation for his writing. His research may not have been as extensive as that of Thucydides, but Herodotus did not simply repeat local oral traditions and legends he had heard. Modern historians have generally considered looking at **primary and secondary sources** of information about the past a crucial element in good history writing. A primary source is from the actual context of the investigation. It might be a document relating to an event or written by a witness or participant. It might be archaeological evidence from the time. By contrast, a secondary source is from someone who knows of the event "secondhand," such as an expert today writing about a battle of the Civil War.

Close-up of a Black Obelisk of Shalmanezer III showing Jehu, king of Israel, bowing before the Assyrian king.

© Kevin L. Welch

Third, although the gods feature in Herodotus's narrative, he pays significant attention to the normal processes of cause and effect. Things that happen are not discussed simply as the will or intervention of the gods, but in terms of real conflict and chains of events as a result of human decisions in conjunction with their circumstances. Later, we will return to this issue of whether supernaturalism has a place in the writing of history.

Finally, the form in which Herodotus wrote would become an established pattern for later "histories." To be sure, kingdoms had long kept chronicles and annals of the deeds of their kings. The Old Testament books of Samuel and Kings regularly mention the "Annals of the Kings of Judah" (e.g., 1 Kings 14:29) and the "Annals of the Kings of Israel" (e.g., 1 Kings 14:19). We have such annals from other ancient kingdoms, including Assyria. These annals presented the exploits and victories of kings throughout their reigns—certainly from a very flattering perspective.[5] By contrast, the *Histories*, also called the *Inquiries* of Herodotus, took a more dynamic and broader form than some incredibly biased listing of a king's exploits.

In more recent times, historians have looked to **Leopold von Ranke** (1795–1886) as the originator of historical investigation in the modern sense. In a famous line, Ranke indicated that the task of a historian was to present history "as it really happened,"[6] an approach to history that we might call **historicism**. At the end of this section we will question Ranke's "modernist" idea that it is possible for anyone but God to know "what really happened" in any fully meaningful sense.[7] Nevertheless, several features of his method of doing history are central to the way we approach history today.[8]

Leopold von Ranke, by Adolf Jebens (1819–1888), 1876 (oil on canvas), Schrader, Julius Friedrich Anton (1815–1900) (after) / Deutsches Historisches Museum, Berlin, Germany / © DHM / The Bridgeman Art Library

OLD TESTAMENT
HISTORICAL BOOKS

Upon hearing the idea that Herodotus was the originator of history writing, a Christian or Jew might immediately think, what about 1 and 2 Samuel or 1 and 2 Kings in the Bible? For that matter, what about Genesis? Asking these questions sheds light on a number of the issues of this chapter.

For one, it highlights the *regional* nature of the construct we call Western civilization. Cicero may never have heard of the Old Testament, and he is the first one on record to call Herodotus the "father." Until recent times, those who traced the story of Western civilization followed a construct that started in Greece, went to Rome, then skipped the Middle Ages to the Renaissance in certain parts of Europe.

© istockphoto.com

It also illustrates the way in which power affects the interpretation of history. In the past two hundred years, those in power over interpretations of history largely have not allowed for the supernatural to be part of historical explanation. For this reason, historical material in the Bible was largely excluded from solid history; it includes numerous accounts of God or other powers intervening in the chain of "natural" causes and effects.

Since we now acknowledge that *all* history telling inevitably takes place from a perspective, we cannot limit the genre of history to those accounts that try to take an objective point of view toward the writer's own people and other parties in the story. Further, the books of Kings relied on other sources, so this criterion of a history using primary sources cannot exclude them. All in all, the postmodern critique of knowledge breaks down the starkest distinctions that historians of the 1800s made between the historical accounts of Scripture and those of individuals like Herodotus and Thucydides.

The historical books of the Old Testament certainly meant to tell about people and events that actually happened. It is true that the narratives of the Old Testament are more theological than most modern histories. In a modern history, someone like Jeroboam II (2 Kings 14:23) would receive at least a whole chapter. He reigned for forty-one years over Israel in perhaps its most materially prosperous and territorially expansive time. He gets seven verses in 2 Kings.

For one, far more than even Herodotus and Thucydides, Ranke insists that historical writing must be based on evidence. Ranke thought mainly of documents when he spoke of evidence. But those that followed rightly expanded our sense of evidence and primary sources to include "material culture," the physical remains from a particular time and place. For example, if we want to investigate what people at the time of Christ in Israel thought about the afterlife, we will look at the relatively few writings that have survived from that time; we will also want to look at things like the way they buried their dead.[9]

Primary sources: sources from the actual context you are investigating (e.g., documents, archaeology).

Secondary sources: sources from other contexts that are about the context you are investigating (e.g., contemporary experts).

Historicism: modernist approach to the past that aims to present it "as it really happened," with complete objectivity.

Supernaturalism: in terms of history, the belief that God and perhaps other spiritual forces sometimes participate in the cause-effect flow of events.

Perhaps more important is the emphasis in Ranke's method of questioning the sources. One must not simply take the word of one's primary sources but approach them with a critical eye. For example, when reading the *Jewish War* by the Jewish historian Josephus, we cannot simply assume that he is giving us an unbiased presentation of events. We need to be aware that he was a general in the war who surrendered to the Romans. Is there a hidden agenda of defending himself? We need to be aware that he was writing for a Roman audience and those who won the war. Does he make them look better than he would have in private conversation? Does he modify his descriptions of groups like the Pharisees, to make them intelligible for his audience?

We are now far more aware of bias than Ranke was in his day. You might say that while he set us on a good course for questioning the biases of sources, today we realize that it is just as important for us to question our own biases. I grew up in a "conservative" group in the Methodist tradition. How does this fact affect the way I read the writings of John Calvin? I like ideas and theology. How does this theological interest affect what jumps out at me when I read a source like Josephus?

Ranke emphasized a third, very important, insight: the historian should let the concrete historical phenomenon drive interpretations of history rather than some abstract ideological framework in which the historian wants to fit that historical data. His thoughts here were probably a direct response to G. W. F. Hegel's theories, which were very dominant at the time and which we will consider later in the chapter. Sometimes we as Christians have this tendency—to take the very complex currents and opinions of various periods of history and put them into a box that says, "this was the era in which people believed x because they had turned from God," or, "this was the time when y happened because people served God."

Ranke thus anticipated what **Jean-François Lyotard** (1924–1998) would say in the late twentieth century about *grands récits*, "grand frameworks" or metanarratives by which we organize the complex phenomena of the world. We are far more likely to be accurate in our descriptions of the world if we stick to the *petits récits*, the smaller stories where we are better able to account for more data. It is much easier to capture the essence of a meeting you had this morning than to summarize the way meetings went in the twentieth century. And it is easier to say how meetings went in the twentieth century than to demonstrate that meetings tend to go better for Christians than for non-Christians, which tries to put an ideological grid over meetings.

One of the most important issues in historical method to arise in the late 1800s and early 1900s was the question of **supernaturalism**—whether a good historian could allow for the possibility of divine intervention in

© istockphoto.com

history. Of course this issue had been around in philosophy for a long time, with the deism of the 1700s in effect bracketing the idea of God's involvement in the world. But with the rise of modern historiography, excluding God from one's explanations of historical events became a dogma.

Perhaps no one captured the spirit of the age better than **Ernst Troeltsch** (1865–1923) in his 1922 book *Historiography*. For him, no explanation of nature is allowed to resort to metaphysics (what is supposed to stand behind or above nature), which includes God. The historian and scientist must stick to concrete, material causes and effects. Notions of ultimate reality have no business in historical description.

Accordingly, he formulated three basic principles for critical history. First, all decisions regarding history are open to revision. They are never a matter of certainty but of varying degrees of probability. Second, historical events today happen similarly to the way they took place in the past. This is a principle of analogy. So if people do not come back from the dead today, he rejected any suggestion that someone might have come back from the dead in the past. Finally, historical events are intertwined (they correlate) with what comes before and after them. They must be explained in the flow of clear historical causes and effects.

Christians today would reject the complete exclusion of God and the supernatural from Troeltsch's historical method. However, it is just as clear that he well describes the way most of us approach our daily lives. If we cannot find our keys, we do not initially think, what demon has taken my keys? especially if we are always losing them, if we have a roommate with a mischievous bent, or if we have a child who likes to put keys in his mouth. And as much as we believe that Jesus rose again from the dead, few of us would go to a cemetery three days after the death of a friend to see if she will rise.

Indeed, different Christians see the level of God's direct involvement in the world differently, as we saw in chapter 10 when we discussed determinism. Some see God steering everyday events down to small details, often working in and around people and events to accomplish his hidden purposes.[10] Such believers spend time trying to guess what God is trying to teach them by causing them to catch a cold or forgetting to call someone. Those taking this approach seem hard pressed to see much of anything that happens simply as the normal flow of cause and effect that God has built into the creation (i.e., the rules that scientists and inventors have capitalized on to give us cell phones and laptops). Rather, for them things that happen are primarily God behind the scenes, orchestrating everything.

Others think that, while God does act in history, his purposes and interventions are much more mysterious. They might suggest that God wants us to think more for ourselves, to take responsibility for the consequences of our choices, and be able to accept the unpredictable ebb and flow of the world. Those taking this approach expect to be able to explain most things by normal causation and would conclude a miraculous intervention only when the normal paths of explanation were exhausted.

In the mid-twentieth century, **R. G. Collingwood** laid out the next major moment in the philosophy of history. Collingwood calls the historical method prior to modern times a "scissors and paste" method.[11] To present a particular moment in history, these historians found an appropriate figure from the time they wished to describe and "pasted" an appropriate quote from that figure as an *authority* on the event. One problem, as we have already seen, is that these "premodern" historians largely did not take into account the biases of the people they were quoting. Collingwood sees a move forward when such individuals were seen as *sources* rather than *authorities* on the day.

BIOGRAPHY

"GREAT MAN" THEORY OF HISTORY

Thomas Carlyle (1795–1881) is especially known for his claim, in *On Heroes, Hero-Worship, and the Heroic in History,* that "the history of the world is but the biography of great men." In his view, we can mostly account for the history of the world by examining the impact of highly influential individuals, including figures such as Muhammad, Martin Luther, William Shakespeare, and Napoleon.

Herbert Spencer (1820–1903) is the best-known opponent of this view, arguing that such leaders can emerge only if the social situation is right. In "The Social Organism" (1860), he said that such individuals "are the products of their societies." In *Social Statics* (1851) he noted that they are "merely the tools with which it [social change] works."

His main claim in *The Idea of History* is that the task of the historian is to "re-enact the past in his [sic] own mind."[12] It is to bring the past into the present by reliving it. To do so, one must go well beyond the "outside" of an event, the individual facts.[13] The historian must instead get into the "inside" of the event, what the thoughts and intentions were of the individuals who took part in these events. Why did they do the things they did? Collingwood wanted to get beyond thinking of cause and effect as a simple matter of events and get into the minds of the individuals participating in the events. What was the human question to which the action was the answer?

As we look back at Collingwood, his focus on human intentions seems a bit ambitious and perhaps overstated. On the one hand, his sense that we have access to the past only in the present is potentially insightful for the historical task. **Hans-Georg Gadamer** (1900–2002) would later argue that we do not have access to the intentions of the authors *of texts* (let alone the thoughts of people from the past themselves).[14] We have only the effects of texts as they have played out over time and reached us in the present. And

even then, we come to the text with our own sociocultural influences. Reading a text is thus a process of "fusing" two horizons, our horizon with that of a text as it comes to us (see chap. 4). We have no certain way of knowing how well that fusing relates to the original intentions of the authors of those texts.

© istockphoto.com

Collingwood's focus on human intention also seems myopically focused on ideas. What of the *experiences* of people and their feelings as the events of the world play themselves out in their lives? Why make rational intentionality the primary focus?[15] More recent times have seen a focus on narrative as more fundamental to human ways of identifying ourselves and thinking about the world. Arthur Danto's *An Analytical Philosophy of History* (1965) rightly argued that the historical significance of any event can be unfolded only in the context of a story because "history tells stories."[16] Story seems potentially to capture in proper perspective all the elements that previous historians sought to incorporate and balance—including ideas, intentions, and natural cause and effect. We will return to this potentially fruitful idea at the end of the chapter.

To bring approaches to history current we must briefly engage the thinking of **Michel Foucault** (1926–1984), whom we will consider more fully in our final chapter as a prominent figure of postmodernism. Predictably, Foucault resisted labels of this sort, but we wish to discuss him from our perspective rather than from his own. In particular, Foucault saw his discussions of history mostly as discussions about language as an expression of power and certainly not "what really happened."

From the critical realist perspective we have adopted in this textbook (see chap. 8), Foucault is helpful in calling our attention to historical paradigms and how they shift over time. He moves us from thinking merely

© Kevin L. Welch

of individuals and their intentions (Collingwood) to the societal assumptions and matrices by which we assign meanings to events. Further, he helps us see how structures of human power affect the way we look at the world and history.

Foucault's historical studies include looking at how societal understandings of punishment, insanity, and sexuality have changed over time. For example, at one point insanity or "madness" was considered almost a blessing from the gods.[17] In the 1400s, a common image was that of a "ship of fools"; society saw a wandering ship sailing unpredictably from port to port as an appropriate image of the wandering minds of these "mad" individuals on the borders of society. Foucault then pursues changes in conceptions of madness until he reaches modern society, where we diagnose and treat insanity as an illness.

With regard to sexuality, Foucault argues that the very category of sexuality as we think of it is a recent invention.[18] In previous days, people did not divide human sexuality into the categories of hetero- and homosexual with distinct "orientations." Homosexual activity was exactly that—sexual activity that some people engaged in. Such individuals would likely have been married and had children as well. Using our language, earlier generations would have assumed that everyone was a heterosexual but that some people also engaged in homosexual behavior. But they did not have a category "heterosexual" in their minds.

A good deal of what Foucault had to say about such things seems to work when we apply them to history. For example, the Bible arguably never addresses the question of homosexual *orientation*—attraction to the same sex. It seems only to address homosexual *activity*. The category of a homosexual arguably did not exist until the 1800s. It is our contemporary way of thinking about sexuality that leads us to assume that the men of Sodom and Gomorrah must have been homosexuals because they wanted to have homosexual sex. In the thought world of Genesis, these are more likely men who wanted to *rape* the angels. Judges 19 confirms this conclusion; in this very similar story, the men of the city go so far as to rape a concubine to death.[19]

Foucault thus corroborates what the cultural anthropologist Clifford Geertz (1926–2006) taught when he advocated what he called a **thick description** of culture.[20] Indeed, as Collingwood indicated, true historical understanding cannot think it has explained the meaning of some event by telling the facts of what happened and certainly not if we assume the key players thought exactly the way we do. This is a major issue when we as Christians read the Bible. When we read of a biblical figure doing something or even saying something, we must explain the meaning of those actions and words in terms of the sociocultural matrix in which they were done or spoken, which will not at all likely be the same as our sociocultural matrix. Further, this warning applies even to the very nature of the narratives themselves; we cannot assume that we are seeing a straightforward presentation of what happened in the biblical narratives, since this is also an assumption of *modern* historical narratives.

Although he did not come up with the saying, a second caveat emphasized by Foucault is that "history is told by the winners." In a set of public lectures in 1976, Foucault postulated that those who emerge the winners in societal struggles often try to eliminate competing versions of the past. Paul Ricoeur (1913–2005) more accurately noted that various versions of history can be at play at the same time. We use them. We abandon them. We start using them again, like a chess player who is playing several games at once, now playing one game, then the other.[21] In short, those in power tend to use their power to propagate their version of the past to justify who they are in the present and what they wish to do in the future. Of course, there are instances where historical narratives give even the warts of their heroes. We can marvel that the books of Samuel tell of King David's weakest moments.

We end our treatment of historical theory with brief mention of **new historicism**, which is not so much a movement in historiography as a movement in literary theory.[22] As a perspective on literature, new historicism represents a return to trying to read literary texts in terms of their original meanings, although not from the narrow historicism of the past but with an understanding of history that takes onboard Foucault's "insights" into how broad cultural dynamics and power structures affect meaning. It is known significantly for its interest in "lost histories" and mechanisms of repression and dominance. But it can represent for us a "chastened" approach to historical inquiry that has learned from the postmodern critique without abandoning a sense that we can still legitimately investigate the past and come to valid conclusions.

> **Thick description:** Clifford Geertz's term for a description of culture that goes beyond simple causes and effects to include sociocultural frameworks.

> **New historicism:** a literary movement that returned to taking historical context and authorial intent into consideration, but with greater recognition of interpretive bias and the tendency for interpretation to favor those with power.

> He who controls the present, controls the past. He who controls the past, controls the future.
>
> **George Orwell, *1984* (1948)**

Aztec calendar stone in Mexico

14.3
A CYCLICAL VIEW OF HISTORY

The default human sense of history would seem to be cyclical, a perspective captured well in the memorable words of Ecclesiastes 1:9–11:

What has been is what will be,
     and what has been done is what will be done;
there is nothing new under the sun.
     Is there a thing of which it is said,
"See, this is new"?
     It has already been,
in the ages before us.
     The people of long ago are not remembered,
nor will there be any remembrance
     of people yet to come
by those who come after them.

Cyclical view of history: the sense that history is not on any kind of a clear trajectory but is more an endless set of similar stories repeated over and over.

Linear view of history: the sense that history is on a certain trajectory toward an ultimate destination, that it has an overall storyline.

It is well for us to remember that these words came before the New Testament, and they express the perspective of perhaps all cultures prior to the centuries just before Christ, as well as most cultures to this day outside the influence of the three great monotheistic religions: Judaism, Christianity, and Islam. This perspective is what we might call a **cyclical view of history**, a sense that the story of the past is merely a series of repeated vignettes in which the same basic types of things happen over and over again. People are born. People die. In between they find food, find shelter, raise children, and grow old.

For many, maybe most, aspects of our daily living, this view of the world has much to commend it. Perhaps we are so used to technological developments being introduced every two or three years that we forget that most of what we do as humans is what humans have always done. Because of the massive scientific improvements of the past century, we have come to expect the *way* we live to improve quickly. But the basic categories remain the same as always: food, shelter, pleasure, clothing, and so forth.

Those who cannot remember the past are condemned to repeat it.

George Santayana,
The Life of Reason (1905–1906)

In a purely cyclical view, history is not "headed" anywhere. It is not waiting for some day when all the dead will come back to life. It is not waiting for Christ to come back to earth and set up an eternal kingdom. In other words, the cyclical view contrasts with a **linear view**, where history as a whole is moving toward some ultimate culmination and "end" of some sort. The vast majority of the Old Testament authors, like the people of their day, understood the world in a cyclical way.[23] This is a significant insight into the original meaning of the Old Testament.

Scale model of Herod's Temple including the courtyard, The Holy Place, and the Holy of Holies whose nearly cubical shape and large size rises far above the surrounding temple walls.

© Kevin L. Welch

In the previous section we noted Foucault's emphasis on taking into account the paradigms of a culture at a point in history. The historical paradigm of the bulk of the Old Testament was, in its original meaning, cyclical. We tend to read the Old Testament in linear terms because that is how the New Testament recasts the individual stories of the Old Testament. It takes what to the original readers were fairly localized *petits récits* (small stories; see earlier in the chapter) and reinterprets them in the light of a *grand récit* (larger metanarrative).

For example, we do not find Solomon in 1 Kings talking about the temple as a temporary solution to the problem caused by Adam in Genesis, to be solved once and for all in Jesus Christ. This sort of large narrative understanding of history was completely foreign to the time of 1 Kings. Rather, people have always offered sacrifices to secure good relationships with God and the gods. And important kings build big temples. Only when we get to the time of Christ are such events recast in the light of an overall story of salvation planned by God before the creation of the world.[24]

Consider also Troeltsch's rule that says we should try to account for an event in terms of the things that happened before and after it. Unlike Troeltsch, historic Christians believe that miracles have taken place in history, but we still might apply his rule in relation to what biblical texts *most likely* meant. If we can account for the meaning of a biblical text in terms of the thought categories of its day, we might well see that meaning as what the original authors and audiences were likely thinking. This also applies to reading the Old Testament texts in cyclical terms of history.

We might use 2 Samuel 7:16 as a case in point. Here God tells David, "Your house and your kingdom shall be made sure forever before me; your throne shall be established forever." But what did "forever" mean at the time? Because most of us come to this text with a linear and absolute sense of history, we assume "forever" means that even three thousand years later—indeed a million years later—we will find a descendant of David ruling. This plays into our sense that Jesus is that descendant of David and that, yes, he will rule forever, literally.

This is certainly something Christians believe and affirm—that Jesus will be king forever, literally. The New Testament understands the Old Testament in this way and that makes this interpretation legitimate, indeed the Christian perspective. But this is not likely anything intended in the *original* meaning of 2 Samuel 7 because its author would have understood "forever" more in the sense of "for a really long time." This example brings together a number of key points. It brings together what we have said in chapter 4 and will say in the next chapter about words being capable of multiple meanings; it brings together our sense in chapter 8 and this chapter that we interpret things from within paradigms, so that the same words might have quite different connotations in different contexts.

14.4
A LINEAR VIEW OF HISTORY

How then did linear interpretations of history emerge? One pattern emerged in the first millennium before Christ, when a people group would divide its *past* history into stages, looking back to a Golden Age that deteriorated over time.[25] The Greek poet Hesiod in the 600s BC was already dividing up the past into successive stages of gold, silver, bronze, and so forth. The Roman poet Ovid in the century before Christ followed suit. They looked to the earliest age of human history as an ideal time that had only deteriorated with successive periods.[26]

We find this same pattern in Daniel 2:31–35 in a dream of the Babylonian king Nebuchadnezzar. In his dream, he sees a statue with a head of gold, a chest of silver, a middle and thighs of bronze, legs of iron, and feet of iron mixed with clay. Daniel interprets the head of gold to be the king's own kingdom, that of the Babylonians. Interpreters of Daniel then disagree on what empires the rest of the metals in the figure originally represented.

In the traditional view, the silver represents the Medes and the Persians. The bronze represents the Greeks. The iron represents the Romans, with the mixed kingdom that follows being the divided kingdom of the Romans. One might then equate the kingdom that will never be destroyed (2:44) as the church, which rose to become the dominant force in Europe during Rome's divided kingdom. This view of course takes the statue as a prophecy about the future.

Outside evangelical circles, the dominant view is that the book of Daniel is largely a type of literature known as **apocalyptic** and that most writings in this genre write about the present by having important figures from the past predict events that were actually taking place at the time the document was written.[27] In other words, in this view, the statue would mostly describe the past for its author, until we get to the feet, which would have been about the author's present. Interpreted from this perspective, Daniel was largely written to speak to a crisis in Israel in the years 167–64 BC, the "Maccabean crisis."[28] No doubt some scholars take this position because they do not believe it is possible to predict the future. Others think this is simply the literary form that God used to present the message of Daniel.

In this interpretation, the silver would represent the Medes, the bronze the Persians. The iron would be the Greeks, with the division of the Greek Empire between the Ptolemies in Egypt and the Seleucids in Syria as the iron

Apocalyptic: a particularly Jewish and Christian perspective on the world that sees history moving toward a climax in which God will ultimately intervene and address the injustices and wickedness of the world.

mixed with clay. God would then set up an everlasting kingdom for Israel at the end of that time, the time when the author was writing the book of Daniel. In this view, the unfolding ages of the past are still much like the pattern of the poet Hesiod, only told in a creative way.

In both interpretations, Daniel is a striking development in linear thinking/writing about history.[29] Daniel looks to a time when God will hit the reset button on justice, bringing back the righteous dead to be rewarded while reviving others to be condemned (12:2–3). Whatever conclusion we reach on the dating of Daniel, we can also agree that the origins of linear thinking about history, as we know it, generally arose from Jewish apocalyptic literature.

For example, the Apocalypse of Weeks was written just after 200 BC, and it divides up all human history into ten "weeks." As with most apocalypses, it tells this history in the mouth of someone from the past, in this case Enoch from Genesis 5:24 (1 Enoch 93:1–10; 91:11–17). Scholars agree that most of these "weeks" of history were well in the past for the author and that he was writing in what he hoped was the beginning of the eighth week. The key is that this anonymous author mapped out three more epochs of human history *in the future* until history reached its finality.

It was probably during this time, the second century before Christ, that the idea of resurrection became a significant force within Judaism.[30] Apocalyptic literature often was written in times of crisis. Accordingly, the expectation of the "end of history," the resolution to the evils of the world, was hoped for imminently. After such crises were over, the literature remained and continued to be read. Thus also remained hope that one day in the indefinite future God would indeed set the world straight. A linear view of history was born that saw a trajectory not only for the near future but potentially for the distant future.

In this period just before Christ it seems that a linear view of history emerged within Judaism. Christianity emerged from Judaism, and Islam later emerged from the matrix of both. The three great monotheistic religions all thus share in common a linear view of history. Because we can trace the origins of the view does *not* mean that it is an incorrect view. We as Christians, for example, believe that this is the means by which God brought the idea forward.

The Christian view of history is thus a linear view. It is not only the fundamental view of the New Testament—belief in a future resurrection of the dead and the return of Christ to judge the world. It is also captured well in the fundamental creeds of Christianity. The Apostles' Creed says, "I believe . . . he [Christ] ascended into heaven . . . From there he will come to judge the living and the dead . . . I believe . . . in the resurrection of the body and the life everlasting."

The first individual we know to formulate an extensive, linear philosophy of history was **Augustine** (AD 354–430). His major work *The City of God* addressed accusations that the gods had allowed Rome to be sacked by the Goths in 410 because Rome had become an exclusively Christian nation.[31] Augustine claimed, rather, that society was witnessing the ongoing conflict between two cities that existed side by side in the world.

The one was the "city of God," a city of heaven made up of the righteous angels as well as the "elect," those whom God has chosen to be saved. While the city of God has a special connection to the "visible church" (the people who gather together and call themselves "Christians") one cannot see clearly who is truly a citizen of the city of God and who is not. The visible church is like the Parable of the Weeds in Matthew 13; the wheat and the weeds are mixed together in this world, and we cannot know definitively which is which until the judgment.

The other city entangled with the "city of God" is the "city of humanity," a city of earth made up of fallen angels and the majority of condemned humanity. Those who ultimately belong to this city are oriented around themselves and their own pleasure, rather than God. These two cities are in constant conflict in this age until Christ finally returns, but the trajectory of history is toward the definitive separation of the two at the final judgment. A significant portion of Augustine's work goes through biblical and secular history to demonstrate the progress of the two cities throughout history. The implication is that we should not be surprised when earthly cities like Rome fall, especially when they are associated with the city of earth.

Augustine's approach to history is sometimes called **amillennial**, because he does not interpret the "thousand years" of Revelation 20:4 literally. For him the number is symbolic and refers to the entire period between Christ and the final judgment.

Augustine thus has a linear view of history; he sees it headed toward a particular destination. But he does not have a clear sense that events will develop in a certain way in the intervening time. He does not clearly indicate whether the city of God will increasingly overcome the city of earth.

Two other Christian perspectives do. **Premillennialism** is a Christian perspective on history that tends to take the thousand-year period of Revelation 20 literally and says this millennium has not yet taken place. Christ will reign on earth for a thousand years *after* he returns to earth in the future. Generally, premillennialists have a pessimistic view of the trajectory of history; they expect the forces of evil to fight harder and harder against God up until the time of the end. They might quote passages like Mark 13:19: "For in those days there will be suffering, such as has not been from the beginning of the creation that God created until now, no, and never will be."

By contrast, **postmillennialism** agrees with Augustine that the millennial age has begun, but this perspective is more specific than Augustine; the city of God is taking over the city of earth, as it were, as time progresses. Things will improve more and more leading up to Christ's return. Christ will thus return after the millennium (not necessarily a literal thousand years) is over. It is perhaps not surprising to find that Christians in different periods of time have tended to lean in one direction or the other. Prior to Augustine, many though not all Christians were chiliasts, from the Greek word for thousand. These were individuals who looked for a literal thousand-year reign of Christ after his return. From Augustine to recent times, postmillennial and amillennial approaches dominated. It is not surprising to note that the optimistic spirit of human progress evident after the Renaissance and Reformation would gravitate toward a postmillennial perspective.

At the same time, we should not be surprised to see that premillennialism would return to the fore in popular circles in the uncertain times of the Industrial Revolution. John Darby (1800–1882), a British evangelist, almost singlehandedly gave birth to **dispensationalism**, a Christian perspective that sees history divided up into a series of periods in which God had a unique relationship and expectations of his people. The culmination is usually a seven-year "tribulation" leading up to Christ's return and judgment, followed by a literal thousand-year reign of Christ on earth.

We thus cannot say that there is a distinctive Christian perspective on the direction history will take leading up to Christ's return. Each position cites favorite biblical passages, and each position has critiquing explanations for the favored passages of the other positions. If we are good philosophers, we will be aware of the forces that have influenced us in the past and are influencing us in the present. We will be aware of and reflective regarding our own biases.

Perhaps most important, we will try not to let our biases become **self-fulfilling prophecies**—by which our expectations come true not because they were inevitable, but because our own actions, perhaps inadvertently, made them come true. If you expect things to get worse and worse, there is a fair chance you will not do much to try to make them better. And if you expect things to get better and better, you probably will do things that move them in that direction. Let *God* watch over history. Let *us* work for good in the world.

Premillennialism: the theological view that, usually after things get worse and worse, Christ will return and establish a literal thousand-year reign on earth.

Postmillennialism: the theological view that the thousand-year reign of Christ began literally on earth through the church after his resurrection, often with a sense that things will get better and better before his return.

Amillennialism: the theological view that does not take literally the thousand years of Revelation 20:4 but sees the current age as one in which Christ both rules and the forces of evil continue to fight against him.

Dispensationalism: the perspective that divides up history into several "dispensations" in which God relates to the world in different ways, usually leading up to a seven-year "tribulation" before Christ returns.

Self-fulfilling prophecy: a prediction that a person inadvertently helps make come true by his or her actions.

14.5
Myths of Progress

In popular language, a myth is something we tell ourselves that is not true, a false story, if you would. As we discussed in chapter 8, there are more sophisticated ways of looking at myths. A more meaningful definition of the word would be a fictional story that we use to express something about ourselves and our sense of the world. "A story expressing a mystery" is how we put it in chapter 8.

When we speak of "**myths of progress**," we could be saying something true by both meanings of the word *progress*. In 1932 the psychoanalyst M. D. Eder wrote an article called "The Myth of Progress" in which he used the word *myth* in the first sense, as a false story we tell ourselves. "The myth of progress states that civilization has moved, is moving, and will move in a desirable direction. Progress is inevitable."[32] He was reacting to the idea that the human condition would inevitably improve over time, particularly through scientific progress. He argued on the contrary that scientific developments were making humanity unhappier on the whole and that in some ways they actually threatened its destruction.

We do not wish to linger long on this sense of the "myth of progress." Most of us would agree that progress is not inevitable. From a human perspective, all it would take would be a serious political mishap to wipe humanity from the face of the planet in a nuclear war. Since every child begins the world anew, humanity is always one generation away from the total loss of any knowledge or accomplishments it has accrued in the past. This is the stuff of science fiction, but most of us can imagine it happening on a human level.

As Christians, we believe in more than the human. We believe in **providence**, God's guiding hand for ultimate good in the world. That is not to say that God does not allow evil. We saw at the end of the last section that Christians do not agree on how this age of existence will end. Some believe Christ could return to a world that has been greatly changed for good by the good news of God's coming kingdom. Others believe things will get worse and worse until God intervenes at the last moment, just before humanity completely implodes.

However, in relation to the "myth of progress," we want to explore the more profound sense of the word *myth*. Whether or not it turns out to be literally true, the *idea* that things will get better and better is real and has had a powerful effect on Western society. Although we noted in the previous section that many ancients saw history as a story of deterioration, the idea of

Providence: the Christian sense that God is watching over the course of history and that God sometimes steers it toward good or protects us from evil.

progress was also present in the ancient world as a minority report. It is not entirely a recent invention.[33]

In this section, we will consider ways in which, in the past five hundred years, many in "the West" have conceptualized history in terms of European and American peoples in particular standing at the front of the progress of humanity and civilization. I put "the West" in quotation marks because it would seem that even the very notion of "Western civilization" is part of this story we have told ourselves, part of the myth.

Again, when we use the word *myth* in this way, we are not saying that these ideas are complete fabrications with no relation to reality. It cannot be denied that the scientific revolutions of the past few centuries took place overwhelmingly in Europe and North America in cultures that primarily speak Indo-European languages. It cannot be denied that the beginnings of these advances took place as the power of the church declined and as intellectuals began to think in terms of natural laws of cause and effect rather than in terms of a spirit-controlled world.

But these observations say nothing about superiority of intelligence, and they certainly say nothing of moral superiority. Further, they say nothing about *everyone* in these places. It simply says that the conditions of these regions in these times were fertile ground for massive scientific and technological advances. We have every reason to believe that individuals of the intelligence of Einstein have always lived in every region around the world, from ancient China, Egypt, and Africa to present-day Afghanistan.[34]

Whatever the basis in fact, the "myth" of Western civilization has gone further to tell the history of the world in such a way as to express its sense of superiority over both the past and others in the present. Even the language we use demonstrates such value judgments: the Dark Ages, the Renaissance, the Enlightenment. These are not value-neutral terms; they impose on the very diverse data of history simplistic and power-laden evaluations that exalt those of us who identify ourselves by this story.

An early piece of this historical construct came in 1442 when the Italian historian **Leonardo Bruni** first called the period from the fall of the Roman Empire to his day the **"Middle" Ages** or the **medieval** period.[35] There is an implicit condescension in this terminology. It implies that while things were good and "enlightened" during the Roman Empire, the intervening thousand years were the **Dark Ages**, a period of cultural darkness.

The term *Dark Ages* is particularly biased. Even more, it ignores significant pieces of data, especially when we apply it to Europe as a whole. For example, several of the great universities of Europe quite possibly were already operating around the year 1200: Oxford, Cambridge, and the University of Paris.[36] The theologian Thomas Aquinas (1225–1274), not to

Middle Ages: or the **medieval** period, roughly the time between AD 500–1500, from the fall of the Roman Empire to the Renaissance.

Dark Ages: derogatory term for the Middle Ages, implying a general absence of significance to the period in culture and thinking.

Renaissance: "rebirth" of culture in the 1400s and 1500s, drawing on ancient Greco-Roman models.

Enlightenment: or the **Age of Reason** from about 1650 to 1800, demanding that reason and evidence be used to establish what is true.

mention the Arab Muslim philosophers Avicenna (ca. 980–1037) and Averroës (1126–1198), extensively appropriated the philosophy of Aristotle as they presented their understanding of various theological issues during this period.

Bruni built his three-part division of Italian history out of some hints from the Italian humanist **Petrarch** (1304–1374). In a letter Petrarch wrote in 1359, he called the period since the fall of the Roman Empire an "era of darkness."[37] To his credit, he considered himself still part of this darkness. But what was more or less a passing comment for him became for Bruni a division of history into three parts: ancient, middle, and modern. Thus we have the idea of the "**Renaissance**," the supposed "rebirth" of culture from around the time of Petrarch in the 1300s, a return to the *living* past in contrast to the intervening *dead* years.[38]

However, to demonstrate the degree to which this way of viewing history is a construct, a story we in part have created, the idea of the *Renaissance* as a period of history did not arise until the 1800s. In English, it seems to have been used in this way for the first time in Jacob Burckhardt's 1867 book, *The Civilization of the Renaissance in Italy*.[39] To be sure, the individuals who lived in the 1400s and 1500s knew that momentous cultural changes were taking place. There are facts behind the construct. But the division of history that prevailed was based on generalizations that *evaluated* whole periods of time and labeled them largely after the fact. The Dark Ages are bad. The Renaissance is rebirth of the good. Those from Europe and America are smart. Everyone else is not.

The term ***Enlightenment*** is yet another label that places a value judgment on a period of history. It began as a term that certain French intellectuals used of the ideas they were sharing with each other in public discussions and debates in the mid-1700s.[40] The vast majority of people living in France at the time were not involved in such discussions, and those who disagreed with their ideas did not consider themselves unenlightened. The identification of those years as a distinct period of history was both a matter of self-promotion by those who participated in the movement and an interpretation that was highly selective.

This is not to deny that there were concrete ideological developments taking place in the 1700s among the most influential intellectuals in France, England, and Germany. There was an almost unprecedented rise of critical reflection on things the vast majority of people previously had simply assumed in one way or another. But ideological invention was also involved; there is also some truth in Roger Chartier's claim that the Enlightenment was in some ways invented by the leaders of the French Revolution when they identified a "canon" or definitive list of true Enlightenment thinkers, while excluding others.[41] It is in part an example of how history is told by the winners.

By the 1800s the myth of (European) progress reached new heights. In the 1820s, **G. W. F. Hegel** (1770–1831) claimed that "world history is the record of the spirit's efforts to attain knowledge of what it is in itself."[42] For him, this was a linear trajectory for history in which society became increasingly aware of what true freedom was. Hegel's philosophy is notoriously difficult and abstract, and is usually described as a **dialectical** process, an exchange between conflicting forces or points of view with a view toward resolution. Ironically, Hegel's dialectic has most often been described in terms that Hegel himself almost never used, namely, that of a **thesis** coming up against its **antithesis**, leading to a **synthesis**.[43] One idea, person, society, etc. (thesis) comes into dialogue with its negative (antithesis), with a result that combines or "sublates" the positive of both, while setting aside the rest (synthesis).

In his own terms, the "abstract" comes into conflict or contradiction with its "negative," and the result is the "concrete." In his most relevant example for our purposes, Hegel notes how those in the ancient east (e.g., Persia, China, and India) existed without freedom, knowing only that *one*—their king—was free, but they were not. For such individuals, freedom is a distant (abstract) concept that they understand little about. The negative of the "oriental" was then the Greek and Roman, who came to realize that *some* individuals were free. In their city-states and empires, citizens were free while slaves and others were not. The pinnacle of the concrete synthesis of these two for Hegel was his own Prussian German nation, which recognized that humanity was by nature free.

Hegel saw history as an ever-improving evolution with his own German nation as its highest and purest form. "World history travels from east to west; for Europe is the absolute end of history, just as Asia is its beginning."[44] Herein we see a pattern of thinking remarkably like what would eventually become the table of contents in later American textbooks on Western civilization, often beginning with the Sumerians and Babylonians before making their way to Egypt and finally Greece.[45] For Hegel, this is a single line of development toward the perfection of his own state.

Of the many thinkers who were substantially influenced by Hegel's philosophy, the best known was **Karl Marx** (1818–1883). Although Marx's sense of history's destination was diametrically opposed to Hegel's, Marx built his philosophy from the basic structure of Hegel's dialectic. The first key difference between the two was that Marx was a materialist (see chap. 7). As a materialist, Marx did not believe that *ideas* were evolving and progressing in history, as Hegel somehow did.[46] What was evolving was a

Dialectic: a process of moving toward truth by dialogue between conflicting forces or points of view.

Thesis: the first idea or force put forward in a dialectical exchange.

Antithesis: the force or point of view in conflict with the thesis.

Synthesis: the advancement after the conflict between thesis and antithesis, incorporating positive elements of both and discarding other elements.

world in which resources were shared by everyone as each had need, a society without rich and poor, without powerful and powerless.

For Marx, ideas were a by-product (an "epiphenomenon") of concrete, material forces in the world. People might say they are arguing over ideas, but they are really arguing over stuff. He saw the materials used to produce things, the people who produce things, and the know-how to produce things as being the real forces of society. Beyond these sorts of very concrete things, ideas were like a game people played that only obscured what they were really arguing over.

His version of Hegel's dialectic is thus called **dialectical materialism**.[47] History is a series of conflicts between various classes within society. Hegel in his own way had argued that one of the earliest conflicts was between king (thesis) and slave (antithesis). The king has complete freedom but cannot appreciate it. The slave has no freedom but has complete appreciation for it. Eventually, we find a synthesis in the medieval "lord," who does not have complete freedom but has immeasurably greater freedom than the serf who works on his land. Thus a new dialectical conflict has arisen in later history. The synthesis of the previous conflict (the lord) becomes a new thesis with a new antithesis (the serf).

From the conflict of the lord and the serf had emerged the aristocracy, which had less power than a lord but still considerably greater status than the merchants who arose as their new antithesis. Merchants also had far more status than the medieval serfs who were bound to the land of the feudal lord who protected them. The centuries just before Marx had seen the decline of the power of the aristocracy and the rise of what he called the bourgeoisie, the middle class that owned the businesses of the Industrial Revolution.

When Marx and Friedrich Engels wrote *The Communist Manifesto* in 1848, they believed they were about to witness the final "class struggle" in history, between the bourgeoisie and the proletariat or working class. They believed that the capitalism of the bourgeoisie was unstable and oppressive, that it would eventually lead to bloody revolutions by the proletariat worldwide resulting in a classless society in which all the materials and resources were held in common. The productions of society would then be distributed to each according to his or her need.

History has not substantiated Marx's ideas, although they did become self-fulfilling prophecies in the hands of revolutionaries in countries such as Russia and China. But no society reached anything like the utopia he expected, and most systems have had to return to some degree of capitalism. What is important in this discussion is that Marx represents yet another linear perspective on history in the late 1800s that saw history basically culminating in the Europe of his day.

Dialectical materialism: Marx's sense that the progression of history was an evolving conflict over who controlled the materials and goods of society.

Zeitgeist: the "spirit of the age," the prevailing ideas and perspectives of a particular time and place.

At the end of the 1800s, the spirit of the age (or **zeitgeist**, as Hegel called it) generally bought into a myth of historical progress, even if the specific expressions of that story differed. Regardless of its scientific merits, it is no coincidence that in the late 1800s the progressive theory of evolution gained dominance in the scientific community. It is said that it took devastations like World War I (the "war to end all wars") and the Great Depression in the early twentieth century to burst the optimistic bubble of the age. The twentieth century had many reminders of the ignorance and evil that have demonstrated themselves in all other centuries of history and will almost certainly find expression again in this one.

The second half of the twentieth century saw many attempts to recognize that "civilization" has never been the exclusive possession of the West. Initially the very notion of civilization arguably developed as a way of saying that *we* are intelligent, cultured, and sophisticated in contrast to those in other parts of the world.[48] And the idea of Western civilization arguably developed in part to distinguish the European colonizers from the people they were colonizing.[49] Today we would speak of multiple civilizations in history rather than the singular thread of civilization that typified Hegel's thinking.

If we think about it, why would a history book tracing the background of European culture start with Babylonia? The region now occupied by Iraq is hardly "Western" by anyone's definition nor is Egypt. Arguably the presence of these areas in the early chapters of Western civilization textbooks is an artifact of an age when these societies were seen as the beginning of a thread of the one "true" civilization evolving into us. These places were seen as antecedents to Europe as the current location of civilization, singular. The presence of Israel in some such textbooks might be justified because of Christianity's later dominance in Europe, but the Semitic culture of the *Middle East* is again curious to find as part of the history of something called *Western* civilization.

The lines that such tables of contents draw around the West often have more to do with us looking back than with the way lines were drawn at the time each culture flourished. The apostle Paul did not enter *Europe* when he left what is now Turkey for what is now Macedonia. At the time the coast of Turkey was thoroughly Greek and had been colonized by the Greeks for centuries. Even more, the whole area was Roman at the time. Our general exclusion of Turkey from Western civilization thus has more to do with distinctions made in the Middle Ages, when the area was conquered by Islam, than with location.

We look to Athens as part of our heritage and perhaps forget that it was only one city in Greece—and not always the dominant one. The fact that we look to the Athenians and not to the Spartans as our cultural forebears is yet another indication of how selective our construct of the Western thread is. It was perhaps appropriate for the Italian Renaissance to look back to Rome for the thread; it was at least in the same location. But on what basis might I as an American claim the Romans? Indeed, on what basis might I as an American claim the Italian Renaissance as a significant part of my cultural heritage? These places, events, and movements in history are part of my heritage as an American because historians of the past two centuries made them so.

The myth of Western progress has thus often been part of American self-identity. **American exceptionalism** is the idea that in some way the United States is distinct, perhaps superior to all the other nations in the world. Some Christians consider the United States almost equivalent to Old Testament Israel, God's favorite nation out of all the current nations of the earth. Many American churches have an American flag on the platform, implicitly associating the United States with God. America is commonly thought of as a Christian nation, even though the U.S. Constitution explicitly prohibits a national religious identity. We can interpret all these dynamics as continued manifestations of the myth of Western progress, albeit with a religious twist.

> **American exceptionalism:** the sense that America is distinct from, perhaps superior to, the other nations of the world in some significant way.

© istockphoto.com

14.6
A CHRISTIAN PERSPECTIVE ON HISTORY

A critical thinker should always hesitate to say something akin to "this is *the* Christian view of . . ." Historically and currently, if one were to canvass people who consider themselves Christians, one would find multiple viewpoints on most issues. And, of course, it is ultimately God who gets to decide who really is a Christian. In this chapter we have seen that there is some variety of thinking about history among Christians. In particular, some view history as a downward spiral till the end, while others look more to the potential of Christianity to change the world for the better, leading up to Christ's return. Other Christians, perhaps without much thought, may operate more cyclically: you live, you die, you go to heaven or hell . . . next in line.

Nevertheless, among those who hold to the historic beliefs of Christendom, we can sketch out some common elements to a Christian view of history, despite disagreements on the details. First, I suggest that a helpful approach to the question is to think of history as a story. Since I as a textbook author cannot see my own blind spots, I hesitate to say that this is *the* way to view history. I can only say that of all the approaches to history mentioned in this chapter I personally find it the most appropriate.

To think of history as a story allows us to incorporate the key elements of historiography. For example, it reminds us that, although we are talking about events we think actually happened in the past, we inevitably have to be selective in what we choose to tell about. Think of the nearly infinite amount of data from the past! Only God could hold it all in his "mind," with every bit in proper relationship to every other bit. How ridiculous for us to think for a moment that we have it all sorted out!

When we tell or relive history as a story, we are inevitably skewing it by selecting only some data and "deselecting" other data. But that is the nature of the game. There is no history that is not told from a perspective. There is always more than one way to tell a story, and there is always more than one way to tell about history.

A story has characters; it has events; it has settings.[50] So does history. The characters are not only the people, but all the "actors" in the drama. If we wanted, we could look at history playfully from the standpoint of certain ideas as characters wending their way through the story. For Christians, the most important character of all is God, and the hero of the story is Christ.

Events form the backbone of a story—its plot. What are the key events of a Christian understanding of history? Surely the creation is very important as the beginning of history for us.[51] And for those who are in continuity with Christianity historically, the central event of the plot has to do focally with Christ's incarnation, death, and resurrection. Again, different Christians may emphasize one of these more than another, but historic Christians will see some or all of these events as at least the beginning of the resolution of the plot's tension, the focal event of all history.

A traditionally Christian view of history is thus a *linear* view of history. It sees the whole of human history starting from a beginning and headed toward a particular destination. The beginning is the creation. The historic destination for Christians is when God sets everything right in the world, leading to eternity. Traditionally Christians have seen a fundamental problem to be resolved in the story, a problem that goes back at least to the first humans. It is this problem that Christ resolved, although the final working out of that resolution is yet to come.

We should be careful about the details. There are Christians who think of Adam and Eve as poetic expressions of the human situation. There are Christians who do not await a literal return of Jesus to the earth in judgment. They stand outside the historic beliefs of Christianity, but God will be the judge. "Blessed are those who have no reason to condemn themselves because of what they approve" (Rom. 14:22).

Believing that Christ was God come into history, Christians are not historically deists. That is, Christians believe that God has and does intervene

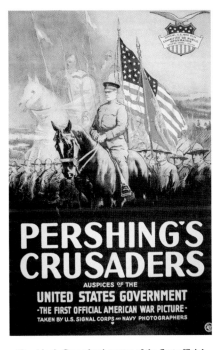

'Pershing's Crusaders', poster of the first official American War Movie, 1918 (colour litho), American School (20th century) / Private Collection Peter Newark Pictures / The Bridgeman Art Library

in the events of history. We are theists. We may differ in the extent to which God intervenes, but Christians believe that God can become part of the cause-effect flow of history. We believe at least that miracles have taken place in the past, and most of us believe they can take place in the present and in the future.

Historic Christians look to the Bible for the most important content of the story: its key characters, events, and settings. Christians differ on a multitude of interpretations of that content, but the story of Israel in the Old Testament and the story of Jesus and the early church are the most important elements of the overall story. As someone once quipped, "History is 'His-story,'" meaning the story of God.

We are part of that story too. So are all the people before and after the Bible. So are all the people who were not in Israel in ancient times. So are all the people who have not been part of the church after those times. So is all the creation and all the "settings" of the story in space in time. The rocks cry out in praise to God (Luke 19:40); the heavens declare the glory of God (Ps. 19:1). Or as the Nicene Creed says, God is the Creator of all that is, "seen and unseen," which includes all spiritual powers.

A narrative- or story-perspective on history is helpful for a Christian in yet another way, as we acknowledge that stories are always told from a particular point of view. Inevitably, we are forced to tell the Christian story from our point of view. For this reason, no version of Christian history any of us gives will be *the* Christian view. Any version we create will be inevitably partial and tainted, including this one.

Nevertheless, we believe by faith that the authoritative point of view on the story, what literary critics call the "evaluative point of view," is that of God. God's perspective on history is *the* Christian perspective on everything that has happened. By the end of this book, we will have made our case that we do not have direct access to God's full perspective on the story for several reasons.

For example, Scripture covers only the core of the story. It does not cover World War II or the next presidential election. A foundational reality is also that *I* am still the one interpreting Scripture, and a trip down an average city street will quickly illustrate how many Christian denominational "I's" there are. Reading the Bible in context also reveals that the Bible itself has multiple narratives on the key events, each with a distinct perspective. Further, the narratives were revealed in ancient categories, meaning that I am forced to translate them into our categories. Finally, because narratives are selective, they by their very nature cannot give an absolute perspective on any story.

We thus believe by faith that God has an evaluative point of view on the story. We believe Scripture gives us the most important indications of what that point of view is. But we will never have direct or complete access to God's point of view. We have to wait till the end of the story for him to reveal such things more clearly to us.

One question in ongoing Christian debate over the story asks whether the key to understanding God's role in history is God's love or God's justice. While most of us would want to say that these two do not contradict each other, there are clear differences among Christians as they play out love or justice in their sense of God's action in history.

To simplify things, those who lean toward love as the key to God's point of view tend to see God creating a world that is somewhat free to go its own way while longing for the world to move toward him. History is thus the story of God wooing the creation back to himself.

Those who lean toward justice as the key to God's character tend to see the creation more in terms of its guilt and sin before God. History is God punishing humanity for the sin of the first human, while making a way through Christ for his justice to be satisfied, so that some of humanity can escape his judgment. It should be clear that this text leans toward viewing love as God's key impulse in relation to history.

14.7
CONCLUSION

Philosophy of history asks second-order, metaquestions about history, such as how one should go about reconstructing history and whether history has a certain trajectory. In the Western tradition, Herodotus is often said to be the father of history writing because he used multiple sources with contrasting points of view and because he did not primarily use the gods to explain the causes of events. However, we also noted in this chapter that even the idea of "Western civilization" is to some extent a construct created by historians by selecting certain individuals and people groups (and not others) as part of "our" past. Herodotus and the Greeks are part of that selection.

Michel Foucault rightly emphasized that the way we tell history often has something to do with the "winners." Those who have the power to control the telling of the story shape our perspective on how history has unfolded, what the most important events were, who were positive and negative figures, and what lessons we should draw. While Leopold von Ranke suggested that a historian should tell history "as it really happened," all telling of history is selective and involves human perspective.

Recognizing that human perspective is an unavoidable element in history telling does not mean that there are not right and wrong perspectives, nor does it mean that we should abandon the quest for objectivity. But ultimately only God has a bird's-eye view of history.

Christians have a linear perspective on history, as opposed to a merely cyclical one. In a cyclical view, history is not headed anywhere in particular but is largely the repetition of similar types of events over and over again. By contrast, Christians believe that the incarnation, death, and resurrection of Jesus Christ was the focal event of all human history and that the end of history as we now know it will come with the return of Christ from heaven and the establishment of his eternal kingdom. Christians sometimes disagree on how events will play out leading up to those final events, as well as on how God engages the world in the meantime. But the focal point and the end point of history are matters on which Christians largely agree.

KEY PHILOSOPHERS

- Herodotus
- Thucydides
- Augustine
- Petrarch
- Leonardo Bruni
- Leopold von Ranke
- Thomas Carlyle
- Ernst Troeltsch
- R. G. Collingwood
- G. W. F. Hegel
- Karl Marx
- Hans-Georg Gadamer
- Jean-François Lyotard
- Michel Foucault

KEY TERMS

- philosophy of history
- historiography
- primary sources
- secondary sources
- historicism
- new historicism
- supernaturalism
- "great man" theory of history
- thick description
- cyclical view of history
- linear view of history
- apocalyptic
- premillennialism
- postmillennialism
- amillennialism
- dispensationalism
- self-fulfilling prophecy
- myth of progress
- providence
- Middle Ages/medieval
- Dark Ages
- Renaissance
- Enlightenment/Age of Reason
- dialectic
- thesis
- antithesis
- synthesis
- dialectical materialism
- zeitgeist
- American exceptionalism

PHILOSOPHICAL QUOTATIONS

- History is told by the winners.
- "He who controls the present, controls the past. He who controls the past, controls the future." (Orwell)
- "Those who cannot remember the past are condemned to repeat it." (Santayana)

KEY QUESTIONS

1. Do you agree with Cicero and others that Herodotus was the father of history? Give reasons for your answer.

2. What do you think the role of the supernatural should be in historical reconstruction? Evaluate Ernst Troeltsch's three criteria for historical investigation.

3. Articulate your viewpoint: To what extent can we be objective or complete in our reconstructions of the past? To what extent is history inevitably told by the "winners"?

4. Personally evaluate this chapter's presentation of myths of progress. To what extent do you think Western civilization is a construct rather than a historical reality? To what extent has history telling in Europe and America made unreasonable value judgments in its terminology and choice of material?

5. If you are a Christian, what is your perspective on issues over which Christians have differing viewpoints, such as the degree of God's involvement in history, whether God primarily acts in love or justice, and whether things are likely to get better and better or worse and worse?

NOTES

1. Cicero, *Laws* 1.5.
2. Lucian of Samosata, *How to Write History* 39.
3. Thucydides, *History of the Peloponnesian War* 1.22.
4. R. H. Barrow, *Plutarch and His Times* (Bloomington: Indiana University, 1967), 157.
5. Such as the famous comment in the chronicles of the Assyrian king Sennacherib, where he can boast only of shutting up King Hezekiah in Jerusalem like a "bird in a cage." As 2 Kings 19 indicates, God did not allow Sennacherib to defeat Jerusalem the way the Assyrians had defeated Samaria to the north.
6. Leopold von Ranke, *Geschichte der romanischen und germanischen Völker von 1494 bis 1514* [History of the Romantic and German Peoples from 1494 to 1514] (1824).
7. See the next chapter for a description of what we mean here by "modernist."
8. For the paragraphs that follow, I am deeply indebted to Mark Day, *The Philosophy of History: An Introduction* (New York: Continuum, 2008), 6–9. Perhaps an even better overview is Elizabeth A. Clark, *History, Theory, Text: Historians and the Linguistic Turn* (Cambridge, MA: Harvard University, 2004).
9. Although the evidence is far from conclusive, the fact that Jews at the time of Christ buried their dead in a tomb and then after a year removed the bones and reburied them in a more compact stone box (an ossuary) is sometimes taken to indicate a belief that those bones would one day come back to life.
10. A good example of this approach is Rick Warren, *The Purpose Driven Life: What on Earth Am I Here For?* (Grand Rapids: Zondervan, 2003).
11. Roger Collingwood, *The Idea of History* (1946; repr., Oxford: Oxford University, 1994). I am thankful again in what follows for Day's presentation of Collingwood in *Philosophy of History*, 16–18, 121–29.
12. Collingwood, *Idea of History*, 282.
13. Ibid., 213.
14. Hans-Georg Gadamer's classic work, published in German in 1960, is *Truth and Method*, trans. J. Weinsheimer and D. G. Marshall (London: Continuum, 1975).
15. A similar, almost bizarre, ideological perspective on history was that of Arthur O. Lovejoy (1873–1962), who might be considered the originator of a field known as the "history of ideas." In *The Great Chain of Being: A Study of the History of an Idea* (Cambridge, MA: Harvard University, 1936), he laid out the notion of a "unit-idea" or individual concept—like an atom of thought. He saw the history of thought as the assembly of such unit-ideas into various combinations.
16. Arthur Danto, *An Analytical Philosophy of History* (Cambridge: Cambridge University, 1965), 111.
17. Michel Foucault, *Madness and Civilization*, trans. R. Howard (New York: Vintage, 1961).
18. Michel Foucault, *History of Sexuality*, trans. R. Hurley 3 vols. (New York: Vintage, 1978, 1985, 1986).
19. Indeed, if we look at the way Jesus discusses Sodom and Gomorrah in the light of the sociocultural categories of the day (Matt. 10:11–15), the way Sodom treated *guests* is the most significant wrong in the story. The context is talking about cities and villages that might reject the disciples, just as Sodom and Gomorrah rejected God's messengers. The wrong of the homosexual act in the passage compounds the wrong to be sure, but it is our current cultural paradigm that makes this act the central point of the passage.
20. Clifford Geertz's best-known work is *The Interpretation of Cultures* (New York: Basic Books, 1973).
21. Paul Ricoeur, *History and Truth*, trans. C. A. Kelbey (1955; repr., Evanston, IL: Northwestern University, 1965), 186.
22. Stephen Greenblatt (b. 1943) is generally considered the originator of the movement.
23. Jostein Gaarder's philosophical novel, *Sophie's World*, trans. P. Møller (1991; repr., New York: Berkley Books, 1996), 149–63, understandably lumps Judaism, Christianity, and

NOTES

Islam together as having "linear" views of history without seeming to realize that it is really not until the time of Christ that some Jewish groups began to have a linear view.

24. The same principle applies to the way most of us look at prophecy about Jesus in the Old Testament. The New Testament applies many words to Jesus from the Old Testament in new ways, but the nature of Old Testament prophecy originally was not to speak to the far-off *distant* future but to the immediate present and near future. Isaiah 7:14 provides us with a good example: "Therefore the Lord himself will give you a sign. Look, the young woman is with child and shall bear a son, and shall name him Immanuel." Matthew 1:23 reads these words in relation to the virgin birth of Jesus. As Christians, most of us would affirm that this is a completely legitimate way for Matthew to read the words, even an inspired way for him to read it.

    At the same time, Isaiah 7:14 also likely had an original meaning that spoke to the present and immediate future of the prophet. In the flow of its own text, the verse seems to promise Ahaz, a king *at that time*, that the child of a young woman *already pregnant* would not reach maturity before the kings to the north (who were troubling him) were removed from power. Both in terms of the flow of the words (the literary context) and the way history was understood at the time (cyclical paradigm), it is extremely unlikely that *Ahaz* would take a sign *to him* to be about something that would take place more than seven hundred years after he was dead!

    The original meaning is a *petit récit*, a small story. The New Testament then legitimately gives those words a "fuller sense" (a *sensus plenior*) and places them into the perspective of a *grand récit*. For more on New Testament interpretation in a "fuller sense," see Walter Kaiser, Darrell Bock, and Peter Enns, *Three Views on the New Testament Interpretation of the Old* (Grand Rapids: Zondervan, 2008), 167–225.

25. Many Christians today still have this tendency when they think of the early church as the ideal church and assume that a primary task for Christians is to "get back" to the way things were in the golden age of the disciples.

26. An exception for Hesiod was what he called the "Heroic Age" of the Greeks who fought the Trojan War, the Greeks of legend and story.

27. The subject of apocalyptic literature is complex and involves a number of considerations. To dig in deeper, see John J. Collins, *The Apocalyptic Imagination* (Grand Rapids: Eerdmans, 1998). Our definition here is very partial so that it relates specifically to our discussion.

28. For example, Daniel 11 reads like a blow-by-blow account of the Maccabean crisis, but then Daniel 12 skips to the resurrection at the end of history in a very linear sense.

29. G. B. Caird and many influenced by him (e.g., N. T. Wright) would remind us that even language about the end of the world may have been less linear in its original context than we might suppose. See G. B. Caird, *The Language and Imagery of the Bible* (London: Duckworth, 1980), 201–71.

30. The only Old Testament passage that everyone agrees refers to resurrection is Daniel 12:2–3, although there are other candidates (e.g., Ps. 73). The bulk of the Old Testament is either silent on the topic or denies resurrection (Job 14:14) or a meaningful afterlife (Eccl. 9:2–5).

31. By decree of the Roman emperor Theodosius I in AD 380. Constantine had made Christianity only a *legal* religion in AD 313.

32. M. D. Eder, "The Myth of Progress," *The British Journal of Medical Psychology* 12 (1932): 1.

33. Cf. J. B. Bury, *The Idea of Progress: An Inquiry into Its Origins and Growth* (London: Macmillan, 1920). Cf. also Robert A. Nisbet, *History of the Idea of Progress*, 2nd ed. (Piscataway, NJ: Transaction, 1994).

34. This claim follows naturally from Herbert Spencer's critique of the "great man" theory of history we mentioned in a sidebar earlier in the chapter. Great leaders do not emerge

NOTES

simply because they are great; they emerge under certain conditions and situations. A George Washington would have been just another anonymous farmer at another time in history.

35. *History of the Florentine People*, sometimes called the first modern history book. Because Leonardo Bruni did not divide up history with a clearly Christian perspective, he is sometimes called the first modern historian.

36. Cf. Charles H. Haskins, *The Rise of Universities* (Ithaca, NY: Cornell University, 1923). In his *The Renaissance of the Twelfth Century* (Cambridge, MA: Harvard University, 1927), he questioned the stark division Jacob Burckhardt made between the "Dark" Ages and the "Renaissance" (see later in the section).

37. Cf. Theodore E. Mommsen, "Petrarch's Conception of 'The Dark Ages,'" *Speculum* 17 no. 2 (1942): 226–42.

38. Although historians debate the precise dates of the beginning and end of the Middle Ages, it will suffice for us to broadly think of them as the years from 500 to 1500.

39. He drew the term from Jules Michelet, who first coined the word *Renaissance* in French in 1855 in his book *Histoire de France*. Cf. M. C. Lemon, *Philosophy of History: A Guide for Students* (London: Routledge, 2003), 74-106, esp. 78.

40. For suggestions on the significance of the public nature of the Enlightenment movement, see Jürgen Habermas, *The Structural Transformation of the Public Sphere* (Boston: MIT, 1989).

41. Roger Chartier, *The Cultural Origins of the French Revolution*, trans. L. G. Cochrane (Durham, NC: Duke University, 1991).

42. G. W. F. Hegel, *Lectures on the Philosophy of World History*, trans. H. B. Nisbet (Cambridge: Cambridge University, 1975), 54.

43. This language more properly comes from Kant and then Johann Gottlieb Fichte (1762–1814) but was made popular in relation to Hegel's philosophy by Heinrich Moritz Chalybäus in 1837, published in English as *Historical Development of Speculative Philosophy, from Kant to Hegel*, trans. A. Edersheim (Edinburgh: T & T Clark, 1854), 361–77.

44. Hegel, *Lectures*, 197.

45. Just to pick a random example, see the table of contents in Jackson J. Spielvogel, *Western Civilization*, 7th ed. (Florence, KY: Wadsworth, 2008).

46. Hegel somehow saw the state as the embodiment of evolving spirit/mind.

47. See chapter 12 for Marx's critique of capitalism and basic sense of communism.

48. According to Émile Benveniste, the word *civilization* first appeared in English in 1767 referring to that part of humanity that is more advanced than the rest. Émile Benveniste, *Problems in General Linguistics*, trans. E. Meek (1954; Miami: University of Miami, 1973).

49. Although it is perhaps extreme, a focal critique along these lines is Silvi Federici, ed., *Enduring Western Civilization: The Construction of the Concept of Western Civilization and Its "Others"* (Westport, CT: Praeger, 1995). Lawrence W. Levine, *The Opening of the American Mind: Canons, Culture, and History* (Boston: Beacon, 1996), has also pointed out that it was not really until the lead up to the United States entrance into World War I that the U.S. really began to consider itself connected to Europe. In this period especially, "Western Civilization" began to be taught with the U.S. as the culmination of this European stream.

50. An excellent overview of the elements of a story is Mark Allan Powell, *What Is Narrative Criticism?* (Minneapolis: Fortress, 1990). An excellent examination of the Christian story from a similar point of view can be found in N. T. Wright, *The New Testament and the People of God* (Minneapolis: Fortress, 1992).

51. God's story no doubt went on in eternity before our story, but presumably it is mostly beyond our comprehension.

CHAPTER 15
THE FUTURE OF TRUTH:
POSTMODERNISM

© istockphoto.com

15.1
DEFINING
POSTMODERNISM

If we were to flash back to the year 2000, we would find a lot of voices announcing that we had entered a new stage of human history, the "postmodern" age. Many were likening the shift of this age to the shifts that took place around the year 1500 with the invention of movable type and the beginnings of the Renaissance. Predictably, in the years that followed, the buzz of the latest hot idea at the turn of the millennium subsided in broader culture. Postmodernism was pronounced dead, and talk of post-postmodernism followed.

Some argued that these sorts of trends are a predictable by-product of a culture that has come to expect a constant flow of technological innovation and is programmed for introspection, self-significance, and a

What to Get from This Chapter

- Postmodernism is a recent trend in philosophy that denies our ability to be fully objective or have absolute certainty in knowledge.
- The history of philosophy these past two hundred years is largely a footnote to what Immanuel Kant had to say about metaphysics and epistemology.
- Jean-François Lyotard called postmodernism "incredulity toward metanarratives."
- Michel Foucault saw truth as an exercise in power and who controls the story.
- Jacques Derrida believed that the meaning of texts deconstructed in the process of us trying to construct it.
- Richard Rorty believed that truth was no more than a compliment we paid to ideas with which we are pleased.
- Hilary Putnam argued that in order for our ideas to work in the world, both the world must exist in some way and our ideas must be true in some way.
- Critical realism accepts by faith the existence of the world despite our partial and/or skewed perception of it.

Questions to Consider

- To what extent can we really see the world as it really is?
- To what extent is truth a function of power?
- To what extent do texts have stable meanings?
- What are the best Christian "take-aways" from postmodernism?

Key Words

- Metanarrative
- Postmodernism
- Pragmatism

penchant toward dividing history into major epochs. But the attempt to put postmodernism into this mold was somewhat ironic, as if postmodernism were part of the Western "myth of progress." Postmodernism properly understood is a critique of such cultural stories. It is the latest instance of a recurring footnote in the history of ideas that says, "You don't know as much as you think you know."

Postmodernism is, more than anything else, doubt that we as humans can know truth in an absolute sense. **Jean-François Lyotard** called it "incredulity toward **metanarratives**," by which he meant having serious questions about any overarching system of truth.[1] Accordingly, you can see that anyone who speaks of postmodernism as if it were the newest and best system of truth to date has not really understood what postmodernism is as a philosophy. We thus have to distinguish postmodernism as a cultural trend and postmodernism in philosophy. The former is a passing phase, like all cultural trends; the latter is an enduring question mark.

Postmodernism is the rejection of claims to complete objectivity or certainty in knowledge. Its most extreme voices tried to reject any sense that the meanings of texts could be stable (e.g., Jacques Derrida). They argued that theories inevitably change and have to do with social dynamics rather than "truth" in any ultimate sense (e.g., Michel Foucault, Thomas Kuhn). Some argued that the very notion of truth itself does not make any sense in the first place (e.g., Richard Rorty). The intensity of their critiques has subsided, but philosophy got the point. Their voices join those of the ancient Skeptics and the medieval nominalists as a recurring reminder that what we believe usually says as much about us as it does about "the truth" per se.

The **Skeptics** were proponents of an ancient philosophical tradition that questioned our ability to know or be certain of just about anything.[2] They reportedly trace their origins to one Pyrrho of Elis (ca. 360–ca. 270 BC); Skeptics are sometimes also called Pyrrhonists. During one period, Plato's Academy had completely converted to Skepticism (ca. 266–90 BC). Carneades (ca. 214–ca. 129 BC), perhaps the best known of the Skeptics from this period, is reported to have said, "Nothing can be known, not even this claim." On an official trip from Athens to Rome (155 BC), he is reported to have given a speech in favor of justice, then to have completely argued against justice the next day. As a consequence, he was sent home by the Roman Senate.

Another movement that anticipated postmodernism emerged in the medieval period. It would be safe to say that the philosopher who had the greatest impact on Christianity in its first thousand years was Plato. The most significant theologian during that period was Augustine (354–430), whom

Postmodernism: philosophical movement that denies the possibility of human objectivity or certainty in knowledge.

Metanarrative: an overarching system of truth by which one organizes particular ideas or data.

Skeptics: ancient philosophical school that questioned our ability to know what is true.

Nominalism: philosophical position that argues that only particular things, not universals, really exist.

Family resemblances: the notion that particulars group more on the basis of loose collections of frequent similarities rather than on characteristics that *all* members of a group universally have in common.

Plato undeniably influenced.[3] Then in the later Middle Ages, Aristotle gained the upper hand, largely through the work of Thomas Aquinas (1225–1274). The late Middle Ages also saw the rise of a third option: **nominalism**.

Let's say you have two cats: Tipper and Miley. On what basis can we say that these two distinct, *particular* bodies belong together in the same general or *universal* category we call cat? Plato thought it was because the idea of a cat existed independently of any physical cat; these two particular cats were "copies" of that ideal cat, a "cat pattern" to which we have access through our minds. Aristotle also believed that these two cats shared the universal form of a cat within them, although unlike Plato he did not believe it existed separately from actual, particular cats.

By contrast, nominalists deny the ultimate existence of any universal cat at all. "Universal categories" do not really exist except as "names" we give things we group together (*nomen* is Latin for "name"). Their point is to deny the existence of anything other than concrete, individual things. If we leave aside the more extreme versions of nominalism, we can see it as an appropriate refinement to Aristotle's view. Aristotle believed that the universal forms of things were *actually in* things like cats. A version of nominalism (e.g., the Christian thinker **William of Ockham** [ca. 1288–ca. 1348]) would say that cat-ness is a concept we create by looking at characteristics that specific cats often have in common.

These characteristics are not actually something in the cats, as Aristotle believed. In fact, as the twentieth-century philosopher Ludwig Wittgenstein (1889–1951) put it, it is more likely to be a collection of **family resemblances** that many specific cats share rather than a core list of universal characteristics that all cats have. For example, most specific cats have four legs, but we would still consider a cat to be a cat even if it met with an unfortunate accident. In that sense, we cannot consider four legs to be a universal characteristic of catness shared by all particular cats. Rather, there is a collection of features shared by most cats, even if not all specific cats have all these features.[4]

If the Skeptics resembled postmodernists in that they questioned whether we can know anything for certain, nominalists resembled postmodernism in that they questioned the overarching ideological schemes into which we place events, ideas, and things. For example, a nominalist might critique Karl Marx's philosophy of history by saying he has imposed general patterns on what was in reality countless diverse individual people, places, and events. As we saw in the last chapter, this is exactly the kind of critique the postmodernist Michel Foucault made. Similarly, a nominalist might critique any sense that a book has a unified theme or message that is not personal to a reader. This is the kind of thing that postmodernist Jacques Derrida said. Through these examples, we can see postmodernism as simply the most recent expression of the nominalist critique of universal truths.

In the contemporary version of nominalism, the word *postmodernism* harks back to **modernism**, which in turn harks back to **premodernism**. These labels are constructs that a hard-core postmodernist would reject. Look at how we have vastly oversimplified the thoughts of hundreds of years with these artificial groupings, they might say!

But this version of the story categorizes history in these terms: modernism largely originates with René Descartes, whose agenda of doubt aimed for certainty in knowledge. Descartes concluded that he could doubt everything but his own existence: "I think; therefore, I am." For the next four hundred years, so the story goes, philosophers sought objectivity in knowledge, to divest themselves of all bias. It is no coincidence that the age of science ran parallel to this quest. The scientific method of Francis Bacon required a person to collect evidence impartially and to form objective hypotheses that could be tested against the evidence.

The term **premodern** or *precritical* is thus a slam against the age before, the age of religion, the "Dark Ages," the "Middle Ages" between the ancient Greco-Roman world and the Renaissance. Such terminology, whatever truth it may relate, is itself riddled with bias of its own sort. The truth of the term *premodern* is the sense that most human cultures have tended to be *unreflective* toward the reasons underlying what it believes to be true. The human animal tends to assume that the way its "herd" views the world is in fact the only way to view the world.

For example, when those in the Western world draw lines around the world, they draw cats and dogs on the domesticated side of the line, the human side. It is thus unthinkable to most Westerners that a person would eat cat or dog. And how uncivilized of those from other parts of the world to do so! But this ethic is unreflective, unexamined for those in the West. We cannot justify it by rational argument; we simply find it disgusting. It is a view of the world we have inherited from our culture.

The impulse of "modernism" was thus to become aware of all biases and become objective about the truth. Like Spock from *Star Trek*, the perfect modernist divests him- or herself of emotional reasoning and forms conclusions based only on the evidence.[5] The perfect modernist would thus be *completely reflective* and objective.

Postmodernism—*after* modernism—correctly recognizes that the perfect modernist does not exist on the human plane. God is the only true "modernist" who knows all the evidence and can process it with complete objectivity in relation to all the other evidence. Postmodernism tells the

Premodernism: often used to label the period before modernism, in which people allegedly did not think objectively or critically about the world.

Modernism: often used to label the period beginning with Descartes, after which emphasis was put on coming to truth objectively without bias.

modernist that he or she at best is only *partially reflective* at any time. And what is worse, by the very definition of the word, we cannot know the points at which we are unreflective.

The next section presents some of the key changes in thinking that took place after Immanuel Kant. In the section after it, we will meet some of the key postmodern thinkers of recent times and attempt to process their ideas from a Christian perspective. The chapter ends with some suggestions for how Christians might think about thinking as we look toward the rest of the twenty-first century.

15.2
PHILOSOPHY AFTER KANT

Alfred North Whitehead once said that the history of European philosophy was basically a series of footnotes to Plato.[6] In a similar way, we might say that the history of philosophy for the past two hundred years is one long footnote to **Immanuel Kant** (1724–1804). We have already discussed the impact of his thinking on the key debates of philosophy. In chapter 4 we met his understanding of knowledge. In chapters 7 and 8 we processed the implications for what we might know about reality.

In this section we will fill in some blanks, further explaining how his ideas about knowledge and reality played out in the key thinkers of the past two hundred years, most of whom we have met in previous chapters. This will set up the context within which the key players of postmodernism emerged, the thinkers we will discuss in the next section. At the end of the chapter, we will argue again that some version of a critical-realist approach to the world is both justifiable and an appropriate Christian understanding (see chap. 8).

Kant, if you recall, was wrestling with the competing claims of rationalism and empiricism. Rationalists argued that truth was a matter of clear thinking; they tended to see our senses and experiences as potentially misleading. Empiricists emphasized the importance of our senses in coming to truth. David Hume took empiricism to its most extreme form, showing that ideas we have about things like right and wrong or about cause and effect cannot ultimately come from our experience. For that reason, he rejected them.

Hume woke Kant from his unexamined assumptions. Kant's conclusion, as we have seen, was that the *content* of our thinking does indeed come from our senses and experiences. But the *organization* of that content takes place according to certain innate categories in our minds—categories like space and time, cause and effect, and the moral law. As a consequence, we cannot know the world as it actually is in itself (*das Ding an sich*). We know the world only as our minds organize it.

For Kant, humans had good reason to trust the way our minds organized things. God was trustworthy. Many of the philosophers who followed Kant were not so convinced. Some were not convinced that it made sense even to speak of a "world as it really is." Others thought we could know the world as it is by some other means. These philosophers share in common uncertainty about what we can be certain of, even if their answers might differ.

The first thinker we note after Kant is **Arthur Schopenhauer** (1788–1860), who reflected the influence of Romanticism on his thinking (see chap. 13). If Kant argued that we cannot know the world as it actually is in itself, Schopenhauer believed that we could know the world, just not through our reason. Rather, our will—the drives and desires in us—gives us direct knowledge of the world as it is on an intuitive rather than rational level. There is a prethinking, emotional intuition that gives us direct knowledge of the world as it actually is.

We are less likely to have heard of Schopenhauer than some of those he influenced. For example, in the field of psychology Sigmund Freud and Carl Jung took cues from Schopenhauer's sense that our rational minds were directed by the preconscious forces of our desires. Further, Schopenhauer believed that the most significant motivation of our lives is our "will to live"—the drive to survive. This idea was a major influence on Friedrich Nietzsche in the late 1800s, who argued that a "will to power" was our most basic drive, a drive to achieve, gain power, and dominate. These individuals then directly and indirectly influenced the existentialists of the 1950s (see chap. 9), who believed that the primary human task is to determine who we are and why we want to continue living.

A second reaction to Kant was that of **G. W. F. Hegel**, whose theory of history we discussed in the previous chapter. Now here we will process those ideas in terms of his reaction to Kant. It is possible to see Hegel as presenting a sense in which philosophy over time is indeed coming to know the world as it actually is, truth in itself. Up to this point in history, such understandings had been partial. The whole point of his thesis-antithesis-synthesis process is the refinement of ideas, with each synthesis removing partial untruths and synthesizing ideas that are increasingly pure. Eventually these ideas would reach the point of absolute truth, true knowledge of reality as it actually is.

It is fascinating to see that Hegel has had such an astounding influence on later thinkers, especially when so much debate exists over what he actually meant to say. Karl Marx is the best-known example; he took Hegel's ideas and applied them to his sense that the world would eventually evolve into a society without class distinctions (see chaps. 12 and 14). But Hegel's ideas also had a significant impact on other fields, including biblical studies in the later nineteenth century through the so-called Tübingen school.[7]

The name of Hegel's masterpiece is often translated as *The Phenomenology of Spirit*. The word **phenomenology** has to do with the way things appear. In Kant's language, the world-in-itself, as it is apart from us thinking about it, is the world of the *noumena*. He thus used the word *phenomena* to refer to the world as it appears to us. Therefore, when Hegel spoke of the phenomenology of spirit, he was writing about the manifestation or the unfolding appearance of Spirit in history.

An example of an image that can be viewed quite differently based on one's perspective.

Indeed, in the twentieth century, **Edmund Husserl** (1859–1938) and **Martin Heidegger** (1889–1976) started what is known as the phenomenological school of philosophy. Husserl tried to "bracket" consideration of things-in-themselves as Kant had understood them. Our *experiences* were the things-in-themselves worthy of consideration. So Husserl tried to analyze how our minds relate to objects as they appear in our minds and ignore Kantian questions about what they might be without minds looking at them.

Heidegger developed Husserl's approach and took it in an existentialist direction.[8] Heidegger defies the traditional use of the word *being* as some external world distinct from ourselves and defines *being* entirely as a matter of being-in-the-world (*Dasein*). Husserl was still very much focused around our *intentions* toward the world as it appears to us. For Heidegger, the key issue is our concern or "care" (*Sorge*) about being in the world. The goal is for us to take responsibility for our being in the world, to embrace our mortality and the cares of living. It is for us to be in the world authentically.

The way in which these approaches flow directly into French existentialism is fairly easy to see. In chapter 9 we saw that the French existentialists Jean-Paul Sartre and Albert Camus were focused on inventing a meaning for your life, a reason to exist. This is much the same as Heidegger's goal of us being in the world authentically. We embrace the world as it is for us and choose an existence to embrace. When people speak of **continental philosophy**, they are largely referring to the phenomenological school and existentialism.

> **Phenomenology:** philosophical school that gained prominence on the European continent in the early twentieth century, bracketing or rejecting classical metaphysics and focusing on the world as we experience it, as it appears to us.
>
> **Continental philosophy:** a shorthand way of referring to the philosophical schools of Europe in the twentieth century, featuring especially phenomenology and existentialism.

> There are no facts, only interpretations.
>
> **Friedrich Nietzsche**

> About those things that one cannot speak, one must be silent.
>
> **Ludwig Wittgenstein**

As we saw in chapter 9, the nineteenth-century philosophers Søren Kierkegaard (1813–1855) and Friedrich Nietzsche (1844–1900) were even greater influences behind the twentieth-century existentialists. They both embody the spirit of the philosophical times after Kant, which shunned classic questions about what reality is (apart from our perception of it). For Kierkegaard, the most important questions were not about abstract existence of this sort, but about my own existence in this world. Nietzsche went so far as to say, "There are no facts, only interpretations." Although Nietzsche had a flare for hyperbole (exaggeration in expression), the quotation denies any access we might have to "facts" beyond our perception of reality.

"It sort of makes you stop and think, doesn't it?"

Also in keeping with the spirit of metaphysical uncertainty (uncertainty about reality-in-itself), another philosophical school arose in the late eighteenth century that would come to be known as **analytical philosophy**. In keeping with the spirit of Kant, this school of thought makes a strong distinction between what philosophy can say and what it cannot. At the end of his *Tractatus Logico-Philosophicus*, Ludwig Wittgenstein (1889–1951) famously wrote, "About those things that one cannot speak, one must be silent."[9] For Wittgenstein in this early phase of his life (he would shift significantly later on), the role of philosophy was to critique and bring clarity to our thinking, not to talk about meaningless concepts like *noumena*.

Analytical philosophy had its origins on the Continent (e.g., German Gottlieb Frege [1848–1925]), but its best-known proponents were British philosophers including Bertrand Russell (1872–1970). It has leaned toward a somewhat mathematical orientation and with a focus on logic, the sense being that one can find certainty about such philosophical processes. Interestingly, philosophy in the late twentieth century was often divided into two camps, between the continental philosophy of mainland Europe and the analytical philosophy of England and the United States. This regional divide illustrates the fact that even a discipline like philosophy draws on sociocultural influences.

One prominent offspring of analytical philosophy was **logical positivism**, which we encountered briefly in chapter 8. Probably its best-known proponent was Rudolf Carnap (1891–1970), and his group is often called the Vienna Circle for the place where these ideas first gained popularity.[10] This school claimed that only ideas that can be empirically verified make any sense. Talk about things like Kant's *noumena* or "things-in-themselves" is purely speculative and thus makes no sense.

Analytical philosophy: school of philosophy that dominated England and the United States in the first part of the twentieth century, focusing on breaking down claims into clear, logical statements and eliminating nonsensical or confused claims.

Logical positivism: also known as the Vienna Circle, a school of early-twentieth-century philosophy that focused on the importance of being able to verify claims empirically or scientifically for them to be meaningful.

Scientism: in philosophy, a tendency to reduce truth to matters that can be verified scientifically.

Chapter 15 The Future of Truth: Postmodernism

Things-in-themselves cannot be tested or verified. The logical positivists thus are the best illustration of a kind of **scientism** that looks at science as the only legitimate path to truth.

The fatal error of the Vienna Circle was that their fundamental claim is not empirically verifiable; there is no way to test or verify the claim that only things that can be tested and verified are meaningful. The very basis for the earliest version of positivism is thus based on something positivism itself says is meaningless. Various philosophers who followed attempted to modify positivism while rejecting its most simplistic form. For example, A. J. Ayer (1910–1989) distinguished between being able to prove something and being able to show it is probable. Strongly critical of logical positivism was Karl Popper (1902–1994), who argued for the task of truth being about what we are able to *falsify* rather than about the problematic quest to verify claims (see chap. 8).

15.3
THE FACES OF POSTMODERNISM

It can be argued that postmodernism flowed naturally from Kant and the various philosophers who followed after him. In the late twentieth century, a sense of uncertainty played itself out in every area of epistemology. We have already met many of the key players. Uncertainty played itself out in science in individuals like Thomas Kuhn (see chap. 8). It played itself out in the field of history through Michel Foucault (see chap. 14). It played itself out in the field of literature through Jacques Derrida. All share in common a sense that we impose meaning on these areas of knowledge far more—or even rather—than deriving meaning from them. The things we say about truth say far more about us than they do about the things we are analyzing.

Here we will look once more at some of these figures in postmodernism. We start with **Michel Foucault** (1926–1984).[11] You might remember that Francis Bacon in the 1500s is noted for saying that "knowledge is power." The more truth you know, the more you are able to do in the world. Foucault turned this expression on its head to say that "power is knowledge." For Foucault, what we say is true in society is far more a matter of ever-changing perspectives and the influence of people with power than the way things actually are.

In chapter 14 we cited examples of how Foucault played with history. We can now look at them from the perspective of postmodernism. Foucault predictably resisted being labeled, but others have consistently called him

poststructuralist. As *post*modernism comes *after* modernism, so *post*-structuralism came after structuralism.

Structuralism was a phase in literature and other disciplines that sought to find universal patterns behind stories, the way culture works, and other social phenomena. For example, structuralists analyzed stories in terms of a mechanical pattern they believed all fell into: basically some unfulfilled goal is eventually achieved through the intervention of a hero. The fundamental idea of *post*structuralism is that one either cannot find such universal patterns or that they have little to do with the real significance of stories, since patterns aren't universal but change over time.

Foucault's historical explorations highlighted periodic shifts in the way various subjects were understood and used. More important, he tried to show how the various ways of looking at punishment, madness, sexuality, and so forth were expressions of power by the dominant forces of society. For example, at one time, those with power used punishment to shame criminals publicly as a deterrent. By contrast, Foucault believed that in the late twentieth century those with power used punishment to exact revenge.

One label that Foucault did accept for himself was genealogist. Following the lead of Nietzsche, who thought he could explain how people invented good and evil (i.e., genealogy of morals), Foucault tried to demonstrate how people invented truth (i.e., genealogy of knowledge). He argued that some assertion of power is behind any claim that something is true. The implication is that any conflict of ideas is more fundamentally a power struggle between individuals with various underlying interests. The presenting ideas are serving other deeper interests; they are embodiments of power being exerted by someone.

Very similar to the ideas of Michel Foucault are those of **Thomas Kuhn** (1922–1996) (see chap. 8).[12] Kuhn suggested that what we perceive to be the progress of science is a somewhat random cycle of theory replacing theory. All scientific paradigms leave some data unaccounted for. "Normal science" does its best to accommodate such data within the prevailing paradigm.

But eventually someone suggests a new paradigm. Normal science resists, often successfully for some time because it holds the *power* over what is allowed to be considered truth. But if the new paradigm can gain traction or power, and as those holding to the older paradigm die off, a new "truth" emerges that becomes the new normal science, and the cycle continues.

The parallels with Foucault are fairly straightforward. In both cases knowledge takes place within a certain **paradigm**, a way of structuring knowledge. And in both cases that structure is not fixed or absolute. It is, rather, a function of power: those who have power—whether they realize it or not—are able to set the terms for what is allowed to be considered as plausible

Poststructuralism: the rejection of universal patterns behind stories, cultures, and other social phenomena.

Paradigm: a framework within which we organize data in a particular area; a lens through which we prioritize data and assign it significance.

or true. Both Foucault and Kuhn held somewhat extreme positions, but there seems to be some truth to their claims, as we have noted in previous chapters.

Christians of course do believe that there are fundamental truths beyond the "social construction of knowledge" that Foucault and Kuhn represent.[13] But it's hard to deny the realities of the way power plays itself out in our fallen world. For example, some people may think that universities are places where professors in all subjects simply pursue the truth wherever it may lead. But in reality there are structures of power that, depending on where you are, inevitably make certain conclusions off limits. Even revisions to the first draft of this textbook involved a (friendly) interchange between individuals with slightly different ideologies and an interplay of various centers of power.

© istockphoto.com

A president of Harvard in the twenty-first century would not do well to conclude that a certain race or gender was inferior in some way to another *even if* he or she did a study that pointed in that direction. A professor at an evangelical college would not do well to conclude that God does not exist even if he or she sincerely believed it. And of course there are a host of colleges and schools from particular "traditions" where one could not teach or do certain things and keep one's job. In one university, a teacher might get fired for favoring evolution. In another, one might be denied tenure for favoring intelligent design. In one college, a teacher might get fired for having an affair. In another, one might not get tenure because he or she expressed disapproval of homosexual practice. A well-known book on Christian leadership came to the inevitable Foucaultian conclusion in such matters: "In a power conflict the leader with higher power will usually win regardless of rightness of issue."[14]

Perhaps the best-known face of postmodernism is that of **Jacques Derrida** (1930–2004).[15] If Foucault doubted the way we structure knowledge and Kuhn doubted the objectivity of science, Derrida doubted that words had stable meanings. He is the "father" of **deconstruction**, an approach to literature that tries to demonstrate that the meanings of words unravel just as quickly as we try to create them. Derrida playfully tried to show that any attempt to "construct" understanding of words inevitably self-destructs in the process.

If Nietzsche believed that "there are no facts, only interpretations," Derrida hardly believed that there were even interpretations. The meaning of a word is simply other words, whose meaning simply *defers* to yet other words. One never arrives at any definite content, only at "traces" of meaning to be found in the *difference* between the signs, the squigglies we call words. As part of his flamboyant personality, Derrida combined these two words, *defer* and *differ,* to make his own French word: *différance.*

Like Nietzsche, Derrida did not restrict this problem to written texts. To him, the entire world was a text, and its meaning was just as uncertain as was the meaning of written texts. He thus is known for saying that "there is nothing outside the text." You probably have not missed the irony that Derrida wrote texts and at times argued over their meaning. He of course was well aware of the irony and at times tried to write vaguely so that his texts embodied the ambiguity he claimed they had.

Nevertheless, Derrida did a good job of reminding us that almost any text can be misunderstood. We already argued in chapter 4 that the meaning of words can be stable. But we also highlighted there that one of the most fundamental issues facing Christians today is *which interpretation* of the Bible is the right one. The fact that we have more than twenty thousand Christian denominations in itself demonstrates that there is some truth to Derrida's point! Derrida is thus an important warning about the potential ambiguity of language. At least to that extent, his thoughts deserve to be taken seriously. But we could not take him seriously if we did not also disagree with him. Because we believe texts can effectively communicate meaning, we are free to disagree with the meanings he intended his texts to have.

Of all the figures of postmodernism, perhaps **Richard Rorty** (1931–2007) demonstrates best its place at the end of the long road that started with Kant.[16] For him, the problem with both the phenomenological and analytical schools is that they are both still talking about truth. Truth, for Rorty, is "simply a compliment paid to the beliefs we think so well justified that for the moment further justification is not needed."[17] He reaches back into the **pragmatist** tradition of **John Dewey** (1859–1952) and **William James** (1842–1910) and builds on it to reject any question of our language representing the world. In particular, he modifies the claim of William James that "truth is what works."[18]

But at least James was still talking about what works as we live in the world. Rorty disregarded even the thought of the world as something we can discuss. Our language is not really about the world; it is a kind of game we play with each other according to certain rules we agree on. Even to ask the questions Kant did about the world in itself is meaningless and confused. When Rorty accepts the idea that "truth is what works," he means what works in our language with each other.

An arguably saner perspective than Rorty is the **pragmatic realism** of **Hilary Putnam** (b. 1926). Like Rorty, Putnam reached back into the pragmatic tradition of the late 1800s and early 1900s to philosophers like

Deconstruction: the idea that the meaning of texts unravels in the very process of trying to construct it, that words do not have any stable meanings.

Pragmatism: school of American philosophical thought that considers concepts to be meaningful in relation to how well they "work" in real life.

Pragmatic realism: an approach that argues that both the external world must be real in some way and our ideas must be true in some way if our ideas "work" in real life.

Critical realism: an approach that affirms that the external world is real even if our understanding of that world is partial and/or skewed.

Charles S. Peirce (1839–1914), a founding member of the American pragmatist tradition (also called the **Metaphysical Club**).[19] We might paraphrase Peirce's "pragmatic maxim" in this way: "Consider the practical impact that—you think—the things you are thinking about might have. Do not think those things amount to anything more than that."[20] This paraphrase of John Dewey perhaps defines pragmatism even more clearly: pragmatism "evaluates concepts by considering what difference they might make in real life if adopted or denied."

For Putnam, the outside world must actually exist in some way for "what works" to make sense. He tries to avoid two extremes: (1) denying that it is meaningful to speak of the world outside ourselves (Rorty) and (2) thinking that we can be more or less objective about that world (modernism). Yes, truth is what works. But for truth to work, we must actually be engaged with a world outside ourselves that is real, a world that limits our conceptions of what does and does not work. This "pragmatic realism" seems very compatible with some version of the critical realism we are advocating in this book.

© istockphoto.com

Christians have responded to postmodernism in various ways. Some have strongly rejected it. They might claim that the Bible more or less directly tells us how God looks at the world and thus how the world actually is in itself.[21] Others have seen in postmodernism an opportunity for Christians to reaffirm the central role that faith—as opposed to reason—plays in what we believe. Some, including James K. A. Smith (b. 1970) and Nicholas Wolterstorff (b. 1932), have seen the situation as ripe for a radical orthodoxy (see chap. 2)—in which Christians affirm the core truths of Christian faith without feeling any need to prove them on the basis of rational argument. For them, postmodernism makes room for Christianity at a table from which modernism tended to bar it.

In this book, we have tended more toward the approach called **critical realism**. Critical realists recognize that our perspective on reality is clouded by our rational limitations. But by faith we believe that reality exists and that God in some way guarantees that our knowledge of that reality "works" in a way that is connected to that reality in a way that Rorty said was nonsensical. Like Kant, we believe that the world exists and that we inevitably see it as it appears to us. Unlike Kant, we are far more aware of the limitations of how it appears to us.

15.4
AFTER POSTMODERNISM

I suspect that most of you readers will have found in this chapter some ideas that seem bizarre and some that seem extreme. The question is whether you can see anything in this chapter of value. In chapter 8 we argued for what we called a critical-realist hermeneutic, and we set out some commonsense principles for deciding between better and worse reconstructions of truth. These included (1) the more data—and the more data accounted for—the better the hypothesis; (2) the simplest and most elegant explanation is the better one; (3) a logically coherent hypothesis is better than an incoherent one; and (4) a hypothesis that predicts future data while accounting for past data is much to be preferred.

Postmodernism has highlighted the fact that such things are not foolproof. That is to say, these principles will not always "work" the best. When we are trying to find patterns in a world of immense complexity, there will almost always—if not always—be data that is unaccounted for or that does not fit. We have learned at least this lesson from Foucault and Kuhn. A more complex explanation can sometimes be the right one. These rules are good rules because, as Rorty reminds us, they usually "work" better than throwing the idea of reality entirely out the window.

We have called our hermeneutic a critical-realist one. Critical realism accepts that the world exists outside of our perception of it and that there are better and worse understandings of that world. Most critical realists are relatively optimistic about the human ability to say true things about the world, even if they accept that our perception of the world inevitably involves skew and a finite perception. Some critical realists lean more toward saying that our understanding of the world is partial rather than skewed. By contrast, another critical-realist perspective sees our understanding as much skewed as it is partial. Both would affirm that we can consider hypotheses better not only because *they work* better but because they may actually say something *true* about the world, especially in a symbolic or poetic way.

At the same time, with Foucault critical realists can be open-eyed about the fact that history is often told by the winners, by those with power. With Kuhn, we can acknowledge the extent to which the way we conceptualize the world and various fields of knowledge is to a large degree a matter of ever-changing paradigms. With Berger and Luckmann, we can accept that our understandings of culture are extensively a matter of social construction. With Derrida, we can recognize the incredible flexibility of meaning that texts of all kinds can have. With the Skeptics, we can embrace the eternal

POSSIBLE CHRISTIAN INFERENCES

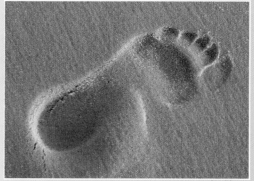

© istockphoto.com

1. None of us has a God's-eye view of the world.

Perhaps the most important Christian take-away from postmodernism is the strong reminder that we are not God. It is not only that our finite minds have a partial understanding of the world. Even the partial view of the world we have is filled with blind spots and skew of which we are not aware. Our minds cannot see the world as it is, for we inevitably see it from the perspective of where we sit in our localized contexts. This situation calls for an "epistemological humility" on our part, a humility about what we think we know for certain.

2. Faith is far more fundamental than reason.

The evidence does not demand a verdict, but what we believe as Christians is far more a matter of faith than of proof. That is not to say that faith is irrational. It is to say that even the most fundamental elements of Christian belief are more a matter of faith than of evidence. It pushes us to see God as far more interested in our attitudes than in the specifics of what we believe.

3. The Bible as a text is polyvalent (susceptible to multiple interpretations).

No matter how perfect a truth the Bible might represent in God's mind, we as finite, contextualized humans can never escape our situation in order to know it as God does. We cannot arrive at a God's-eye view of truth from the Bible because *we* are incapable of having one. We see the Bible through our partial, skewed lenses just as we see the rest of the world.

Further, as texts encapsulated in human language, the words of the Bible are susceptible to a multitude of interpretations and configurations of meaning. Even more, reading the Bible in context reveals that God intended to speak to its individual audiences in their own context-dependent categories. The result is that we as readers of the Bible are inevitably forced not only to interpret individual texts, but also to organize their particular meanings into a coherent whole. This situation calls for our having a more robust sense of the role of the Holy Spirit and God's speaking through the church than many Christians have.

4. The larger a system of ideas is, the more likely the skew.

The more particular data we try to sweep up into a generalized system or "worldview," the more likely we are oversimplifying and in the process omitting or skewing individual bits of data. This is true of our generalizations about the Bible ("The Bible says . . ."), and it is true of our theological systems. Given number 1 above, this is true even of systems that are largely deductive (e.g., Calvinism), because it is likely that our starting premises are already somewhat figurative in ways we could not comprehend. This situation calls for increased Christian conversation among believers who come from different Christian traditions with different theological systems.

5. Power plays a role in what we call truth.

We should acknowledge it openly so that it does not play out secretly. What is considered true at any time and place, not to mention how ideas are policed, involves a significant element of power. The best ideas are not always the most popular, nor can we trust those in authority to police ideas with justice. Once again, we are pushed toward seeing the attitudes of others as usually far more significant than the specifics of what they believe.

footnote to all knowledge: we probably do not know nearly as much as we think we know. With the nominalists, we can recognize that the universal connections we see are often a matter of us seeing them rather than them actually being there.

Notice how we have learned from extreme postmodern individuals without embracing their pessimism. We have used qualifying words like *usually*, *to a large degree*, *extensively*, *probably*, and *often*. It is the faith that these warnings are not the end of the story that makes the difference between critical realism and epistemological despair. The word *faith* seems especially appropriate for us as Christian thinkers. It is perfectly Christian to believe that our understanding of the world is not only partial but "fallen," fundamentally skewed.[22] And it is perfectly Christian to believe, by faith, that God and reality exist apart from my perception of God and the world.

As we saw in chapter 2, as Christians we believe many more things by faith than did any of the leaders of postmodernism. We believe that Jesus rose from the dead, indeed, that he is God the Son. Most of those reading this book will believe that God has spoken and continues to speak to us through the words of Scripture. One possible take-away from this discussion of postmodernism is that we should recognize that our understanding of these things will inevitably be colored by assumptions of which we are not completely aware. Our understandings even of faith are inevitably entangled with paradigms and socially constructed understandings of the world we have inherited. We probably know about God best intuitively and symbolically, far more than we will ever know about him literally.

We are all in a sense premoderns, moderns, and postmoderns at the same time. There will always be areas of our lives where we are unreflective, where we do not even realize there are other ways of looking at things. From time to time, we become "modernists" and can see that we have not been objective, that there are other, better ways to think about certain topics than we previously have. And we are postmodernists when we embrace that while we have become more objective about something, we almost certainly have some blind spot about it that we have not yet realized.

15.5
CONCLUSION

This chapter is a fitting conclusion to the book because it summarizes where philosophy currently stands on many of the subjects treated throughout the book. The central question of philosophy at the beginning of the twenty-first century is the question of certainty in knowledge. When Immanuel Kant drew attention to the inevitable role our minds play in the way we organize our perception of reality, he set in motion a chain of philosophical reactions. Some have disagreed with him and claimed that we *can* know the world on its own terms (e.g., Schopenhauer). Others have slipped into complete uncertainty about everything (e.g., extreme postmodernism).

Jean-François Lyotard once described postmodernism as an "incredulity toward metanarratives," by which he implied that the bigger a system of ideas we use to organize the data of the world, the more likely we are skewing that world. Similarly, Michel Foucault would highlight the extent to which what we call truth is really an expression of power, especially the power to promote your ideas over others. Jacques Derrida tried to argue that texts have no stable meanings at all and that even statements whose meanings seem obvious to us often "deconstruct" and unravel into other meanings. Richard Rorty went so far as to say that it is nonsensical even to speak of truth as something real. For him, saying that something is true is simply paying a compliment to ideas we like.

We can learn from these individuals, even as Christians, without surrendering to their pessimism. The critical realism we have advocated in this book affirms the central role that faith plays for us, not only as Christians, but as people who live in the world in general. Hilary Putnam argued that the world must exist in some way for our ideas to work. So we step out of the way of moving traffic whether we are certain the cars exist or not.

As Christians we believe in much more. We believe that God is real outside ourselves. We believe that God knows absolute truth and that he has created the world in such a way that what "works" in the world is a reflection of that truth, even though we can only partially see it. Faith in truth is a reasonable faith.

KEY TERMS

- postmodernism
- metanarrative
- nominalism
- "family resemblances"
- premodernism

- modernism
- phenomenology
- scientism
- poststructuralism
- paradigm

- deconstruction
- pragmatism
- pragmatic realism
- critical realism

KEY PHILOSOPHERS / MOVEMENTS

- Skeptics
- William of Ockham
- Immanuel Kant
- Arthur Schopenhauer
- G. W. F. Hegel
- Edmund Husserl
- Martin Heidegger

- continental philosophy
- analytic school
- Vienna Circle
  (logical positivists)
- Metaphysical Club
  (pragmatists)
- C. S. Peirce
- William James

- John Dewey
- Hilary Putnam
- Thomas Kuhn
- Jean-François Lyotard
- Michel Foucault
- Jacques Derrida
- Richard Rorty

PHILOSOPHICAL QUOTATIONS

- Postmodernism is "disbelief in metanarratives." (Lyotard)
- "Nothing can be known, not even this claim." (Carneades)
- "There are no facts, only interpretations." (Nietzsche)
- "About those things that one cannot speak, one must be silent." (Wittgenstein)
- "Power is knowledge." (Foucault)
- "There is nothing outside the text." (Derrida)
- "Truth is what works."

KEY QUESTIONS

1. What is your response, especially if you are a Christian, to the "postmodern critique" of our commonsense assumptions about the reality of the world and the categories within which we process it? How might it affect the way you read the Bible or the way you relate to people who think differently than you about something? How might it change or not change your attitude toward your sense of what is true and what is real?

2. We have now finished the final chapter of the book. Take a moment to look back through the book's table of contents. Are there areas in our journey where you have moved from being unreflective ("premodern") to being more reflective or more objective ("modern")? Are there areas where you have a sneaking suspicion that areas of unreflectiveness may soon come to light?

3. At the end of this book, what would you say is your "theory" of what is real and what it means to say something is true?

NOTES

1. Jean-François Lyotard, *La condition postmoderne: rapport sur le savoir* (Paris: Minuit, 1979). Popular-level introductions to postmodernism include James K. A. Smith, *Who's Afraid of Postmodernism? Taking Derrida, Lyotard, and Foucault to Church* (Grand Rapids: Baker Academic, 2006); Stanley J. Grenz, *A Primer on Postmodernism* (Grand Rapids: Eerdmans, 1996); and Carl Raschke, *Next Reformation: Why Evangelicals Must Embrace Postmodernity* (Grand Rapids: Baker Academic, 2004).

2. The classic treatment of ancient philosophy in the centuries immediately following Aristotle is now in its second edition: A. A. Long, *Hellenistic Philosophy: Stoics, Epicureans, Skeptics*, 2nd ed. (London: Duckworth, 2010).

3. The influence of Plato was mediated on Augustine through neo-Platonism, whose most prominent figure was Plotinus (ca. AD 204–270).

4. Certainly if we introduced DNA into this discussion, it would complicate the argument, but one hopes the reader sees the point.

5. Stanley Grenz uses Spock as the consummate ideal for how modernism aimed to look at the world. See *Primer*, 5.

6. Alfred North Whitehead, *Process and Reality* (New York: Free Press, 1978), 39.

7. The Tübingen School of the late 1800s applied Hegel's ideas to the evolution of thought in both the Old Testament and New Testament. For the Old Testament, Julius Wellhausen suggested that the first five books of the Bible evolved through a process of thesis and antithesis between sources known as J, E, D, and P. For the New Testament, F. C. Baur suggested that the early church involved a dialectic between those who insisted on believers converting to Judaism and the apostle Paul, synthesizing into the early catholic church.

8. The personal relationship between Heidegger and Husserl has been a notorious topic of interest since World War II. Heidegger was Husserl's student, and Husserl arranged for Heidegger to take over his post when he retired. Heidegger even dedicated the first edition of his famous book *Being and Time* to Husserl. At the same time, Husserl was Jewish, even though he had early on become a Lutheran. Meanwhile Heidegger publicly supported Nazism. Some have accused Heidegger of doing nothing to try to help Husserl after the 1933 race laws in Germany removed all his academic privileges at the University of Freiburg. Heidegger later indicated that the two had already split well before that time. Husserl died in 1938 before Hitler's anti-Jewish agenda gained full force.

9. Typically Wittgenstein's philosophy is divided into earlier and later periods. His earlier work clearly fits into the category of analytical philosophy, the time from which this quote comes. Arguably his later work was most significant, the period during which he published on topics we have discussed such as language games (chap. 4) and family resemblances (this chapter).

10. They were largely dispersed by the advent of Nazism in the mid-1930s. The founder of the Vienna School, Moritz Schlick, was murdered in 1936 by a disturbed student who considered Schlick's ideas to have corrupted his morals.

11. Perhaps the best starting point for Foucault's epistemology, originally published in French in 1969, is *The Archaeology of Knowledge* (New York: Pantheon, 1972).

12. Thomas Kuhn's classic work again is *The Structure of Scientific Revolutions*, 3rd ed. (Chicago: University of Chicago, 1996).

13. Here alluding to another book we have mentioned previously by Peter Berger and Thomas Luckman, *The Social Construction of Reality: A Treatise in the Sociology of Knowledge* (New York: Doubleday/Anchor, 1966).

14. J. Robert Clinton, *The Making of a Leader: Recognizing the Lessons and Stages of Leadership Development* (Colorado Springs: NavPress, 1988), 188.

15. Jacques Derrida's most famous work, originally published in French in 1967, is *Of Grammatology*, trans. Gayatri Chakravorty Spivak (Baltimore: Johns Hopkins University, 1974).

NOTES

16. Richard Rorty's most famous work is *Philosophy and the Mirror of Nature* (Princeton, NJ: Princeton University, 1979).
17. Richard Rorty, *Truth and Progress: Philosophical Papers III* (Cambridge: Cambridge University 1991), 24.
18. William James, *Pragmatism: A New Name for Some Old Ways of Thinking* (1907; repr., New York: Cosimo, 2008), 38.
19. In 1905 Charles Peirce would later invent the term *pragmaticism* to distinguish himself from fellow pragmaticists like William James and John Dewey.
20. See Charles S. Peirce, "Issues of Pragmaticism," *The Monist* 15 (1905): 481–99.
21. E.g., Douglas Groothius, *Truth Decay: Defending Christianity against the Challenges of Postmodernism* (Downers Grove, IL: InterVarsity, 2000).
22. Cf., e.g., James K. A. Smith, *The Fall of Interpretation: Philosophical Foundations for a Creational Hermeneutic* (Downers Grove, IL: InterVarsity, 2000).

GLOSSARY

a posteriori: "from afterward"; in epistemology, the idea that knowledge only comes after experience.

a priori: "from beforehand"; in epistemology, the idea that certain knowledge or categories exist in our minds prior to experience.

Absolute: in ethics, a principle of action that applies in every situation, time, and place.

Act-based ethics: ethics oriented around what we should *do* or not do.

Adiaphora: things that are morally neutral, being neither morally positive or negative.

Aesthetics: that branch of philosophy that asks what the nature of beauty and art is.

Affective: having to do with feelings and the emotional dimensions of human life.

Agnostic: one who is uncertain whether God exists, especially one who does not believe it is possible to know for certain.

Alvin Plantinga: along with Nicolas Wolterstorff, one of the originators and main proponents of Reformed epistemology.

American exceptionalism: the sense that America is distinct from, perhaps superior to, the other nations of the world in some significant way.

Amillennialism: the theological view that does not take literally the thousand years of Revelation 20:4 but sees the current age as one in which Christ both rules and the forces of evil continue to fight against him.

An end in itself: if we say something is an end in itself, we do it or value it regardless of whether it causes something else good or bad to happen. It is good for its own sake.

Analytical philosophy: school of philosophy that dominated England and the United States in the first part of the twentieth century, focusing on breaking down claims into clear, logical statements and eliminating nonsensical or confused claims.

Anarchy: chaos, the absence of order.

Antithesis: the force or point of view in conflict with the thesis.

Apocalyptic: a particularly Jewish and Christian perspective on the world that sees history moving toward a climax in which God will ultimately intervene and address the injustices and wickedness of the world.

Apologetics: the study of how to defend your faith, usually on the basis of rational argument.

Argument from necessity: the argument that if all entities had only a possible existence then conceivably nothing might exist. Since something does, there must be at least one Necessary thing.

Aristocracy: in theory, rule by the most virtuous in a society. In recent centuries, the word has come to refer to the "landed gentry," those with inherited status in a society and often wealthy.

Aseity: God is self-sufficient.

Atheist: one who does not believe that God exists.

Austrian school: a heterodox school of economics that opposes using mathematical models for understanding economies (macroeconomics) and strongly opposes governmental regulation of economies (central planning).

Axiology: the branch of philosophy that asks questions about value.

Balance of power/checks and balances: where the power of one entity is held in check or balanced by the power of another, so that no one power has absolute authority or can abuse its power.

Behavior modification: the shaping of behavior by associating reward or withholding of reward with certain choices (also called "operant conditioning").

Bourgeoisie: members of the managerial, business class of a society who control the production and distribution of goods.

Calvinism: Christian school of thought derived from John Calvin, in particular the idea that God chooses those who will be saved from hell.

Capital: all the resources a person has at his or her disposal for production and exchange, including money, equipment, products, and land.

Capitalism: an economic system in which individuals and companies accumulate wealth by selling their resources for profit.

Categorical imperative: Kant's idea that if something is a "must do," an imperative, then it is always something you must do, without exception.

Chaos theory: the idea that pockets of random complexity tend to develop as a virtual mathematical certainty.

City-state: cities as the unit of independent governance in the ancient world, usually with each city having its own king.

Classical liberalism: in economics, another name for the approach that favors a free-enterprise system.

Coherence test: an approach to truth that asks whether a claim is coherent both with itself and with your prior assumptions.

Collectivist culture: culture in which your identity is largely a function of the groups to which you belong, especially family, ethnicity, and gender.

Commonsense realism: an approach to reality that avoids theoretical questions and takes a what-you–see-is-what-you-get attitude.

Communism: in theory, "from each according to his ability; to each according to his need," a system in which everything is held in common, where everyone contributes as much as he or she can to society and takes only what he or she needs.

Compatibilism: the philosophical position that sees determinism and free will as logically compatible, if free will is defined as the freedom to act in accordance with what you want to do.

Continental philosophy: a shorthand way of referring to the philosophical schools of Europe in the twentieth century, featuring especially phenomenology and existentialism.

Correspondence test: an approach to truth that asks whether a claim corresponds to the evidence.

Cosmological argument: the argument that God must exist in order to explain where the world came from.

Courage: being willing to do the right thing, despite obstacles.

Creation ex nihilo: creation of the world "out of nothing."

Critical realism: an approach to reality that affirms by faith that reality exists, even though our perception of that reality will always be skewed by the fact that we inevitably view it from a certain perspective.

Cultural relativism: the idea that right and wrong is a function of the culture in which you are located.

Cyclical view of history: the sense that history is not on any kind of a clear trajectory but is more an endless set of similar stories repeated over and over.

Dark Ages: derogatory term for the Middle Ages, implying a general absence of significance to the period in culture and thinking.

Darwinism: the idea that evolution has taken place gradually over millions of years simply by nature "selecting" organisms better equipped to survive in particular environments.

Deconstruction: the idea that the meaning of texts unravels in the very process of trying to construct it, that words do not have any stable meanings.

Deductive reasoning: reasoning to what *must* be true given certain assumptions.

Defense mechanism: a way of protecting one's conscious mind from repressed feelings and drives.

Deism: the perspective that God created the universe and set up its rules but does not currently interact with it.

Determinism: the belief that everything that takes place has to happen exactly as it does because of the laws of cause and effect.

Dialectic: a process of moving toward truth by dialogue between conflicting forces or points of view.

Dialectical materialism: Marx's sense that the progression of history was an evolving conflict over who controlled the materials and goods of society.

Direct democracy: rule by the people where individuals directly make a community's decisions.

Dispensationalism: the perspective that divides up history into several "dispensations" in which God relates to the world in different ways, usually leading up to a seven-year "tribulation" before Christ returns.

Divine right of kings: the idea that since kings are appointed by God, their authority cannot be questioned or undermined.

Dualism: the belief that the universe consists of two basic types of "stuff" (e.g., the material and the immaterial).

Duty-based ethics: an act-based approach to ethics that focuses on acts that are universally right or wrong in themselves (e.g., lying, stealing).

Economy: the system of producing and distributing goods in a society.

Efficient cause: the most immediate and direct cause of an event.

Egoist ethics: an act-based approach to ethics that looks to consequences and focuses on what will most benefit me.

Empiricism: an approach to knowledge that views experience as the principal path to truth.

Ends justify the means: the idea that the goal we are moving toward is so good or valuable that it does not matter how we achieve it, even if we have to "break a few rules" in the process of getting there.

Enlightenment: period from roughly 1650 to 1800 when many intellectuals in France, England, and Germany questioned all previous assumptions and tried to rely on reason and evidence alone (not revelation) to arrive at the truth.

Epistemology: the branch of philosophy that asks questions about truth.

Essence: what something is.

Ethics: a branch of philosophy that asks how we best live in the world.

*Eudaimonia***:** happiness.

Evil: an act of will whose objective is inappropriate given its context.

Evolution: the idea that complex organisms developed from less complex ones.

Existence: that something is.

Existentialism: the philosophical view that sees meaning as self-created, created as a matter of individual human will and choice.

Fact-value problem: the difficulty of finding an intrinsic connection between the "facts" of the world and the "values" we assign to them.

Fall, The: the event when Adam and Eve disobeyed God in the Garden of Eden, with the subsequent entrance of death, evil, and suffering into the world.

Family resemblances: the notion that particulars group more on the basis of loose collections of frequent similarities than on characteristics that *all* members of a group universally have in common.

Fatalism: an attitude toward life that sees the future course of events as inevitable.

First-order question: asks about something.

Foreknowledge: God's prior knowledge of the future.

Form of life: Wittgenstein's way of referring to a specific context in which words are used.

Formal fallacy: a fallacy where the logical structure of the argument is invalid.

Free will (compatibilist view): the capacity to make choices undetermined by forces perceived to be outside your "self."

Free will (libertarian view): the capacity to make choices undetermined by all the forces at work on you.

Free-enterprise system: an economic system that allows individuals to start their own businesses in which they set their own prices and the terms of trade, with limited governmental intervention.

Freudian slip/parapraxis: when words someone did not intend to say slip out of his or her subconscious.

Fundamentalism: In American Christianity, a movement that arose in the early twentieth century in reaction to certain developments in biblical studies (e.g., higher criticism), science (e.g., evolution), and broader American culture (e.g., women's rights). It is thus perhaps best characterized in terms of what it opposes, often militantly, or that from which it is separated.

Fusing the two horizons: in Gadamer's hermeneutic, the idea that readers inevitably bring their world to a text, including any traditional interpretations of that text that have impacted them; readers then engage in a hermeneutical circle in which the "horizon" of their world fuses with the "horizon" of the text.

Generational poverty: a cycle of poverty passed on from generation to generation to the point that it becomes a conditioned way of life.

Geocentric solar system: the view that the earth is at the center and the sun moves around it.

Gnostics: early Jewish and Christian movement that believed the material world is evil in contrast to spirit which is good.

God's directive will: God's active and explicit command to make certain things to happen.

God's permissive will: God's allowance for things to happen that God does not actively determine.

Golden Mean: moderation in all things.

Golden Rule: Do to others what you would have them do to you.

Hard determinism: the idea that we cannot help but will and act the way we do, that humans are not free in any meaningful sense.

Heliocentric solar system: the view that the sun is at the center and the earth moves around it.

Hermeneutics: the branch of philosophy that asks how meaning takes place and is communicated; the philosophy of language.

Historicism: modernist approach to the past that aims to present it "as it really happened," with complete objectivity.

Historiography: the genre of literature that writes about history and people writing about history.

Immaterial: not material, usually applied to heavenly "substances" such as the soul or that of which angels consist.

Indeterminism: the idea that reality is fundamentally random and unpredictable.

Individualist culture: culture in which individuals largely determine their own identity apart from their inherited status, ethnicity, or gender.

Inductive reasoning: reasoning to what is *probably* true given certain data.

Industrialization: the process of becoming a society that functions off of manufactured products rather than farm products.

Informal fallacies: fallacies that involve false assumptions and problems with the content of an argument.

Innate: "born with"; in epistemology, the idea that we are born with certain knowledge or categories a priori.

Instrumental good: something that is good only because it leads to something else that is good.

Intelligent design theory (ID): a more recent Christian approach to scientific evidence that suggests it cannot be explained adequately without recourse to an intelligent Designer, namely, God.

Intrinsic good: something that is an end in itself, good for its own sake.

Justice: doing the right thing at the right time.

Keynesian economics: an approach to economics that focuses on governmental intervention to make sure that the total spending of the private and governmental sectors is in equilibrium with the total demand for goods and services.

Laissez-faire capitalism: "to allow to do," another name for free-enterprise systems.

Language game: a particular way that a word or set of words is used in a particular form of life.

Law of supply and demand: the basic pattern that prices go up when supply is low or when demand is high.

Leap of faith, blind faith: phrases commonly used to refer to the idea that faith is not based on evidence or reasoning but is rather a "leap" without sure footing, made without seeing where we are leaping.

Limited good: the sense that only a certain amount of materials or goods exist and therefore that for one person to have more, another must have less.

Linear view of history: the sense that history is on a certain trajectory toward an ultimate destination, that it has an overall storyline.

Logic: the branch of philosophy that explores the nature of good thinking.

Logical positivism: also known as the Vienna Circle, a school of early-twentieth-century philosophy that focused on the importance of being able to verify claims empirically or scientifically for them to be meaningful.

Macroevolution: the idea that over millions of years, complex organisms like human beings have evolved from the smallest of micro-organisms.

Marxist communism: utopian vision of a classless, stateless society in which all resources are held in common by a people.

Marxist-Leninism: an approach to communism that saw socialism as a necessary transition to a classless society, led by a professional class of revolutionaries.

Materialism: the belief that the universe consists only of matter and energy.

Metanarrative: an overarching system of truth by which one organizes particular ideas or data.

Metaphysics: the branch of philosophy that asks questions about existence and reality.

Microevolution: the idea that variation (such as with the peppered moth) does occur on a small scale, such as within a species or genus, but not on a larger scale.

Middle Ages: or the **medieval** period, roughly the time between AD 500 and 1500, from the fall of the Roman Empire to the Renaissance.

Middle knowledge: knowledge of all the possible outcomes depending on human choice.

Miracle: an event that is not explicable on the basis of normal scientific, cause-effect reasoning.

Modernism: often used to label the period beginning with Descartes, after which emphasis was put on coming to truth objectively without bias.

Modernist hermeneutic: interpretation that attempts to read words in their original contexts, often with overconfidence in the result.

Molinism: the perspective that holds God knows the definite outcome of what must be true and of how he will act, but that he has only middle knowledge of the outcome of human choices.

Monetarism: a mathematical approach to economics that sees equilibrium between the money supply and the gross domestic product of a nation as the key to economic health. It otherwise opposes governmental attempts to manipulate an economy.

Monism: the belief that the universe consists of only one basic type of thing, such as matter, ideas, etc.

Moral argument: the idea that the fundamental human sense of right and wrong cannot be explained without recourse to a moral Creator.

Moral evil: bad events that occur because of human or "supernatural" intention.

Moral nihilism: a position that holds that "right and wrong" does not truly exist.

Mutation: a change in the fundamental molecular structure of an organism.

Nation-state: the modern sense of nations where a relatively large group of people in a significant space embrace a common identity and governance.

Natural "evil": bad events that occur apart from human or "supernatural" intention, perhaps better called natural pain or suffering.

Natural selection: the idea that nature "selects" those organisms that are best suited to survive in a particular environment over time.

Natural: things we can explain on the basis of matter/materials and "laws."

Naturalism: the belief that the natural realm is all that exists.

Negative reinforcement: the demotivation of certain behavior by withholding or withdrawing reward or desired consequences.

Negative theology: an approach to God that focuses on what God is not rather than on what God is.

Neo-Darwinism: a revision of Darwin's theory that understands mutation as the method by which organisms arise that are better equipped to survive in particular environments.

Neoplatonism: the form of Platonism at the time of Augustine, whose chief founder was Plotinus. It taught that evil was the absence of good.

New historicism: a literary movement that returned to taking historical context and authorial intent into consideration, but with greater recognition of interpretive bias and the tendency for interpretation to favor those with power.

Nihilism: the philosophical view that sees no intrinsic meaning to the world.

Nominalism: philosophical position that argues that only particular things, not universals, really exist.

Non sequitur: Latin for "it does not follow," when a person's conclusion does not follow from his or her argument.

"Normal" science: science operating under the assumptions of a dominant paradigm.

Objective: a matter of fact rather than opinion, pertaining to things that would be true even if no person were involved.

Objectivity: the idea that we can form conclusions without bias and thus attain somewhat of a "God's-eye" perspective on truth.

Occam's razor: the idea that the simplest explanation is usually the better explanation.

Oligarchy: rule by a few individuals, sometimes with a pejorative sense.

Omnibenevolence: God is entirely good.

Omnipotence: God is all powerful.

Omnipotent: all powerful.

Omnipresence: God is everywhere present.

Omniscience: God is all knowing.

Omniscient: all knowing.

Ontological argument: the argument that if we can conceive of the greatest possible Being, it must also therefore exist.

Ontology: the sub-branch of metaphysics in philosophy that asks what the nature of being or existence itself is.

Open theism: the view that God intentionally suspends his foreknowledge of what we will choose so that we can be free to choose.

Original sin: for Augustine, the first sin of Adam and Eve that corrupted human nature, a corruption they passed down to all their human descendants.

Panentheism: belief that the world is a part of God.

Pantheism: the belief that everything is god, that the world equates to god.

Paradigm shift: a radical shift from one way of looking at a particular topic to a significantly different perspective.

Paradigm: a framework within which we organize data in a particular area; a lens through which we prioritize data and assign it significance.

Pascal's Wager: a thought experiment proposed by Blaise Pascal in which a person has to wager in life whether to believe or not to believe in God. He proposed that belief in God was a much better bet than choosing not to believe in God.

Personal relativism: the idea that right and wrong is a function of one's individual values and convictions.

Phenomenology: philosophical school that gained prominence on the European continent in the early twentieth century, bracketing or rejecting classical metaphysics and focusing on the world as we experience it, as it appears to us.

Philosophy: asks questions about the nature of reality, truth, and value as well as about the nature of all other subjects.

Philosophy of art: asks questions about the nature of art.

Philosophy of history: asks questions about the nature of history.

Philosophy of religion: asks questions about the nature of religion and God.

Philosophy of science: asks questions about the nature of science and scientific inquiry.

Positive reinforcement: incentive for certain behaviors by connecting them with reward or positive consequences.

Postmillennialism: the theological view that the thousand-year reign of Christ began literally on earth through the church after his resurrection, often with a sense that things will get better and better before his return.

Postmodern hermeneutic: interpretation that in one way or another recognizes the limitations of our ability to know the intended meaning of texts with absolute certainty.

Postmodernism: philosophical movement that denies the possibility of human objectivity or certainty in knowledge.

Poststructuralism: the rejection of universal patterns behind stories, cultures, and other social phenomena.

Pragmatic realism: an approach that argues that both the external world must be real in some way and our ideas must be true in some way if our ideas "work" in real life.

Pragmatic test: an approach to truth that asks whether a claim "works" on some level, whether it is a useful or beneficial idea.

Pragmatism: school of American philosophical thought that considers concepts to be meaningful in relation to how well they "work" in real life.

Predestination: God's prior determination of the future, usually, in particular, whether or not we will be saved from his judgment.

Prejudice: an attitude that tends to draw conclusions or make judgments before examining relevant information on the basis of irrelevant biases.

Premillennialism: the theological view that, usually after things get worse and worse, Christ will return and establish a literal thousand-year reign on earth.

Premise: the assumptions you make when making an argument.

Premodern hermeneutic: unreflective interpretation in which a reader is largely unaware of the difference between how the words strike him or her and their original meanings.

Premodernism: often used to label the period before modernism, in which people allegedly did not think objectively or critically about the world.

Presuppositions: beliefs that one *assumes* before reasoning rather than for which one argues on the basis of evidence or reasoning.

Primary sources: sources from the actual context you are investigating (e.g., documents, archaeology).

Problem of evil: the question of why evil exists if God is both good and powerful enough to stop it.

Process theology: a form of panentheism that sees God evolving and developing along with the world.

Projection: accusing others of things for which someone subconsciously feels guilty.

Proletariat: the workers of a society.

Properly basic: beliefs without which we could not even function in the world. Such beliefs are "warranted" without argument.

Proposition: a truth claim.

Protestant Reformation: the movement of protest against the beliefs and practices of the medieval Roman Catholic Church in the early 1500s, ultimately resulting in the more than twenty thousand other church denominations in the Western world today.

Providence: the Christian sense that God is watching over the course of history and that God sometimes steers it toward good or protects us from evil.

Psychoanalysis: the school of psychology Freud founded that tries to bring forces of the unconscious to the conscious mind to deal with them.

Psychology (in the philosophical sense): asks questions about the nature of the human mind and/or soul.

Radical orthodoxy: a postmodern approach to truth claiming that, since we cannot be objectively certain about what is true, we should assume all the essential beliefs of Christianity without argument.

Rationalism: an approach to knowledge that views reason as the principal path to truth.

Rationalization: making excuses so someone does not have to face something or accept blame.

Reader-response hermeneutic: an approach to texts that focuses on the way a particular reader or group of readers understands it.

Reductio ad absurdum: a line of deductive thinking that results in a false conclusion, thereby implying that one or more of the premises in the argument is false.

Reformed epistemology: an approach to truth that considers certain beliefs, such as the existence of other minds, as properly basic.

Relative: in ethics, a principle of action that varies depending on the situation, time, or place.

Renaissance: "rebirth" of culture in the 1400s and 1500s, drawing on ancient Greco-Roman models.

Representative democracy: rule by the people where individuals elect representatives to make most of the direct decisions for them.

Repression: suppressed drives or desires.

Republic: a form of representative, democratic government in which individual rights are protected from the whims of the majority.

Scientific creationism: a Christian approach to scientific evidence that arose in the 1970s to counter belief in macroevolution. It assumes a literal seven-day creation and explains the earth's geology by recourse to a worldwide flood.

Scientific method: A method for developing explanations for the way the natural world works by generating and testing hypotheses in order to account for the data of the world.

Scientism: in philosophy, a tendency to reduce truth to matters that can be verified scientifically.

Secondary sources: sources from other contexts that are about the context you are investigating (e.g., contemporary experts).

Second-order question: asks about asking about something (i.e., about a first-order question).

Self-control: controlling passions that would lead to doing the wrong thing.

Self-fulfilling prophecy: a prediction that a person inadvertently helps make come true by his or her actions.

Sins of commission: wrongs a person does by doing something.

Sins of omission: wrongs a person does by *not* doing something (see James 4:17).

Skeptics: ancient philosophical school that questioned our ability to know what is true.

Social and political philosophy: that branch of philosophy that tries to ascertain the best (and worst) ways we might live together.

Social construct: a way of understanding something not intrinsic to the thing itself but generated by a social group.

Social contract: an implicit or explicit agreement among the members of a society to abide by certain common rules for everyone's mutual benefit.

Social Darwinism: the application of the idea of "survival of the fittest" to its "haves" and "have nots," justifying the domination of the powerful over society's weak.

Socialism: economic system in which the state owns everything and directs the production and distribution of goods.

Soft determinism: compatibilism, the view that while everything we do is ultimately determined, we at least experience life as having free will.

Sovereignty: in relation to God, absolute authority and control over everything.

Stoicism: ancient philosophical school that emphasized rationality and accepting one's circumstances. One should have *amor fati*, "love of fate," with *apatheia*, nonemotional acceptance.

Subconscious/unconscious: the forces of one's human mind of which one is not completely aware.

Subjective: a matter of personal or group perspective rather than "fact," pertaining to the observer rather than the thing observed.

Sublimation: repression that is redirected and expressed in a healthy way.

Supernatural: things that seem to stand outside the normal rules of nature and are best explained by recourse to forces outside or beyond the natural.

Supernaturalism: in terms of history, the belief that God and perhaps other spiritual forces sometimes participate in the cause-effect flow of events.

Survival of the fittest: popular way of describing natural selection—the organisms best equipped to survive in a particular environment tend to advance in competition with those less well equipped.

Syllogism: a pattern of reasoning in which the conclusion must follow if your assumptions are true.

Synthesis: the advancement after the conflict between thesis and antithesis, incorporating positive elements of both and discarding other elements.

Tautology: two statements that say the same thing.

Teleological argument: an argument for the existence of God that suggests the existence of an intelligent Designer is necessary to explain the complexity and order in creation.

Theater of the absurd: dramas of the mid-twentieth century that were meant to portray the meaninglessness and irrationality of human existence.

Theism: the perspective that God created the universe, set up its rules, and continues to be involved with it.

Theistic evolution: the idea that God in some way directed the evolutionary process or at least that macroevolution is compatible with belief in God.

Theocracy: rule by God or certain gods.

Theodicy: an explanation of God's justice in the light of the existence of evil.

Thesis: the first idea or force put forward in a dialectical exchange.

Thick description: Clifford Geertz's term for a description of culture that goes beyond simple causes and effects to include sociocultural frameworks.

Total depravity: the idea that humans are unable to will or do any good at all in their own power.

Trinity: the classical Christian belief that, while there is only one God and that God is one in substance, God is at the same time three persons: Father, Son, and Holy Spirit.

True syllogism: a syllogism for which both the logic is valid *and* the conclusion is true because your premises are true.

Universal rights and wrongs: as we are defining them, ethical duties that are universal and timeless, but not exceptionless.

Utilitarianism: an act-based approach to ethics that looks to consequences and focuses on what will bring about the greatest good for the greatest number.

Valid syllogism: a syllogism whose logic works correctly, whether the conclusion is true or not.

Virtue-based ethics: ethics oriented around who we should *be* or not be.

Wesleyan-Arminian theology: the perspective that holds that God potentially empowers everyone to be saved from judgment if he or she responds favorably.

Wisdom: knowing the right thing to do.

Worldview: the lenses through which a person understands reality.

Zeitgeist: the "spirit of the age," the prevailing ideas and perspectives of a particular time and place.

INDEX